Assertion

Assertion

On the Philosophical Significance of Assertoric Speech

Sanford C. Goldberg

OXFORD
UNIVERSITY PRESS

Great Clarendon Street, Oxford, OX2 6DP,
United Kingdom

Oxford University Press is a department of the University of Oxford.
It furthers the University's objective of excellence in research, scholarship,
and education by publishing worldwide. Oxford is a registered trade mark of
Oxford University Press in the UK and in certain other countries

© Sanford C. Goldberg 2015

The moral rights of the author have been asserted

First Edition published in 2015

Impression: 1

All rights reserved. No part of this publication may be reproduced, stored in
a retrieval system, or transmitted, in any form or by any means, without the
prior permission in writing of Oxford University Press, or as expressly permitted
by law, by licence or under terms agreed with the appropriate reprographics
rights organization. Enquiries concerning reproduction outside the scope of the
above should be sent to the Rights Department, Oxford University Press, at the
address above

You must not circulate this work in any other form
and you must impose this same condition on any acquirer

Published in the United States of America by Oxford University Press
198 Madison Avenue, New York, NY 10016, United States of America

British Library Cataloguing in Publication Data
Data available

Library of Congress Control Number: 2014950697

ISBN 978–0–19–873248–8

Printed and bound by
CPI Group (UK) Ltd, Croydon, CR0 4YY

Cover image: *Senegalese*, 2012, by Sam Nhlengethwa. Mixed media on canvas, 90 × 120 cm.
Courtesy of the artist and Goodman Gallery

Links to third party websites are provided by Oxford in good faith and
for information only. Oxford disclaims any responsibility for the materials
contained in any third party website referenced in this work.

This book is dedicated, with love, to my mother, Gail Krebs, who taught me the speech act of assertion (and much else besides).

Preface

This book concerns the speech act of assertion: what it is, and why it matters. Although the term 'assertion' is perhaps somewhat removed from everyday talk, the phenomenon it denotes is familiar. The sort of speech act in question is the act by which we *state, report, contend,* or *claim* that such-and-such is the case. It is the act through which we *tell* others things, by which we *inform* an audience of this-or-that, or in which we *vouch* for something. We find it in the act in which we *affirm* or *attest to* something's being the case. And it is present as well when we *avow* that this-or-that is true.

In this book I will be asking about the nature of this speech act. I do so with an eye on exploring what I will call its philosophical significance. By this I understand its relations to other philosophically interesting topics. These include topics in epistemology (testimony and testimonial knowledge; epistemic authority; disagreement), the philosophy of mind (belief; the theory of mental content), the philosophy of language (norms of language; the method of interpretation; the theory of linguistic content), ethics (the ethics of belief; what we owe to each other as information-seeking creatures); and other matters which transcend any subcategory (anonymity; trust; the division of epistemic labor; Moore-paradoxicality).

Assertion is not a new topic to philosophers. In fact, in the past two decades there has been a good deal written on the subject. For reasons that I will explore, many philosophers have become convinced that the speech act of assertion can be individuated—distinguished as the particular speech act that it is—by reference to the rule (or "norm") that governs acts of this type. Those who pursue this line of inquiry develop something like the following hypothesis:

Assertion is the unique speech act that is governed by a rule, to the effect that one must not perform acts of this type unless . . .[1]

where we replace '. . .' with a statement of the condition that captures the content of the rule in question. Accordingly, the philosophical literature has focused on two related issues: the content of the rule (that is, what it requires of us; what fills in the '. . .' slot), and the case for thinking that the speech act of assertion *can* be individuated in this way. Of these, the former issue—the content of the rule—has loomed large. If you want to know what an assertion is, this line of thinking goes, it suffices to know that it is the unique speech act which is governed by a rule which requires speakers not to produce speech acts of that kind unless . . . (where one fills in the blanks according to one's

---

[1] Most writers have put the rule in the affirmative, as in *one must: assert p, only if* . . . By contrast, I have put the rule here in negative form: *one must **not** assert p, unless* . . . I intend for this to be equivalent to the affirmative form; I use the negative form for stylistic reasons only.

favored version of the rule). Various candidate rules have been suggested: one must not assert the proposition that p unless (a) one *knows* that p, (b) one is *certain* that p, (c) one is *justified* in believing that p, (d) one is *rational* in believing that p, (e) one *believes* that p, or (f) it is *true* that p.

While the present book does attempt to contribute to the literature I have just described, this is not my main aim. On the contrary, the book emerges out of a kind of double dissatisfaction with that literature.[2]

First, and most centrally, I worry that this literature risks obscuring the proverbial forest for the trees. My thought has always been that if assertion is the unique speech act governed by a rule requiring something in the ballpark of (a)–(f), then the fact that assertion is so governed should be of great philosophical interest *whatever the actual content of the rule*. Underlying this thought is another idea. As a linguistic (more specifically: speech act) phenomenon, assertion is connected to all sorts of topics of philosophical interest. The underlying idea is to explore the extent to which we can *explain* or *account for* these connections by reference to the fact that assertion is governed by a rule mandating something in the vicinity of (a)–(f). No doubt the particular details of the connections between assertion and these other phenomena will depend on the precise content of the norm. Still, the broad sense of assertion's connectedness to these other phenomena should not. And when we see the extent to which the connections themselves can be discerned and accounted for prior to engaging in the debate over the precise content of the norm, to that very extent we will have appreciated the full philosophical significance of the hypothesis that assertion is governed by a norm. What is more, we will have made clear why it is worth devoting so much time and energy to thinking about the norm of assertion. Or so, at any rate, I think, and it is this thought that animates the present book.

This animating idea is connected to my second dissatisfaction with the current state of the literature. A good many people who advance a thesis regarding assertion's norm do so on the basis of cases:[3] they argue that their norm best explains the data in a battery of situations (or situation-types) in which assertions are produced and responded to. By contrast, most of the argumentation I will present in connection with the hypothesis that assertion has a norm does not argue by appeal to cases. Rather, I defend this

---

[2] I should acknowledge that I have contributed to that literature, so this dissatisfaction is self-directed as well.

[3] Not everyone argues for the norm of assertion on the basis of cases. Thus, the knowledge norm has been defended (by Williamson 2000, for example) by appeal to its account of a certain subclass of Moore-paradoxical sentences (those of the form 'p, but I do not know that p'). More recently, the discussion of assertion's norm has been connected to that of the norm of action, and more generally to considerations of practical interests and concerns, where particular proposals have been defended on the grounds of their happy implications on this score (see Hawthorne 2003; Cohen 2004; Stanley 2005; Maitra and Weatherson 2010). I regard these sorts of argument as in the spirit of the present project: the particular epistemic norm of assertion is defended as giving us a plausible account of a phenomenon—Moore-paradoxicality, the link between assertion and action, or what have you—that is of independent and distinctly philosophical interest.

thesis on the basis of the connections it enables us to discern. Insofar as these connections (between assertion and other issues of philosophical interest) can be described in an illuminating fashion in terms of the hypothesis of assertion's norm, to just that extent the hypothesis earns its keep in philosophy, and to just that extent the effort to discern the precise content of that norm is a worthwhile activity.

I should be clear that I do have opinions about the content of the norm. I will be advancing these opinions in the last part of the book (its final three chapters). But I have organized the book so as to bring out as much as I can *prior* to engaging in that debate. Hence in the first three sections of the book (the first eight chapters) I will be assuming only that assertion has an epistemic norm, and seeing what we can derive from this fact alone. The defense of regarding the norm as epistemic, and hence as ruling out (e) and (f),[4] for example, will proceed in Chapters 2 and 3, where I argue that we need a norm with a robustly epistemic content in order to capture the epistemic significance of assertion. After I have explored as much as I can without weighing in on the debate over the precise content of the (epistemic) norm, I will weigh in on that debate as well. I do so in the last section of the book. For reasons that I will develop there, I favor a context-sensitive account of the norm—one which regards the core rule for assertion as requiring one to have the relevant epistemic authority, but where what counts as the relevant authority will vary according to what is mutually manifest (better: what is reasonably regarded as mutually manifest) in context.[5]

My proposal comes at a cost: it is a more complicated rule than the other (context-invariant) rules that have been defended by others, and this complication will force us to revisit some of the topics that have been treated by the simpler rules. But I will argue that the various virtues of the account should make us willing to pay the cost. Still, I am under no illusions about this part of my proposal: it is a competitor in a very well-traversed terrain. I will be satisfied if in presenting my case I succeed in bringing to others' attention a source of data that I think have been underappreciated in the literature on assertion's norm, even if my account of those data is rejected.

---

[4] It may not rule out (e). Bach and Harnish (1979) endorse something like the hypothesis that assertion is governed by a norm the content of whose rule is given by (e), but they point out that this norm can mirror an epistemic norm insofar as we assume that the phenomenon of belief itself is governed by an epistemic norm. (See also Bach 2009.) This strikes me as an intriguing suggestion to which I will return at various points in the book.

[5] Interestingly, the claim that the epistemic strength required to warrant assertion varies with context is one that several people have recently advanced, albeit on very different grounds, and in defense of a different sort of account. Such a claim is discussed in connection with contextualism about knowledge in DeRose (1996, 2002) and Leite (2007); and is considered, albeit briefly, in Lackey (forthcoming) and Maitra and Weatherson (2010: 114). One person who explicitly defends a context-sensitive account—although different in important ways from the one I will develop in ways described in later chapters—is McKinnon (2013).

Acknowledgments

This book is the result of many, many discussions over the years. A good number of people have helped me think hard about this topic. Special thanks go to Matt Benton, who read and provided feedback on large portions of this manuscript, to my colleague Jennifer Lackey, with whom I have had more conversations about assertion than I can remember, and to three anonymous referees at Oxford University Press, who gave me a great deal to think about in revising this manuscript. I am also grateful to others for many detailed discussions about assertion over the years: my Northwestern colleagues Mark Alznauer, Fabrizio Cariani, Kyla Ebels-Duggan, Sean Ebels-Duggan, Michael Glanzberg, Richard Kraut, Cristina Lafont, Peter Ludlow, Baron Reed, Gregory Ward, and Stephen White; my friends and professional colleagues Jessica Brown, Lizzie Fricker, Miranda Fricker, Richard Fumerton, Mikkel Gerken, Alvin Goldman, Peter Graham, Mitch Green, Thomas Grundmann, Ted Hinchman, Clare Horisk, Jesper Kallestrup, Klemens Kappell, Tim Kenyon, Igal Kvart, Michael Lynch, Duncan Pritchard, Geoff Pynne, Mike Ridge, Rob Stainton, Tim Sundell, John Turri, and Åsa Wikforss; and Northwestern graduate students Amy Flowerree, Lauren Leydon-Hardy, Matthew Mullins, and Nick Leonard, as well as graduate students Casey Johnson (University of Connecticut) and Andrea Kruse (University of Bochum, Germany). I am indebted to each of them. Finally, I would also like to thank the various people who over the years have encouraged, challenged, and cajoled me, enabling me to clarify my thinking on matters of assertion. These include Scott Aiken, Ben Almassi, Louise Antony, Brendan Balcerak Jackson, Magdalena Balcerak Jackson, David Barnett, Heather Battaly, J. C. Bjerring, Martijn Blauw, Paul Bloomfield, Larry Bonjour, Tad Brennan, Paul Carelli, Anjan Chakravarti, Dave Chalmers, David Christensen, Matthew Christman, Ryan Davis, Mark Dechesne, Jeroen de Ridder, Ciann Dorr, Ray Elugardo, David Enoch, Don Fallis, Jeremy Fantl, Kati Farkas, Rich Feldman, Carrie Figdor, Arthur Fine, Hans Fink, Bryan Frances, Marilyn Freidman, Axel Gelfert, Brie Gertler, Heidi Grasswick, Al Hajek, Mitch Haney, John Hardwig, Ali Hasan, Jim Hawthorne, John Hawthorne, Stephen Hetherington, Joachim Horvath, Sherri Irvin, Alex Jackson, Tom Kelley, Jenz Kipper, Dirk Koppelberg, Arie Kruglanski, Greg Landini, Pierre le Morvan, Christian List, Diego Machuca, Jon Matheson, Larry May, Matt McGrath, Rachel McKinnon, Ben McMyler, Boaz Miller, Seamus Miller, Martin Montminy, Philip Nickel, Daniel Nolan, Nikolaj Pederson, Rik Peels, Ted Poston, Dani Rabinowitz, Paulo Santorio, Eric Schwitzgebel, Johanna Seibt, Daniele Sgaravatti, Russ Shafer-Landau, David Simpson, Barry Smith, David Sosa, Ernie Sosa, Kai Spiekermann, Jason Stanley, Asbjørn Steglich-Petersen, Daniel Stoljar, David Stern, Bob Talisse, Jeff Tlumak, Deb Tollefson, Rico Vitz, Michael Williams, Timothy Williamson, Christian Wirrwitz, Sarah Wright, and Linda Zagzebski. I also would like to thank the audiences at various places where I have presented talks which now form parts of this book: the Arché workshop on Assertion at the University of St Andrews (St Andrews, Scotland); the *Episteme* Conference on "Epistemological Problems of Privacy and Secrecy" (The Hague, Netherlands); the Epistemology of Groups conference (University of London, England); the Summer School in Philosophy at the University of Cologne (Cologne, Germany); the Kentucky Philosophical Association Fall 2011 meeting (Highland Heights, Kentucky); the A. David Klein Philosophy Symposium on "The Ethics of Belief" (University of North Florida); the Orange Beach Epistemology Workshop (Orange Beach, Alabama); Aarhus University (Aarhus, Denmark); Australian National University (Canberra, Australia); Hebrew University (Jerusalem, Israel); LOGOS at the University of Barcelona (Barcelona, Spain); Magdalen and Oriel Colleges, Oxford University (Oxford, England); Monash University (Melbourne, Australia); Northwestern University (Evanston, Illinois); Notre Dame (South Bend, Indiana); the University of Colorado (Boulder, Colorado); the University of Iowa (Iowa City, Iowa); the University of New South Wales (Sydney, Australia); the University of Oklahoma (Norman, Oklahoma); the University of St Andrews (Scotland); the University of Stockholm (Stockholm, Sweden); the University of Washington (Seattle, Washington); the University of Wollongong (Wollongong, Australia); and Vanderbilt University (Nashville, Tennessee).

Special thanks also go to my home university, Northwestern, whose support during the writing of this book was tremendous; to the Philosophy Department and the Eidyn Research Center at the University of Edinburgh, where I revised this manuscript during my time as a Professorial Fellow; and to Peter Momtchiloff, for his suggestions, good judgment, and support, and the rest of the team at Oxford University Press, with whom it is always a pleasure to work.

Another special thanks goes to my family: my best friend and partner Judy, and my children, Gideon, Ethan, and Nadia. They keep me honest and ensure that my nuttiness does not overflow its proper boundaries.

Parts of this book borrow from previously published work, and are reproduced here, in part or in whole, with the kind permission of the original publishers. Chapter 2 borrows several pages from my paper "Testimony and Reasons," which is forthcoming in D. Star (ed.), *The Oxford Handbook of Reasons and Normativity* (Oxford University Press). Chapter 3 is a heavily revised version of my paper "Putting the Norm of Assertion to Work: The Case of Testimony," originally published in J. Brown and J. Cappelen (eds.), *Assertion: New Philosophical Essays* (Oxford University Press, 2011), pp. 175–95. Chapter 4 borrows several extended passages from my paper "Interpreting Assertions," originally published in G. Preyer and C. Amoretti (eds.), *Triangulation: From an Epistemic Point of View* (New York: Ontos Publishers, 2011), pp. 153–76. Chapter 7 is based on my paper "Assertion and the Ethics of Belief," originally published in J. Matheson and R. Vitz, *The Ethics of Belief* (Oxford University Press, 2014). Chapter 8 is a shortened version of my paper "Anonymous Assertion," *Episteme* 10:2, 135–51. Chapter 9 is a heavily revised version of my paper "Disagreement, Defeaters, and

Assertion," originally published in D. Christiansen and J. Lackey (eds.), *Disagreement* (Oxford University Press, 2013), pp. 167–89. Chapter 10 is a slightly revised version of my paper "Mutuality and Assertion," forthcoming in M. Brady and M. Fricker (eds.), *The Epistemic Life of Groups* (Oxford University Press). Finally, Chapter 11 borrows several pages from my paper "Defending Philosophy in the Face of Systematic Disagreement," originally published in D. Machuca (ed.), *Disagreement and Skepticism* (New York: Routledge: 2012), pp. 277–94, and which is reproduced here by permission of Taylor and Francis Group, LLC, a division of Informa plc.

Contents

Part I. Introduction   1

  1. What Is Assertion? In Defense of the Norm-Based Account   3

Part II. The Epistemic Significance of Assertion   37

  2. Assertion and the Spread of Knowledge   39
  3. Assertion and Testimony   72

Part III. Other Applications: Mind, Language, and More   93

  4. Assertion and the Method of Interpretation (Radical and Otherwise)   95
  5. Assertion and Assertoric Content   123
  6. Assertion and Belief   144
  7. The Ethics of Assertion (and Belief)   171
  8. Anonymous Assertion   204

Part IV. A Case for Context-Sensitivity in the Norm of Assertion   223

  9. Assertion and Disagreement   225
  10. Mutuality and Assertion   250
  11. The Costs of Context-Sensitivity   272

Bibliography   291
Index   301

Detailed Contents

Part I. Introduction — 1

1. What Is Assertion? In Defense of the Norm-Based Account — 3
   1.1 The Nature of My Project — 3
   1.2 Assertoric Practice: Examples — 4
   1.3 The *Explananda*: Features of Assertoric Speech — 6
   1.4 Theories of Assertion: Four Approaches — 9
   1.5 Applying the Approaches to the *Explananda* — 12
   1.6 The Constitutive Rule Account: Objections and Replies — 21
   1.7 Conclusion — 35

Part II. The Epistemic Significance of Assertion — 37

2. Assertion and the Spread of Knowledge — 39
   2.1 Assertion's Role in the Spread of Knowledge — 39
   2.2 Two Framing Assumptions — 39
   2.3 Varieties of Evidentialism Regarding Assertion's Role in the Spread of Knowledge — 43
   2.4 Strong Evidentialism and the Positive Reasons Requirement — 46
   2.5 Against the Positive Reasons Requirement — 50
   2.6 On the Very Possibility of Non-Evidential Accounts — 58
   2.7 Non-Evidential Accounts: Interpersonal Views (Trust and Assurance) — 62
   2.8 Non-Evidential Accounts: The Norm of Assertion — 66
   2.9 Conclusion — 70

3. Assertion and Testimony — 72
   3.1 Overview — 72
   3.2 Assertion-Generated Expectations: Entitlements and Responsibilities — 73
   3.3 Assertion's Norm and the Buck-Passing and Blame Phenomena — 75
   3.4 Assertion and the Act of Testifying — 77
   3.5 The Norm of Assertion as Common Knowledge — 80
   3.6 The Norm-Based Account vs. the Assurance View — 82
   3.7 Are Testimony-Constituting Assertions Evidence? — 89
   3.8 Conclusion — 91

Part III. Other Applications: Mind, Language, and More — 93

4. Assertion and the Method of Interpretation (Radical and Otherwise) — 95
   4.1 The Mutually Manifest, Robustly Epistemic Norm of Assertion: MMENA — 95
   4.2 Davidson's Characterization of the Task of Interpretation — 97

4.3	From Davidsonian Radical Interpretation to the Norm of Assertion	100
4.4	MMENA and the Epistemology and Methodology of Interpretation	103
4.5	In Defense of the Norm-Based Account of Interpretation: AIP	112
4.6	Interpretation, Comprehension, and the Epistemology of Testimony	118
4.7	Conclusion	122

5. Assertion and Assertoric Content   123
    5.1 A Role for MMENA in the Determination of Assertoric Content   123
    5.2 MMENA and the Hypothesis of Face-Value Interpretations   124
    5.3 The Idea of Face-Value Interpretations as a Useful Fiction   130
    5.4 Against Idiosyncrasy   132
    5.5 Against Internalism about Assertoric Content   137
    5.6 Conclusion   143

6. Assertion and Belief   144
    6.1 The Link between Assertion and Belief: Contingent or Essential?   144
    6.2 MMENA and the Assertion–Belief Connection   146
    6.3 Does Warranted Assertion Require Belief?   150
    6.4 Belief-Worthiness, Assertion, and the Pragmatics of
        Epistemic Self-Representation   155
    6.5 Assertion and Moore's Paradox   157
    6.6 The Norm of Assertion and the Norm of Belief   162
    6.7 In Defense of Different Standards for Assertion and Belief   164
    6.8 Conclusion   170

7. The Ethics of Assertion (and Belief)   171
    7.1 MMENA and the Ethics of Assertion and Belief   171
    7.2 The Ethics of Assertion, Part I: What the Speaker Owes to the Hearer   172
    7.3 The Ethics of Assertion, Part II: What the Hearer Owes to the Speaker   180
    7.4 The Obligation to Assert: "You Should Have Told Me So!"   189
    7.5 Deriving (some) Ethics of Belief from the Obligation to Assert   192
    7.6 Conclusion   203

8. Anonymous Assertion   204
    8.1 Paradigmatically, Assertion Is a Public Act   204
    8.2 Anonymity   205
    8.3 The Gap: Reductionism and Non-Reductionism Revisited   207
    8.4 Minding the Gap: Assessing Assertions   209
    8.5 Anonymity and the Impoverished Mechanisms for Policing and Assessing
        Assertoric Responsibility   213
    8.6 Effects of Anonymity: Mutually Diminished Expectations   216
    8.7 Relativized Anonymity and Anonymity-Policing Regimes   219
    8.8 Conclusion   221

Part IV. A Case for Context-Sensitivity in the Norm of Assertion — 223

9. Assertion and Disagreement — 225
   9.1 The Problem: The Persistence of Assertions under Conditions of Systematic Disagreement — 225
   9.2 Preliminaries — 227
   9.3 Systematic Peer Disagreements as Evidence of Unreliability — 231
   9.4 Systematic Peer Disagreements and Grounds for Self-Doubt — 237
   9.5 Systematic Peer Disagreements and Epistemic Defeat — 241
   9.6 Philosophical Disputes as Systematic Peer Disagreements — 242
   9.7 The Persistence of Assertions in Systematic Peer Disagreements — 245
   9.8 Conclusion — 248

10. Mutuality and Assertion — 250
    10.1 The Challenge of Disagreement: Some *Desiderata* Regarding an Answer — 250
    10.2 Cooperativity, Mutual Belief, and the Fixation of Standards of Assertoric Warrant — 255
    10.3 Epistemic Groups and Assertoric Practice — 259
    10.4 Objections and Replies: What Is Reasonably Regarded as Mutually Believed — 264
    10.5 Conclusion — 271

11. The Costs of Context-Sensitivity — 272
    11.1 Implications of Context-Sensitivity in the Standard for Warranted Assertion — 272
    11.2 The Significance of Speech Context — 273
    11.3 The Epistemic Significance of Assertion, Reconsidered — 276
    11.4 Sincerity in Assertion, Reconsidered — 278
    11.5 Assertion and Moore's Paradox, Revisited — 285
    11.6 Children's Assertion — 288
    11.7 Conclusion — 289

Bibliography — 291
Index — 301

PART I
Introduction

The speech act of assertion is introduced with examples. Its main characteristics are then identified. Four accounts of this speech act are then described, and their ability to account for the main characteristics is explored.

1
What Is Assertion? In Defense of the Norm-Based Account

1.1 The Nature of My Project

This book concerns the speech act of assertion. Although the term "assertion" itself is perhaps somewhat removed from everyday talk, the phenomenon it denotes is familiar. Consider the sort of speech act by which we *state, report, contend,* or *claim* that such-and-such is the case; through which we *tell* others things, by which we *inform* an audience of this-or-that, or in which we *vouch* for something; in which we *affirm* or *attest to* something's being the case; or through which we *avow* that this-or-that is true. In standard cases, such acts are performed by way of asserting—performing the speech act of assertion.

In this book I will be asking about the nature of this speech act. I do so with an eye on exploring what I will call its philosophical significance. By this I understand its relations to other philosophically interesting topics. These include topics in epistemology (testimony and testimonial knowledge; epistemic authority; disagreement), the philosophy of mind (belief; the theory of mental content), the philosophy of language (norms of language; the method of interpretation; the theory of linguistic content; Moore-paradoxical sentences), ethics (the ethics of belief; what we owe to each other as information-seeking creatures), social philosophy (anonymity; trust; the division of intellectual labor), and philosophical practice itself.

I want to use this chapter to introduce the topic of assertion itself. I will begin by introducing it by way of examples, which I present in order to fix the subject-matter. I will then go on to characterize various features we might hope to illuminate with our account of the nature of the speech act of assertion. Having done that, I will then list the four main competitor accounts of assertion that have been offered, and will provide some initial reasons for favoring one of them. The one I favor holds that assertion is the unique speech act that is governed by a particular rule: the so-called norm of assertion. I cannot pretend that the reasons I offer in defense of such a view suffice to compel those already committed to the other views to change their minds. I offer these reasons, rather, to provide a brief overview of the variety of virtues I see for the norm-based view. (I will be spending the majority of this book developing these virtues.) I will conclude by addressing several objections that have been pressed against the norm-based account, finding each of them wanting. This will pave the way for the rest of the book, where I discuss the philosophical significance of assertion (Parts II and III), followed by a concluding foray into my own take on the content of assertion's norm (Part IV).

1.2 Assertoric Practice: Examples

Let us start with some examples of the kind of speech act that will be the topic of this book. In each case, an assertion is made by way of the utterance of a declarative sentence.

YANG: The Yankees won last night, 2–1.
FITZPATRICK: Wow, they've really been on a roll recently. They've won 5 games in a row.

MCSORLEY: What time is it?
VELAZQUEZ: It's 5:15.

WALLACH: The banking system in the US is deeply flawed. We are in need of more regulation.
FRANKLIN: You're wrong. What we need is less regulation, not more.

SORIANO: Plato was the first philosopher to offer a coherent theory of knowledge.
RIVERA: What makes you say that?

These examples could be multiplied. And there are many ways we might describe the speech acts: the speakers "advance claims," they "make statements," they "tell" their audience things, they "report" on a given state of affairs, they "express judgments" they have made, and so forth.

A salient feature of each of the foregoing cases is that one or both of the speakers performs the speech act in question by uttering a declarative sentence.[1] It may be worth observing, however, that not all utterances of declarative sentences are assertions. The following example will serve to establish this.

PITZER: Now, class, I want you to practice the art of sounding like you mean it. So I want each of you to say something as if you were stating a fact. Only I want you to make it up; nothing real. OK? Jones, you go first.
JONES: Hmmm. Ok, here goes. [clearing her throat] Boston has more hair salons than does New York.
PITZER: Excellent! Now you, Smith. Go ahead.
SMITH: [thinking] The dance last night was a success.
PITZER: Good!

---

[1] Alternatively: a sentence in the indicative mood.

In these cases, both Jones and Smith utter declarative sentences, but they are not making assertions.[2] They are only pretending to do so (and pretend assertions are not real assertions any more than play money is real money). Nor is this the only sort of example in which the utterance of a declarative sentence fails to be an assertion. Consider actors producing their lines on a stage: they too utter declarative sentences, but they are not really asserting anything. We might then wonder: insofar as we exclude all cases of pretense (including play-acting), is the (sincere) utterance of a declarative sentence sufficient for making an assertion? It would seem not. Here is an example:

ZINZER: What time is it?
WETHERINGTON: I have no idea.
ZINZER: If you had to guess.
WETHERINGTON: Well...
ZINZER: [waiting] Yes?
WETHERINGTON: [uttered with a shrug of the shoulders] It's 5 o'clock.

Wetherington's last speech act is an utterance of a declarative sentence, but it is not an assertion. In particular, it lacks the *force* of an assertion: it is presented with the force of a guess.

In light of this, it is tempting to offer the following as an initial characterization of what assertions have in common. At a minimum, they are all speech acts in which a given proposition is *presented as true*, where this presentation has certain *force* (what we might call *assertoric force*). Unfortunately, this characterization is not particularly helpful.

To see this, consider the claim that assertions are speech acts in which one *presents a proposition as true*. It is plausible to think that lies involve assertions. If so, then by extension *bald-faced* lies involve assertion.[3] But bald-faced lies are lies made under conditions in which it is mutual knowledge that the claim being made is false. So if assertions are speech acts in which a given proposition is presented as true, then to present something as true in speech is something one can do even under conditions in which it is mutual knowledge that no one believes or will believe that the proposition is true. We might then wonder what is involved in presenting a proposition as true, beyond uttering a sentence in the declarative mood. But if nothing further is involved, then it would not appear that the notion of presenting a proposition as true adds anything distinctive. Keep it in your account if you would like; just be aware that it is not particularly illuminating to be told that assertions are speech acts in which a proposition is presented as true.

---

[2] It is tempting to think that a better case of the phenomenon of sentences uttered in the declarative mood that nevertheless do not constitute assertions is the case of irony. I refrain from using this sort of case here as it introduces complications I would prefer not to introduce at this point. I will discuss irony a little further later. (With thanks to an anonymous referee for indicating the need for this point.)

[3] I owe this example to an anonymous referee.

Next, consider the notion of assertoric force. It is natural to suppose that an account of the nature of assertion will focus on the nature of assertoric force. If one follows that route, then an analysis of assertoric force is in order. But it is also worth pointing out that it is possible as well to reverse the order of analysis here, so that assertoric force is whatever force is distinctive of acts of assertion. Clearly, if one were to employ this order of analysis, one would need an independent characterization of the speech act of assertion. And this is indeed what I propose to offer in this book.

It will be helpful, however, not to begin with such a characterization (for how would we know what would count as a good one?). Rather, we should begin with what we would hope such a characterization could explain. To this end, what I propose to do is to enumerate the characteristic features of assertoric speech. These are the features that we might hope will be explained by our account of assertion. If the account that does best by this standard adverts to a notion of assertoric force or of a presentation-as-true, then so be it; in that case, the theoretical notion of assertoric force (or that of a presentation-as-true) earns its keep. But if the account that does best by this standard does not advert to either of these notions, then we need not attribute very much significance to them—at least not insofar as our aim is understanding the nature of the act itself. On the contrary, we might hope to acquire some insight into these notions from our independent characterization of assertoric speech itself.

1.3 The *Explananda*: Features of Assertoric Speech

As a type of speech act, assertion has various features which we might hope to be able to explain. These pertain to assertion's role in communication and the spread of knowledge, its role in generating what I will call *entitlements* and *responsibilities* for speakers and hearers, its availability as a vehicle for the expression of belief, and its foundational role in the method by which one would go about interpreting a speaker whose language one does not understand.

I begin with those features of assertion that are bound up in its role in communication and the spread of knowledge—assertion's *epistemic significance*, so to speak. It is uncontroversial, I suppose, to say that it is by way of assertions that one can (and typically does) communicate one's knowledge to others. Stronger, assertions are *apt* for such a knowledge-communicating use. That is to say, assertion is the sort of speech act which is such that both speaker and hearer are aware of the knowledge-communicating use, and both are prepared to treat the act accordingly. Thus speakers are prepared to employ the act—that is, to make an assertion—when they aim to communicate knowledge, and hearers are prepared to comprehend the act of assertion in terms of a default (albeit defeasible) assumption that the speaker is aiming to communicate knowledge. I will call assertion's aptness for communicating knowledge its *CK-aptness*. An account of assertion ought to explain the fact that assertion is CK-apt.

Several other features of assertion are bound up with assertion's CK-aptness, and so are related to assertion's epistemic significance—its role in the communication of knowledge. For example, consider that it is common for a speaker who makes an assertion to do so with the aim that her audience accept the proposition she presents as true in this way. What is more, a speaker who does assert with this aim has a reasonable chance of realizing the aim. To be sure, not all speakers whose assertions are intended to get the audience to believe what they have asserted succeed; sometimes their assertions are rejected. What is more, not all assertions made with this intention *should* be accepted: some are insincere or incompetent. But the very fact that the issue of assertion's belief-worthiness arises in the first place is an interesting feature of assertion. For we might well wonder: how does the performance of a certain type of speech act result in the salience of the question regarding the *belief-worthiness* of the (content of the) act? And how is this related to the fact that speakers who assert things have a reasonable expectation to be believed? An account of assertion ought to explain the purported belief-worthiness of assertion.

Still in keeping within assertion's epistemic significance (its role in the communication of knowledge), consider yet another feature of assertion: assertions can be challenged by querying the speaker's epistemic standing on the proposition she has asserted. Thus, if a speaker asserts something, a hearer can ask how the speaker knows that, or what evidence she has for thinking that, or on what basis she makes that claim, and so forth. What is interesting here is that it is no part of the explicit content of the assertion that the speaker knows, or has relevant evidence; yet querying such things appears to be a perfectly appropriate way to challenge the assertion. I will call this assertion's susceptibility to epistemic challenge, or its *EC-susceptibility* for short. An account of assertion ought to explain why it is that the performance of an assertoric speech act renders that act EC-susceptible.

Relatedly, many writers describe assertions as involving the speaker's *representing herself* as knowing, or at least having evidence for, what she has asserted. I will call this the *conveyed self-representation* implicit in assertion. That assertion conveys this sort of self-representation would explain why an appropriate reaction to an assertion is to query how the speaker knows or has proper evidence. At the same time, the speaker does not explicitly claim to know, nor does she explicitly claim to have evidence for her assertion. She merely asserts what she does. Consequently, we might hope to be able to explain how it comes to pass that a speaker who asserts something represents herself as knowing, or at least as having evidence for her claim. How does assertion succeed in conveying such a self-representation?

I move now to several other features of assertion which, though still related to assertion's epistemic significance, nevertheless deserve to be called out separately. The first of these has to do with the sort of entitlements and responsibilities that assertion generates for speakers and hearers. Suppose that you believe something on the basis of Jones's say-so, and then are queried regarding the grounds of your belief. You might well have reasons for regarding Jones's say-so as credible. Still, after you have exhausted these reasons you have not exhausted your resources in dealing with the challenge; it remains open to you to defer the challenge to Jones herself. Stronger, we might say that Jones's assertion *authorized* or *entitled* you to do so; and when you do "pass the buck" to her in this way,[4] Jones then has the *responsibility* to address the challenge herself. It would thus appear that in asserting that p, the speaker *authorizes* the hearer to defer any legitimate challenge to the truth of the claim to her, and generates the *responsibility* for taking up that challenge. An account of assertion ought to explain these "interpersonal" aspects of the speech act.

Another feature of assertion which, though not unrelated to assertion's epistemic significance, nevertheless deserves to be called out separately, has to do with assertion's relation to belief. Simply put, when they are performed sincerely, assertions express or manifest one's beliefs. In fact, it is natural to think that the sincere performance of this speech act *just is* a matter of manifesting one's belief. This seems to be a feature of assertion that is common knowledge among all competent speakers. I will call this the *sincerity* aspect of assertion. An account of assertion ought to explain how an assertoric utterance, when sincere, (typically) counts as the expression or manifestation of belief.[5]

Yet another feature of assertion which, though not unrelated to assertion's role in communicating knowledge, nevertheless deserves to be called out separately, has to do with the *retractability* of assertion.[6] A speaker might retract an assertion when she regards herself as no longer entitled to believe what she previously asserted, or else when she no longer regards herself as in a position to vindicate her assertion (whether or not she continues to believe the asserted content).[7] An account of assertion ought to make sense of the rectractability of assertion.

Not all of the features we might hope to explain in an account of assertion are directly relevant to its aptness for communicating knowledge. I want to close with one such feature. (While this feature may ultimately be connected to assertion's aptness for communicating knowledge, the connection will be indirect.) It is this: assertions play a particularly prominent role in the method through which a hearer would go about interpreting a language she did not understand. This generic task was labeled "Radical Interpretation" by Donald Davidson. As he conceived of it, Radical Interpretation was the task of cracking the code of a heretofore uninterpreted

---

[4] I employed the notion of buck-passing to characterize a feature of testimonial belief in Goldberg (2006).
[5] One might think that the sincerity feature of assertion is not something to be explained, but rather is a condition on assertion itself—that to be "felicitous" in Austin's sense, assertions must be sincere, hence must express one's belief. One who thinks this way will take the sincerity condition as something that is part of the account itself, rather than as something that the account can be used to explain. This may be; but perhaps we can all agree that if one's account of assertion can actually explain why the sincerity condition on assertion is belief, so much better for the account.
[6] This point has been emphasized by Bach and Harnish (1979) and MacFarlane (2003, 2005, 2010).
[7] MacFarlane (2003, 2005, 2010) notes that the retraction of assertion is compatible with the continuation of belief. Kvanvig (2009) agrees, distinguishing between the retraction of an assertion (the act) from the retraction of its content. For a discussion, see Chapter 6.

language without assuming knowledge of either the meanings of the speaker's words or the beliefs she expressed with them. Davidson himself made clear that the speech act of assertion—as well as its mental analogue, assent (in the face of a prompting by a query formulated in the target language)—constitutes a core part of the evidence on the basis of which one would perform this task. If you know nothing of another's language or what she believes, and your aim is to crack the code, it would seem that you will need to start by observing her assertions (or, perhaps equivalently, her assent-manifesting behaviors), and will then need to correlate these acts with the conditions that prompted them. Call this feature of assertion whereby it constitutes the foundational evidence for the task of Radical Interpretation the *RI-evidential* feature of assertion. Davidson himself famously theorized about the RI-evidential feature of assertion, using this to ground his Principle of Charity. For our part, we might wonder whether we can shed light on the nature of Radical Interpretation by way of a prior understanding of assertion: the idea would be to explain the role speech acts of this kind can play in Radical Interpretation, by way of the nature of these acts (and the task one faces in Radical Interpretation).

I do not claim that a theory of the speech act of assertion must be able to explain all of these features of assertion. (Indeed some might want to challenge the presuppositions I have been making, in speaking of these as features of assertion.) Nor do I claim that all of these features are equally important. I can see a case to be made for thinking that, while some of these (presumably the ones bound up with assertion's CK-aptness) are the core features of assertion which any adequate account will need to explain, others are not (so that their explanation, while perhaps something to be desired, would not constitute an adequacy condition on an account). I also think that the most uncontroversial of these features are those that are a core part of what I have been calling assertion's epistemic significance. (These are so important that I will single them out in my extended treatment: they occupy my attention in Part II of the book.) Still, we can say this: to the extent that an account explains these features, to that extent the account enjoys independent support. By extension, if there is any single account that explains them all, this account is thus to be preferred to the others. But is there such an account? To answer this question it will be helpful to have before us the main competitor accounts of the speech act of assertion. I turn to this now.

1.4 Theories of Assertion: Four Approaches

In a recent paper, John MacFarlane (2010) has usefully identified four main accounts of assertion.[8] I will call these the *attitudinal* account, the *common ground* account, the *commitment* account, and the *constitutive rule* account. I do not pretend that this list is

---

[8] This entire section is deeply indebted to MacFarlane's paper; I follow him not only in his taxonomy but also in how I am presenting the four views. I will indicate where my formulations are his by citing page numbers from his paper when I do borrow heavily from him.

exhaustive (it may not be), nor that the categories are mutually exclusive (presumably hybrid accounts are available). Still, in this section I will present simplified versions of each. This will help us see whether there is any single approach that can lay claim to being the best hope for a theory of assertion. If there is, simplicity considerations would favor such an approach over any hybrid.[9] Here I will present the four approaches themselves, and in the next section (1.5) I will consider how well they explain what we would like explained.

I begin with the attitudinal account. According to this account, to assert is to express an attitude (MacFarlane 2010: 80). Perhaps the most well-known version of this view is developed by Bach and Harnish (1979). They write that

In uttering e, S asserts that p if S expresses (i) the belief that p, and (ii) the intention that H believe that p. (1979: 42)

Bach and Harnish go on to characterize the notion of expressing an attitude in terms of R-intentions, where R-intentions are intentions to bring something about in an audience by way of the audience's recognition of this very intention. (Their inspiration for this notion is, of course, Grice's (1957, 1968a) account of meaning.) Here is how Bach and Harnish gloss the notion of expressing an attitude:

For S to express an attitude is for S to R-intend the hearer to take S's utterance as a reason to think that S has that attitude. (1979: 15)

Putting these points together we can characterize the Bach–Harnish version of the attitudinal account as follows: to assert a proposition is to utter a sentence expressing that proposition, with the intention that the utterance be regarded by one's audience as a reason both to think that one believes the proposition and that one intends the audience to believe it as well. (It is perhaps worth noting that this view yields a natural characterization of assertoric force itself, where assertoric force is the property a speech act has in virtue of the sort of illocutionary intention just described.)

A second account of assertion, the *common ground* account, construes assertion in terms of what Robert Stalnaker (1978) calls its "essential effect."[10] According to this account, to assert is to propose to add information to the conversational common ground (MacFarlane 2010: 80). Here is Stalnaker's seminal description of the approach:

... [A]n assertion should be understood as a proposal to change the context by adding the content to the information presupposed. This is an account of the *force* of an assertion, and it respects the traditional distinction between the content and the force of a speech act. Propositional content is represented by a (possibly partial) function from possible worlds to truth values; assertive

---

[9] This is not to say that simplicity considerations alone would settle the matter; only that they would offer one sort of consideration to favor a given theory over others.
[10] It is worth noting that Stalnaker (1978) takes the notion of assertion to be primitive; in saying that his aim is to capture the "essential effect" of assertion, he means to be distancing himself from the idea that his proposal serves as an analysis of the notion of assertion.

force is represented by the way in which any such function is used to change the context that the speaker shares with those to whom he is speaking. (Stalnaker 1999: 10–11)

As MacFarlane points out, both this proposal and the commitment account (to be discussed later) take their inspiration from David Lewis' (1979) suggestion that speech acts can be understood in terms of how they alter the "conversational score." Stalnaker's suggestion is that the conversational score can be represented as the common ground of accepted propositions, and that speech acts can be thought of in terms of how they alter the common ground. Assertions do so by adding information to the common ground; this is what assertoric force consists in, according to this view.

A third account of assertion—the commitment account—holds that to assert is to undertake a commitment (MacFarlane 2010: 80). First articulated by C. S. Pierce (1934: 384), such a view has been defended more recently by Searle (1969, 1979), Brandom (1983, 1994), Wright (1992), MacFarlane (2003, 2005), Watson (2004), and Rescorla (2009). Like the common ground account, the commitment account characterizes assertion in terms of its "essential effect." But unlike the common ground account, the commitment account regards this effect as an alteration in deontic status (to borrow Brandom's (1994) way of putting the point). That is, one who asserts that p undertakes a commitment to the truth of [p], which involves inheriting the obligation to vindicate one's entitlement to [p] if queried.[11] Equipped with such a view, we might go on to characterize assertoric force as the property of a speech act that manifests this sort of commitment.

Finally, we move to the constitutive rule account of assertion—the one I will be developing in this book. According to this account, to assert is to make a move defined by its constitutive rules (MacFarlane 2010: 80). Tim Williamson, one of the key defenders of this account, characterizes the key idea as follows: "... the speech act [of assertion], like a game and unlike the act of jumping, is constituted by rules" (Williamson 1996: 489). The idea that assertion can be characterized in this way is the idea that this type of speech act can be picked out as the unique speech-act type governed by a particular rule, or set of such rules: *all* and *only* assertions are governed by the rule(s) in question. As presented by Williamson, the rule takes the following form:

RA   One must: assert that p, only if φ.

The most popular version of this approach holds that there is only one such rule—referred to as "the norm of assertion." Candidates for φ include the condition that (i) one knows that p (Unger 1975; Slote 1979; Williamson 1996; and many others), (ii) one is (epistemically) certain that p (Stanley 2008), (iii) one is justified in believing that p (Lackey 2007b;[12] Kvanvig 2009), (iv) one is rational in believing that p (Douven 2006),

---

[11] Here and throughout I adopt the practice of referring to a proposition by putting square brackets around a sentence that expresses it: [p] = the proposition that p.

[12] Lackey's "reasonable to believe" norm does not require that one believe on the basis of the reason in question; only that one have the reason that would render the belief reasonable.

(v) it is reasonable for one to regard oneself as knowing that p (Neta 2009; Lackey 2007b anticipates such a view), (vi) one believes that p (variants on Bach and Harnish 1979),[13] and (vii) it is true that p (Weiner 2005, 2007). (This list is not exhaustive, though it covers the main proposals.) The point behind this approach is that assertion is to be characterized in terms of the rule(s) that tell(s) us when one is warranted in performing a speech act of this kind. MacFarlane (2010: 85) notes that it is unclear whether this proposal aims to characterize assertoric force.

Each of these accounts has its strengths and its weaknesses. It is to these that I now turn.

1.5 Applying the Approaches to the *Explananda*

Having introduced the sort of data we might expect an account of assertion to explain (that is, the various features of assertion), as well as the four accounts of assertion that we might examine by reference to these data, we can now proceed to determine how well each of these four accounts does with the eight features described previously. As before, I will be considering only pure versions of these accounts, rather than hybrids.

1.5.1 *The Attitudinal Account*

The attitudinal account is well-placed to explain a good many of the previous features. It has no problem explaining the *sincerity* phenomenon; that is, how it is that making an assertion counts as manifesting one's beliefs. The explanation would be this: to express a belief (in the Bach–Harnish model) is to R-intend that the hearer take one's utterance as a reason to think that one has the belief in question. Assuming that sincerity involves having the attitudes one is representing oneself to others as having, sincerity in this intention would then be a matter of (among other things) having the belief in question. Hence sincere assertion manifests belief.

Next, consider the other features of assertion bound up with its aptness for communicating knowledge. The proponent of the attitudinal account can explain these so long as she assumes, plausibly, that there are epistemic standards for belief.[14] In this light, consider first what I called previously the *belief-worthiness* of assertion: why those who assert in the hope of being believed stand a reasonable chance of realizing this hope. If assertion expresses belief and belief itself is governed by epistemic standards, then one who makes an assertion expresses something governed by epistemic standards. But then the audience who regards the assertion as sincere (and so as manifesting the speaker's belief) will naturally raise the question whether the standards for belief have been met. If she has reasons to think that the standards have been met (and she has no

---

[13] As I noted, Bach and Harnish's view can be taken to be a version of the attitudinal account; but a close variant can also be represented within the constitutive rule framework, where the rule in question is the belief rule to the effect that *one must: assert that p, only if one believes that p*.

[14] Bach and Harnish do make this assumption. See also Bach 2008.

relevant defeaters), this will rationalize her acceptance of the proposition asserted—with the result that if she is rational, she will accept the assertion and so believe what was asserted. This, in turn, explains the aptness of assertion to communicate knowledge: insofar as the manifested belief amounts to knowledge, then the hearer who (out of the conviction that the manifested belief satisfied the epistemic standard governing belief) properly accepted the assertion thereby acquires the knowledge in question. So, too, we might explain why assertion is susceptible to epistemic challenge. If assertion expresses belief and belief itself is governed by epistemic standards, then epistemic challenges to assertion are intelligible as challenges to the belief expressed—that is, as querying whether the belief expressed meets the governing epistemic standards.

Finally, we might also explain why assertion should play such a prominent evidential role in Radical Interpretation. Radical Interpretation aims to recover both what a speaker believes and what she means by her utterances. So, insofar as assertion expresses the speaker's beliefs and these in turn are governed by epistemic standards, the Radical Interpreter may then try to interpret the speaker's expressions of her beliefs—her assertions—in such a way as to aim whenever possible to construe her as conforming to the relevant standards. But this will mean interpreting her speech so as to maximize her justified belief and knowledge—or perhaps to minimize cases involving the unexplained lack of these.[15] And it is plausible to think that the best way to do this is by correlating (where possible) the assertions made with the environmental conditions prompting them. Such a methodological proposal seems very attractive; and insofar as it is, the attitudinal account can explain the RI-evidential feature of assertion.

However, the attitudinal account appears to face challenges in explaining some of the other phenomena associated with assertion. I begin with the claim that the attitudinal account will have difficulty explaining the entitlements and responsibilities generated by assertion. This is because it is unclear on the attitudinal account why one whose own belief was formed through accepting another's assertion would be entitled to defer the challenge to the source speaker. After all, even if you believe something because I indicate to you that I believe it, this alone does not entitle you to defer challenges to me. Nor is it clear how my expressing a belief authorizes or entitles you to defer to me any challenges to your entitlement to believe as you do.

In fact, it is tempting to see the problems facing the attitudinal view on this score as indicating a central weakness: the attitudinal view *does not have enough normativity in the picture*. I have assumed previously that the attitudinal picture could help itself to the idea that belief is governed by an epistemic standard; and I assumed as well that if it does help itself to this idea, then the attitudinal account inherits the normativity attaching to belief. The present difficulty is that neither the normativity attaching to belief, nor the normativity involved in expressing belief in the manner

---

[15] This is a variant on Richard Grandy's (1973) Principle of Humanity.

of Bach and Harnish, suffices to explain the normative dimension of assertion. (In bringing this out here I anticipate a theme that I will be developing at greater length in Chapter 6.)

To see that the attitudinal view does not explain the normativity attaching to assertion, let us focus on the phenomenon whereby assertion generates an entitlement to a hearer to defer a challenge to the asserter. Let H believe that p, and let H's belief be formed on the basis of S's assertion that p. According to the attitudinal view, in asserting that p, S expressed the corresponding attitudes, and so gave H a reason to regard S as (i) believing that p and (ii) intending that H believe that p (through this very recognition) as well. But does S's having given H such a reason also entitle H to defer challenges to S when these arise regarding his (H's) own belief that p? There seems no reason for H to think that he enjoys this entitlement. To be sure, H can reason that if S's assertion was sincere, then S herself has the belief that p, and she intended H to believe that p as well. So, assuming belief is answerable to epistemic standards, S intended H to do something that itself was answerable to such standards. But nothing would prevent S from shrugging her shoulders and saying to H, "Oh, well, so the belief I intended you to form fails to satisfy epistemic standards. So sorry." H might then accuse S of having led him to form an unwarranted belief; but S could reply that the decision to believe what she (S) believes was his (H's) and his alone. Compare: I may know that these cookies are for Ralph, and even so I may place them in a spot where I know you will encounter them, intending that you eat them (by way of your recognizing my intention). Still, if you do, it is no excuse to say that I authorized you to eat them—I did no such thing! To *tempt* a person to φ (by doing something with the intention that they φ by way of their recognizing this intention) is not the same as *authorizing* her to φ. In short, even if the asserter intends the hearer to form the belief in question, intending is one thing, *authorizing* is another, and it would seem that the attitudinal view has no basis for moving from the former to the latter. What is missing here, and what the attitudinal view seems to fail to deliver, is a sense that S *ought not* to have asserted as she did—and that the reason she ought not to have done so is that in so asserting she *authorized* H to believe as he did.

A diagnosis in the same spirit is appropriate in connection with MacFarlane's (2010) contention that the attitudinal account fails to be able to explain the phenomenon of retraction as well. MacFarlane notes that retracting one's assertion that p is not the same as, and does not imply, making it clear that one no longer believes that p. He writes:

One can, without any insincerity, retract an assertion of something one still believes. One might do this, for example, because one realizes one cannot adequately defend the claim, or because one does not want others relying on it. (MacFarlane 2010: 83)[16]

---

[16] Compare again Kvanvig's (2009) distinction between retracting an assertion (the act) and retracting what was asserted (the content).

MacFarlane goes on to note that the attitudinal account might try to construe retraction in terms, not of no longer believing the asserted proposition, but of no longer wanting to be taken as *committed* to the proposition, or as holding the proposition to be *adequately grounded*.[17] But even so amended the account fails, according to MacFarlane, for failing to have the resources to capture the normativity of the assertion: "the notions of epistemic groundedness and commitment that are invoked here are foreign to the expressive account" (2010: 84). Again, the problem appears to be a lack of materials with which to capture a normative aspect of the assertion.

I conclude, then, that even if it is supplemented with the assumption that there are epistemic standards governing belief, the expressive account of assertion faces challenges, and its apparent inadequacy reflects its lacking the resources to account for the normativity distinctive of assertion.

1.5.2 *The Common Ground Account*

Let me now move to the common ground account, according to which the speech act of assertion is the act through which one proposes to add information to the conversational common ground.

We can begin with the assertion's aptness for communicating knowledge (and the other properties bound up with this one). An initial complication is that a speaker can propose to add information to the common ground for all sorts of reasons, only one of which is that the speaker knows the asserted proposition to be true. But perhaps the proponent of the common ground account can say this: it is often mutually manifest that the aim of the conversation is to exchange information about what is the case, and in such cases the hearer is entitled to presume that the speaker's motive for proposing to add to the common ground is to add information she (believes that she) knows to be true.[18] If this explanation is plausible, perhaps it can do double duty as an explanation for the *belief-worthiness* of assertion: the speaker's hope of being believed is reasonable, and is likely to meet with success, to just the extent that the hearer regards the speaker's proposal to add to the common ground as deriving from her knowledge of the proposition asserted. Still, it must be said that the common ground account does not regard the requirement to speak only from knowledge (or justified belief) as essential to the speech act of assertion (but see Schaffer 2008). Consequently, it is not entirely clear why speakers are rational in hoping to be believed when they assert. Perhaps the best that can be done on the common ground account is to explain the belief-worthiness of assertion *conditional on* the hearer's recognition of the knowledge-communicating aim of the speaker. By the same token it is not obvious why assertion should be susceptible to distinctly epistemic challenge; after all, the proposal to add to the common

---

[17] As MacFarlane notes, the retraction should also be seen as expressing the speaker's intention that H *not* believe that proposition on the basis of the previous assertion.

[18] For an interesting and novel view which combines the common ground approach with a knowledge standard for assertion, see Schaffer 2008.

ground may have been made on non-epistemic grounds. But again it may be that the common ground proposal can explain assertion's EC-susceptibility at least in those instances where it is mutually manifest that the point of the conversation is to exchange true information. On this view, not all assertions are EC-susceptible; but assertions are susceptible to epistemic challenge when they are taken to be part of an information exchange aimed at communicating knowledge.

The fact that there are many potential motives for wanting to add information to the common ground also appears to make it harder for the common ground account to explain *other* phenomena associated with assertion. These include the conveyed self-representation of the speaker as knowing (or at least having good evidence for) the proposition asserted, the entitlements and responsibilities generated by assertion, and the central evidential role assertion plays in the method of Radical Interpretation.

Consider the feature whereby one who asserts that p represents herself as knowing that p (or at least as epistemically authoritative on the matter). Insofar as a speaker can propose to add a proposition to the common ground for any of a variety of purposes, it would seem that the mere fact that one is asserting that p does not convey that one represents oneself in this way. In response, the proponent of the common ground account might hold that, at least when it is mutually manifest that the aim of the conversation is to exchange information that is (believed to be) known to be true, one's assertion will succeed in representing oneself as knowing. But it would seem that there are occasions on which this would-be explanation gets things *precisely backwards*: it is not that we recognize the assertion's conveyed self-representation because we have prior knowledge that the aim of the conversation is to exchange known truths; rather it is because we recognize that in asserting the speaker is representing herself as knowing (or at least as authoritative), that we apprehend that the aim of the conversation is to exchange information regarded as (known to be) true! Take a case in which you take your seat on an airplane, only to find that the person seated next to you begins asserting all sorts of things about this and that. You need not ask yourself first what the conversational point of his doing so is, prior to knowing that he is representing himself as knowledgeable on the matters. You might wonder *why* he is doing so—what the *point* of his doing so is. Still, the order of explanation goes against what the common ground account would predict: on the strength of your knowledge of the conveyed self-representation implicit in assertion, you can conclude that the purpose of his monologue, whatever it is, must involve his desire to tell you various things he takes to be (known to be) true. Essentially the same point might be put this way: at least sometimes, and arguably always, the knowledge that a speaker has made an *assertion* is all the context we need in order to determine that she is representing herself as knowledgeable regarding (or at least as justifiedly believing) what she says.

Consider too the feature whereby asserting something generates an entitlement in the hearer to defer challenges to the speaker. Perhaps the proponent of the common ground account will think to explain this phenomenon as appropriate, on the grounds that it was the speaker (after all) who proposed to add the proposition to the common ground. But again, if assertion involves proposing to add information to the common ground, and if this sort of proposal can be made on non-epistemic grounds, then it is not clear that the speaker has so entitled the hearer. Nor is it clear that the speaker is under any obligation to take up the deferred challenge: after all, she merely proposed to add it to the common ground, and may not even regard the proposition as true.

What is more, the common ground view appears without recourse to any explanation for why the speech act of assertion would figure so centrally in the method of Radical Interpretation. The proponent of this account can say this much: the reason assertion is central in the interpretation of heretofore uninterpreted languages has to do with its role in representing what the speaker takes to be the case. Insofar as what she takes to be the case on a given occasion can be determined by examining the conditions that prompt her assertion on that occasion—as when what she takes to be the case is something she determined by her perception of features of her environment—we can then see why the task of Radical Interpretation will typically begin by focusing on assertions. Still, we might wonder: how can the Radical Interpreter tell when her assertions are advanced for this conversational purpose, as opposed to some other conversational purpose? Standardly, the assumption is that any assertion is to be regarded as aiming to communicate what the speaker takes to be the case; but it is not obvious that the proponent of the common ground view is warranted in making this assumption. Certainly, her conception of the speech act of assertion does not warrant this assumption.

In sum. It is not entirely clear how many of the features bound up with our assertoric practice can be explained by the common ground approach to assertion. I do not say that these features cannot be explained; only that it is not obvious that they can be. I can also say that even if this approach can provide the explanations sought, the explanations themselves will be complicated, appealing to a variety of factors beyond the nature of assertion itself to explain what wants explanation.[19] If we find that we can provide a plausible account of these features in some other way, without the need for the various auxiliary hypotheses, such an account is to be preferred.

1.5.3 *The Commitment Account*

Next, let us consider the commitment account, according to which to assert is to undertake a commitment. This view does quite well with explaining the interpersonal features of assertion bound up with its aptness to communicate knowledge. It clearly explains the susceptibility of assertions to epistemic challenge, as well as the feature whereby the speaker authorizes the hearer to defer challenges to her. After all, the commitment undertaken is conceived to include the commitment to vindicate one's entitlement to the asserted proposition (if appropriately queried). Since the entitlement in question is an epistemic one, we can explain assertion's

---

[19] Arguably, one of these factors will be a feature whereby assertion is answerable to an epistemic standard!

belief-worthiness as well as its aptness for communicating knowledge. In particular, the asserter conveys that she stands ready to vindicate her entitlement to the proposition. This will suffice, when the hearer is entitled to regard her as able to vindicate that entitlement, to render the assertion belief-worthy, and insofar as the speaker spoke from knowledge, she will thereby have passed this on to anyone in her audience who, on the basis of their entitlement to regard her as able to vindicate her entitlement, accepted what she said.

I note, too, that this account appears to have the resources as well to explain the conveyed self-representation implicit in assertion. The commitment account might explain this on the assumption that, as an account of a speech-act type, the commitment account is itself implicitly known by all competent language users. In that case, one who observes another's assertion will know that the speaker conveys her readiness to vindicate her entitlement to the proposition in question. Since the speaker herself is also aware of this feature of assertion, and will regard it as common knowledge, she will be aware that the hearer will be in a position to draw this inference on observing the assertion. And all of this, taken together, appears to capture a sense in which the asserter represents herself as being epistemically authoritative regarding the proposition asserted.

Finally, the commitment account appears to have a very simple, and highly plausible, account of retraction. To retract is simply to undo one's commitment to a proposition. One can do so even though one continues to believe the proposition in question. The "undoing" of the commitment can be conceived as a change in deontic status: one who retracts an earlier assertion that p is no longer "on the hook" to vindicate her entitlement to [p]. This account also has a nice explanation for why assertion has a correlative act in retraction: both are public acts, one in which the speaker manifests her commitment to defending a given proposition, and one in which she manifests her cancellation of that commitment.

Still, it is unclear how the commitment account will explain the sincerity aspect of assertion—the way in which assertion expresses belief. The proponent of the commitment view might think to explain this feature by identifying belief with the sort of commitment that figures (in her account) in assertion. On such a view, belief just is (or involves) a commitment to the truth of a proposition, such that, when one is legitimately called upon to do so, one stands ready to vindicate one's entitlement to the proposition to which one is so committed. The difficulty, though, is that it is not clear that this singles out the attitude of belief. On the contrary, it seems that one might be committed to the truth of a proposition in this way for all sorts of reasons, even when one does not believe it. Consider, for example, what is involved in defending a philosophical claim. One's commitment to the view in question might be likened to the commitment of one who *champions* the view—something one can do even if one does not believe it.[20]

[20] See Chapter 11 for further discussion.

So, too, the commitment view appears to leave us at a bit of a loss as to why assertion would play so central a role in Radical Interpretation. Why the focus on the speaker's avowed commitments, when the aim is to interpret her speech? Perhaps we could make sense of this if we could identify these commitments with the speaker's beliefs. But again we have seen that a speaker might be committed to the truth of a proposition she does not believe. So it is unclear whether the commitment view can make sense of the central role assertion plays in Radical Interpretation.

I raise these objections for the commitment view, but I should say that I regard this view as perhaps the best of the views I do not endorse. I have two reasons for preferring the constitutive-rule-based account (to which I will shortly turn): first, I think that the rule-based account does a better job explaining these various features; but second and perhaps more importantly, I think the rule-based account can provide the mechanisms by which one commits in this fashion—thereby enabling us to *derive* the core features that the commitment view would ascribe to assertion.

1.5.4 The Constitutive Rule Account

I turn, then, to the constitutive rule account itself. According to this approach, to assert is to perform an act defined by its constitutive rules. Here I am going to assume that the rule in question provides the standard against which the warrantedness (propriety) of assertions is to be judged. Let us assume, too, that the standard is a robustly epistemic one. I submit that this view does the best job with the phenomena discussed previously.

Let us begin with the explanation for assertion's features that are bound up with its aptness for communicating knowledge. Assume that the norm of assertion is a rule of language, and so is something that is common knowledge among all competent language users. Then, when a speaker asserts something in a hearer's presence, both the speaker and hearer know that the speaker's act was warranted only if the standard was satisfied. Since the standard is robustly epistemic, the result is that insofar as the hearer regards that standard as being satisfied, she will regard the speaker as being epistemically authoritative regarding the truth of the proposition, in which case she will regard the proposition as belief-worthy (since her doing so is likely to lead to knowledge or epistemically authoritative belief).[21] So, too, we can explain the conveyed self-representation implicit in assertion: since both the hearer and speaker know that an assertion is warranted only if the speaker satisfies the epistemic norm, the act of assertion itself can be seen as conveying that the speaker *does* satisfy this norm.[22] (This, then, is the content of the idea that the asserter represents herself as being relevantly epistemically authoritative.) In like fashion, we can explain the feature

---

[21] To see how one can get this sort of result even if the norm is not knowledge but instead some other robustly epistemic property, see Chapter 11.

[22] Here I assume that one who performs an act regarding which it is mutual knowledge that the act is governed by rules conveys to those who observe the act that the rules have been satisfied. For an articulation and defense of something like this view, see Ross (1986: 77–78).

whereby assertion authorizes a hearer to defer challenges to the speaker. Were the hearer to accept the assertion on the strength of the speaker's say-so, she would then be in a position in which she regarded the speaker as satisfying the norm of assertion, under conditions in which the speaker conveyed precisely this. Thus, were the hearer to be challenged to defend his belief, the fact that the speaker conveyed that *she* satisfies the epistemic standard warranting assertion of the proposition in question would entitle him, the hearer, to defer any challenges to her. Thus, on this view the fact that assertion involves a commitment to defend is itself a natural implication of assertion's rule-governed nature. (See Chapter 3 for details.)

Finally, we can also make sense of (sincere) assertion as the expression of belief: if assertion is governed by a robustly epistemic norm, then insofar as one is sincere in one's assertion one aims to satisfy that norm, and since the norm requires things—knowledge, justified or rational belief—all of which involve belief, sincere assertion involves belief in the asserted content. It must be admitted, however, that several recent accounts of assertion's norm are robustly epistemic without requiring belief,[23] and so, strictly speaking, only some versions of the rule-based account can provide this simple explanation of the sincerity of assertion. (See Chapter 11 for a complete discussion.)

Next, consider the role of assertion in the method of Radical Interpretation. The constitutive rule account has a simple explanation of this as well: since assertion is governed by a robustly epistemic norm, the Radical Interpreter who discerns the making of an assertion can then follow the method of trying to render the assertion in such a way as to satisfy the norm. This will inevitably point the Radical Interpreter to the speaker's environment, since the interpreter must render the speaker so that she knows (or justifiably or rationally believes). In this way we see that if assertion has a robustly epistemic norm, that it does so grounds a certain principle of interpretation which would have us maximize the speaker's satisfaction of a robustly epistemic standard—or at least to minimize the (unexplained) occasions in which this standard is not satisfied.

Finally, consider the retractability of assertion. Insofar as assertion is governed by a norm whose standards must be satisfied if the assertion is to be warranted, and given that making an assertion conveys that one satisfies the standard in question, we would predict that retraction would be called for whenever one asserts under conditions in which one did not, in fact, satisfy the norm. And retraction itself would be a matter of indicating something to this effect (that is, that one did not satisfy the rule). The effect of doing so would be to communicate that one is no longer representing oneself as

---

[23] In order to handle her own cases of selfless assertion (Lackey 2007b), Lackey has discussed a view on which knowledge-relevant (propositional) justification warrants assertion, where one can have this without belief. So, too, MacKinnon's (2013) "supportive reasons" norm does not require belief. And insofar as he would apply his norm of action to assertion, Neta's (2009) view, that the relevant standard is reasonableness regarding whether one knows, also does not require belief. In Chapter 11 I discuss how rule-based accounts of assertion whose rule does not require belief might handle the sincerity of assertion.

relevantly authoritative—with the further result that this would make clear that one is no longer available to shoulder the epistemic burden for the proposition in question.

I cannot pretend that this quick run through the four main accounts of assertion, and several of the features characteristic of assertions, secures the case for the constitutive rule account. But I do think it should increase our interest in that account: given the totality of the explanatory work that it appears to be able to do, which none of its competitors can do equally well and equally simply, we ought to take it seriously. Of course, it remains to be seen whether we can make good on all of these explanations. In the rest of this book I will be developing these explanations in much greater detail. For now, however, I tentatively conclude that the hypothesis in question—to the effect that assertion is to be understood in terms of the constitutive rule that governs it—has much going for it. In the rest of this book I will be suggesting that the explanatory power of this hypothesis is significantly greater than has heretofore been recognized.

1.6 The Constitutive Rule Account: Objections and Replies

The foregoing comparison appears to give us some initial reason to favor the constitutive rule account of assertion over the other accounts: it handles more of the data to be explained, and does so in a simpler fashion, than they do. Still, it might be thought that the constitutive norm account faces some important challenges. In this penultimate section of this chapter I reply to what I regard as the main challenges.

1.6.1 *Is the Norm of Assertion a Constitutive Rule?*

First, there are generic reasons for thinking that the rule embodied by the "norm of assertion" is very different from paradigmatic instances of things we all recognize as constitutive rules (such as the "three strikes and you're out" rule in baseball). This criticism has been forcefully defended by Ishani Maitra (2010: 282–84), who identifies three distinct differences between paradigmatic instances of constitutitive rules (on the one hand) and the norm of assertion (on the other).

One difference which Maitra highlights is in the form of the rules. Where the "three strikes and you're out" rule identifies what outs *are* (or rather one way to acquire the status of being out), the norm of assertion ("You must: assert p, only if you satisfy E") states the condition (not on what an assertion *is*, or what it is to count as being an assertion, but rather) on an assertion's being warranted. In response, I find myself agreeing with the claim that Maitra is making here but failing to see this as grounds to question the hypothesis that assertion is governed by a constitutive rule.

I can say two things in defense of my attitude on this score. First, the aim of the norm of assertion proposal is to individuate assertion as a type of speech act. If it succeeds in this aim—if assertion is the unique type of speech act governed uniquely by the proposed rule—then we can use the norm of assertion to say what assertions are (alternatively: what it is to count as an assertion). To wit: to assert is to perform the unique type of speech act that is subject to the norm in question. Admittedly, this does not add very much illumination beyond what was already present in the hypothesis that assertion is individuated by a constitutive rule. Even so, it is not unilluminating. (Quite the contrary: the rest of this book is aimed to show that if this is true we can understand the variety of connections that exist between assertion and a host of other phenomena of interest to philosophers.) My second point is this: while Maitra is right that the norm of assertion does not have the same form as the "three strikes" rule in baseball, it is not clear what significance we should attach to this fact. Unless we have reason to think that constitutive rules come in only one form, this is an interesting point which nevertheless does not undermine the hypothesis of assertion's having a constitutive rule. Perhaps what Maitra has in mind is something like this: it is only when a rule tells us when the satisfaction of some condition "counts as" the having of a certain status in the game—when something counts as an *out* in baseball, or *being in check* in chess—that the rule is recognizable as a constitutive one. If so, then I would say that the norm of assertion fits the bill—or at least that it is natural to understand it as doing so. A move in a language game counts as an assertion just in case (i) the move is properly assessed along the dimension of warrantedness, and (ii) the condition on the move's being warranted is uniquely specified by the rule that one must not make a move of that sort unless … (Fill in the lacuna with your favored account of the standard provided by the norm of assertion.)

A second difference Maitra highlights is in the relative prevalence of what she calls "breaches" of the rules in question. She writes:

… [T]hough there are no doubt some breaches of the three-strikes norm in games of baseball, it seems likely that these are extremely rare. For example, by and large, batters are indeed ruled out when they earn three strikes. By contrast, if either the knowledge or the truth norm were a constitutive norm of assertion, then … breaches of the constitutive norm of the speech act would be common indeed. (Maitra 2010: 282)

I worry that this objection is based on confusing two very different things that might be described as "breaches" in a rule. On the one hand, one might have in mind a case in which a move in a game *fails to satisfy a rule's standards*—something that would result in a verdict that the act in question is not good, or unwarranted, or results in a penalty, or what-have-you. On the other hand, one might have in mind a case in which a rule on the books is *incorrectly applied to the case at hand*. The result here is that a verdict is rendered, but it does not reflect the actual rules that govern the game. I submit that the "three strikes" example Maitra gives is of the latter sort, whereas the case of assertion is of the former sort.

To bring out the significance of the distinction I am making, it will be helpful to have another constitutive rule from baseball on our hands. We might define a "pitch" as a throw by the pitcher towards home plate, where the trajectory of the ball itself is governed by a 'strike zone' standard of goodness (so that throws in the strike zones are *strikes*, while those not in the strike zone are *balls*), where we can then define other baseball statuses (*strikeout, walk*) in terms of these. In what sense can a "pitch" be defined in this way? Well, consider that not all throws by the pitcher to the catcher at home plate are pitches: sometimes the pitcher will throw to the catcher in the middle of a play (trying to get someone out at home plate), or during practice, or . . . in which case the throw is not a pitch. We might thus say that pitches are the throws from pitcher to catcher that are governed by the 'strike zone' standard. (While this may not be particularly informative—we might want to know when this standard is appropriately applied—the rule in question does effectively mark the contrast between throws that are pitches and throws that are not.) To be sure, there are other ways to assess pitches: it is usually considered poor pitching for a pitcher to throw a ball right down the middle of the strike zone (since it is easy for the batter to hit), and in certain pitch counts it is sometimes good to throw pitches that are not in the strike zone at all (in an attempt to get the batter to swing at an unhittable pitch). But these assessments do not speak to the issue of whether a thrown ball is a pitch or not; a thrown ball is a pitch only if it is properly assessable by reference to the 'strike zone' standard.

Now, it is an obvious empirical truth about baseball that in the course of a game many pitches fail to satisfy the 'strike zone' standard. But does this claim—that many pitches fail to satisfy the 'strike zone' standard—amount to an objection to the claim that the 'strike zone' standard is part of a constitutive rule regarding what it is to count as a pitch? Clearly not: no one would be moved by such an objection. Rather, the pitches which fail to meet the standard are all *balls* (in the sense of *bad pitches*, as defined previously). The prevalence of such pitches does not undermine the thesis that the 'strike zone' standard governs pitches; to suppose otherwise is to confuse the normative with the descriptive. But nor does the prevalence of such pitches undermine the claim that this standard is part of a constitutive rule regarding pitches; to suppose otherwise is to confuse the failure to satisfy a rule's standard (something that happens with some frequency) with the failure to properly apply a rule (which is a less common, though still not non-existent, phenomenon; more on this later).

Now, I submit that, in effect, Maitra's second objection is guilty of precisely this sort of error, and should be rejected accordingly. I want to say: of course there are lots of assertions that violate the norm's standard. These are unwarranted assertions. But the fact that there are lots of these does not undermine the thesis that the standard itself governs assertions; to suppose otherwise is to confuse the normative with the descriptive. Nor does the prevalence of such assertions undermine the thesis that the norm's standard is part of a constitutive rule for assertion; to suppose otherwise is to confuse the failure to satisfy a rule's standard, with the failure to properly apply a rule. It is akin to thinking that the fact that there are lots of pitches that do not satisfy the 'strike zone' standard undermines the thesis that the 'strike zone' standard is part of a constitutive rule for pitches.

Still, Maitra might think to recast her objection as follows: even after we are clear about the distinction between violating a rule's standard and misapplying the rule, still, a constitutive rule such as the "three strikes" rule is misapplied less frequently than is the norm of assertion. After all, it is rarely the case that a batter is considered out even though she only had two strikes, or only after she was given a fourth strike;[24] yet for any plausible candidate for the norm of assertion, there are many cases in which hearers regard an assertion as warranted when in fact (by the lights of the rule) it was not, or as unwarranted when in fact (by the lights of the rule) it was warranted. And we might add that there will even be cases in which hearers regard something as an assertion even when it was not appropriate to assess it by reference to the norm of assertion in the first place. Unless these can be explained in a plausible way, consistent with the hypothesis that the norm of assertion is a constitutive rule, it will suggest that the rule in question is not a constitutive one.

Happily, the explanation we seek is near to hand. Consider what is involved in applying the "three strikes" rule to a case at hand: you need to be able to distinguish balls from strikes at game speed, you need to be able to count to three, and you need to remember what "the count" is prior to each pitch. With the exception of the capacity to distinguish balls from strikes at game speed, these are relatively rudimentary capacities that are easy to apply in practice. Now consider what is involved in applying the rule in the norm of assertion: arguably, you need to be able to discern speaker intentions, and you also need to be able to discern whether the standard of the norm of assertion was met. The satisfaction of these conditions is harder to discern than are the conditions relevant to applying the "three strikes" rule. So it is no strike against the hypothesis that assertion has a constitutive rule, that it is harder to apply this rule than it is to apply the constitutive "three strikes" rule in baseball.

On this point it is also worth underscoring that, *strictly speaking*, the "three strikes" rule *is* misapplied with some frequency. This is because it is hard to discern balls from strikes at game speed. To a rough approximation, a pitch (when not offered at by the batter) is a strike if and only if it crosses over the plate at a height between the batter's knees and his waist. Yet umpires get this wrong with some regularity. In fact, having reviewed slow motion replays of roughly 700,000 pitches, Braydon King and Jerry Kim have concluded that "about 14 percent of non-swinging pitches were called erroneously" ("What Umpires Get Wrong," *New York Times*, March 28, 2014). Of course, the game of baseball is played by counting as a strike whatever the umpire calls a strike, even when the umpire is "wrong" in this way. Here we have a case in which a constitutive rule tells us that something is an X (here, a strike) iff condition C is satisfied (here, facts about the location of the ball when crossing over or near the plate), yet this rule is "breached" (in the sense of misapplied) with some frequency. This does not undermine the claim that the rule for counting as a strike is constitutive. The explanation for this is obvious: with a ball coming in at a speed between 75 and 95 miles per hour, often with a good deal of spin, the judgment must be made instantly, and the umpires

---

[24] Here I disregard the various ways a batter can get out beyond by striking out.

are only human. None of this calls into question that the rule for counting as a strike is a constitutive rule. So, too, I suggest, we have an explanation in the assertion case. Here too we have a case in which a constitutive rule tells us that something is an X (here, a warranted assertion)[25] iff condition C is satisfied (here, the satisfaction of the norm's standard), yet this rule is "breached" (in the sense of misapplied) on occasion. But again this fact can be explained by reference to the challenge of discerning when the conditions on warranted assertion are satisfied. Only here the challenge derives not from the speed at which the judgment has to be made, but from the difficulty of discerning others' intentions and the difficulty of epistemic assessment generally. There is no mystery here; the case is analogous to that of the constitutive rule for being a strike in baseball.

I turn, finally, to the third difference Maitra claims to find between the constitutive rules of baseball and the allegedly constitutive rule of assertion. It was this: whereas flagrant failures to conform to constitutive rules indicate that one is in fact not playing the game defined by those rules, "flagrant failures to conform to either the knowledge or the truth norm can nevertheless count as assertions" (Maitra 2010: 283). But this objection fails to mark a principled contrast between the two cases (baseball and assertion). Let us assume that what she has in mind with a "flagrant failure to conform" is a case of the following sort: a speaker makes (what any good theory should recognize as) an assertion, but the speaker knows full well that what she is saying is false or otherwise unsupported by evidence. (Bald-faced lies would be an excellent example.) In response, I note that we can find an analogue in baseball. These will be cases in which the pitcher throws (what any correct theory of baseball ought to recognize as) a pitch, but the pitcher does not even pretend to try to conform to the 'strike zone' standard. I refer, of course, to cases of the "intentional walk." There, a pitcher flagrantly fails to conform to the 'strike zone' standard, intentionally throwing pitches that are several feet out of the strike zone. Such a pitcher is flagrantly (deliberately; on purpose) failing to conform to the 'strike zone' standard, but is still playing the game of baseball for all that, just as a person who engages in bald-faced lying is flagrantly (deliberately; on purpose) failing to conform to the norm of assertion, but is still asserting for all that. To be sure, in the baseball case there are some rules which are such that a violation of *those* rules (flagrant or not) would indicate that the person is no longer playing baseball. (If you allow five strikes for an out then it is not baseball you are playing.) But in parallel fashion we can come up with cases of flagrant violations of the standard of assertion's norm where this fact alone suggests that the speaker is not, in fact, making an assertion. Consider cases in which people make clear that they are practicing their lines in a play, or have repeated an utterance to get their accent right, or . . . These are cases in which the flagrancy of the violation of the rule would itself be grounds for thinking that the act was not one in which the rule was, in fact, applicable. Again, there

---

[25] An assertion that is warranted is the analogue of a pitch that is a strike.

is no principled difference between assertion and other constitutive-rule-governed activities. Maitra's case against the constitutivity hypothesis fails.

1.6.2 Can One "Cheat" at Assertion?

Many critics of the hypothesis that assertion has a constitutive rule contend that, unlike other cases where there is a constitutive rule, with respect to assertion there is no notion of cheating, nor is there any sense to the idea of being better or worse at following the rules (Cappelen 2010). But these objections can be met directly: while there is nothing that we *call* cheating, and nothing that we *describe* in terms of doing better or worse at following the rule(s) of assertion, there certainly are phenomena in the area.

Consider first the objection that there is no analogue in assertion for cheating. It is worth noting that there are at least two ways in which one can cheat. I think that there can be versions of both sorts of cheating in the practice of assertion.

In the first form of cheating I want to consider, one violates a rule whose violation is associated with a sanction, but one covers one's tracks so that one "gets away with it" (whereas if one had been caught violating that rule one would have been penalized). Let us call this sort of cheating the "avoidance of sanction." The following example illustrates. Holding one's opponent is illegal in football; so if one holds one's opponent but covers it up, so that one gets away with it, one might be said to have been cheating. It is clear that this sort of cheating does have an analogue in the case of assertion: lying. Lying, very much like the avoidance-of-sanction type of cheating, is a matter of violating the rule (failing to have the epistemic authority to satisfy the norm of assertion), where one covers one's tracks and so is not seen as doing anything sanctionable. True, we do not describe lies as cases of "cheating"; but the similarity remains.

But this is not the only sort of cheating. What is more, arguably this is not the sort of cheating Cappelen had in mind, since it involves rules that are regulative rather than constitutive (whereas the rule governing assertion is supposed to be constitutive).[26] For constitutive rules, the violation of the standard itself calls, not for a sanction, but for a recognition that *the agent did not perform the act she purported to perform*. Thus, imagine one who purported to castle in chess, but where she did not follow the rules of castling (and indeed did not follow any of the rules of chess), where she was aware of this and moved the piece where she did only to gain maximal advantage, and where she tried to keep the rule violation hidden from her opponent. This sort of "move" is not a chess move, and so not a castling move, at all. To be sure, she might get away with it, but she cheated nevertheless. Let us call this sort of cheating "constitutive-rule cheating." But I submit that even here there can be forms of "cheating" at assertion. I present two cases, but these could be multiplied.

---

[26] I thank an anonymous referee for this suggestion.

FAKE WEBSITE Intending to get another person to believe that the President is in Honolulu, Gonzalez goes to the trouble of faking a website that looks exactly like the website of the *New York Times* online (albeit with a slightly different URL), and posts a story about Obama being in Honolulu.

COMPUTER-GENERATED ILLUSIONS Simpson is a computer whiz who has recently learned to program her computer so that it produces arbitrary but intelligible sentences and "utters" them through its voice synthesizer. Anyone hearing the computer who did not know that the "utterances" were computer-generated would be duped into thinking someone had said something.

In both of these cases, I submit, we have the appearance of assertion but not the reality. This is because (roughly put) in neither case is there an utterance of a sentence by a speaker who performs the act in such a way as to invoke his or her own epistemic authority. In FAKE WEBSITE, Gonzalez has not put his own epistemic authority on the line; indeed, he has not even *purported* to do so. Rather, what he has done is make it seem as if a writer for the *New York Times* has done so, whereas in point of fact no one has done so. In COMPUTER-GENERATED ILLUSIONS Simpson has generated the appearance of assertoric speech, but again no one has produced an act invoking one's own epistemic authority on anything (the sentences were arbitrarily generated). These cases amount to constitutive-rule cheating, since they purport to follow a constitutive rule—they purport to be cases in which a speech act or inscription is properly assessed by reference to the norm of assertion—but they are no such thing. The proof of this is that there is no one, group, or institution who is properly held responsible for having the relevant epistemic authority. It can be allowed, of course, that we would hold Gonzalez and Simpson responsible for producing these would-be assertions; but this point is parallel to the point that we would hold the subject who cheats in chess responsible for violating the rules of chess. The point remains that in neither case was the act what it purported to be. I will acknowledge as well that, when it comes to assertion, such cases are highly unusual, and any actual cases of this sort will be rare. But presumably Maitra's cheating objection is not that cases of assertoric cheating will be rare, but that there can be no such cases; and I have just argued that there can be such cases.

Next, consider the objection that there is nothing we would describe as "doing better or worse" at following the rules of assertion. Again, while this is true, it says more about our descriptive practices than it tells us about any significant disanalogy between assertion and other constitutive-rule-governed activities. For surely there are people who are better or worse informants, and one aspect of being better or worse as an informant is how reliable one is. Now, we can understand reliability along two dimensions: the reliability of a particular assertion, and the reliability of a speaker in the assertions she makes (or would make) overall (or perhaps in some restricted domain).

Consider, then, one way for a speaker to be "better" as an asserter: be more reliable in the particular assertions she makes. To spell out this notion we can follow a process-reliabilist account of reliable belief, so that the reliability of an assertion is construed as the reliability of the process-types through which the speaker represented, stored, and then asserted the proposition in question.[27] This contention is based on the claim that the more reliable an assertion, the more likely it is to satisfy the norm of assertion (and the greater the margin of error for those assertions that do satisfy the norm). Indeed, this might even be endorsed by one who thought that truth is the norm of assertion. After all, the more reliable one's assertion, the more likely it is that one's assertion is true, and so the more likely it is that one's assertion satisfies the norm. But the point holds for the other candidate norms as well. To see this, suppose that the norm of assertion is an epistemic standing requiring reliable belief. Then, on the assumption that reliable assertion typically reflects reliable belief, the more reliable one's assertion, the easier it will be for the assertion to satisfy even a demanding epistemic norm. And even if the norm of assertion is an epistemic standing that does not require reliable belief—say, rational belief (construed so as not to require reliable belief)—even so, on the empirical assumption that satisfying this epistemic standing is highly correlated with reliability in belief, the result is that reliable assertion increases the chances that one satisfies the norm of assertion. In short, whatever the norm of assertion is, the more reliable one's assertion, the more likely that one's assertion satisfies the norm of assertion, the greater the margin for error—and so the "better" one is as an asserter on this occasion. The basic idea here is clear enough: a speaker whose assertion is produced by processes that are 97% reliable is "better" than one whose processes are 90% reliable—even if both speakers' assertions satisfy the norm of assertion—if only because the former asserter has a greater margin for error, and so exposes her audience to a lesser risk of falsehood (and a lesser risk of accepting an assertion that did not satisfy the norm of assertion).

But there is a second way for a speaker to be "better" as an asserter, and that is simply to have more assertions satisfying the norm of assertion. An asserter 98% of whose assertions satisfy the norm of assertion is better than an asserter 65% of whose assertions satisfy the norm. To be sure, we may not readily talk this way, in terms of better and worse asserters. But again this reflects more a point about how we talk than it does a point about the nature of assertion.

I conclude, then, that while it is true that assertion is unlike other constitutive-rule-governed activities, insofar as we do not speak about "cheating" in assertion or about being "better or worse" as an asserter, this does not provide us with a reason to abandon the hypothesis that assertion is governed by a constitutive rule.

1.6.3 Does the Constitutive Rule Have Unacceptably Strong Modal Implications?

Cappelen (2010) contends that the constitutive rule account is too modally robust: it implies that there can be nothing recognizable as assertion in the absence of the rule

---

[27] This is the approach I take to reliable testimony in Goldberg (2010a).

in question, and this can be called into doubt. Thus he imagines that, given any candidate standard for the norm of assertion φ, we can imagine nearby worlds in which there is a speech practice just like our practice of assertion, with the sole difference that φ is not the standard that governs the practice. So if it is actually the case that knowledge is the standard by which we assess assertions for warrantedness, we can imagine a community in which rational belief is the standard for (apparently) assertoric speech. But (Cappelen argues) insofar as assertion has a constitutive norm, then any speech act governed by a different norm *cannot be assertion*. Since this conclusion seems wrong in the imagined scenario case, we should reject the hypothesis that assertion is governed by a constitutive norm.

Although I will not be in a position to respond to this objection until I present my own account of assertion's norm, here I will anticipate that account (a full defense of which will have to wait until Chapters 9–11). I will be arguing that we do best to think of assertion's norm as requiring that one assert that p, only if one has *the relevant epistemic authority* with respect to [p]. (I will be arguing that what counts as the relevant epistemic authority will be determined in context.) If this is correct, then Cappelen's objection turns on the existence of the following possibility: a speech community engages in a practice of assertion, even though the speech acts are never properly assessed in terms of the epistemic standing of the speaker (where what counts as sufficient standing is fixed in a context-sensitive way). But can we make sense of this? Can we make sense of a practice of assertion where it is never appropriate to query the speaker's epistemic credentials, never appropriate merely on observing the assertion to hold the speaker responsible for having had appropriate epistemic credentials, and so forth? I submit that, whatever is going on in this community, we would not recognize such a speech act as one of assertion—precisely as the constitutive norm hypothesis would lead us to suppose.

It might be thought that this proves too much. Consider game theorists interested in signaling games, as well as evolutionary biologists studying communication systems. Both study something that can reasonably be regarded as information transactions, yet there need be nothing in the picture like a constitutive norm of assertion. As a result, insofar as at least some of these information transactions can be thought of on the model of assertions, we will thereby have made Cappelen's point: not only is it possible for there to be assertions with different norms than those actually used in the assessment of assertion, it is *actually the case* that there are assertions even when there is *no constitutive rule at all*.

In response, I deny that these scenarios involve assertion. To be sure, they are cases of information exchange. But not all cases of information exchange are cases of assertion. Although I will not be in a position to spell out fully my reasons for thinking this here—again, it will have to await my full account of the norm of assertion—still, I can anticipate those reasons here. First, these information exchanges have none of the interpersonal trappings of assertion. (In particular, the observer inherits no entitlement to hold the signaler responsible for the truth of the content of the signal itself.)

Second, these signals are not apt for the expression of belief on the part of the signaler. This is certainly true for the case of communication systems in biology: these systems (typically) operate below the level of conscious awareness. And even in the sorts of signaling games of interest to game theorists, the signals themselves, while part of communication systems, constitute a move in a competitive game in which the aim is merely to get the observer to believe something (or perhaps to act in a certain way). There need be no interesting connection to the signalers' beliefs at all. Third, and relatedly, these signals need have no connection whatsoever to any communicative intention on the part of the signaler. I say that they "need have" no such connection; to be sure, some of the signaling games studied in game theory do have such a connection, only there they begin to seem as if they are appropriately assessed by reference to a standard appropriate to assertion, and so do not count as a counterexample to the constitutive rule hypothesis. In short, while signaling games and evolved communication systems exist even in the absence of any norm of assertion, they do not amount to anything recognizable as assertoric practice; and insofar as they do amount to something recognizable as assertoric practice, this will be precisely because it is highly plausible to think that they are governed by the standard provided by the norm of assertion. In short, these cases fail to undermine the constitutive norm thesis. I conclude, then, that Cappelen's contingency objection can be met.

1.6.4 Does the Constitutive Norm Account Get Cases Right?

A fourth objection to the constitutive rule hypothesis comes in the form of cases. The cases in question are meant to be examples of assertions which we do not think are unwarranted merely because the speaker is not in an epistemically authoritative position with respect to the asserted content. (They would thus count against the most popular versions of the constitutive rule view, on which the norm of assertion has either an epistemic or a truth standard.) Cappelen's examples include the philosophy seminar room, as well as the law court. Bernard Williams' example is the student who in the course of sitting for an examination makes many assertions in response to her teachers' questions. Another example that has been suggested to me by several people (in conversation) involves the act of teaching, when one speaks on behalf of Descartes (or whomever is the author one is teaching at the moment).

In each case, it appears that it is perfectly proper to assert even when no substantial (epistemic or truth) standard is satisfied. In the philosophy seminar room, where there is ample disagreement, one is often not in a position to claim knowledge (or even justified belief) of the claims one makes, yet one makes them all the same. (See Chapters 9–11 for full discussion.) In a court of law, lawyers for each side make all sorts of assertions—indeed, they are *bound by their profession* to make all sorts of assertions—even under conditions in which they do not so much as believe what they are saying. The student sitting for an examination may make all sorts of assertions in response to the examiners' questions; if the norm of assertion is epistemic, she will often violate that norm—yet there seems nothing wrong with her doing so. Finally, the teacher who is teaching Descartes for the day often occupies Descartes' perspective, and defends his views, by making various claims "in the spirit of Descartes," where she does not believe much if any of what she is thereby asserting. Far from being unacceptable, this sort of assertoric practice appears to be good pedagogy. In short, there appear to be a number of practices in which assertions are made freely, where the assertions seem perfectly in place, yet where on the assumption of a constitutive rule of assertion there is a systematic violation of assertion's norm. This might give us pause with respect to the hypothesis that assertion is governed by a constitutive rule.

Indeed, we might think that these sorts of cases provide supporting evidence for the commitment view of assertion.[28] After all, in each of these cases (philosophy seminar room; court of law; student being examined), by the standards of the relevant context the contribution being made is bound by a distinct professional or institutional norm, involving a commitment to defend the assertion. The proponent of the commitment view might well claim support in the fact that in these sorts of professional settings the commitment is explicitly adopted by the speaker; after all, this is what we would have expected if the commitment view were true.

In response, I have two things to say, one of which is self-standing, and the other of which anticipates the account of assertion I offer in the final three chapters of this book (and so will be provisional here).

The self-standing response is that, in at least three of these cases, the objection appears to confuse two distinct notions of assertoric propriety. Take the case of the lawyer in a court of law. It may well be that, in the course of trying to get her client off the hook, the defense attorney asserts all sorts of things, many of which she does not believe (and some of which she even believes to be false). This may well be proper assertoric practice from a legal perspective. (Whether it is so will depend, in part, on the extent to which it coheres with the total evidence admitted in the case.) But being a proper assertion from a legal perspective is not the same as being warranted as an assertion (*simpliciter*). In fact, those responsible for reaching a verdict will have to decide whether the lawyer's case is a good one, and part of that decision will be based on whether the lawyer's claims on behalf of her client were warranted. But then it seems that an assertion made by a defense attorney in a courtroom can be the sort of thing expected of her as the defense attorney, and hence proper in *this* sense, yet also fail to be the sort of thing that is believable, and hence improper (unwarranted) in *that* sense, where the latter sense is what is articulated by the norm of assertion. For this very reason one should not infer from, for instance, the conditions on a legally proper assertion to the conditions on a proper or warranted assertion *simpliciter*. As developed in connection with claims made in a court of law, the present objection appears to conflate these distinct senses of 'proper assertion.'

---

[28] I thank an anonymous referee for this suggestion (and for the way it is developed in the paragraph).

I note, too, that this response appears to suggest why it would be wrong for the proponent of the commitment view to regard this case as supporting her view. For we might wonder: insofar as the sort of commitment that one makes in making an assertion is determined by, for example, one's professional role as defense attorney, how is it that we (or a jury) can raise the question of the assertion's warrantedness in ways that abstract away from that role, and focus only on the assertion itself (and its epistemic backing)? On any commitment view that claims support from such cases, this phenomenon would appear mysterious. Of course, the proponent of such a commitment view might reply that assertions come with their own sort of commitment, independent of the role that the speaker is taking on. But it is not clear why such a view is motivated if the commitment view is true, and in any case it appears as though at this point the theorist is appealing to the norm of assertion itself.

Similar things can be said about the case involving a teacher who makes claims on behalf of Descartes, trying to get her students to understand the Cartesian perspective. This case is a bit trickier, if only because it is not clear that these should count as assertions in the first place. They seem more like the sort of speech acts that are performed in the theater, albeit with a pedagogical aim in mind. After all, the teacher is not "speaking for herself," but instead is "acting a part." Only here, the part is not that of a character in a play, but rather a philosopher whose work she is trying to impart. But suppose I am wrong about this, and the teacher's claims are assertions after all. In that case, similar things can be said here as were said in connection with the law court case. It may well be that the teacher's (Descartes-inspired) claims are proper for the classroom setting. But even so that does not shed any light on whether they are warranted as assertions. The proof of the distinction here is that we may well regard the teacher as demonstrating good pedagogy—hence as engaging in proper assertoric practice—even as we recognize that this has no bearing at all on the students' task of determining whether the claims are belief-worthy. (It is one thing to understand what Descartes said; it is another to endorse what Descartes said.) Determining whether a claim is belief-worthy requires assessing the evidential support behind the claim—and it is here that the students will have to apply something closer to the standard provided by the norm of assertion. And so we see the same distinction here as we saw in the case of the court of law: an assertion made by a teacher in the course of teaching a philosopher's viewpoint can be the sort of thing expected of her as the teacher, and hence proper in this sense, yet also fail to be the sort of thing that is believable, and hence improper or unwarranted in that sense. And so it would seem that one cannot infer from, for example, the conditions on a pedagogically proper assertion to the conditions on a proper or warranted assertion *simpliciter*.

Consider too the case of the student sitting for an examination. Here we can be quick. It is proper for that student to try to pass the examination; and insofar as this involves making assertions, it is proper for her to do this as well. Still, this does not settle the question of whether her assertions are good ones as assertions. Of course, here the question is not whether they are deemed belief-worthy by her examiners; presumably her examiners already know the answers. Rather, the question is whether they hold up to the sort of scrutiny one brings to bear in an examination. The standards employed here will be epistemic standards—and hence close to the sort of standard that would be provided by the norm of assertion (assuming it is an epistemic one). It would seem, then, that this case, like the previous two cases, does not provide us with any reason to question whether assertion has a constitutive rule.

The analysis I have suggested for these three cases distinguishes the legal and pedagogical norms that bear on the making of claims, on the one hand, and the generic norms that do so, on the other. In effect, I have suggested that whereas an assertion might be proper from a legal or pedagogical point of view, this does not settle the question of whether it is proper *simpliciter*—that is, when evaluated for warrantedness. The norm of assertion provides us with a standard that articulates the latter sort of propriety. Still, this distinction would not appear to help in the case of the philosophy seminar room. This is for the simple reason that there the speaker is neither legally nor pedagogically constrained in her linguistic representations—she really does aim at truth. Insofar as she fails to know or justifiably believe (or state truths), it can thus seem that the cost of the constitutive rule view is the need to say that assertions made in a philosophy seminar room are systematically unwarranted. This is a cost.

It is in reaction to this worry that I present my second response to the objection. This response appeals to my own favored theory regarding the norm of assertion—to be defended in the final three chapters of this book. Here I will be brief.

Suppose that the standard provided by the norm of assertion is itself fixed in a context-sensitive way, by appeal to what is mutually manifest in context. The result will be that in any type of context in which there are mutual expectations between speakers and hearers, we would predict that these can affect the standard for warranted assertion. This seems like an apt description of what goes on in the philosophy seminar room. (This is to anticipate what I discuss at length in Chapter 11.) Insofar as it is mutually familiar to all parties to the discussion that they are doing philosophy, and that epistemically high-quality belief is very hard (if not practically impossible) to come by when doing philosophy, and insofar as it is also mutually familiar to all parties that the practice of philosophy flourishes only when there is a way to advance claims even under these (epistemically adverse) circumstances, the result will be that it will also be mutually familiar that neither side should expect that the standard for advancing claims (making assertions) is as demanding as that for reporting the winner of last night's game. And this, in turn, will adjust the standard that operates in the seminar room.

Still, we might worry: once it is granted that we have little knowledge or justified belief in the seminar room, what possible standards could the norm of assertion have? Is not this just a recipe for "anything goes"? It is not. While there is one sense in which the standard for warranted assertion is *lower* in a seminar room—for example, one needs not know the truth of what one claims—there is another sense in which the standard for warranted assertion is *much more demanding* in a seminar room—one must be in a position to satisfy philosophical standards of reasoning and dialectical defense, which is not typically expected of those who make assertions about the winner of last night's game. A philosopher who asserts under conditions in which she cannot adequately defend her claim in the face of challenge is a philosopher whose assertion is unwarranted. This is not to say that warrant here requires full vindication of one's claims—that would be a recipe for systematically unwarranted philosophical claims. But it is to say that warrant here is not freely given either, but instead must be earned.

Putting my two responses together, I conclude, then, that none of the case-based objections to the constitutive rule hypothesis succeed in undermining the plausibility of that hypothesis. At best, they point to the need to distinguish the most generic sense in which a claim is proper or warranted from other senses in which a claim is proper or warranted; and they give us some reason to suppose that the standard provided by the norm of assertion will have to be fixed in a context-sensitive fashion (a point to which I will return in Part IV of this book).

1.6.5 Does the Constitutive Norm Account Offer Us a Principled Way to Distinguish Assertions from Non-Assertions?

Cappelen (2010) has argued that, while any attempt to develop a constitutive rule account of assertion will need a principled way to distinguish those utterances of declarative sentences that are, and those that are not, tantamount to assertions, there is no principled way to draw this distinction. In response, and anticipating the view that I will be defending throughout this book, I submit that there *is* a principled way to distinguish utterances of declarative sentences which are assertions from those that are not. It has to do with the speaker's implicit invoking of her own epistemic authority.[29] Assertions are those speech acts in which a proposition is presented-as-true in such a way as to be presented as backed by that authority; non-assertions are not. It is true that there may not be a sure-fire way of discerning when propositions are presented in this way; but to just that extent the category of assertion itself is fuzzy at the boundaries. What is more, this way of drawing the line is a principled one, as it marks the distinction between speech acts that *by their very nature* are apt for serving as the vehicle for distinctly epistemic ends (such as communicating knowledge or justified belief or . . .) and those that are not so apt.

1.6.6 Is the Constitutive Norm Needed?

Sixth, several authors (including Pagin 2011) have argued that there is no need to appeal to norms at all in our account of assertion. To this the only thing I can say for now is that the proof is in the pudding: a great deal of what is interesting about the speech act of assertion—a great deal of the connections this speech act bears to other phenomena

---

[29] On the connection between assertion and the invocation of one's own epistemic authority, see Turri (2010a) and McKinnon and Simard Smith (2013).

of interest to philosophers—can be explained by appeal to assertion's norm. I have argued previously that the other accounts of assertion do not fare as well in this regard. If that is so, it gives us a reason to endorse the hypothesis that assertion is governed by a constitutive rule. I will be developing the case for this throughout the rest of this book.

1.7 Conclusion

The foregoing defense of the constitutive rule account of assertion is an initial defense; much more could be said in comparison of it with its competitor accounts. However, I do not intend to say much more by way of comparison. I propose instead to spend the rest of the book focusing exclusively on the constitutive rule account. In this brief concluding section I explain why.

A first point to make is that the constitutive view is already very popular—in fact, it is arguably the view to beat these days. While it may well be worthwhile to further develop the case for this view as against its main competitors, I am going to rest content with what others have said on its behalf (and with the little that I have said so far), so that I can focus my attention elsewhere. In particular, assuming that the view is well-motivated, I want to go on to explore its implications. My hope is that in exploring these implications we will discover that the view has even more going for it than has been appreciated in the literature to date.

Second, my choice—to explore the implications of the constitutive rule account rather than pursue further comparisons between it and its main competitors—enables me to address what I regard as a lacuna in the existing literature. What has been largely missing (in my view) of discussions of proposed constitutive rules for assertion is a sense of what *theoretical work* can be done by the hypothesis that assertion is governed by a constitutive rule. Instead, one finds a good deal written in defense of this or that candidate norm of assertion, with the burden of the argument being that the proposed account gives the right verdicts in particular cases.[30] As I stated in the introduction, I have found this discussion to be wanting: what is wanted is a sense of what further distinctly theoretical work can be done with the hypothesis of a constitutive norm for assertion in hand. This is the question I propose to pursue.

Third, my choice will put us in a position to generate new sources of data regarding the precise content of the norm. In Part IV I will use this to defend my own proposal in this regard.

With this, I proceed to the substance of my account.

---

[30] As I said in the Introduction to this book, there have been theorists who tried to argue for their proposal regarding the norm of assertion, not on the basis of cases, but rather in terms of the theoretical work it can do in connecting assertion with other philosophically interesting phenomena. Williamson (2000) defends the knowledge norm by appeal to its account of a certain subclass of Moore-paradoxical sentences. More recently, various people (Hawthorne 2005; Cohen 2004; Stanley 2005; Maitra and Weatherson 2010) have connected their discussion of assertion's norm to that of the norm of action, and more generally to considerations of practical interests and concerns. But this has been the exception rather than the rule.

PART II

The Epistemic Significance of Assertion

In this part I use the norm of assertion to characterize what I call the "epistemic significance" of assertion: the aptness of assertion as a vehicle for the communication of knowledge and warranted belief.

2

Assertion and the Spread of Knowledge

2.1 Assertion's Role in the Spread of Knowledge

In the previous chapter I introduced the hypothesis that assertion is governed by a constitutive (robustly epistemic) norm. I gave initial reasons to think that this theory of assertion does better than its rivals in enabling us to make sense of the variety of phenomena that are bound up with the practice of assertion, and I suggested that objections to this theory can be met. In this and the next chapter I will be deepening the case for the hypothesis that assertion is governed by a constitutive (robustly epistemic) norm, by suggesting how this hypothesis can be used to account for what I will be calling assertion's "epistemic significance." Under this rubric I will be discussing two features that are associated with assertion: its role in the spread of knowledge (to be discussed in this chapter), and the entitlements and responsibilities that obtain when an assertion is made and observed (in the next chapter).

Perhaps the most salient feature of the speech act of assertion is the role that acts of this type play in the spread of knowledge. The question I will be pursuing here is how assertoric acts play this role. A natural first thought is that they do so by serving as a kind of evidence. In the first half of this chapter I develop and then criticize an evidentialist account of this role. Having made clear the difficulties facing such a view, I then go on to examine three non-evidential accounts; these focus on the phenomenon of interpersonal trust, the act of assurance, and the norm of assertion, respectively. As non-evidential accounts, all three require independent motivation. I will argue, first, that such motivation can be provided by an account of human communication as a basic source of knowledge, and second, that the norm-based account enjoys several advantages over the other two non-evidential accounts. Some of these advantages have to do with the entitlements and responsibilities involved in testimony cases, but I postpone my discussion of these until Chapter 3.

2.2 Two Framing Assumptions

If you (think you) know that p, and you hope to communicate (what you take to be) this piece of knowledge to another person, you will most likely resort to language to do so. And if you do, the speech act of assertion will most likely be the act you employ (whether through the written word or the spoken word). Why should this be? What is it about the speech act of assertion that enables it to play this role as a vehicle for the spread of knowledge?

I will be framing my discussion of these questions in terms of two assumptions. These assumptions are meant merely to enable me to set up the discussion; I do not intend them to be substantial (more on which in a moment). The first of the two is the *Basis Assumption*: I assume that the role played by assertions in enabling the spread of knowledge can be understood in terms of their relation to *the (epistemic) basis* of a hearer's beliefs. The second I will call the *Reasons Assumption*: I assume that the relevant relation assertions bear to the (epistemic) basis of a hearer's belief can be understood in terms of their *providing reasons* for the hearer's belief.

It must be acknowledged that neither assumption is fully innocuous. While it should be relatively uncontroversial, the Basis Assumption might be doubted either by theorists whose epistemology rejects the very notion of epistemic grounds (such as justification coherentists), or by theorists who reject the idea that beliefs formed through another's say-so are based on grounds. (I will discuss one possible rationale for such a view later in this chapter.) And for its part, the Reasons Assumption can seem to be stacking the deck against anyone whose epistemology does not give any prominent role to reasons (or does not give such a role to reasons in the context of beliefs formed through another's say-so). Still, I think these assumptions can be given a reading on which they are relatively uncontroversial, and that they earn their keep in enabling me to set up the issues I want to discuss in a particularly vivid way. I want to begin by spending a few moments spelling this out.

I begin with the Reasons Assumption. It can seem that neither this assumption nor the language of "reasons" itself is innocent in connection with the role of assertion in the spread of knowledge. In particular, while everyone (or at least all non-skeptics) will agree that assertions are vehicles for the spread of knowledge, it is not universally accepted that assertions play this role *by providing reasons to believe*. Several authors regard the communication of knowledge through language as a case of "displaced perception" (to borrow the phrase used by Dretske 1997). On Dretske's account, when information is communicated from a speaker to a hearer, "there is conceptual, but no corresponding sensory, representation" of the state of affairs in question (Dretske 1997: 41–42). A similar "displaced perception" model is endorsed by Ruth Millikan. She writes:

Recognizing a linguistic reference to a substance is just another way of reidentifying the substance itself. It is identifying it through one more medium of manifestation. Think of this medium as like an instrument that aids perception. Like a camera, a radio, a cat scan, or a microscope, another person who talks to me picks up information-bearing patterns from his environment, focuses them, translates them into a new medium, and beams them at me. Or think of living in a language community as like being inundated in one more sea of ambient energy. Like the surrounding light, surrounding people transmit the structure of the environment to me in ways that, barring certain interferences, I can become tuned to interpret. (Millikan 2000: 89)[1]

Here Millikan is giving voice to the view that communication of knowledge through speech operates in a manner akin to perception. If this is correct, it would seem wrong, or at least unmotivated, to burden our account of communication with the assumption that assertion plays its role by way of providing reasons for belief.

This worry is unfounded. In particular, my use of 'reasons' talk is meant to be minimalist. In my sense of 'reason,' someone's assertion that p provides the hearer who observed (and understood) the assertion with a (defeasible) reason to believe that p, in the same way that a subject's perceiving that p provides her with a (defeasible) reason to believe that p. Thus if the best model of knowledge communication is a "displaced perception" model, à la Dretske, then the reasons talk can be adopted to this model at no extra cost. Still, I acknowledge that not everyone thinks of the epistemology of perception in terms of reasons. For those who do not, I suggest that this talk of reasons can be taken as a stand-in for talk of the epistemic basis or ground of belief.

Still, worries might persist. After all, some theorists regard perceptual belief as groundless belief (see, for example, Lyons 2009). If this is correct, and if we continue to assume a model of "displaced perception" for communication-based knowledge, then (not only the Reasons Assumption but also) the Basis Assumption itself will seem objectionable. But I believe that the case I will be making here can be translated even into an austere reliabilist framework of the sort in play in Lyons (2009). First, the issues I wish to address can be stated in a way that begs no question against the reliabilist framework: how does another's assertion that p put one in a position to acquire the knowledge that p through accepting that assertion? And second, the way I propose to address these issues can be framed in a reliabilist-friendly way as well. My main point will simply be that we cannot regard assertions as what I will call *mere evidence*, but instead must regard assertions as themselves linguistic representations answering to an epistemic standard. (For all I have to say here, the standard can be reliabilist.) Indeed, this is a picture I myself have endorsed, and developed at great length, elsewhere,[2] so I will not have much more to say on this here. My present point is only that this talk of 'reasons' and 'bases' is merely an expository tool that can be avoided for those who do not like this talk.

At this point it might be wondered why, if I intend my reasons-talk to be translatable into basis-talk, and if this basis-talk itself is not essential to the points I wish to make in this chapter, I nevertheless persist in employing the language of reasons and bases.

---

[1] See also Millikan (2004: 237). A similar "displaced perception" account is offered by John McDowell, who writes that "[elements of the] communicative repertoire serve as epistemic surrogates for the represented states of affairs" (McDowell 1980: 134). I exclude him from the body of the text, however, since, while he does endorse the displaced perception model of communication, he regards perception, and so (by extension) displaced perception, as providing reasons for belief.

[2] See Goldberg (2010a).

The simple answer is that this talk enables me to make the issues I seek to raise most vivid. The issue before us is essentially this: what sort of epistemic support, and of what strength, is provided by another's assertion that p, and how is this support provided? In this respect both the Basis Assumption and the Reasons Assumption enable us to address this directly. The Reasons Assumption in particular is useful since it enables us to describe in a succinct fashion precisely what we want to have explained. What we want to know is how it is that

> AGRB   Another person's asserting that p gives a hearer a reason to believe that p, where the epistemic quality of the hearer's belief is partly a function of the quality of the assertion-generated reason.

(I label this 'AGRB' for 'Assertion-Generated Reason to Believe.') Using AGRB, we can frame our questions as follows: how does an assertion that p generate a reason (for a hearer) to believe that p, and what strength do such reasons have (that is, are they sufficient for knowledge)? It is a virtue of reasons-talk that it enables us to frame the discussion so naturally and succinctly.

Nor is this the only way that reasons-talk earns its keep in the present context. First, the various accounts I will be discussing in this chapter—evidentialist and non-evidentialist accounts alike—all endorse something like AGRB, so the talk of reasons enables me to represent their views with ease (and without begging any questions against them). Additionally, AGRB itself seems eminently plausible. In fact, it can seem simply obvious that another person's asserting something gives you a reason to believe what was asserted. Suppose you form a belief on the strength of Smith's word. If you were subsequently asked why you believe as you do, it would be natural for you to respond, "Because Smith told me so" or "Because Smith said so." It is plausible to think that this use of "because" identifies your *reason* for believing as you do.[3] So the hypothesis that assertions provide reasons for belief can seem nothing more than a piece of common sense. And if this is correct, it stands to reason that the assertion-based belief a hearer acquires is as epistemically strong as the reason provided by the assertion itself—precisely as AGRB maintains.

So much, then, for the two assumptions that will structure my discussion of assertion's role in the spread of knowledge. I turn, then, to the question before us: *how* can someone's asserting that p provide a hearer with a reason to believe that p, where the reason itself is (or at least can be) sufficiently strong to underwrite knowledge?

---

[3] As we will see, there are debates about the nature of this reason, and in particular whether "because Smith said so" stands by itself as a sufficient (knowledge-supporting) reason for belief, or whether it needs to be supplemented with still further reasons in support of the credibility of Smith's say-so. But both sides agree that "because so-and-so said so" can be *a* reason for belief—the debate being over whether it can stand on its own.

2.3 Varieties of Evidentialism Regarding Assertion's Role in the Spread of Knowledge

A natural first thought is that assertion plays this role by serving as *evidence* for the truth of what is asserted. Assuming that the evidence is "good enough" (more on which later), the result would be that a hearer could then form a belief in what was asserted, on the basis of that evidence, thereby coming to acquire the very knowledge in question. This is the core idea behind what I will call the *evidential* view of assertion's role in the spread of knowledge. According to this view, another's assertion is a kind of evidence, and so the reasons it provides are to be understood in evidentialist terms. As part of an account of the epistemology of communicated knowledge (also known as the "epistemology of testimony"), the evidential view is common among many epistemologists with otherwise different approaches to epistemology. For example, it is common among Bayesian epistemologists (see Sobel 1987), evidentialists (Conee and Feldman 2004), more traditional-style internalist foundationalists (Fumerton 2006), and those who treat the epistemology of testimony on the model of an inference-to-the-best-explanation (Lipton 1998, 2007).

To see how the view that assertions are evidence can provide an account of assertion's role in the spread of knowledge, we will need a generic theory of evidence. To that end, we will need a taxonomy of event-types, together with bridge principles stating which event-types reliably indicate what states of affairs. With this in hand, we will then be able to say the following: that some event, *e*, took place constitutes evidence for H to believe that p when H knows, or is justified in believing, something to the effect of the following two things: (i) *e* took place, and (ii) *e* is a type of event the obtaining of whose tokens reliably indicates that p. By substituting talk of reasons for talk of evidence, and by bringing the foregoing to bear on the question of assertion, we arrive at the evidential account of how an assertion that p constitutes a reason to believe that p: that speaker S asserted that p gives hearer H a reason to believe that p when H knows, or is justified in believing, something to the effect, both that S asserted that p, and that S's asserting that p is a type of event the obtaining of whose tokens reliably indicates that p.

Proponents of the evidential account face two questions. First, what is the relevant event-type under which the S's asserting that p is to be classified? And second, what is involved in H's knowing or justifiably believing that events of this type reliably indicate that p? The latter question will be addressed later, when we take up the core issues in the epistemology of testimony; here I want to address the taxonomic question.[4]

A natural first thought is that the relevant type—the type under which the event of S's asserting that p is to be classified as a piece of evidence—will involve characterizing S's act *as an act of asserting that p*. It is as an act of assertion, after all, that a speaker will

---

[4] My own impression is that the literature on the epistemology of testimony has not given the taxonomic question the attention it deserves. Jack (1994), Fricker (2004), and Rysiew (2007) are interesting exceptions to this. See also Goldberg (2007a: chapter 1).

typically intend her act to be taken; and it is in terms of its status as an assertion, and more specifically as an assertion that p, that H typically makes use of it, epistemically speaking, in arriving at a belief. Still, it is worth emphasizing that nothing in the evidential view itself requires that acts of assertion be characterized as such, when they are regarded as evidence. And it is clear that acts of assertion can be used as evidence for propositions other than that which the speaker asserted.[5] Thus H might regard the relevant event—S's asserting that p—as providing him (H) with reasons to think, for example, that S has a cold (since H recognizes that stuffy-nose sound in S's speech), that S is irritated (since H knows that S never speaks about such topics except when she is irritated), or that S speaks English with a Southern accent (since H recognizes her accent).[6] This present point, to the effect that an act of assertion can be used as evidence for many different propositions, illuminates a key (and often under-appreciated) commitment of the evidential view: when it comes to the status of assertion as constituting evidence, that an act is one of assertion (or, more specifically, an assertion that p) is not the only way to characterize the act, nor does it highlight the only evidentially-relevant feature of the act to which the audience might attend. It may be that acts of assertion are (typically) produced with an eye towards being taken *as an assertion* by the audience; but this is inessential to its status as a reason to believe, according to the evidential view.

Can the proponent of the evidential view recover any sense in which the property of being *an assertion that p* is epistemically special? Well, she might say that hearers typically have background reasons to think that acts of assertion are (at least under certain further conditions) often highly correlated with the truth of the proposition asserted—in which case characterizing these acts *as an assertion that p* highlights a feature of these acts which is both highly specific and highly epistemically significant. She might also say that characterizing the act of assertion in this way reveals that, unlike evidence generally, assertion is special in wearing its own interpretation—what it is evidence *for*—"on its sleeve," so to speak. Still, it is worth noting that even after a hearer H justifiably believes that a speaker S asserted that p, this proposition counts as a reason for H to believe that p (according to the evidential view) only if it is epistemically proper for H to believe that acts of this type—or perhaps of some further, more specific type of which this is an instance[7]—are reliable indications of

---

[5] By this I do not mean to endorse what Cappelen and Lepore (2005) endorse under the name "Speech Act Pluralism," according to which no *one* thing is asserted or said by a given assertion (but instead many things are asserted or said by an utterance). Rather, what I have in mind is that if the acts constituting assertions are evidence, we can learn things from them that have nothing whatsoever to do with the content(s) asserted.

[6] Audi (1997) has an example in which one and the same testimonial event provides two distinct types of evidence for the same belief. The case is one in which a speaker utters "I am an alto" in an alto voice.

[7] It is plausible to think that the relevant type will be more specific than an *asserting that p*; perhaps it will be something like *apparently sincere and seemingly competent asserting that p*. That assertions will have to be so characterized if they are to serve as the basis from which to draw inferences regarding the truth of the asserted content is a point made by many others; see, for example, Dummett (1981) and Fricker (1987) for early versions of this point.

the truth of p. On this score, we might distinguish two distinct versions of evidentialism: one is *non-reductionist* about the status of assertions, in that it holds that another's assertion can be a basic source of justification (and so in this sense is like perception); the other is *reductionist* about the status of assertions, in that it holds that whatever justification one has in accepting another's assertion derives from (and so reduces to) other, non-testimonial sources of justification (such as perception and induction).[8]

Addressing this dispute (between reductionist and non-reductionist versions of evidentialism) takes us into the second of the two questions I raised previously: what is involved in H's knowing or justifiably believing that events of this type reliably indicate that p? Although I will discuss this at length later, still, it is worth anticipating that discussion. Evidentialists who are non-reductionist about the status of assertions will hold that, absent reasons to suppose otherwise, it is epistemically proper for H to presume that assertoric acts of the relevant type are reliable indications of the truth of p. Evidentialists who are reductionists will deny this; they will hold that it is epistemically proper for H to believe that assertoric acts of the relevant type are reliable indications of the truth of p, *only if* H has adequate positive reasons to believe that this linkage holds. According to such a view, the fact that someone asserted that p, by itself, is not a reason to believe anything. It becomes a reason only when the hearer also has evidence (or positive reasons) to believe that the act was of a type that is reliably correlated with the truth of p. When an evidentialist treats assertions like this, I will say that she treats assertions as *mere* evidence. In short, evidentialists who are reductionist about the status of assertions treat them as mere evidence. I will call such a position *Strong Evidentialism*.

As I say, I will discuss the virtues and drawbacks of non-reductive versions of evidentialism later, when I discuss the debate between reductionist and non-reductionist approaches to testimony more generally. For now, though, I want to focus exclusively on reductionist versions (= Strong Evidentialism). I do so for a straightforward reason. In this chapter I seek to defend the idea that the norm of assertion will be part of our best account of assertion's role in the spread of knowledge. Later I will be arguing that the norm of assertion is a natural supplement to non-reductionist positions in the epistemology of testimony. Consequently, if evidentialism is to offer an *alternative* explanation for assertion's role in the spread of knowledge—if it is to offer an explanation that is meant to compete against that provided by the norm of assertion—then it must not be a non-reductionist version of evidentialism. In short, insofar as evidentialism aims to offer an alternative account of assertion's role in the spread of knowledge—one that is independent of, and does not need to be supplemented by, the hypothesis that assertion has a norm—then evidentialism needs to take the form of Strong Evidentialism.

---

[8] The terms 'non-reductionist' and 'reductionist' come from the literature in the epistemology of testimony; I will discuss that literature, and the rationale behind this nomenclature, later in this chapter.

2.4 Strong Evidentialism and the Positive Reasons Requirement

In this section I explore Strong Evidentialism about assertion's role in the spread of knowledge. Here I do so with an eye towards bringing out Strong Evidentialism's implications regarding the nature and strength of the reason generated by another's assertion that p. These will be implications for any view which holds that assertions play their knowledge-communicating role by constituting mere evidence. (In Section 2.5 I will argue that these implications are objectionable.)

To bring out the implications themselves it will be helpful to contrast the Strong Evidentialist's account of these reasons with the sort of reasons that are provided by our basic epistemic sources, such as perception. When it comes to perception, most non-skeptical epistemologists think that the perceiving subject is entitled to accept her perceptual experiences at face value: if it seems (perceptually) to you that p, and there are no specific relevant reasons to question the perceptual appearances, you are entitled to accept that p. To be sure, this entitlement is defeasible: if it perceptually seems to you that p, but you are aware that you just ingested an hallucinogen, you are no longer entitled to endorse the content of your perceptual experience. Still, the important point is that the entitlement is *presumptive*, and does not depend on your having evidence of the reliability of your perceptual system.[9] To be sure, it seems plausible to suppose that the hypothesis of a default-entitlement in perception depends on the reliability of perception, as well as on the sensitivity of our perceptual system to the presence of defeaters. (Had your visual experience been one that you had under conditions that were not conducive to visual acuity—the lights were low, the object was at a distance, and obscured, and so on—you would not have moved to endorse whatever it was that you thought you were seeing.) Still, the entitlement to rely on perception is presumptive, even if it is defeasible.

Now, the Strong Evidentialist's view of assertion's role in the spread of knowledge holds that others' assertions (or testimonies) are not like perception in this regard—in particular, that it is not the case that hearers enjoy a default-entitlement to accept others' (testimony-constituting) assertions at face value. Instead, proponents of the strong evidential view accept a claim which, in the epistemology of testimony literature, is known as the 'Positive Reasons Requirement' (PRR). Framed in terms of assertion (rather than testimony), the Positive Reasons Requirement holds the following:[10]

---

[9] This is why any would-be defeating reason must be *specific*; merely generic skeptical considerations do not count.

[10] I have formulated the principle in terms of the conditions on the rational acceptance of another's say-so, but it is worth bearing in mind that in the epistemology of testimony literature some formulate the Positive Reasons Requirement in terms of the conditions on the doxastic justification of beliefs formed through acceptance of another's say-so. For the purpose of this book I will not bother to distinguish these, though I think a full epistemology of testimony ought to do so.

PRR In order for a hearer H's acceptance of another's assertion to amount to knowledge, it is required that H have (positive, undefeated, epistemically adequate) reasons or evidence for regarding that assertion as credible.[11]

PRR itself has been defended in a variety of ways, but at their core most of these arguments share an idea from Fricker (1994). Fricker argues that accepting another's testimony without having positive reasons for thinking that the testimony was credible exhibits gullibility. On the assumption that gullible acceptance of another's assertion cannot underwrite knowledge, we quickly reach the conclusion of PRR: acquiring knowledge through assertion requires having positive reasons to think that the assertion was credible.[12]

For our purposes here, Strong Evidentialism's commitment to PRR is of interest, since PRR itself amounts to a rejection of the idea that another's assertion that p can generate a *basic* reason to believe that p—that is, as a reason which stands by default, whose status and epistemic strength as a reason do not rest on the hearer's having still further reasons to regard the assertion as itself a reliable indication that p. This implication of PRR, and by extension of the Strong Evidentialist view, is worth developing at greater length.

Those who endorse PRR are committed to a certain view regarding the nature of the sort of reason(s) another's assertion provides. In particular, the proponent of PRR must hold that the reasons another's assertion provide are *unlike* the reasons that, for example, one's own sensory experiences provide.[13] Suppose H believes that p on the basis of a visual experience as of its being the case that p. Most (non-skeptical) epistemologists will allow that, even in the absence of possessing positive reasons for thinking that the visual appearances are a good guide to the truth, one can be warranted in accepting one's visual experiences—that is, in accepting that things are as they are represented in those experiences to be. If we think of experience as providing reasons for belief, the present point can be formulated in terms of the sort of reasons that visual experience provides: as a reason to believe that p, *that it appears (visually) to one as if p* is not in need of further supplementation, but instead suffices by itself to warrant one's acceptance of [p] so long as there are no relevant reasons for doubting that things are as they (visually) appear to be. What is more, so long as there are no relevant defeaters

---

[11] A more careful discussion of the epistemology of testimony would distinguish between three distinct "positive reasons" requirements: one might require adequate positive reasons (i) for the rational acceptance of another's testimony, (ii) for the doxastic justification of testimony-based belief, or (iii) for testimonial knowledge. In addition, one would need to highlight the issue whether, given a view that endorses one or more of (i)–(iii), the reasons that render the acceptance rational (the belief doxastically justified, and so on) are the only materials that provide epistemic support for the hearer's beliefs. While most proponents of a positive-reasons requirement would answer in the affirmative, not all do; so-called "hybrid" views (for example, Faulkner 2000; Lackey 2006, 2007a, 2009) answer in the negative.

[12] See Goldberg and Henderson (2006) for a response to this argument.

[13] For those who deny that sensory experience provides reasons for belief, the same point can be made in terms of the rational support provided by sensory experience.

(and no Gettier conditions), such a reason suffices to underwrite the perceptual knowledge that p. By contrast, if PRR is true, another's assertion is unlike one's own sensory experience in this respect: as a reason to believe that p, *that another person said that p* does not stand by itself, but instead must be supplemented by further reasons—reasons which make it warranted for the hearer to assume that the say-so was credible.[14] Nor can a reason like *that so-and-so said that p*, by itself, underwrite one's knowledge even in cases of no defeaters and no Gettier conditions. It is for this reason that views which endorse the Positive Reasons Requirement are accordingly often labeled as 'reductionist': they hold that, as a reason to believe that p, *that so-and-so asserted that p* is itself epistemically insubstantial unless backed by still further reasons to suppose that so-and-so's assertion was a reliable indication that p. In this respect, assertion— or, to use the category in the epistemology literature, testimony[15]—is not special as a source of reasons: the epistemic support that an assertion- (or testimony-) generated reason provides for the corresponding testimonial belief is "reducible" to the epistemic support provided by other (inductive or abductive) reasons. PRR maintains that in the absence of having such reasons, it is not warranted for a hearer to accept an assertion (and so she is not in a position to acquire knowledge through her acceptance).

If PRR—and so, by extension, Strong Evidentialism's view of assertion's role in the spread of knowledge—is to be a plausible thesis, then the reasons PRR requires must meet two adequacy conditions. First, they must be the sort of reasons which ordinary hearers regularly possess, at least in those cases in which the hearers are correctly regarded as having been warranted in their acceptance of another's assertion; call this the *realisticness* condition. Second, these reasons must be such that a hearer's possession of reasons of this sort warrant her move to accept the assertion in question; call this the *warranting* condition. It is standard to suppose that a set of reasons satisfies the warranting condition if and only if the set of reasons licenses the inference from 'so-and-so asserted that p' to 'p'. But precisely what such reasons must be like to license this inference has been the subject of some discussion. It is worth exploring the recent history of this debate as it has transpired in the epistemology of testimony literature, if only to make clear the epistemological background against which I am making my claims regarding assertion.[16]

---

[14] At this point it is tempting to characterize the issue before us as which sources of justification are properly basic. According to this tempting thought, the Positive Reasons Requirement amounts to a denial of the claim that testimony is a basic source of justification. While there is much to this suggestion, it can create some confusion and so should be treated with care. Simply put, such a presentation encourages the conflation of (a) the reasons that rationalize the acceptance of another's assertion with (b) the materials that determine the doxastic justification of the resulting assertion-based belief. This conflation is one that several proponents of the Positive Reasons Requirement are at pains to reject. For example, Faulkner (2000) and Lackey (2006, 2007a, 2009) hold a "hybrid" position according to which positive reasons are required for rational acceptance, yet those reasons do not exhaust the materials relevant to the doxastic justification of assertion-based (also known as testimonial) belief.

[15] I will discuss the relation between assertion and testimony in Chapter 3.

[16] Except where attending to the difference makes a difference, I will move back and forth between talk of testimony and talk of assertion. Where it might make a difference I will flag this by speaking, not of assertion

Some critics of reductionist approaches (such as Coady 1992) have argued that the reasons one would need to license this transition (from 'so-and-so asserted that p' to 'p') cannot make any unreduced appeal to reasons that derive from *other* testimonies. This can make it seem that the cost of endorsing PRR is nothing short of having to vindicate the reliability of (testimony-constituting) assertions as a class, using only the materials available from the first-person perspective. Since it is arguable that few of us have enough first-personal evidence to perform such a wholesale reduction, this is taken by some to show that PRR should be rejected, on the grounds that there are no reasons that satisfy both the realisticness condition and the warranting condition.

However, defenders of PRR have argued that the task facing those who endorse this requirement is not as robust as Coady's criticism makes it seem. Points have been made in connection with both of the adequacy conditions.

Regarding the realisticness condition, Fricker (1987, 1995), Lackey (2008), and Kenyon (2012) have argued that hearers have far more in the way of relevant (first-personal) evidence than Coady's criticism suggests. They contend that while it may be that we often lack background evidence of a particular speaker's assertoric track record, even so we typically have other evidence with which to assess the relevant assertions. Fricker, Lackey, and Kenyon point out that mature subjects typically have extensive experience with various types of (testimony-constituting) assertion, categorized either by content (testimony regarding the location of a familiar landmark, and so on), by the speaker's relationship to the content (testimony by an expert, testimony by a local resident, and so on), by the probable motives behind the speech act (testimony by someone who was in no position to benefit from a lie, and so on), by the character or other properties of the speaker (testimony by a used car salesperson, testimony by a parent or friend, testimony by someone who appeared to lack confidence, and so on), and/or by the circumstances under which the testimony was produced (under oath, with a great deal on the line, on a topic/under circumstances on which falsehood is easy to detect, and so on).

Regarding the warranting condition, Fricker (1994, 1995) has argued that the task facing the defender of PRR is not the "global" sort of reduction Coady described, according to which each hearer must have reasons, independent of any testimony, to think that testimony *in general* is a reliable way to form beliefs. What is required rather is a more "local" reduction, on which one has reasons *in particular cases of encountered testimony* to regard the testimonial transition (from 'so-and-so said that p' to 'p') as acceptable. What is more, Fricker herself has argued that the more "local" reduction can employ evidence involving others' testimony.

Fricker's distinction between local and global reduction is connected to a second issue that has been discussed in connection with the nature of the reasons that warrant acceptance. Assuming that the requirement of reduction is the "local" rather than the

---

simpliciter, but of *testimony-constituting assertion*. Again, I will return to the relation between assertion and testimony in the next chapter.

"global" requirement just described, what sort of reasons would satisfy this requirement? That is: what sort of reasons warrant the inference from 'so-and-so said that p' to 'p' on a given occasion? Some, such as Peter Lipton (1998, 2007), hold that this inference is an inference to the best explanation. If this is correct, the sort of reasons we seek are those that suggest that the best explanation for why so-and-so asserted that p is that so-and-so wanted to express her knowledge of the fact that p (or something like this). These would be reasons about another's motives, her epistemic position on the matter at hand, and so forth. Related to Lipton's suggestion, Fricker (1987, 1994, 1995) holds that the inference in question is licensed on an occasion when S has evidence that so-and-so's testimony on this occasion was both sincere and competent. In any case, I will assume that Fricker's and Lackey's replies to Coady's original objection to PRR are sound, and that if PRR is objectionable it is not for the reasons Coady cited.

2.5 Against the Positive Reasons Requirement

In this section I want to present some alternative grounds for thinking that the Positive Reasons Requirement, and with it Strong Evidentialism regarding assertion's role in the spread of knowledge, is objectionable.

2.5.1 *In Support of Basic Testimonial Reasons*

I begin with considerations in support of the idea that, contrary to what PRR maintains, a reason such as *that so-and-so said that p* stands on all fours with *that it appears (visually) to me as if p*—namely, as something that, absent reasons for suspecting any unreliability, warrants the move to accept that p on that basis. In effect, such a view denies the Positive Reasons Requirement—that is, it denies that the reasons generated by the making of an assertion are reducible to other, non-testimonial kinds of reasons. Consequently, this view has been called "non-reductionist."

Various considerations have been offered in defense of non-reductionism. (Since I will want to focus in the main on other considerations, here I cite only the traditional ones to get them on the table.) Early arguments (Coady 1992; Stevenson 1993) focused on (what was argued to be) the practical impossibility of satisfying the demand for positive reasons in each and every case in which, intuitively, a hearer was rational in accepting a piece of testimony. (Such an argument can be made even if we grant that the proponent of PRR need not perform the "global" sort of reduction described in Coady 1992. See, for example, Goldberg 2007a: chapter 5.) Other arguments question whether the distinctions typically made (and thought to be needed) by proponents of PRR, such as that between global or local reduction, or between the immature and mature phases of an epistemic subject's life, are well-motivated (Insole 2000). An additional set of arguments aim to give reasons for thinking that we ought to treat testimony as we treat other "basic" sources on which subjects are presumed to be entitled to rely (McDowell 1994b; Strawson 1994; Reid 1997; Goldberg 2007a).[17] Still others offer symmetry considerations in defense of extending the (defeasible but presumptive) rationality of self-trust to the (defeasible but presumptive) rationality of trust in others (Foley 1994, 2001; for a critical discussion see Schmitt 2002). An interesting variant on this idea can be found in Burge (1993), who argued that it is *prima facie* warranted[18] to accept what appears to be an intelligible presentation-as-true, since such presentations-as-true appear to come from a rational source, and a rational source is a source that aims at truth—is a "resource for reason"—and hence is worthy of being presumed trustworthy.

Although I am committed to a non-reductionist view in the epistemology of testimony, and although I think one can use such a view as the basis for objecting to Strong Evidentialism about assertion's role in the spread of knowledge, still, the debate between reductionists and anti-reductionists is sufficiently vexed that it would be great if we could find other grounds for suspicion against Strong Evidentialism. Given that not everyone regards the conflation of testimony and assertion as legitimate,[19] it would be better still if we could find grounds that have to do with assertion as such, rather than with those assertions that are also testimonies. Happily, there are such grounds.

2.5.2 *The Epistemic Significance and De Facto Reliability of Assertion*

In addition to the considerations just described, which offer positive reasons for endorsing a "non-reductionist" approach to testimony (as against PRR), here I want to focus on an objection to Strong Evidentialism—one which focuses on assertion more specifically. Here the objection is that Strong Evidentialism misrepresents the relation between assertion's epistemic significance (as a speech act) and its *de facto* reliability. Strong Evidentialism holds that the epistemic significance of the speech act of assertion is to be traced to the *de facto* reliability of assertions as a speech-act type.[20] This account of the relation between assertion's epistemic significance and its *de facto* reliability, I contend, is objectionable.

For one thing, Strong Evidentialism makes false predictions about what in Chapter 1 I called assertion's promise of "belief-worthiness." This promise was seen in the fact that, when offered, assertions purport to be worthy of belief (by the hearer). But now consider how this purported belief-worthiness can be understood from the perspective of Strong Evidentialism. According to Strong Evidentialism, the fact that someone asserted that p, by itself, is not a reason to believe that p. It is only when that fact is

---

[17] See Section 2.6, where I develop these at greater length.
[18] Admittedly, Burge speaks of "entitlements" where I speak of "warrant." Still, I think that the differences, though real, need not concern us here.
[19] Those who reject this identity include Coady (1992) and Goldberg (2010b); those who endorse the identity appear to include Fricker (1987) and Sosa (1994). I say "appear to," since their comments are made in passing, and so the attribution is not certain.
[20] By the "reliability of assertions as a speech-act type," I mean that, taking the class of all assertions into account, there is a *de facto* preponderance of true assertion over false assertion.

connected to other things that the hearer justifiably believes—things that support the claim that the speaker's having asserted that p makes it highly likely that p—that the speaker's having asserted that p becomes a reason to believe that p. If this is so, then in what sense can assertions *purport* to be belief-worthy—that is, in what sense can assertions purport to provide an adequate reason to believe what was asserted? It would seem that the only option available to the Strong Evidentialist is to treat this purport as itself deriving from the empirical evidence the hearer has in support of the following reliability hypothesis: as a speech-act class, assertions have a high ratio of truth to falsity. But then on such a view it stands to reason that, as a class, assertions themselves hold out the promise of belief-worthiness *only insofar as* hearers already have empirical evidence confirming that as a speech-act class, assertions have a high ratio of truth to falsity. And so it would seem that the only sense that Strong Evidentialism can make of assertion's promise of belief-worthiness is in terms of assertion as mere evidence. On such a view, it is the hearer's background evidence regarding assertions' high ratio of truth to falsity that puts the hearer in a position, on observing another's assertion, to regard it as even so much as purporting to be good evidence for the truth of what was asserted.

I submit that this distorts the epistemic significance of assertion. Simply put, to recognize a speech act as one of assertion is *already* to apprehend it as purporting to say how things are, hence as purporting to be belief-worthy. This is what is involved in *understanding* the speech act; it is not something for which one needs evidence. Admittedly, *purporting to be belief-worthy* and *being belief-worthy* are two different things. (This is why the present point cannot do double duty as an account of the epistemology of testimony.) But even so it would seem that the apprehension of the purport is a core part of what it is to understand the speech act of assertion, and Strong Evidentialism would appear to have no plausible account of this.[21]

I just criticized Strong Evidentialism's account of assertion's epistemic significance, claiming that this account distorts how assertions should be understood. But there is a second, related objection: the Strong Evidentialist account is too demanding. It entails that anyone in a position to regard an assertion as "epistemically significant" must already have substantial evidence of assertoric reliability. This seems to require too much of ordinary language users. Here I think in particular of children at the earliest age of linguistic competence. While they respond to assertions in the way one would expect if they were sensitive to the assertions' epistemic significance, it seems far-fetched to think that at such an age they already have any substantial evidence of assertions' reliability. Arguably, a similar point holds for hearers of any age.[22]

---

[21] Compare Rysiew (2007).

[22] This is probably the most standard traditional criticism of evidential approaches to the epistemology of testimony: hearers (of any age) typically lack the evidence which (by the lights of the evidential approach) they would need if they are to be justified in accepting the speaker's assertion. Argumentative variations on this theme can be found, for example, in Coady (1992), Burge (1993), Stevenson (1993), Dummett (1994), Strawson (1994), and Audi (1997).

It might seem that the foregoing two objections to Strong Evidentialism are merely versions of Coady's original (1992) objection to reductionist approaches to testimony. According to Coady's objection, reductionism requires a wholesale reconstruction of the reliability of testimony, without relying on any testimonial sources. Of course, if the foregoing two objections *are* merely versions of this argument, then presumably they can be met, as that argument was met, by appeal to Fricker's distinction between local and global reduction.[23] But I submit that the foregoing two objections are not merely versions of Coady's original objection. This is because Coady's objection did not call into question something that my two objections do call into question: namely, the Strong Evidentialist's entitlement to assume that assertions are speech acts that purport to represent how things are. Coady's objection did not call into question the reductionist's entitlement to assume, in reconstructing a hearer's right to accept testimony, that the hearer would already recognize a class of speech acts as assertions; that is, as speech acts purporting to represent how things are. The issue Coady raised was that if all one has to go on is one's own (first-personal) evidence and reasons, one cannot confirm that the practice of assertion/testimony in general is as it purports to be. But I am calling into question the Strong Evidentialist's right to assume, without evidence, that there is a kind of speech act that purports to represent how things are (and that hearers can recognize this merely by observing this kind of speech act). My claim is that, short of postulating a norm of assertion, the assumption that there is a kind of speech act of this sort needs to be earned, if the Strong Evidentialist account is to explain what it claims to explain.

Can the proponent of Strong Evidentialism reply to this, and by extension to both of the foregoing objections, by granting that assertion's purport of belief-worthiness is itself something that does not need to be established by evidence, and yet still maintain that, even so, if a hearer is to be justified in accepting an assertion, she must have positive reasons for doing so?[24] Such a position is available. But it goes against the very spirit of Strong Evidentialism itself, and in any case it would not be a *competitor* to the view I will be defending later. The position in question goes against the spirit of Strong Evidentialism, since it no longer regards assertion as mere evidence, but instead treats assertion as already purporting to constitute evidence of a certain sort—where the hypothesis that the act has this purport is itself not in need of further evidence. What is more, the resulting position would not be a competitor to the view I will be defending later. For insofar as one grants that assertion's purport of belief-worthiness is something that does not need to be established by evidence, one needs some account of why this is. I will shortly argue that the best explanation for this fact will appeal to the norm of assertion itself. In short, this reply does not offer a position from which to defend Strong Evidentialism's account of the epistemic significance of assertion, as against that provided by the norm of assertion.

---

[23] I thank an anonymous referee for indicating the need to address this matter.
[24] I thank an anonymous referee for raising this question.

And there is yet a third way in which the Strong Evidentialist's account of assertion's epistemic significance is objectionable: this account makes false predictions about the modal features of assertion. In particular, it allows that there could be a practice of assertion even under conditions in which (i) these "assertions" were systematically and invariably false, and (ii) everyone in the community is aware of (i). But it seems that, on the contrary, any speech act all of whose tokens have been, are, and will be known to be false is not a practice of assertion. The point is related to, but is strictly weaker than, a more familiar point owed to Donald Davidson's reflections on interpretability. The more familiar point, developed in Coady (1992), involved an appeal to Davidson-style considerations regarding interpretability, in order to argue that the activity of reporting—the activity that forms the core of testimony—was by its very nature reliable (see Coady 1992: 85–87). If such a claim could be made regarding the activity (not just of reporting but also) of assertion, then no practice involving a speech act all of whose tokens were false could be a practice of assertion—in which case my present point would be established immediately. However, it is far from obvious that Coady's Davidson-inspired argument is successful even on its own terms (see, for example, Graham 2000c). Happily, the claim I am presently making is much weaker—and so decidedly more plausible—than Coady's claim. My claim is merely that the following is not a possible scenario: there is a speech act A, such that every instance of A that is ever made, and every one that will ever be made, is known to be false—and yet the speech act in question is one of assertion. I suspect that everyone—Graham (2000c) included[25]—can agree with that much. No speech act of type A could be one of assertion, since no such act would be taken as a reason to believe the act's propositional content, and since speakers will be aware of this, no speaker would have a reason to produce an act of this sort in the intention to get a hearer to believe the propositional content in question.

2.5.3 Assertion's Distinctive Contribution in Testimony Cases

I have just presented several reasons, having to do with the speech act of assertion (as distinct from the epistemology of testimony), to support my contention that Strong Evidentialism regarding assertion's role in the spread of knowledge is objectionable. To these I want to add one further objection: Strong Evidentialism regarding assertion's role in the spread of knowledge misconstrues the difference in epistemic significance between assertion and other (non-assertoric) speech acts in which a proposition is presented-as-true. Although this objection will take us back to considerations

---

[25] The target of Graham (2000c) is the claim that reports are necessarily reliable—the claim that it is impossible for there to be a situation in which reports are made which are systematically unreliable. This is a much stronger claim than the claim I am making here, which is that it is impossible for there to be a situation in which reports (assertions) are made which are, one and all, *invariably false*. See also Williams (2002: 85), where he appears to endorse something like the claim I am making. He writes, "... utterances would not be assertions if they were not expected to be true, and they would not be expected to be true if they did not, a lot of the time, express true beliefs" (though he does go on to weaken his commitment a little when he writes that "all of this may be correct").

pertaining to the epistemology of testimony, I think that developing it will take us closer still to the epistemic significance of assertion. We can do so by comparing the conditions on acquiring knowledge through assertion with the conditions on acquiring knowledge through other speech acts in which a proposition is presented-as-true.

Let me begin with something I take to be a datum: another speaker's assertion that it is raining provides a hearer with a stronger reason to believe that it is raining than what is provided by another's *speculation* that it is raining. This is a fact about assertion's relative epistemic strength vis-à-vis speculation, and it requires explanation. Insofar as the proponent of Strong Evidentialism does not rely on the norm of assertion itself in her explanation, she will have to explain this fact in terms of hearers' evidence of the comparative reliability of these speech-act types. On this explanation, hearers have evidence that the ratio of true to false assertions is higher than the ratio of true to false speculations, and it is this evidence that underwrites assertions' greater epistemic punch vis-à-vis that of speculations. But this explanation seems wrong. In addition to misrepresenting the relation between the epistemic significance of assertion and the (*de facto*) reliability of assertion, as described previously, this explanation misdescribes certain cases of reliable speculation.

In developing this objection it will be helpful to have a concrete case before us. Consider, then, the following case, which I will call

RELIABLE SPECULATION (or, WHEN HARRY MET SALLY)
A hearer, Harry, knows that a given speaker, Sally, has extremely high epistemic standards. In particular, Harry knows that Sally asserts something only if she is absolutely (epistemically) certain. (Sally rarely asserts anything, but when she does you can bet your house that it is true.) Harry also knows that Sally's high epistemic standards inform her speculations as well: Sally will not speculate that p unless [p] is true. (Harry knows that even when speculating, Sally hates to be seen as ever having presented-as-true something that is false.) In fact, Harry knows that Sally's track record vis-à-vis her speculations is as good as the track record of highly competent asserters. So when Harry observes Sally speculate that p, under conditions in which Harry has all of this background knowledge regarding Sally's speech dispositions, Harry thereby comes to believe that p on the basis of Sally's having so speculated. Unsurprisingly, [p] is true. What is more, and equally unsurprisingly, Sally's speculation was in fact both sensitive—Sally would not have so speculated had [p] been false—and reliably formed—a preponderance of the speculations she would arrive at through this same process would be true. Finally, there are no relevant defeaters. Under these conditions it seems patent that we can credit Harry with coming to *know* that p on the basis, or at least partly on the basis, of accepting Sally's speculation. There should be no thought to deny this merely because Sally's speech contribution was a speculation: after all, Harry already knows this, and took account of it.

Now, I submit that, by the lights of any Strong Evidentialism that avoids appeal to the norm of assertion, Sally's speculations have roughly the same epistemic significance (for Harry) as other speakers' *assertions* have (for Harry, or indeed for other ordinary hearers). But this, I want to say, is simply wrong. In particular, a speaker who speculates that p engages in an act with a distinctive epistemic significance from one who asserts that p—even in a case like that of Harry and Sally.

An indirect way to bring this out is to consider Harry's likely reactive attitudes to the two acts. Suppose Harry were to find out that Sally's speculation that p was based on very little evidence. Given his background knowledge he would be surprised, of course. (She never does this!) Even so, his reactive attitude to such a scenario would be very different from his reactive attitude on finding out that another speaker's *assertion* that p was based on very little evidence. Whereas he will criticize the asserter who asserts on very little evidence, Harry will show no tendency to criticize Sally for having speculated on very little evidence. (If he does, his doing so is not appropriate: she was *speculating* after all.) This difference in reactive attitudes attests to the fact that hearers have different expectations from speakers who assert, than they do from speakers who speculate. And this point can be made even in a case, like that of Sally, where the hearer has excellent evidence in favor of the high reliability of the speaker's speech behavior when speculating. I submit that this difference in hearer expectations provides indirect evidence for the hypothesis that the epistemic significance of assertion differs from that of speculation: hearers expect—better, they regard themselves as *entitled* to expect—more from speakers who make assertions than they do from those who merely speculate. (This topic of hearer expectations will be revisited at length in Chapter 3.)

Still, it is worthwhile trying to put a finer point on this by considering how the proponent of Strong Evidentialism might try to account for this datum about hearer expectations (without appealing to the norm of assertion). She might try to do so as follows. Given Harry's background knowledge of Sally's super-high epistemic standards and her excellent track record as a speculator, Sally's speculation that p provides Harry with evidence in favor of [p], where this evidence is as good as the evidence that Harry would have in the case that Samantha—a colingual he does not know so well—asserted that p. The explanation for the epistemic significance of Samantha's assertion would be that, while Harry does not have all that much background knowledge of Samantha's track record as an assertor, he has the assertoric track record of many *other* speakers—and so he has evidence that assertions in general are right much more often than not, with the further result that he has strong inductive grounds to think that Samantha is probably right in what she asserts. But, where Harry's expectations of Samantha's assertion are grounded in generic evidence of assertions generally, so that he would have precisely the same expectations of *any arbitrary person's* assertion, Harry's expectations regarding Sally's speculation derive from specific evidence of Sally's track record as a speculator. Since he recognizes this, he would not expect another speaker's speculations to live up to the same standards. In short, there would appear to be an evidential basis for Harry to recognize the difference in epistemic significance between assertion and speculation, as well as for him to have the expectations he does in particular cases of observed speech.

But the view just described, in which the proponent of Strong Evidentialism aims to accommodate the facts about the difference in epistemico-pragmatic significance between assertion and speculation, faces two key objections.

First, it regards as brute something I should think requires explanation: namely, the fact that a hearer who aims to acquire knowledge through the acceptance of another's speculation (in the way Harry did) requires significantly more background knowledge than a hearer who aims to acquire knowledge through the acceptance of another's assertion. Even if it is conceded that some background knowledge (of general assertoric reliability) is needed if one is to acquire knowledge through the acceptance of another's assertion, surely this demand is less burdensome than the demand on someone who hopes to acquire knowledge through acceptance of another's speculation. And if this is so we would like some explanation of this fact. Assuming that one cannot appeal to any difference in the norms governing the acts, Strong Evidentialism would appear to be at a loss here.

Second, and perhaps relatedly, the Strong Evidentialist view just described fails to appreciate what I will call the *division of epistemic labor* involved in the two cases. Let H be a hearer who wants to know whether p. Now suppose that I am right to think that the epistemic requirements on H, if he is to come to know that p through accepting a speaker's speech contribution, are less stringent in the case of H's observing another's *assertion* that p than they are in a case of H's observing another's *speculation* that p.[26] Then it seems plausible to think that there is something like a *division of epistemic labor* going on in the case of assertion: it is because the assertor somehow makes available to the hearer the results of her own epistemic sensibility—results that, in the best case, render her (the speaker) knowledgeable—that the epistemic demands on the hearer, if *he* is to count as knowing, are less stringent than they are in the case of a speculation. To be sure, we need an account of how the speaker can play this role (a topic to which I return in Chapter 3). Still, the point remains that the speaker makes available to the hearer the results of her own epistemic sensibility. This is part of what I have in mind by speaking of the epistemic significance of assertion. The difficulty is that Strong Evidentialism would appear to have no way to acknowledge this. The proponent of Strong Evidentialism might respond that assertion makes the *speaker's evidence* available to a hearer, in a way that speculation does not. But if this were so we would like an explanation of this fact, and there appears to be no explaining this short of by way of appeal to distinctive norms governing these distinctive types of speech act. (Again, this is a topic to which I will return in Chapter 3.)

---

[26] Here I also assume that the epistemic conditions on knowledge remain the same no matter the type of knowledge. That is, knowledge through another's speech is no less (and no more) demanding than knowledge through, for instance, perception.

2.5.4 Assertion and Evidence Again

I want to conclude with one final consideration against Strong Evidentialism regarding assertion's role in the spread of knowledge. This consideration has already been noted in passing and can be dealt briefly with here: when one asserts something, one's speech act is not *offered* as, and is not *intended to be taken* as, a piece of evidence. On this basis, many theorists conclude that any account which thinks of these acts in purely evidential terms misconstrues how they function, epistemically speaking (see, for example, Ross (1986: 72) and Moran (2006: 301)).[27] Such authors often take their inspiration from a point made in Grice (1957): there is a big difference between *saying* something to the effect that p, and revealing a photograph whose content is or includes the content that p. (Grice's original example contrasted the photograph with a drawing; but his point was that the act of saying something was more like drawing something than it was like showing a photograph with that content.) All three non-evidential views of how S's assertion that p can generate a reason for H to believe that p—the trust-based view, the assurance view, and the norm-of-assertion view—will trace testimony's status as a reason-generator to one or another feature bound up with its status as a case of Gricean "saying."

2.6 On the Very Possibility of Non-Evidential Accounts

I have just argued that Strong Evidentialism—the combination of reductionism and evidentialism regarding the role of assertion in the spread of knowledge—cannot hope to account for that role, at least not if it is to avoid all appeal to the norm of assertion itself. My arguments on this score do not address those who endorse the combination of evidentialism and *non*-reductionism. Such a position holds that another's assertion is a form of evidence, but also endorses that this evidence functions like the evidence of one's senses—something that can be accepted by default, without requiring further reasons to regard the evidence as reliable. Such a view is worth taking seriously.[28] However, rather than discussing its merits and drawbacks, I want to consider the possibility of *non-evidential* approaches to assertion's role in the spread of knowledge. My reason for shifting the discussion in this fashion at this point is straightforward. Any version of non-reductionism (whether evidentialist or not) will have a non-evidential component in it. In particular, any version of non-reductionism will regard *assertion's status as a reason to*

---

[27] The claim is that it will not do to construe testimony *wholly* in evidential terms. A stronger claim is sometimes made, to the effect that it will not do to construe testimony in evidential terms *at all*. The former claim is consistent with the idea that testimony can sometimes function as evidence; the latter claim is not. Here I am only considering the weaker version of the claim.

[28] It appears to be the position of McDowell (1994b).

believe as something which itself stands by default, as not in need of the backing of further reasons or evidence. (Even evidentialists who endorse non-reductionism will have to allow this much.) For this reason, it is proper to abstract away from evidentialism itself, to inquire into this non-evidential component in an account of assertion's role in the spread of knowledge. What account can we offer for thinking of assertions in this way—as providing reasons to believe, where the reasons in question stand by default, defeated only in the presence of positive reasons to doubt them?

We can put our central question in terms of other's speech as a basic source of justification. Formulated in this way, the question is this: how can another person's assertion that p, by itself, ever generate a justification-conferring reason to believe that p?[29] More specifically, once the assertion's status as mere evidence is off the table,[30] why should we think that a proposition such as *that so-and-so asserted that p*, when justifiedly believed by a subject, is (or generates) a justification-conferring reason to believe that p? What is owed is an explanation for how assertion (or testimony) can be a basic, irreducible source of justification. If this question is not addressed, the idea that there can be a non-evidential component in our account of assertion's role in the spread of knowledge seems like a non-starter.

There are several different ways one might aim to address this explanatory burden. In what follows I describe these, indicating the strength and drawbacks of each.

One strategy (an early version of which can be found in Coady 1992) is an anti-skeptical one. The form of argument is a *reductio*. Suppose that (the assertions that constitute) another's testimony is not a basic source of justification. Then, on the twin assumptions that (i) a global reduction of testimonial justification to other kinds of justification is impossible, and (ii) testimony is implicated throughout our fabric of belief (for which see Audi 1997 in addition to Coady 1992), much of what we currently believe will turn out, implausibly, to be unjustified. This strategy has two obvious drawbacks. The first is that it assumes that any plausible form of reductionism about testimonial justification requires global reductionism. Of course, this potential flaw could be rectified if the skeptical conclusion could be established without depending on a claim such as (i) (for which see Insole 2000). But there remains the second drawback: even if this strategy succeeds, still it fails to illuminate *why* or in *virtue of what* another's say-so counts as a basic source of justification.

A second strategy, which is more substantial than the bare anti-skeptical strategy, is to endorse a kind of *dogmatism* about testimonial justification. Very roughly put,

---

[29] In this section I am moving from talk of rationality to talk of justification. A full account of the epistemology of testimony would have to connect these. For my own view, see Goldberg (2010a).

[30] By this I mean Strong Evidentialism regarding assertion's role in the spread of knowledge is off the table. Clearly, assertions *are* evidence: that my brother asserted that he would like to leave is evidence that he is unhappy. The point is rather that it is not merely in virtue of being evidence that assertions play their characteristic (testimony-constituting) role in the spread of knowledge.

dogmatism is the view that certain types of appearance states are such that when beliefs are formed on the basis of an acceptance of the appearances, they are *prima facie* justified. (To say that they are *prima facie* justified is to imply that they are *ultima facie* justified unless there are relevant defeaters, in the form of, for example, reasons to think that the sources are malfunctioning, or that conditions are not normal for the use of these sources.) Dogmatism can be thought of as a kind of foundationalist picture of justification, with a dogmatic attitude towards the (appearance-type) sources of basic belief. Dogmatism has been defended regarding perceptual appearances (Pryor 2000), and Chudnoff (2011) argues that if perceptual dogmatism is true, so too is dogmatism about the intuitive appearances. One might then think to extend dogmatism to include the testimonial appearances as well.[31] This strategy is rather more substantial than the bare anti-skeptical strategy, as dogmatism itself is a view that has been motivated and defended on grounds independent of testimony (for which see again Pryor 2000). Still, those who hope to vindicate the basicness of the justification-conferring reason that assertions generate might hope to do more in the way of accounting for this than simply to embrace dogmatism about testimony and assertion.

A third strategy, deriving in the main from the eighteenth-century Scottish Enlightenment philosopher Thomas Reid, offers a broadly reliabilist rationale for (testimony-constituting) assertion as a basic source of justification. This rationale makes two claims. First, the need to communicate in general—and the need to communicate knowledge in particular—is part of human nature (a part of our natural sociality, as it were). And second, the communicational route to belief is by and large reliable—in any case, reliable enough to serve as a basic source of justification (Reid 1997). Thus, in the same way that our natural perceptual endowments (together with the reliability of those processes, and our sensitivity to the conditions under which they are not reliable) render us justified in taking the deliverances of our perceptual faculties at face value so long as there are no relevant grounds for doubt, so too our natural endowments in taking the word of our fellows (together with the reliability of the relevant processes, and our sensitivity to the conditions under which they are not reliable) render us justified in taking the word of our fellow at face value so long as there are no relevant grounds for doubt. (See Goldberg 2007a for a contemporary version of this view.)

According to the foregoing reliabilist rationale for regarding others' assertions as a basic source of justification, it is the reliability of assertions *in general* that is relevant to testimony's status as a basic source of justification. On this view, assertoric exchanges are of a type that reliably produce reliable belief, and hence the speech act of assertion is such that tokens of this type are worthy of being relied upon (and so are defeasibly justification-generating). Here I note, however,

---

[31] See Graham (2006a) for a very interesting discussion of the considerations that one would confront were one to approach testimony in this way.

that even if this sort of rationale is acceptable as an account of assertion's status as a basic source of justification, it would appear to leave out something important in communicative exchanges involving assertions. After all, a hearer H who forms a belief by accepting speaker S's assertion is not relying on the reliability of assertions *in general*, so much as he is relying on the reliability of S's assertion *in particular*: H is relying on S herself to have produced reliable testimony on this occasion.[32] Can we accommodate this point about the *de re* nature of the reliance of a hearer on a speaker, and still accept the reliabilist rationale for testimony as a basic source of justification? It would seem that we can: the resulting picture would be a non-reductionism which is also an *anti-individualism* about the epistemology of assertion-based belief.[33]

According to the envisaged view, the general reliability of assertion renders assertion a basic source of justification—one not reducible to other sources of justification. At the same time, what justifies a hearer's assertion-based belief is not the general reliability of the communicative process alone, but also whatever it is that supports the assertion itself. Such a view can be developed in any number of epistemological frameworks. Suppose that one's framework gives pride of place to reasons or evidence. Then one might try defending the thesis of Transindividual Reasons (Schmitt 2002, 2006; Adler 2002), according to which the reasons that serve to determine the justificatory status of H's assertion-based belief include the reasons that support the speaker S's assertion. Alternatively, suppose that one's framework is in terms of the reliability of belief-forming processes. Then one might try defending a thesis according to which the process of assertion-based belief-formation is an interpersonal process which includes the processes that eventuated in the speaker S's having asserted as she did (see, for example, Goldberg 2010a). Both sorts of view might be defended by appeal to the parallels between memory and testimony. Thus, just as it is plausible to suppose that the justification of a memory-sustained belief is a function of the goodness of the reasons that supported the belief on acquisition (or the reliability of the processes that originally produced the belief), so too it is plausible to suppose that the justification of a testimonial (assertion-based) belief is a function of the goodness of the reasons that support the assertion (or the reliability of the processes that produced it). Such a view is based on a comparison between memory and testimony that others have found to be fruitful and defensible (see, for example, Strawson 1994).

In short, while it can at first seem jarring to suppose that we need a non-evidential component in our account of assertion's role in the spread of knowledge, there are various options available for making good on this idea. This, together with the deficiencies in Strong Evidentialism (noted in Section 2.4), ought to prompt us to take this idea seriously.

---

[32] This point is the centerpiece of the account of testimonial knowledge in Graham (2000a, 2000b).
[33] The label "epistemic anti-individualism," as a label for describing a class of views in the epistemology of testimony, is one I have used elsewhere; see Goldberg (2007a, 2010a).

2.7 Non-Evidential Accounts: Interpersonal Views (Trust and Assurance)

Having argued, programmatically, that we will do well to embrace a non-evidential component in our account of assertion's role in the spread of knowledge, I now move on to describe three particular accounts of this component. All three are motivated by the Gricean idea that there is something distinctive in the act of *saying* something; all three aim to capture what this distinctive feature is in terms of one or another characteristic of (some subclass of) assertions. The first two accounts, which we might label "interpersonal" accounts, claim that the relevant characteristic is bound up with the (moral and prudential) relations between a speaker and the audience to whom she addresses her speech act. Although both of these accounts are first and foremost accounts of testimony rather than assertion, still, on the plausible assumption—which these authors accept—that testimony requires assertion, we can regard these as accounts of the subclass of assertion that constitutes testimony. Insofar as this subclass is then taken to be paradigmatic of assertion, it might be thought to contribute to our understanding of the speech act itself.

In this section I will review the two non-evidential views which can be described as "interpersonal" accounts of the sort of reasons that assertion makes available to a hearer. According to the first of the two interpersonal views, a speaker's assertion that p generates a reason to believe that p, and hence can play its characteristic role in the spread of knowledge, in virtue of its connection to interpersonal trust—a sort of trust on which assertoric communication depends. According to the second of the two interpersonal views, assertion generates a reason to believe, and hence can play its knowledge-spreading role, in virtue of the special nature of the act of *assuring* another of the truth of a proposition (an act that is present in some, though not all, cases of assertion).[34] Both of these accounts have their virtues, but I will argue that both ultimately fail (and for a very similar reason). This will bring me to the third account, which traces assertion's generation of a reason to believe, and hence its role in the spread of knowledge, to the constitutive (epistemic) norm that governs assertion. I will argue (in Section 2.8) that this is the one that we ought to endorse.

According to the trust-based version of the interpersonal view, speaker S's assertion that p generates a reason for a hearer H to believe that p, and hence can play a knowledge-spreading role, in virtue of H's manifest dependence on S for truth—H's *affective trust* in S. The core claim of the trust-based view is that this very manifest dependence generates a reason for H to regard S's assertion—at least when it is mutually manifest that this assertion was offered with the aim of addressing H's need for information—as trustworthy. Proponents of this view (for example, Pettit 1995; Faulkner 2007, 2011) bring out the relevant point in two steps. First, when H's dependence on

---

[34] Beyond being employed by the so-called "assurance views of testimony" that I will consider later, the notion of assurance plays a particularly prominent role in Lawlor (2013).

(or affective trust in) S is manifest to S, this gives S a reason to "live up to" H's expectations (so as to avoid letting down H). Second, the fact that H is aware that S has such a reason to be trustworthy constitutes a reason for H to think that S *will* be trustworthy. This reason—H's reason to think that S will be trustworthy—combines with the fact that the content of the assertion was that p, to constitute a reason for H to believe that p.

The other version of the interpersonal account is the so-called "assurance view" of testimony (Hinchman 2005; Moran 2006; McMyler 2011). The assurance view of (the relevant subclass of) assertion traces these assertions' status as a reason to believe that p, to the fact that in testifying that p the speaker has offered her assurance (to the hearer) regarding the truth of [p]. To be sure, some proponents of the assurance view, such as Moran, require further conditions (such as the actual competence and sincerity of the speaker) if this reason is to count as good enough to justify a hearer's testimonial belief that p; I will return to this issue briefly later. For now, I note only that, on the assurance view, the fact that S told H that p[35] is a reason for H to believe that p in virtue of the fact that S's act amounts to her having offered H a "guarantee" or "assurance" that p. In this respect, acts of assertion, when they amount to "tellings," are analogues of acts of promising (Moran 2006). When S promises H that she (S) will φ, S entitles or authorizes H to expect that S will φ: the promise itself constitutes the basis of H's entitlement. Similarly, on the assurance view, when S tells H that p, S entitles or authorizes H to believe that p: the telling itself constitutes the basis of H's entitlement.[36]

This comparison between tellings and promises underwrites one of the most prominent features of the assurance view: the "second-personal" nature of the reason to believe.[37] According to the assurance view, the nature of the reason that a testimony-constituting assertion provides to a hearer is "second-personal" in that it is the distinctive property of the person addressed by the speaker. An audience who merely *overhears* the assertion (without having been addressed) does not enjoy such a reason, though she might nevertheless exploit the assertion and have a reason of a different sort. This aspect of the assurance view's construal of assertion has been developed by way of the analogy with promising (Moran 2006). To promise someone that you will do something confers a "right of complaint" on your promisee, so that if you fail to do what you promised her she can hold you responsible (and demand redress).[38] In this way the addressee is in a different position than another who simply observed

---

[35] Proponents of the assurance view often prefer to describe the act of testimony as that of "telling," in part because acts of telling are directed at particular audiences, and this feature of testimony is a core part of their account of testimony's status as a reason to believe.

[36] It is worth noting that theorists who do not endorse the assurance view have nevertheless endorsed analogies between assertion and promising. See, for example, Gary Watson (2004) and David Owens (2006). It is also worth noting that the assurance view was to some extent anticipated in the account of assertion found in Brandom (1983).

[37] The notion of a "second-personal" reason is developed in ethics by Stephen Darwall; see Darwall (2006). (Darwall himself suggests analogies between the practical case in ethics and the theoretical case in epistemology, but does not develop this suggestion at any length.)

[38] The phrase "right of complaint" is from Moran (2006).

the promise being made (to another). Similarly, according to the assurance view, hearers who are the intended audience of an act of testimony-constituting assertion have been given the "right of complaint" if it should turn out that the assurance was defective; no such right is conferred on those to whom the assurance was not addressed (even if they happen to overhear the act of assurance). According to proponents of the assurance view, this feature illuminates the nature of the reason the telling makes available: if you promised me to φ, my reason for believing that you will φ is that you promised me (which gives me a reason to hold you to your word); whereas another person who observed your promise to me is not in the same position. If the assurance view is correct, the same asymmetry holds for acts of asserting (when these amount to acts of telling).

I believe that, while both versions of the interpersonal view—the trust-based version and the assurance version—are getting at something, their insights have more to do with ethics than with epistemology. I will discuss the ethics of assertion at greater length in Chapter 7. Here I want to focus my attention on these views, not as claims regarding the ethics of assertion, but rather as claims regarding assertion's role in the spread of knowledge. I find these claims wanting.

Let us assume (as many critics do) that both the trust-based view and the assurance view describe what in fact are interpersonal dimensions of testimonial exchanges. The criticism is rather that these views fail to identify features that render assertion and testimony the sort of thing that can justify belief and underwrite knowledge. Thus Lackey (2008, 2011) argues that even if it is mutually known between speaker S and hearer H that H is depending on S for the truth, and so that S has a reason to live up to H's expectations, even so, this mutual knowledge does not make it reasonable for H to regard S's assertion as credible unless H is also entitled to regard S as actually motivated by this reason (and as competent to meet the expectation). In a similar fashion, both Lackey (2008, 2011) and Goldberg (2011) argue that, absent any entitlement to regard the fact of S's assurance of [p] as a reliable indication of the truth of [p], no hearer should regard S's assurance-manifesting testimony that p as a good reason to believe that p.

These criticisms, I think, succeed in establishing that neither version of the interpersonal view, taken by itself, can serve as an account of assertion's role in the spread of knowledge. In particular, neither the phenomenon of interpersonal trust, nor the phenomenon of assurance, by itself, establishes that testimony-constituting assertions generate a (defeasible) reason to believe. At a minimum, these views must be supplemented with independent reasons to think that assertions do generate such reasons[39]—reasons of the sort I characterized in Section 2.6. Insofar as proponents of

---

[39] My sense is that both Hinchman (2005) and McMyler (2011) intend their assurance view to suffice, by itself, to establish the basicness of testimony-generated reasons. If so, they both fall to this criticism. The assurance view in Moran (2006), however, does not—for the simple reason (mentioned previously) that he adds, as an additional condition on the reasons generated by testimony, that the testimony itself must be reliable. In effect, in conceding this Moran is conceding that the phenomenon of assurance alone cannot be used to establish that testimony-constituting assertions generate an irreducible reason to believe. But in so doing he also weakens the need to appeal to assurance in the first place. (I will return to this in Chapter 3.)

either of these views endorse those reasons, they can continue to appeal to the phenomenon of interpersonal trust (or to that of assurance) in defense of a weaker claim. The weaker claim would be that, *given that there are independent reasons in support of a non-evidential account of assertion's role in the spread of knowledge*, interpersonal trust (alternatively: assurance) is the mechanism enabling assertion to play this role. It is this weaker claim that I now want to consider.

Although there is much to the idea that the act of assurance (alternatively: the link to interpersonal trust) is the mechanism that enables (some) assertions to play their knowledge-spreading role, I want to raise several objections to such a claim. These objections stand even if we allow that these accounts can help themselves to the independent reasons in support of the basicness of assertion-generated reasons to believe. Since the objections I will be presenting here will be developed at length in Chapter 3, where I can connect them to other phenomena of interest, here I will be brief. The basic objection is that both the trust-based view and the assurance view amount to an unnecessary complication: whatever it is that they might be used to explain is better explained by the hypothesis that assertion has an epistemic norm.

Let us begin with the assurance account. I submit that the appeal to assurance is a complication, and it is not needed. It is a complication in that it introduces a distinction between those assertions that constitute an act of assurance, and those that do not. (I will argue later that this distinction does not do the epistemic work that assurance theorists need it to do.) And it is unnecessary, since the appeal to assurance is not needed in order to see how assertions can play their knowledge-spreading role.

These points can be developed in the form of a dilemma. Either all assertions are acts of assurance, or it is not the case that all assertions are acts of assurance. In the former case, the appeal to assurance would be unnecessary on the assumption that we have an alternative, simpler account that does just as well in explaining assertion's role in the spread of knowledge. Later I will argue that the account in terms of the epistemic norm of assertion is just that. Such an account is simpler, since (a) it appeals directly to a feature of assertion that does not involve the postulation of any specifically moral or interpersonal relationship between the speaker and the hearer, and at the same time (b) it can be used to account for the generation of the distinctly moral or interpersonal phenomena attendant to this sort of act.[40] Now take the latter horn of the dilemma, on which it is not the case that all assertions are acts of assurance. The difficulty for the assurance view here is that in this case the assurance view does not explain what needs to be explained. This is because *whether or not an assertion is also an act of assurance*, the assertion is apt for the spread of knowledge. To modify a case presented in Lackey (2008), suppose a person makes a voice recording in which she states all that she observes, but does so without any intention to assure anyone of anything. (She

---

[40] I will develop this idea at length in Chapter 3; and in Chapter 7 I will argue that, despite the fact that the norm-based account does not postulate any specifically ethical dimension to speech, it can be used to illuminate that dimension.

thinks all of this is too boring, that none of this would be of interest to anyone other than herself.) Still, she wants to record things as she observed them, so she aims to be as reliable as possible in her statements. If, despite her intentions, her recordings were to fall into the hands of a colingual, that colingual is then in a position to learn (= come to know) what our verbal diarist observed by accepting her statements. Since by hypothesis she was not aiming to assure anyone of anything, the assurance view cannot obtain the desired result. Nor do we have to resort to private diary cases for this. It suffices to say that the "second-personal" dimension of the assurance view gets matters wrong as well. If Henry overhears Samantha tell Henrietta that they will meet at the movie theater in downtown Evanston, then Henry is in a position to know precisely what Henrietta is in a position to know, and for precisely the same reason: Samantha said so. Here, the assurance view makes a false prediction, since it predicts that Henry's reason cannot be the same as Henrietta's.

Interestingly, an objection with the same form can be made against the interpersonal trust account. Perhaps this is unsurprising: in tracing assertion's role in the spread of knowledge to the relation of *interpersonal trust* associated with assertoric exchanges, the trust-based view will fail to get the cases right when there is no intended audience, or when there is an audience other than the intended audience. Again, we can present the objection in the form of a dilemma, according to whether or not all cases of assertion are cases involving interpersonal trust. Taking the first horn, if all cases of assertion aim at being cases involving interpersonal trust, even so, we have reason to prefer a simpler account of the data than this account, which postulates (over and above what is needed for assertion proper) interpersonal relations of trust as well. And again I will be arguing that an account in terms of the norm of assertion is simpler, since it does not postulate anything beyond what is needed for assertion itself. Taking the second horn, if not all cases of assertion aim at being cases involving interpersonal trust, then this view will deliver the wrong results in the two types of case discussed previously.

Now, these objections to the trust-based view and the assurance view are successful if, but only if, I am right to think that there is a simpler alternative account of assertion's role in the spread of knowledge. And so there is: it is in terms of the hypothesis that assertion has a constitutive (robustly epistemic) norm. It is to that account that I now turn.

2.8 Non-Evidential Accounts: The Norm of Assertion

Those who reject Strong Evidentialism regarding assertion's role in the spread of knowledge, but who also find the two interpersonal accounts wanting as well, might hope to derive assertion's status as a reason for belief from features of the speech act of assertion itself—as distinct from the interpersonal (moral or prudential) relations holding between speaker and hearer(s) in particular assertoric speech exchanges. In this section I argue that we can have what we want by appeal to the hypothesis that assertion has an epistemic norm.[41]

Suppose that assertion is that unique speech act whose warrantedness is specified by a certain standard—that provided by the "norm of assertion." Suppose further that the standard in question is a robustly epistemic one (in the sense defined in Chapter 1). In that case, a speaker must not assert p unless she has the relevant epistemic authority with respect to p. Here I will be neutral on what the content of the standard is. Candidates for this authority include (epistemic) certainty (Stanley 2008), knowledge (Williamson 1996), justified belief (Kvanvig 2009; see also Lackey 2007b, which is a view in the neighborhood), and rational belief (Douven 2006). For my present purposes the key point is this: so long as the norm is robustly epistemic, assertions are not warranted unless the speaker had the relevant epistemic authority. If we make the further assumption that the norm of assertion is a rule of language, it will be mutually known, if only implicitly, by all competent speakers.[42] We would then be in a position to account for assertion's providing a reason to believe. Suppose that S asserts that p, and that she does so in H's presence. Then both S and H will know that the act that S performed was not warranted unless S had the relevant epistemic authority with respect to the truth of [p]. Since this is a piece of mutual knowledge, H knows that S acknowledges as much, and S is aware that H knows this. In light of this, it seems appropriate to speak of the mutual awareness of S's acknowledging the responsibility for having the relevant epistemic authority with respect to the truth of [p]. Then, so long as H is entitled to regard S as (not merely *acknowledging* this responsibility but) *being* responsible in this way, H is entitled to believe that S is epistemically authoritative regarding—has the relevant sort of epistemic goodies supporting—the proposition that p. And this would be the basis of testimony's status as a reason for belief. In effect, it would be a matter of H's being entitled to regard S as having reasons in support of p, where that there are such reasons is itself a reason for H to believe that p.

Two comments are in order regarding this proposed account of assertion's role in the spread of knowledge.

First, the account just presented provides for assertion's generation of a reason to believe, but only in those cases in which the hearer is entitled to regard the speaker as having the relevant epistemic authority. But it might be wondered what entitles a hearer to so regard a speaker. Indeed, this question returns us to the debate between reductionists and non-reductionists. Some—the reductionists—will hold that a hearer

---

[41] Compare what follows to Owens' (2006) "assertion-based" account of testimony, which, while it rejects the assurance view, does not itself appeal to the norm of assertion. Instead, it appeals to the idea that (sincere) assertion manifests belief.

[42] By this I do not mean that hearers will be able to explicitly state this norm, as a piece of knowledge. Rather, their implicit knowledge of the norm is seen in the ways in which they participate in the practice of assertion: the conditions under which they will produce assertions, their reactive attitudes towards the assertions of others under a variety of circumstances, and their reactive attitudes to others' reactive attitudes towards their own assertions under a variety of circumstances.

is so entitled only when he has positive reasons to regard the speaker as epistemically authoritative on this occasion. Others—the non-reductionists—will hold that a hearer is so entitled so long as he lacks reasons to doubt that the speaker is epistemically authoritative on this occasion. I will have more to say about this debate in Chapter 3. For now, however, I want to point out only that, whatever side is ultimately correct on this score, the point remains that *both* sides will need to appeal to the norm of assertion, if they are to explain assertion's role in the spread of knowledge. For it is (hearers' implicit grasp of) the norm of assertion that entitles hearers to regard assertions as speech acts in which the speaker purports to represent how things are, as backed by her relevant epistemic authority. Without appeal to the norm of assertion, the hypothesis that there is a speech act of this type is itself something that would have to be established through evidence—with all of the troubles that such a view involves.

Second, there is a further complication that arises at this point, regarding the norm-based view of assertion's role in the spread of knowledge. It is very tempting to think that, given only the fact that an assertion was observed, a hearer H is not entitled to expect anything more in the way of the speaker S's epistemic authority than what the norm entitles him to expect. Thus, if the norm is knowledge, then H is entitled to expect that S is (responsible for being) knowledgeable; but if the norm is less than knowledge, then H is entitled to expect only what the norm provides for. Does this dimension affect the strength of the reason that testimony provides for H (according to the assertion view)? If it does, then we might have a novel argument for knowledge being the norm of assertion. The argument in outline form would be as follows. Assertion is the speech act whose nature makes it apt for the transmission of knowledge; but it can only play this role if the hearer who observes an assertion is *ipso facto* entitled to expect that the asserter knows whereof she speaks; and the hearer is entitled to expect as much only if (something at least as strong as) knowledge is the norm of assertion. Of course, this sort of argument might be resisted by denying one or more of the premises. But to my mind this is a topic that has not received the attention that it deserves. (See Goldberg 2010b for an initial exploration of this strategy.)

Since I do not at this point want to descend into details about the content of the norm of assertion, beyond assuming that it is robustly epistemic, I do not want to address this matter here. (I will do so in Chapters 9–11). Instead, I want to consider what programmatic reasons there may be for favoring the norm-based approach. In doing so, the only assumption I make is that the content of the norm is robustly epistemic. My answer is that, if it is combined with non-reductionism, such an account can explain what is attractive about the two interpersonal accounts, without having any of their flaws.

On the twin assumptions—first, that assertion has a robustly epistemic norm, and second, that hearers are (defeasibly but presumptively) entitled to regard speakers as satisfying the norm when they assert—we can explain assertion's role in the spread of knowledge. For on these two assumptions, a hearer is entitled to regard the speaker as satisfying the norm of assertion so long as there are no relevant reasons to suppose she has not done so. In that case, the hearer is entitled to regard the speaker as having whatever epistemic goodies she needed to have to satisfy the robustly epistemic norm. But in that case the hearer is entitled to draw the trivial inference that there is adequate support for the proposition asserted—adequate to satisfy whatever the robustly epistemic standard is. This would be sufficient to rationalize the hearer's move to accept what she asserted. Then, whether his assertion-based belief satisfies the conditions on knowledge would depend, presumably, on the strength of the speaker's own position regarding the asserted proposition. But in any case this would explain *both* why it is rational for a hearer to accept what was asserted, and why, when it is rational for him to do so, it is often the case that the hearer's belief will amount to knowledge. The latter explanation is simply that the speaker's satisfaction of the norm of assertion makes it more likely that the hearer's assertion-based belief satisfies the conditions on knowledge. This explanation will be stronger or weaker in accord with the strength of the norm of assertion itself. If the norm is knowledge, then the speaker's satisfaction of that norm, together with the hearer's entitlement to suppose that it is satisfied, is a knowledge-sufficient ground for the hearer's belief based on his acceptance of that assertion. If the norm is merely rational belief of the sort described in Douven (2006), then the speaker's satisfaction of that norm, together with the hearer's entitlement to suppose that it is satisfied, only makes it likely that the hearer's assertion-based belief is grounded in a knowledge-sufficient basis. Either way, however, we have made sense of how assertion can play a role in the spread of knowledge.

What is more, with the two previous assumptions in hand we can explain the attractiveness of the assurance view without running into the objections faced by that view. According to the norm-based view, when an assertion is made it will be mutually manifest to the speaker and the hearer that the speaker's performance is warranted only if the speaker satisfies a robustly epistemic standard vis-à-vis the content asserted. We might thus say that to assert is to do something regarding which it is mutually manifest that anyone who observes the assertion will regard it as warranted only if the robustly epistemic standard in question was satisfied. Consequently, one who observes an assertion is entitled to assume that either the standard was met or the performance was unwarranted. Since the speaker can know in advance that the hearer is entitled to assume as much, and since the sincere speaker does not intend the hearer to regard the performance as unwarranted, we might say that in asserting that p a speaker conveys her own relevant epistemic authority vis-à-vis [p]: she conveys that she satisfies the standard set down by assertion's norm. This might be put succinctly by saying that in making an assertion a speaker implicates her own epistemic authority.[43] It is this, I submit, that constitutes the core insight of the assurance view: one who asserts does something that conveys her own epistemic authority to her audience. But this is something that is conveyed to anyone who observes the assertion, not merely to those to whom it

---

[43] Compare this account of the invocation of one's own epistemic authority with that in McKinnon and Simard Smith (2013).

was offered—and it is conveyed whenever an assertion is made, not only in the special case in which the assertion constitutes a "telling." In this way, the norm-based account is not susceptible to the objection to which the assurance view was susceptible.

What is more, equipped with just those two previous assumptions we can also appreciate what is attractive about the interpersonal trust view without running into the objections which that view faces. Since to convey one's own authority is compatible with not having the authority one represents oneself as having, to assert that p is compatible with not having the authority one conveys in the act of asserting. Thus, there will always be an element of risk involved in accepting another's assertion. Interpersonal trust is simply one consideration, perhaps among others, that enhances the epistemic position of one who runs the risk of accepting another's assertion. However, it is not this trust, but rather the conveyed authority, that underwrites assertion's role in the spread of knowledge. The sort of trust that is in play in the interpersonal trust view is too weak to play this underwriting role. This sort of trust is *generic*: it is not based on evidence regarding the speaker's trustworthiness (Faulkner 2007, 2011), and hence provides the same sort of reason no matter the speaker to whom it is applied. In this way, the reason it generates is very different from the sort of reason generated by the norm of assertion. In the latter case, the reason derives from the hearer's entitlement to think that on this occasion of assertion the speaker herself satisfied the robustly epistemic norm. The result is that a belief formed through an acceptance of the assertion, under conditions when the hearer was entitled to regard the norm as satisfied, will be more or less likely to satisfy the requirements on knowledge, according to the actual epistemic position of this speaker.

I conclude, then, that, of the non-evidential accounts of assertion's role in the spread of knowledge, the account which makes use of the (epistemic) norm of assertion is to be preferred. What the norm of assertion offers is a plausible (non-evidential) account of assertion's purport of belief-worthiness: it provides us with a non-evidential account of why hearers are entitled to understand acts of assertion as acts whereby the speaker purports to represent how things are, in a way backed by her (the speaker's) own epistemic authority. Knowledge can be spread by assertion, then, when, in addition to understanding that an act of this kind has been performed, the hearer is entitled to regard the speaker as actually *having* the relevant authority she purports to have. In the next chapter I will argue that the norm of assertion itself is silent on the conditions on the hearer's having such an entitlement: we are free to endorse either a reductionist or an anti-reductionist account of that entitlement. (I regard this as a virtue of the norm-based account.)

2.9 Conclusion

In this chapter I have been discussing one aspect of the epistemic significance of assertion: namely, assertion's role in the spread of knowledge. My claims have been several.

First, the Strong Evidentialist account of this significance is objectionable, and so we have reasons to favor an alternative. Second, I argued that any alternative form of evidentialism will need to regard assertion's *belief-worthiness purport* as itself not something that requires to be established by evidence—it is rather something that is part of what is understood when one understands that an assertion has been made. Third, among the non-evidential accounts of assertion's role, only one of them—the one that traces assertion's epistemic significance (and its role in the spread of knowledge) to the constitutive (robustly epistemic) norm that governs this speech act—derives from the distinctive nature of assertion. What is more, that account, I argued, is the best of the three non-evidential accounts on offer. If this is correct we have a first example of a case in which the hypothesis that assertion is answerable to a (robustly epistemic) norm earns its keep by way of its explanatory power, and in particular by way of its connecting assertion to another phenomenon of philosophical interest (the spread of knowledge through speech).

3
Assertion and Testimony

3.1 Overview

In the previous chapter I suggested how the hypothesis that assertion has an epistemic norm might be used to account for one feature bound up with the "epistemic significance" of assertion: its role in the spread of knowledge. I argued that this account was to be preferred both to the Strongly Evidentialist account and to alternative non-evidential accounts of assertion's role in the spread of knowledge. As developed in the preceding chapter, the main selling point of the norm-based account was its ability to model the *belief-worthiness purport* of assertion. According to the norm-based account, the fact that assertion enjoys this feature is not something that needs to be confirmed by evidence; rather, it is a core part of the act itself. In particular, the act of assertion is one in which a speaker represents things as being a certain way, where this act of representation is presented as *backed by her (the speaker's) own epistemic authority*.[1] In arguing for this, I had occasion to argue that the norm-based account outperforms two other non-evidential accounts: the interpersonal trust account and the assurance account. At least when it comes to this aspect of assertion's "epistemic significance," then, the norm-based account earns its keep.

In this chapter I use the norm of assertion to account for another feature of assertion's "epistemic significance," having to do with the epistemic entitlements and responsibilities that arise in certain speech exchanges involving information exchange. Although these entitlements and responsibilities are typically presented (when they are presented at all) in terms of the speech act of *telling* (rather than in terms of assertion), here I argue that we do better to see the phenomena in question as deriving from assertion: if we do so we can account for them in terms of assertion's norm. Doing so has two selling points. First, we make do with claims we need anyway, independent of issues of testimony and telling, and in this sense have an account that is simpler than its rivals. And second, we avoid other difficulties to which the rival accounts (which trace these phenomena to interpersonal features of *tellings*) are susceptible.

---

[1] Of course, even if we agree that to assert that p is (among other things) to present that p as worthy of belief, even so, we can wonder when a hearer is entitled to accept that things are as they are presented to be in the assertion. However, this is the task of an epistemology of testimony; it is not something to be settled by an account of assertion. I will return to this later in this chapter, arguing that it is a virtue of this account that it does not settle that issue.

3.2 Assertion-Generated Expectations: Entitlements and Responsibilities

In the previous chapter I argued that the hypothesis that assertion has an epistemic norm can be used to give an account of one dimension of assertion's "epistemic significance": assertion's role in the spread of knowledge, and in particular its *belief-worthiness purport*. My discussion there concluded by pointing in the direction of a series of questions which relate to another dimension of assertion's epistemic significance. In particular, I spoke of speakers' and hearers' expectations of one another in assertoric exchanges, and contrasted this with their expectations in cases involving other speech acts (such as speculation). This chapter deepens my account of those expectations.

The expectations themselves are clearly part of the story regarding assertion's role in the spread of knowledge. In particular, it is because of what speakers typically expect of hearers' reactions to assertions, that the choice of an assertion (as a type of act by which to communicate knowledge) is a rational one; and it is because of what hearers typically expect of speakers' assertions, that another's assertion is typically regarded by a hearer as a possible opportunity to acquire knowledgeable belief in the asserted content. In this way, we might see the present investigation into these expectations as a continuation of the story of assertion's role in the spread of knowledge.

However, I propose to treat the assertion-generated expectations separately, in their own chapter. One of my reasons for doing so is that, while these expectations are related to assertion's role in the spread of knowledge, they are only *indirectly* related to that role. After all—and contrary to what (in Chapter 2) we saw the two "interpersonal" accounts maintaining—it is not the expectations themselves that underwrite a hearer's knowledge, when he comes to know something through accepting another's assertion. That underwriting role is played, rather, by the epistemic quality of the particular assertions the hearer accepted.[2] But there is a second reason why the expectations generated in assertoric exchanges deserve their own treatment. This is because in so doing we can highlight the distinctly *normative* dimension of assertoric exchanges. It is not merely that hearers and speakers form expectations of one another when a speaker makes an assertion; it is that both sides are, and in any case regard themselves as, *entitled* to these expectations. The fact that both sides are (and regard themselves as) *entitled* to form these expectations has tremendous significance in its own right. In this chapter I will be exploring the epistemic significance of this fact. This significance is seen in the distinctly epistemic entitlements and responsibilities that are bound up in the act of asserting something.[3] (In Chapter 7

---

[2] As I noted in Chapter 2, one proponent of the "assurance" view—Moran (2006: 289)—appears to recognize this. I argued that this recognition comes at the cost of rendering the assurance itself much less significant from an epistemic point of view.

[3] In speaking of distinctly epistemic entitlements and responsibilities, I mean only that the contents of these entitlements and responsibilities are epistemic. It may be, for example, that our responsibilities in speech are *moral* responsibilities—that we are morally responsible for living up to an epistemic standard in

I discuss the ethical dimension of this fact; there I will appeal to the norm of assertion to suggest that there is an ethics of assertion, and that this can be fruitfully connected to the ethics of belief.)

In this chapter my aim is to use the hypothesis that assertion is answerable to a robustly epistemic norm, in order to give an account of the mutual expectations that speakers and hearers have of one another in contexts of assertoric communication. If assertion has such a norm, we would expect that hearers and speakers would have precisely these expectations of one another. While I will not be arguing that there is no other way to account for these assertion-generated expectations, I will be arguing that the account on offer has important virtues.

I should make clear that I am not the first to try to link the debate over assertion's norm to issues regarding testimony. Various people have already done so. So, for example, one might wonder whether the knowledge norm of assertion, together with considerations regarding the conditions under which assertion can be used to transmit knowledge, can be used to make difficulties for contextualist views about knowledge (Williamson 2005; Turri 2010a).[4] Alternatively, one might appeal to assertion's role in expressing belief to account for various features of the epistemology of testimonial belief (Owens 2006; David Sosa, forthcoming).

My proposal, by contrast, will be to use assertion's norm in order to account for features of the testimonial exchange which, though prominent, have received much less attention in the literature on testimony. The features I have in mind have to do with the *responsibilities* and *entitlements* that are generated by a speaker's testifying that p. What little discussion there has been of these features has accounted for them in terms of the specific nature of the act of telling someone something, and of the relation between teller and addressee.[5] Such views were mentioned in my discussion (in Chapter 2) of the "interpersonal" accounts of assertion's role in knowledge communication. In this chapter I complete the work that I started there; I will be arguing that we do better to regard the responsibilities and entitlements in testimonial exchanges as generated by the act of assertion, and to account for them by appeal to assertion's norm. As in the previous two chapters, so too here I will be neutral as between the epistemic candidates for the norm of assertion: I will be assuming only that, whatever the standard is that the norm lays down, it is a robustly epistemic one.

In a nutshell, the position I will be defending is this. Given that assertion is governed by a robustly epistemic norm, it is in terms of this norm that we should characterize the sorts of responsibilities a speaker accrues in virtue of testifying, and the sorts of entitlements that a hearer acquires in virtue of observing and understanding testimony. My

---

our asserting practices. (I thank the members of Fritz Warfield's Fall 2010 Testimony seminar at Notre Dame for indicating to me the need to make this point explicit.) I discuss this matter in greater detail in Chapter 7.

[4] Although not on testimony *per se*, there is also a lively debate concerning whether the hypothesis that knowledge is the norm of assertion can be used to establish a contextualist view of knowledge (yes: DeRose 1996, 2002; no: Leite 2007).

[5] One exception to this is Brandom (1983).

claim will be that an account of testimony that appeals to the norm of assertion in this way is in a position to give a simple, plausible, independently motivated account of these features—one that outperforms its rivals.

3.3 Assertion's Norm and the Buck-Passing and Blame Phenomena

The bundle of features in question pertain to what I have elsewhere called the phenomena of *epistemic buck-passing* and *blame* (Goldberg 2006). To a first approximation, we can characterize these features as follows:

BUCK-PASSING
Suppose that hearer H accepts speaker S's testimony that p, under conditions in which H had the epistemic right to accept that testimony; that some individual T later queries H regarding the truth of H's testimony-based belief that p; that, in response, H exhausts all of her reasons for regarding S's testimony as trustworthy; and that even so, T remains unsatisfied. In this situation H is epistemically entitled—is within her epistemic rights[6]—to pass the epistemic buck to S (by representing S as having more in the way of epistemic support for the truth of p).

BLAME
Suppose that H accepts speaker S's testimony that p, under conditions in which H had the epistemic right to accept that testimony; and that it turns out that S's testimony to this effect had insufficient epistemic support. In this situation H is entitled—is within her epistemic rights—to blame S for the insufficient epistemic support of her (H's) own belief.

These features, I submit, are a familiar part of our assertoric practice; they are seen in that part of our practice in which we take something on the strength of another's assertion.[7]

Something in the neighborhood of these phenomena has been highlighted by some authors, in the course of trying to establish one or another version of anti-reductionism, according to which hearers enjoy a presumptive (albeit defeasible) entitlement to accept what others tell them. For example, Ross (1986) makes a point about responsibility and blame in testimony cases, as part of an attempt to argue for anti-reductionism from the rule-governed nature of language use. In addition, Hinchman (2005) and Moran (2006) make various points about speakers' responsibility to hearers, and hearers' reliance on speakers' fulfilling their responsibilities. They do so in their respective

---

[6] I am not entirely happy with this construal of "entitled," but I confess that I do not know a better one at present.
[7] Compare Williamson (in Greenough and Pritchard 2009: 344) and Turri (2010b), both of whom describe conversational patterns in assertoric practice that correspond to the blame phenomenon.

attempts to establish what in Chapter 2 I called the "assurance view" of testimony, on which the rationality and justification for accepting another's say-so derives from (what they allege is) the fact that offering testimony constitutes a way of offering one's *assurance* regarding the truth of the attested proposition. In Chapter 2 I expressed my doubts about these moves. In particular, while these authors appear to think that the assurance view itself can be used to *establish* an anti-reductionist thesis, I think rather that their accounts *presuppose* the viability of anti-reductionism. In this chapter I will be furthering my suspicions against the assurance view of testimony; only here I will be presenting my doubts about these as accounts of the buck-passing and blame phenomena. For now, I simply note that, insofar as these authors aim to accommodate the features involved in the phenomena of buck-passing and blame, their accounts are needlessly complex. Their complexity is seen both in that they make substantial claims about the nature of testimony and the relations between testifier and hearer. This complexity is needless: the norm of assertion affords us a simpler, more plausible, and less ideologically committed account of the features in question.

My proposal, then, is that we can make use of the claim that assertion has an epistemic norm, in order to account for the phenomena I have called buck-passing and blame. The idea behind this strategy is simple. Suppose that (i) in order to constitute a case of testifying (or a case of one person "telling" another something), a speech act must have the assertoric force of straight assertion. In that case, such speech acts will answer to the norm of assertion. On the further assumption that (ii) this norm is a robustly epistemic one, we will then have all that we need to explain the phenomena of epistemic buck-passing and blame. In particular, there is no need for further auxiliary assumptions[8] about the nature of testimony, tellings, or the relation between testifier/teller and audience.

The norm-based account of buck-passing and blame can be developed as follows. Assume (i) and (ii) (and assume that (i) and (ii) are common knowledge; I will return to this further assumption later). Now take a speaker S who testifies that p. Such a speaker knows—or, at any rate, is in a position to know, and should know—that she has performed a speech act whose warrant *qua* assertion depends on the satisfaction of a robustly epistemic norm. What is more, S knows that her audience H knows this, and that H knows that S knows that H knows, and so on. Since S and H know all of this, each knows—or, at any rate, is in a position to know, and should know—that if S's epistemic position vis-à-vis p is such that the epistemic norm fails to be satisfied, then S's speech act is unwarranted. It would be unwarranted *qua* assertion; and this unwarrantedness would attach to her testimony as well, since testimony involves speech acts with the assertoric force of assertion. Herein lies the source of the blame phenomenon. What is more, the point at issue—that testimony can be criticized on epistemic grounds, and its producer blamed, when it fails to satisfy assertion's norm—is a special case of a more

---

[8] That is, assumptions that go beyond those that we need anyway, as part of a correct account of assertion's norm.

general point. The more general point is this: since S and H both know (and know that the other knows, and so on) that, in testifying, S has performed a speech act whose warrantedness depends on the satisfaction of an epistemic norm, both know—or, at any rate, are in a position to know, and should know—that if the speech act was warranted, the epistemic norm was satisfied. But then it is easy to appreciate that once H exhausts his reasons for thinking that S's speech act was warranted *qua* testimony,[9] there remains more to which H is entitled to appeal in the way of support for the attested proposition H came to believe—namely, whatever epistemic goods S needed in order to satisfy the norm of assertion.[10] The buck-passing phenomenon is a reflection of the hearer's recognition of this point.

I submit that, despite its schematic nature, this account of the buck-passing and blame phenomena is both natural and simple. Even so, in the next section I will assume the burden of defending the claims on which the account depends. It depends on three crucial claims: that testimony-constituting speech acts must have the assertoric force of straight assertion; that, as such, these speech acts, like assertoric speech acts generally, answer to an epistemic norm; and that these first two points are common knowledge. In the next two sections I defend these claims.

3.4 Assertion and the Act of Testifying

How should we regard the relation between testimony and assertion? Whether or not we identify the two (as in Fricker 1987 and Sosa 1994), it would seem that on any plausible view of what is involved in the act of *testifying to the truth* of a proposition—and we can say the same thing about *telling* someone something—for a speech act to so count it must have the assertoric force of straight assertion. This will be true if the act in question is thought to be as a speech act aimed at settling a question before an audience (see Coady 1992). But it will also be true if the act in question is seen as a speech act aimed at giving one assurance (as in Moran 2006 and Hinchman 2005). Arguably, the hypothesis that these speech acts involve assertion can be established by reflecting on what is involved in attesting to the truth of a proposition. To attest is not merely to perform a speech act in which the proposition is presented-as-true; otherwise speculations and guesses, which present a proposition as true, would count as testimony. What distinguishes attesting from speculating or guessing is that the former involves presenting a proposition as true in such a way as to implicate one's own epistemic authority on the matter. It is precisely for this reason that testimony-constituting speech acts must have the assertoric force of assertions themselves: a speech act that fails to have the

---

[9] These will consist in H's reasons for regarding the testimony as credible—reasons which, I submit, are also reasons for regarding the speech act as appropriate *qua* assertion. I will return to this point later.

[10] In effect, H's entitlement to accept the testimony was *ipso facto* an entitlement to regard the testimony as satisfying the norm of assertion, and so was an entitlement to regard S as having whatever epistemic goods she needed in order to satisfy that norm. For more discussion of this point, see Goldberg (2007a: 16–20).

assertoric force of assertion will not involve the implication of the speaker's own epistemic authority, and so will lack a feature that is characteristic of cases of testimony.

Our conclusion, on which testimony-constituting speech acts require assertoric force, can be doubted. I can imagine two ways to do so.

The first concerns religious testimony.[11] Do those who attest to religious propositions invoke their own epistemic authority? Perhaps it will be said that a "belief-only" norm is the most appropriate one for such cases. I disagree: it is legitimate to assess these testimonies, like testimony more generally, from the epistemic point of view. Thus the skeptical scientist in the audience might well think that religious testimony as such is unwarranted, since none of the speakers has the requisite epistemic authority to *assert* the claims they make; and the now-skeptical adult who reflects on what she was told as a child might well blame her parents for the various assertions they made in the course of her religious upbringing. In both cases, blame attaches insofar as these sources engaged in flat-out assertion ("I was visited by God last night") as opposed to the mere expression of belief. Thus it would seem that even religious testimonies answer to a robustly epistemic norm of assertion. If audiences typically refrain from blaming religious testifiers, this is not because their testimonies answer to a non-epistemic standard, but rather because those who are skeptical of the testimonies typically see no point in voicing their epistemic reservations. In saying this I do not mean to belittle religious testimony; only to account for the otherwise anomalous fact that most people do not react to such testimony as an epistemic norm of assertion would predict.

The second way one might doubt my claim that testimony-constituting speech acts require assertoric force concerns the speculation case I introduced in Chapter 2 (WHEN HARRY MET SALLY). To review, Sally has super-high epistemic standards, including when she speculates, so that she will only speculate that p under conditions in which she has the sort of evidence that would warrant assertion (and she only asserts when she is epistemically certain). Harry knows all of this about Sally, having assembled a track record of her reliability in speech (both assertions and speculations). Our question is this. When Harry regards Sally's speculation that p as a good basis for coming to believe that p, is he not regarding Sally's speculation as a case of testimony?[12] If so, this falsifies the claim that in order to count as testimony, a speech act must have the force of an assertion.

My response will have been anticipated. Whether or not we regard this as a case of testimony, it is clearly not a case of Sally's *having testified*. For one thing, Sally would not regard herself as having testified. She did not implicate her own epistemic authority on the matter. She did nothing to indicate to Harry that he could "take it from her" that the proposition was true. She did nothing to "assure" him of the truth of the proposition. She certainly did not *tell* him that p. On the contrary, in making clear that she was speculating, she was explicitly distancing herself from being taken as offering any

---

[11] This case was brought to my attention by an anonymous referee for an earlier version of this chapter.
[12] Compare Lackey's (2008) notion of *hearer testimony*.

assurance, from being taken as having told him. If, despite all this, we still want to regard Sally's speculation as testimony—and I can see reasons why we might[13]—then (following Lackey 2008) we need to distinguish between hearer testimony and speaker testimony: not all *hearer testimony* (= things regarded as testimony by a hearer) will be *speaker testimony* (= speech acts performed with the intention of informing, of testifying). In cases of speaker testimony (in which the speaker testifies), the speaker performs a speech act through which she *aims* to be attesting to the truth of p. Such a speaker is not warranted in having so attested unless she is at least as well placed, epistemically, as one would need to be in order to be warranted in asserting p. Sally's speculation could then be described as a case in which she presents a proposition as true under conditions in which she is warranted in testifying to the truth of that proposition, even though she herself does not take herself to be, and so presumably is not, testifying in the first place. My previous claim—that in order to count as testimony, a speech act must have the force of an assertion—should be read as restricted to speaker testimony; that is, to those cases that involve the act of *testifying*.

In the context of an attempt to forge a link between testimony and assertion, the restriction to cases of testifying is well motivated. For my aim here is (not to characterize testimony as such, but rather) to characterize a core feature of *familiar cases* of testimony. The fact that there might be cases of testimony without the associated praise and blame phenomena, as there would be if the previous speculation case counts as a case of (hearer) testimony, should not obscure our interest in accounting for these phenomena when they *do* arise. As such, I will be restricting myself in what follows to considering cases of testifying; and it is with respect to these that I claim that testimony-constituting speech acts must have the assertoric force of straight assertion. (From now on, except where indicated otherwise, when I speak of testimony I should be taken to mean the restricted class of cases where the testimony is given through an act of testifying.)

Granting that speech acts constituting a case of testifying must have the assertoric force of straight assertion, what should be said about the sort of force that is in question? My assumption on this score is that it is characterized at least in part in relation to the norm of assertion. In particular, a speech act has the force of an assertion when it is appropriately assessed in terms of the norm of assertion. (This is not intended as an informative characterization—still less as an analysis!—but only as capturing a truth about assertion.) If this is correct, then whatever assertoric force comes to, it involves performing a speech act in such a way as to make the following condition hold: the warrant of one's having performed that speech act depends on one's having

---

[13] Suppose that Harry comes to know that p through accepting Sally's speculation that p. On what basis does Harry know? He is relying heavily on Sally's epistemic sensibility, as expressed in a speech act in which she presented-as-true the results of that sensibility. While she did not assert that p, and so did not manifest that sensibility in the standard way, nevertheless she manifested it by another species of presentation-as-true: speculation. Insofar as we think of testimony as a presentation-as-true of a proposition, which this is, or purports to be, the output of an epistemic subject's epistemic sensibility, Sally's speculation counts as testimony.

the requisite epistemic goods regarding the truth of the proposition presented-as-true, so as to satisfy assertion's robustly epistemic norm in the case at hand.[14]

3.5 The Norm of Assertion as Common Knowledge

My previous account assumes not only that testifying has this feature, but that its doing so is common knowledge. I take it that this assumption will be shared by virtually everyone who thinks that assertion has a norm (and that testimony must satisfy that norm). After all, explorations of assertion's norm are part of a more general exploration of the familiar conventions of language use; and if our theories of these conventional features do not aim to capture something that is (or approximates) common knowledge, it is unclear how our theories explain the conventional aspect of these features. Even so, it is worthwhile exploring how we might defend the common knowledge hypothesis. (Anyone who already grants this hypothesis should skip the next three paragraphs.)

Let us first ask the question as it pertains to straight assertion: why suppose that it is not only true, but also a piece of common knowledge, that assertion involves a speaker's presenting a proposition as true in such a way that her speech act is warranted (*qua* instance of that speech-act type) only if she occupies a happy epistemic position vis-à-vis the truth of the proposition presented-as-true? The answer is that the common knowledge aspect of our hypothesis is needed in order to explain what we want to explain. We want to explain why it is that, as a matter of fact, criticism of assertions not backed by adequate grounds is commonplace; and why it is that speakers whose assertions are criticized in this way will react by producing their grounds (rather than, say, by calling into question the legitimacy of the challenge). The common knowledge hypothesis regarding assertion would explain the relevant data in an elegant fashion: hearers criticize such assertions, and speakers react in characteristic ways to such criticisms, because all parties to a discussion recognize (and regard as legitimate) the expectations generated by making or observing an assertion—and all parties recognize that the other parties recognize this as well, and so on.[15]

What is more, it is doubtful that the same data can be explained without the common knowledge hypothesis regarding assertion. Since the data have to do with matters of perceived responsibility and perceived susceptibility to blame, an explanation for hearers' and speakers' systematic reactions will presumably have to appeal to some

---

[14] What constitutes the requisite epistemic goods on the matter will depend in the main on two points: the content of the norm of assertion itself, and the correct theory of the supervenience base for the epistemic properties that figure in the norm of assertion. I am trying to remain neutral on both of these.

[15] If speakers were not aware that hearers are aware of these expectations, then (contrary to what we observe) speakers should be surprised by the systematic and characteristic way in which hearers will criticize assertions on epistemic grounds; and if hearers were not aware that speakers are aware of these expectations, then (contrary to what we observe) hearers should be surprised at the systematic and characteristic way in which speakers will respond to these criticisms.

norm or standard to which participants in a speech exchange are appropriately held. And since the responsibility/blame in question is responsibility/blame generated by the speaker's having made an assertion (as opposed to some other type of speech act in which a proposition is presented-as-true), the norm in question will presumably be the (or a) norm *of assertion*. Otherwise, it will be quite mysterious why our reactions to cases systematically track the difference in speech act kinds; for example, why the praise and blame phenomena associated with assertion are very different from those of other speech act kinds such as speculation.[16] Thus it would seem that whatever explains these reactions must appeal in some way or another to the (or a) norm of assertion. Further, it would seem that hearers who accept an assertion must regard the speaker as satisfying that norm;[17] for unless hearers hold speakers responsible for satisfying that norm, the appeal to the norm itself, as part of an explanation of the responsibility and blame phenomena, is idle. And it would seem that speakers who make assertions must recognize that they have spoken in such a way that they are appropriately assessed against that norm, and that their audience knows this, and so on; there would appear to be no other explanation for the characteristic sort of reaction speakers have to challenges to their assertions (which is to manifest their relevant epistemic authority). Admittedly, the foregoing considerations do not prove the common knowledge hypothesis regarding assertion; but they do place the burden of proof squarely on the shoulders of those who would deny it.

We can extend the common knowledge hypothesis regarding assertion to the category of testimony (through testifying) so long as it is common knowledge that, in order to be warranted as testimony (through testifying), a speech act must satisfy a norm that is at least as demanding as that of assertion. (In that case, a speaker who intends to be offering testimony will know what is expected of her speech act, if it is to be warranted *qua* testimony.) As evidence for the common knowledge hypothesis regarding testifying I submit the following: given any case that a hearer recognizes as involving a speech act through which the speaker intends to be offering testimony, the hearer will react to the news that the speaker lacks relevant grounds in precisely the way she would react to the same news in cases involving assertion. I take it that our reactions here are both common and systematic. The prevalence and systematicity of these reactions are explained on the assumption that each of us knows that testimony is answerable to the norm of assertion, and that this is a robustly epistemic norm. This knowledge becomes common knowledge when we move back and forth between our roles as hearers and speakers. In reflecting on what we can demand (in our role as hearer) from another speaker's testimony, and then reflecting that they (in their role

---

[16] For example, you would be properly criticized if you speculate to be true something you know (or even believe) to be false; but you would not be properly criticized if you speculate to be true something regarding which you have some evidence, even if the evidence in question does not pass some threshold for warrant or justification.

[17] This is not quite right: see Goldberg (2007a: 20–25). But as the complications involved in handling exceptions are not relevant to my present concerns, I ignore them.

as hearer) can demand the same of our testimony, it becomes clear that what we know of the practice of testifying, they know of the practice of testifying, and we know they know it, and know that they know it of us, and so on. I note, though, that if it is not common knowledge that the act of testifying answers to a robustly epistemic norm, it is unclear how the data are to be accounted for, since in that case it is unclear what could warrant our making the assumptions we do regarding the entitlements generated by a testimonial exchange. It would appear, then, that the claim, that a speech act that constitutes the act of testifying must satisfy a norm that is at least as strong as that governing assertion, is common knowledge.[18]

3.6 The Norm-Based Account vs. the Assurance View

The foregoing concludes my defense of the proposal to use the norm of assertion to account for the buck-passing and blame phenomena generated in testimony cases. I turn now to what I regard as the two main virtues of this account. First, it makes do with claims we already need anyway, independent of present considerations. Second, it is not susceptible to the objections to which the assurance view of testimony (arguably its only competitor in the present domain) is susceptible.

First, the account makes do with claims we need anyway, independent of present considerations. It traces the phenomena of buck-passing and blame to the hypothesis that testimony involves assertion, together with the hypothesis that assertion answers to a robustly epistemic norm. To most people, the first of these claims will be relatively uninteresting (because obviously true), and the second, while more controversial, is the core thesis of this book. What is more, since the core thesis itself—that assertion answers to a robustly epistemic norm—is an hypothesis for which we have independent grounds, the account of these buck-passing and blame phenomena is economical as well. So, insofar as the resulting account is plausible and attractive in its own right, this is still further support for that core thesis.

In addition to being simple and economical, the present account is not susceptible to the objections to which its main and (arguably) only competitor is susceptible. I refer here to the assurance view of testimony, encountered in Chapter 2. To appreciate those objections, we will do well to revisit that account. Only here we do so, not in connection with the role of testimony in the spread of knowledge, but rather in connection to the topic of blameworthiness and testimony.[19]

---

[18] I should be clear about the content of the common knowledge here. Few of us have any *de dicto* knowledge to the effect that the norm governing testimony is at least as strong as the norm of assertion. (Few of us besides philosophers and linguists think about assertion as such.) Rather, the knowledge in question is implicit in our practice; I suspect that some relevant piece of knowledge (sufficient to rationalize our testimony-relevant behaviors) could be elicited on reflection.

[19] I restrict myself to blameworthiness since, to the best of my knowledge, there has been little on the topic of buck-passing beyond Brandom (1983) and Goldberg (2006).

On this topic there is no better place to begin than with Angus Ross's very interesting discussion (Ross 1986). Ross's characterization of the phenomenon of blameworthiness in testimony cases derives from what he sees as speakers' responsibilities, which responsibilities derive from the fact that "speech is a rule-governed activity and its rules impose certain normative requirements on speakers" (77). He goes on to identify this as the source of the sort of blame that can attach to a speaker who attests in a way that violates these rules:

> It is a quite general feature of rule-governed life that the responsibility for ensuring that one's actions conform to the rules lies primarily with oneself and that others are in consequence entitled to assume, in the absence of definite reasons for supposing otherwise, that one's actions do so conform. Thus where the rules are such that one may perform a certain action only if a certain condition obtains . . . then to perform the action is to entitle witnesses to assume that the corresponding condition obtains. If that assumption proves false and others act upon it with unfortunate consequences, at least part of the responsibility will lie with oneself for having entitled them to make that assumption. The use of signs to which truth-conditions are attached is clearly a case in point. Given the requirement that one speak truly, to utter 'P' is to entitle hearers with no reason for supposing otherwise to assume that P, not in the sense of having provided them with evidence which justifies that conclusion but in a sense more akin to moral entitlement. The hearer possesses a justification for believing what is said which stems directly from the speaker's responsibility for its truth. (Ross 1986: 77–78)

In tracing the phenomenon of blameworthiness to the violation of the rules governing the use of language, Ross's account is on all fours with mine. At the same time, there are important differences.

For one thing, the rule to which he appeals is the rule enjoining us to speak truly. Since this is not an epistemic rule, I regard it as a poor candidate for the norm governing testimony. Surely there is something wrong with a person testifying that p when she is merely guessing that p, even if her guess happens to be right. (I also think that the truth rule is not a good rule for assertion; but see Weiner 2005 for a robust defense of that rule.)

Second, Ross's argument calls into question a contention I made in Chapter 2. There, I argued that non-evidential accounts of assertion's knowledge-spreading role *presuppose*, and so cannot be used to *establish*, non-reductionism about the conditions on rational acceptance. Ross's argument calls this into question. His claim is that, in the absence of evidence to the contrary, one is entitled to regard a speaker as having conformed to the rules of language, and so as having spoken truly. He uses this claim as the basis for his conclusion that the hearer's "justification for believing what is said . . . stems directly from the speaker's responsibility for its truth." Since the hearer's entitlement to regard the speaker as responsible in this way flows from a "quite general feature of rule-governed life" (Ross 1986), the result (Ross contends) is that the hearer's entitlement to assume that the speaker is playing by the rules (in this case, speaking truly) is defeasible but presumptive: hearers are "entitled to assume, in the absence of definite reasons for supposing otherwise, that one's [speech] actions ... conform" to the relevant rules of language. Ross's account is thus aimed at establishing a robust form of non-reductionism. (I will return to the success of his account on this score later in this chapter.)

A third difference between Ross's account and the one I sketched in Section 3.2 concerns the distinctly moral flavor Ross sees in the sort of blame a speaker deserves when she testifies in a way that is unwarranted. (It is for this reason that Ross's account is best seen as a forerunner of the assurance view.) For Ross, the relevant sort of blame derives from the moral relation in which speaker stands to hearer. He writes that proffered testimony generates a "moral entitlement" for the hearer to regard the testifier as having spoken truly. Ross goes on to elaborate:

> The speaker, in taking responsibility for the truth of what he is saying, is offering his hearer not evidence but a *guarantee* that it is true, and in believing what he is told the hearer accepts this guarantee. (Ross 1986: 79–80; italics in original)

In effect, this guarantee is what, from the speaker's point of view, corresponds to the hearer's entitlement to suppose that the speaker is speaking truly. And it is for this reason that Ross thinks that the sort of blame attaching to improper testimony is moral: we might gloss it as a violation of *trust* (attending to one's having given a false guarantee). And, as we saw previously, it is this guarantee, generated through the rules for proper language use, that underwrites Ross's non-reductionist view regarding the justified acceptance of testimony.

I argued previously that the blameworthiness of faulty testimony can be accounted for as a species of the violation of assertion's norm. Locating the source of blame here has one important virtue: it makes clear that the speaker's failure is one that is *essentially* bound up with epistemic considerations, and so makes clear that the blame to which she is susceptible is the sort of blame that involves the violation of an epistemic standard. That is, she is properly criticized for having failed to conform to the hearer's (entitled) expectation that she occupy a certain epistemic position—one of having the goods required to satisfy the robustly epistemic norm of assertion. The same cannot be said for Ross's account of the source of blame, which derives from the moral character of the interpersonal relation holding between speaker and hearer. If this is the source of the blame, the following question arises: Why should the *moral* relation in which a speaker stands to a hearer, when the former testifies to the latter, be such as to provide to the hearer with anything approximating an entitlement to regard the speaker as occupying a certain *epistemic* position? Granted that it would be immoral of you to testify inappropriately to me; does this alone give me the epistemic right to expect that you occupy the relevant epistemic position? It is unclear why this should be.[20]

To this I want to add another point in favor of my proposed account over Ross's. Ross's account commits us to strong claims that are not needed to account for the

---

[20] The assurance account of Moran (2006), which builds on Ross's seminal treatment, aims to rectify this problem; but, as I will go on to argue later, it suffers from its own difficulties.

epistemic entitlements and responsibilities generated in testimonial exchanges. He traces these to the nature of rule-governed activity in general, and that of language use in particular. Rule-governed acts, he argues, generate for their audience the entitlement to believe that the rules have been followed; and in the case of language this entitlement is the entitlement to believe that the speaker has spoken truly. Waive the recent criticism that it is unclear how a speaker's moral responsibility generates for the hearer an entitlement to a certain epistemic expectation. And let it be granted that Ross is right about the nature of rule-governed activity itself. Even so, it is worth highlighting that for the purpose of grounding an ascription of blame, we do not need to suppose (with Ross) that the hearer is entitled to regard the speaker as having *satisfied* the relevant rules of language; it suffices that the hearer is entitled to regard the speech act as *appropriately assessed by reference to those rules* (whether or not the speaker has satisfied them, and indeed whether or not the hearer regards the speaker as having satisfied them). Given a speaker S who has spoken in such a way as to have rendered her speech act properly assessable in terms of, for example, the norm of assertion, a hearer is entitled to blame S if S's speech act fails to satisfy that norm. If you have done something that warrants me in holding your action to some norm, then I can blame you (your action) for failing to satisfy that norm, even if I am not tempted in the least to believe that you actually satisfied it (still less to act upon that assumption). Compare: if you write me a check for $100 and you do not have the money in your account to cover this (with the result that the check bounces), I can hold you responsible for this even if, in receiving your check, I regarded you as highly unlikely to have had the money in your account to cover it. This makes clear that, with respect to the aim of accounting for the phenomenon of testimonial blameworthiness, the entitlement to which Ross appeals—that in the absence of determinate reasons to the contrary, hearers are entitled to suppose that a given speaker spoke truly (or, more generally, that she followed the relevant rules)—is overkill. In particular, one need not be a non-reductionist, or (like Ross) endorse a view entailing non-reductionism, in order to account for the phenomenon of the blameworthiness of unwarranted testimony. We can detach the issue of blameworthiness from the issue of the conditions on justified acceptance of testimony.

There are various other reasons that favor the norm-of-assertion-based account over Ross's account. One of them lies in the general methodological preference for a simpler, deeper account. We need the norm of assertion in any case (or so I am arguing throughout this book), so appealing to it to explain the phenomenon of testimonial responsibility does not add any theoretical commitment. Ross's account, by contrast, postulates distinctively moral relations between speaker and hearer in cases of information exchange. Now, I agree that there are such moral relations. But I believe (and will argue in Chapter 9) that these relations, too, can be understood in terms of the norm of assertion. If this is correct, then we can account for all that Ross wants in terms of an hypothesis which we have independent reasons to accept anyway.

Another reason to favor the norm-of-assertion-based account over Ross's is related to this first one. We have already noted that Ross's account is presented as explicitly committed to non-reductionism about the conditions on rational acceptance of testimony. Bracketing for the moment the cogency of Ross's argument on this score, I want to focus only on the suggestion implicit in his account. He suggests that the proper way to account for the phenomenon of testimonial blame is by endorsing a version of non-reductionism. This suggestion is not credible. Are reductionists (those who reject non-reductionism) really ideologically committed to being blind to the blameworthiness of unwarranted testimony? It would seem not. So long as we can make out an account in which the materials that make for praise or blame in (the warrantedness of) a speaker's assertion are not the materials that determine the rationality of the hearer's testimonial belief, reductionists too can account for the blame phenomenon. The norm of assertion makes clear that the reductionst can do so: for the reductionist might appeal to the norm of assertion to account for testimonial blame, while simultaneously endorsing even the Strong Evidentialist view of assertion's role in the spread of knowledge, discussed in Chapter 2. I do not endorse such a view; I merely cite its possibility to suggest that one need not endorse non-reductionism to account for the blame phenomenon. And this gives us our second reason to prefer the norm-of-assertion-based account, since that account does not depend, as Ross's account does, on a strong claim about what the audience is entitled to believe of a given case of rule-governed behavior.

Yet another reason to prefer the norm-of-assertion-based account over Ross's is that the former is more economical. Anyone who agrees that assertion has an epistemic norm will *ipso facto* acknowledge that there is a kind of blameworthiness associated with unwarranted assertion. It does not require any further substantial assumptions to regard the sort of blameworthiness that attends to unwarranted testimony as an instance of the blameworthiness of unwarranted assertion.

One final reason to prefer the norm-of-assertion-based account is that it does not burden us with any auxiliary assumptions about the nature of testimony; that is, that it involves a special kind of speech act that implicates the moral relations in which we stand to our fellows. This last virtue is one that the present proposal enjoys relative to the more recent "assurance" views of testimony, which have developed out of Ross's views. I close this section with a brief discussion of the more recent versions of the assurance view; I focus on Richard Moran's development of it, as this is the most developed version of the position.

In his development of the assurance view, Moran (taking up Ross's idea) is keen to show how what he calls the speech act of telling differs from the offering of evidence for the truth of a claim. Moran notes that a key difference between telling someone that p, and presenting evidence for p, is that in the former the subject "presents himself as *accountable* for the truth of what he says, and in doing so he offers a kind of guarantee for this truth" (Moran 2006: 283). It is noteworthy that Moran originally traces this feature of telling to the speaker's "presenting his utterance of an *assertion*, one with the force of *telling* the audience something" (283; italics in original). This makes it appear that Moran's view is very similar to the one presented here.

Differences arise, however, when we consider Moran's further views about the nature of telling. Although Moran sees the speech act of telling to be an instance of the speech act of assertion (288), he nevertheless has a very different account of the epistemic significance of assertoric speech acts. On Moran's view, the epistemic significance of assertoric speech is a function of the speaker's "invest[ing] his utterance with a particular epistemic import"—something which itself is accomplished by the speaker's "explicit assumption of responsibility for his utterance's being a reason for belief" (291). This can seem curious: why think that an explicit assumption of (epistemic) responsibility on the speaker's part invests her (assertoric) speech with epistemic import—with the qualities it needs in order to count as a reason for a hearer to believe what was said? To be sure, Moran recognizes that in order for the speech to succeed in having this sort of import, "the appropriate abilities and other background conditions must be assumed to be in place for it to amount to anything" (289). These conditions require "that the speaker does indeed satisfy the right conditions for such an act (for example, that he possesses the relevant knowledge, trustworthiness, and reliability)" (289). But then we can wonder: given that assertion has a robustly epistemic norm, does not the assumption of "the appropriate abilities and other background conditions" itself suffice to account for the buck-passing and blame phenomena? Why burden our account with the further assumption that assertion involves the "explicit assumption of responsibility for [one's own] utterance's being a reason for belief"?

Not only is this claim (about the explicit assumption of authority in assertion) not needed to account for the buck-passing and blame data; it appears to be false to the facts. For it would seem that there can be cases of someone (such as a liar) who asserts that p, but who explicitly repudiates any epistemic responsibility in connection with the epistemic standing of p. (Of course, she hides this repudiation from her audience.) Not only has such a person asserted; what is more, she is still legitimately criticized *qua* asserter, and can be blamed by those who (having been justified in accepting her assertion[21]) come to acquire the false belief that p through their reliance on her assertion. This would seem to show both that the explicit acknowledgment of epistemic responsibility by the speaker is not a necessary feature of assertion as such, and that such a feature is not needed to account for the phenomena of buck-passing and blame. Moran would dismiss the liar case as one in which "the appropriate abilities and other background conditions" are not in place; but this would only succeed in showing that it is in connection with these conditions, rather than in the nature of the speech act of telling (understood to require the explicit acknowledgment of epistemic responsibility), where we find the things that explain buck-passing and blame. This favors an account in terms of the norm of assertion, since such a norm, taken to be robustly epistemic, explicitly requires that the speaker occupy a certain happy epistemic position vis-à-vis what she asserted to be the case.

---

[21] Suppose the liar were a consummate deceiver, and expertly concealed her perfidy.

We might put the contrast between Moran's account and the account that proceeds in terms of the norm of assertion as follows. Moran holds that assertion involves a person's intention to provide (something like) a guarantee of the truth of what she says. His account is thus faced with an awkward question: In virtue of what does this intention confer on the speech its epistemic significance? As we have already seen, Moran's official answer to this awkward question—that it is in virtue of the speaker's explicit assumption of responsibility for the truth of what she says—leans heavily on the behind-the-scenes assumption of the required "background conditions."[22] The account I have proposed, by contrast, avoids the awkward question at the outset. Given that the speaker (in testifying) made an assertion, she performed a speech act whose warrantedness requires that she occupy some happy epistemic position vis-à-vis the truth of the asserted content. This is so, whether or not she explicitly assumes the responsibility of occupying this position. The epistemic significance of the assertion then can be accounted for in terms of this normative characterization of assertion, together with the facts relevant to characterizing her epistemic position vis-à-vis the truth of the asserted content.

I have just indicated two differences between the assurance view's account of the blame phenomenon, and that offered in terms of the norm of assertion, arguing that these differences favor the latter account. But the latter is also favored by another important difference. As Moran notes, the assurance view (like Ross's earlier view)

> makes much of the fact that in its central instances speech is an action *addressed to a person*, and that in testimony in particular the kind of reason for belief that is presented is one that functions *in part by binding speaker and audience together*, and altering the normative relationship between them. (295; italics in original)

The result is that, while one who overhears another person tell a third party that p "improves his epistemic situation in this way, without entering into the normative relationship of the two parties involved," nevertheless the overhearer "himself has not been told anything... and no right of complaint has been conferred upon him" (295). Here I note that this implication—that the overhearer has no "right of complaint" against an unwarranted telling[23]—can be sustained only at the cost of a distorted account of the norm of assertion. To see this, suppose that assertion has a robustly epistemic norm. Then a speaker who makes an assertion has performed a speech act that is warranted (*qua* assertion) if and only if the norm was satisfied. Note that this condition *introduces no restriction to the intended audience*. Thus it would seem that the making of any assertion, whether directed at its intended audience or overheard by a third party,

---

[22] This point is emphasized by Lackey (2008: chapter 8).
[23] Moran speaks of no right of complaint being "conferred on" the hearer, but I take it that he holds that it is only through being conferred such a right that the hearer would acquire such a right in the first place—in which case it is correct to say that the overhearer has no right of complaint.

generates a "right of complaint" to those who form a belief through their acceptance of the assertion.[24] Since such a conclusion is inconsistent with the assurance view's description of matters, Moran must resist it. But it would appear that he can only do so either by relativizing the norm of assertion to the assertion's intended hearer, or else by maintaining that assertion (as distinct from telling) has no proper norm to speak of. Neither of these positions is happy.

The foregoing point can be generalized. Moran appears to think that the sort of cases that generate the blame phenomenon—cases in which a speaker *tells* a hearer something—are a (perhaps not proper) subset of cases of assertion. But Moran faces a dilemma, according to whether he endorses or rejects that all cases of assertion have the relevant speech-act force for being a case of telling. In the former case, his appeal to the distinctiveness of the speech act of *telling* is superfluous, as we can account for all of his data (it would seem) merely in terms of the norm of assertion. If (on the other hand) he holds that some cases of assertion do not have the relevant speech-act force to be a case of telling, his theory makes false predictions. For in that case his theory would predict that there can be cases of assertion without the corresponding sort of blame that attaches to cases of telling. This prediction would appear to be unsustainable. For, to repeat what was stated previously, if assertion really does have a robustly epistemic norm—something many people, including perhaps Moran himself, appear to accept—then any case of assertion is a case in which the speaker can be blamed, and so is a case in which the hearer has the "right of complaint" against the speaker, for asserting in violation of the norm.[25] Of course, Moran might respond that this sort of blame is different from the sort of blame attaching to unwarranted tellings; but this seems to me to be a difference that makes no difference.[26] If I am correct about this, it would then be evidence that (insofar as he treats tellings as a special case of assertions) Moran has mislocated the source of the blame phenomenon itself.

3.7 Are Testimony-Constituting Assertions Evidence?

Before concluding, there is one final point that is worth taking up. Following Grice (1957) and Ross (1986), the assurance view of testimony is explicitly motivated by the

---

[24] This is not to say that it will always be practical for the speaker to act on this right, or that the hearer's having this right shows that the assertion was improper all-things-considered. See Williamson (1996) for related points.

[25] To repeat what was said in the previous footnote: to say that an assertion in violation of the norm of assertion is *ipso facto* blameworthy is not to say that the hearers in such cases will always act on their entitlement to blame the speaker, or that there will never be any countervailing considerations rendering the assertion acceptable all-things-considered.

[26] This verdict is supported by the idea that all of the uncontroversial data accounted for by the assurance view can be accounted for by the norm of assertion. This suggests that the account of telling proffered by the assurance view, which aimed to account for the relevant data, is superfluous.

idea that there is a key difference between telling someone that p, and presenting evidence for p. Ross writes:

Given the requirement that one speak truly, to utter 'P' is to entitle hearers with no reason for supposing otherwise to assume that P, *not in the sense of having provided them with evidence which justifies that conclusion* but in a sense more akin to moral entitlement. The hearer possesses a justification for believing what is said which stems directly from the speaker's responsibility for its truth. (Ross 1986: 77–78; italics added)

The speaker, in taking responsibility for the truth of what he is saying, is offering his hearer not evidence but a *guarantee* that it is true, and in believing what he is told the hearer accepts this guarantee. (Ross 1986: 79–80; italics in original)

Moran describes the difference between telling and offering evidence as that in the former case the subject "presents himself as *accountable* for the truth of what he says, and in doing so he offers a kind of guarantee for this truth" (Moran 2006: 283). It might be reckoned a virtue of the assurance view that it rejects the Strong Evidential view of assertion's role in the spread of knowledge (discussed in Chapter 2).

I note, though, that the norm-based account, too, can recognize the difference to which Ross and Moran are gesturing. After all, and as we saw in Chapter 2, the norm-based account of assertion's role in the spread of knowledge traces this role to the fact that assertion is governed by a robustly epistemic norm. On this view, to assert is to perform an act regarding which it is mutual knowledge that the act was warranted only if the speaker satisfied a robustly epistemic standard vis-à-vis the proposition asserted. It is this that rationalizes the hearer's acceptance of the assertion: insofar as he is entitled to regard the speaker as (not merely answerable to but also) satisfying that standard, the hearer is rational in accepting the assertion. Of course, one can argue over the conditions on being entitled to so regard the hearer; this is to recapitulate the dispute between reductionists and non-reductionists. But I have argued that it is a virtue of the norm-based account that it does not require a commitment to either position. If one thinks that a reductionist answer is best, one can combine one's endorsement of the norm-based account with a commitment to reductionism. On the other hand, if one thinks that we have independent grounds to favor non-reductionism, as I do,[27] then one can combine the norm-based account with a non-reductive approach to the epistemology of testimony. The resulting view agrees with the assurance view that we should reject Strong Evidentialism; but it disagrees with the assurance view in what it is that underwrites the hearer's testimonial belief. Whereas the assurance view would trace this to the speaker's assuming responsibility for the truth of the assertion, the norm-based account would trace this to the speaker's actually satisfying the robustly epistemic norm of assertion (together with the hearer's entitlement to assume as much). In this way, the role of the epistemic goodness of the assertion is not a mere

---

[27] I have not argued for this here, though I reviewed some of the arguments in Chapter 2. See also Goldberg (2007).

add-on to the account, as we saw it was in the case of Moran's view, but rather emerges directly from the hypothesis that assertion is answerable to a robustly epistemic norm.

In short, if one's reason for endorsing the assurance view of testimony is simply that one thinks that testimony should not be construed as Strong Evidentialism construes it, then this is a better reason to endorse the norm-based view than it is to endorse the assurance view.

3.8 Conclusion

In this chapter I have been arguing that the responsibilities and entitlements generated by testimonial exchanges can be accounted for by appeal to the norm of assertion; and I have defended this proposal as better than what is arguably its only competition: the assurance view of testimony. If I am correct about this, then the norm of assertion can be used to explain both of the features that I described as part of assertion's "epistemic significance."

PART III

Other Applications: Mind, Language, and More

In this part I use the norm of assertion to account for assertion's connections to the method of interpretation, the theory of speech content, belief, the ethics of assertion, and more.

4

Assertion and the Method of Interpretation (Radical and Otherwise)

4.1 The Mutually Manifest, Robustly Epistemic Norm of Assertion: MMENA

I started this book by arguing that we can understand the speech act of assertion in terms of the hypothesis that assertion is governed by a constitutive (robustly epistemic) norm. Having presented this sort of initial case for this hypothesis in Chapter 1, I went on to the task I set for myself for the remainder of this book: to reinforce my case for the norm-of-assertion hypothesis by using this hypothesis to discern and explain connections between the nature of assertion and other topics of philosophical interest. In Chapters 2 and 3 I went on to argue that we can use this hypothesis to understand the distinctive epistemological significance of this type of speech act. This significance is seen both in the role assertion plays in the spread of knowledge (Chapter 2) as well as in the characteristically normative expectations that speakers and hearers have of one another in testimonial speech exchanges (Chapter 3). In both cases, I argued, the best account of these phenomena appeals to the hypothesis that assertion answers to a robustly epistemic norm. This chapter is the first of five in which I will bring the hypothesis of assertion's norm to bear on topics beyond epistemology proper. In particular, I will be using this hypothesis to explore assertion's connections to a variety of topics in the philosophy of language, philosophy of mind, ethics, and social philosophy.

The aim of this chapter is to argue that the hypothesis that assertion is answerable to a robustly epistemic norm has implications for the nature and method of what Donald Davidson called "the task of radical interpretation." This is the task of interpreting another's speech contributions, and thereby solving for their "beliefs and meanings" without assuming prior knowledge of either. I argue that the resulting norm-of-assertion-based account of the nature and method of interpretation, which differs from that offered by Davidson himself, is to be preferred to Davidson's own account.

Before proceeding to this discussion, however, it will be helpful to have a clearer statement of the norm-of-assertion hypothesis to which I will be appealing. As before, my aim here is to remain neutral on the precise content of the norm of assertion, beyond holding that it is robustly epistemic (where this means that it is at least epistemically strong enough to rationalize or justify belief). Consequently, I will have to be schematic in formulating the hypothesis in question. I begin with the claim that assertion is governed by a norm.[1] I will understand this to amount to the claim that there is a completion of the following rule-schema which governs assertions ('NA' for 'Norm of Assertion'):

NA   One must: assert that p, only if C.

Here, 'C' is replaced by a description of the standard that must be met if the assertion is to be warranted (proper). To say that assertion's norm is robustly epistemic, then, is to say that the standard, C, itself is a robustly epistemic one, in the sense that one's assertion is warranted only if one satisfies that epistemic standard with respect to the proposition asserted. We might put this as follows:

ENA   One must: assert that p, only if E(one, [p]).

Here, 'E' is replaced by a description of the relevant epistemic standard; this is a matter on which I will remain neutral—at least until Part IV of this book.[2] But I will be adding one additional feature to the hypothesis to which I will be adverting: for reasons I discussed in Chapter 3, Section 3.5, I will be assuming that ENA itself is mutually manifest to all competent participants to a speech exchange. With this point understood, I can formulate the hypothesis to which I will be referring throughout these next few chapters as follows:

MMENA   It is mutually manifest to participants in a speech exchange that assertion has a robustly epistemic norm; that is, that one must: assert that p, only if E(one, [p]).

('MMENA' is the chosen label as it designates the Mutually Manifest nature of the robustly Epistemic Norm of Assertion.)

My claim in this chapter will be that MMENA can be used to account for aspects of the nature of language interpretation (radical and everyday). In subsequent chapters I bring MMENA to bear on the relation between assertion and belief (Chapter 5), to the determination of assertoric content (Chapter 6), to the ethics of assertion and belief (Chapter 7), and to the sense in which assertion is a public act (Chapter 8).

---

[1] In presenting the norm in terms of various schemes, I am following Williamson (2000). The formulations here differ a little from his, however.

[2] Leading contenders are (epistemic) certainty, knowledge, doxastically justified belief that one knows, doxastically justified belief *simpliciter*, and rational belief.

4.2 Davidson's Characterization of the Task of Interpretation

Our present topic—the nature and methodology of interpretation (in particular, of the speech of others)—is familiar to philosophers from the work of Davidson and Quine. Davidson's own account of interpretation is (I hope) a familiar one, at least in broad outline. Since Davidson's conception of the task of interpretation sets the background for the contribution I aim to make in this chapter, and since my proposal will be contrasted with Davidson's own, I begin with a brief review of the main contours of his account. (Readers familiar with this account should feel free to skip the remainder of this and the next section.)

As Davidson conceived of the task of interpretation, interpreting another's language involves arriving at a manual which enables one to assign truth conditions to any sentence in the language under interpretation.[3] This claim reflected several of Davidson's core theses: first, that to interpret a sentence is to assign to it a set of conditions under which the sentence is true;[4] second, that the interpretation of sentences affords us a way to determine the interpretation of each subsentential part of the sentence, as what that part contributed to the truth conditions of sentences in which it figured; and third, that the resulting interpretation manual should take the form of a recursive theory of truth for the language in question (as it was only in this way, Davidson thought, that we could guarantee that a finite manual might be systematic in its assignment of truth conditions to the infinity of sentences in the language).

In addition to thinking about the form that such a theory would take, Davidson also thought a good deal about the sort of evidence against which the adequacy of a theory (= interpretation manual) might be tested. Here Davidson followed Quine in holding that, at least at the outset of this process, the interpreter ought not assume that she knows either the meanings of the speaker's words or the beliefs she is expressing with her utterances. On the contrary, conclusions about what words mean or what the interpretee believes would be reached by way of arriving at an empirically adequate theory of (interpretation manual for) her language. The evidence for such a theory would be characterized in terms of the set of sentences held-true by the speaker, correlated with the worldly conditions prevailing at the time at which the speaker manifested her attitude of holding-true. As Davidson conceived of it, the task of interpretation, then, was essentially that of trying to discern correlations between sentences held-true and the worldly conditions that prompted the speaker's assent. It was in connection with this task that Davidson argued for the so-called Principle of Charity: when seeking to assign truth conditions (interpretations) to sentences, the interpreter must do so

---

[3] I disregard here the role of context in interpretation. Everyone recognizes that this topic is of central importance to the interpretation of language, and especially spoken language, but as it is not directly relevant to the points I want to make here I will place it to one side.

[4] Alternatively: the conditions under which that sentence can be *used* to make a true *statement*.

in such a way as to maximize the number of truths (true beliefs and true statements) that become attributed to the interpretee.⁵ An interpretation is correct, by Davidson's lights, only if it does better in meeting this condition than any of its rivals.

Now, like Davidson, I too will be interested here in the epistemological dimension of interpretation. What is more, I accept that this dimension is best approached in a Davidsonian spirit: the task of interpretation should be seen as that of devising a theory that would systematically assign truth conditions to each of the sentences from the language under interpretation; and evidence for the theory would take the form of correlations between the acts through which the interpretee manifests that she holds-true particular sentences, and the prevailing worldly conditions at the time and place of these manifestations. Where I will differ with Davidson is over the nature of the constraint that we ought to impose as we devise our theories on this basis. In particular, where Davidson defended the Principle of Charity, I will motivate and defend a constraint that derives from MMENA itself. This will involve a slight shift in how we think of the correlations that are the evidence for our theories. Where Davidson spoke of correlations between assent behavior and eliciting conditions, I will speak of correlations between assertions and eliciting conditions. The legitimacy of this shift will be defended in due time.

To anticipate, my main contention will be this: in a situation in which one subject, H, is warranted in regarding another subject, S, as having made a sincere assertion, H is entitled to assume that S regards herself (if only implicitly) as satisfying some robust epistemic standard regarding the truth of the claim she (S) made.⁶ This entitlement, which derives from MMENA, can be seen as imposing a substantial constraint on interpretation: on the assumption that assertion has a robustly epistemic norm (and that this is mutually manifest to all parties to a speech exchange), we can justify a methodological injunction that requires the interpreter to minimize the number of occasions on which she sees the interpretee as inexplicably violating this standard.

Three further comments or clarifications are in order before proceeding to develop these ideas further.

First, I will be speaking throughout this chapter of the *sincerity* of an assertion. Many readers will hear this and will assume that, by definition, an assertion is sincere if the speaker believes what she says.⁷ But this is not what I have in mind. I will understand sincerity in assertion in terms of the hypothesis of MMENA itself. On this view, an assertion is sincere just in case it is made with the aim of conforming to the standards

---

⁵ Davidson: "Charity is forced on us; whether we like it or not, if we want to understand others, we must count them right in most matters" (1974a; as reprinted in 1984a: 197).

⁶ It is important to underscore that sincerity is simply a matter of aiming to fulfill the conditions on warranted assertion. If these require belief, then sincere assertion requires belief. If these do not require belief—and even if we restrict ourselves to "robustly epistemic" norms, not all accounts of the norm of assertion require belief—then sincere assertion does not require belief. I will discuss this at length in Chapter 11.

⁷ I thank an anonymous referee for indicating this, and for indicating the need to address this at the outset of this chapter.

of warranted assertion. Indeed—as I will go on to argue in Chapters 6 and 11—it is a virtue of the constitutive norm approach that it enables us to *derive* the hypothesis that belief is a sincerity condition on assertion. Or rather, the constitutive norm approach enables us to do so on the further assumption (which most defenders of this approach endorse) that the norm of assertion is one whose satisfaction by a speaker requires belief.[8] In sticking with my neutrality regarding which robustly epistemic candidate norm is the norm of assertion, I will not weigh in on this here (but see Chapter 11, where I do weigh in on it). My only point is that, in the first instance, sincerity in assertion will be understood as the condition in which an assertion is made with the aim of conforming to standards of proper assertion.

Second, the idea that the norm of assertion might be used to motivate constraints on linguistic interpretation is not new. It is suggested in Williamson (2000). He writes that the proposal to regard knowledge as the norm of assertion

has repercussions in the methodology of interpretation. The appropriate principle of charity will give high marks to interpretations on which speakers tend to assert what they know, rather than to those on which they tend to assert what is true, or even what is reasonable for them to believe. (Williamson 2000: 267)

(See also Williamson 2007: chapter 8, where he develops an account of interpretation along roughly these lines.) As a defender of the knowledge norm, Williamson's suggestion is not as generic as the present one (which holds only that the norm is robustly epistemic, but is otherwise neutral on its content). But I intend the present proposal to be a weaker version in the spirit of his suggestion nevertheless. (It is weaker in that, whereas Williamson urges us to maximize attributed knowledge, my version will have it that we ought to minimize unexplained unwarrantedness in assertion.)

Third, a core assumption of this chapter, to the effect that we should illuminate the role that assertion plays in interpretation by appeal to the norm of assertion itself, is not entirely uncontroversial. In a recent book, Jary (2010) discusses at length the role of assertion in interpretation. He notes that hearers naturally react to assertions as the expression and communication of belief (Jary 2010: 38).[9] The result is that insofar as a hearer can tell when an assertion is made, a hearer can tell when there is an opportunity for the interpretation of a speaker's beliefs. Since Jary himself makes no appeal to any norm of assertion in his account of its role in interpretation, one might think that such an appeal is otiose in this context.

Despite this, I do not think Jary's view of assertion does support such a conclusion. To bring this out, I note that Jary follows Dummett in regarding the declarative

---

[8] I should acknowledge that even if we restrict ourselves to candidate norms that are "robustly epistemic" in my sense, not all candidates do require belief: consider, for example, a propositional justification norm, or the supportive reasons norm of McKinnon (2013).

[9] Jary's view is rather unorthodox in that, at the same time that he holds that this is how hearers standardly react to assertion, he also thinks (with Dummett) that we cannot define *belief* save in terms of assertion (Jary 2010: 36). I will not try to reconcile Jary's two commitments here.

mood as the (default) sign of assertoric force: given certain paradigmatic background conditions, any sentence uttered in this mood is an assertion (for which see Jary 2010: chapter 4). In keeping with this, Jary characterizes assertion as follows:

Canonically, assertion is a case of a speaker presenting, by linguistic means, an explicitly expressed proposition as relevant to the hearer (i.e. as relevant to an individual) in its own right. (Jary 2010: 163)

However, it is noteworthy that right after this "canonical" characterization, he goes on to offer this hedge:

Assertion cannot be defined thus, though. In order for an utterance to have assertoric force, it must also be subject to the cognitive and social safeguards that distinguish assertion ... It is the applicability of these safeguards that distinguishes assertion both from other illocutionary acts and from other forms of information transfer. (163–64)

By my lights this is an acknowledgment of a theoretical need that must be addressed by any theory of assertion. Since this need is precisely addressed by the hypothesis that (it is mutually manifest that) assertion answers to a robustly epistemic norm, MMENA appears to enjoy this advantage over a position, like Jary's, which adverts to assertion as playing a central role in interpretation, but which does not try to understand this role in terms of anything like MMENA.

I conclude, then, that when it comes to illuminating assertion's role in the task of interpretation, there is no principled reason to resist an appeal to the norm of assertion. Precisely what work such an appeal can do remains to be seen, however. It is to this that I now turn.

4.3 From Davidsonian Radical Interpretation to the Norm of Assertion

As noted, Davidson thought that the best way to investigate the evidence for and methodology of language interpretation is to focus on the situation of "radical interpretation,"[10] in which the interpreter does not assume knowledge either of the speaker's beliefs or of the meanings of her words, but instead aims to solve for both simultaneously. This situation is made vivid if we assume that the hearer/interpreter is observing the speech behavior of a subject who speaks a heretofore untranslated language. In this sort of circumstance, the hearer/interpreter cannot take for granted her understanding of the utterances she is observing or the beliefs being manifested in those observed utterances; she must construct her "interpretation manual" from scratch. To

---

[10] For another view about the epistemological dimension of Radical Interpretation, see McGinn (1986). But compare Lewis (1974/1983: 110–11), where Radical Interpretation is regarded as a way of making vivid how the intentional properties of mind and language supervene on the non-intentional states of the world.

investigate how this is to be done, Davidson thought, is to lay bare the presuppositions and methodology of interpretation itself.

As Davidson conceived of it, the project of Radical Interpretation is the project of "solving for" the beliefs and meanings of another (would-be) speaker, without assuming knowledge of either. The Radical Interpreter solves for these by prompting the interpretee with sentences from her (the interpretee's) own language, and then correlating the interpretee's assent and dissent behaviors with the salient environmental conditions prevalent at the time. Following Quine, Davidson held that there are certain ineliminable assumptions a hearer-interpreter would have to make if she is to "break into the belief-meaning circle" in this way. Most salient among these assumptions was the Principle of Charity. Very roughly put, this principle maintains that interpretations of a subject's language are to be preferred to the degree that they maximize the number of truths (in speech and thought) that would be attributed to the speaker.

Extrapolating from the simplest cases, Davidson himself was very clear about the demands of such a method of interpretation. He wrote:

Torn between the need to make sense of a speaker's words and the need to make sense of the pattern of his beliefs, the best we can do is choose a theory of translation that maximizes agreement. (Davidson 1969/1984a: 101)

This method [of Radical Interpretation] is intended to solve the problem of the interdependence of belief and meaning by holding belief constant as far as possible while solving for meaning. This is accomplished by assigning truth conditions to alien sentences that make native speakers right when plausibly possible, according, of course, to our own view of what is right. (Davidson 1973/1984a: 137)

The general policy ... is to choose truth conditions that do as well as possible in making speakers hold sentences true when (according to the theory and the theory builder's view of the facts) those sentences are true. (Davidson 1974a/1984a: 152)

A key question that arises in this connection concerns the justification for this interpretative procedure. The familiar Davidsonian response is that it is only by following something like this procedure that we can render the other speaker *intelligible*: "What justifies the procedure is the fact that disagreement and agreement alike are intelligible only against a background of massive agreement" (Davidson 1973/1984a: 137). Interpretability, then, is the crux on which the method's justification turns.

As I noted previously, the focus on Radical Interpretation is meant to highlight the nature of the evidence available to an interpreter—*any* interpreter, including those that are already familiar with the language in question. In this sense, Davidson's early discussions of Radical Interpretation[11] can be seen as a contribution to what we might call

---

[11] By "early discussions" I mean those collected in Davidson (1984a). Davidson's "later" work on these topics, collected in Davidson (2001), differ in emphasis, if not in substance. There he focuses a good deal on what he calls "triangulation" at the heart of the interpretative process. I will return to discuss this a little later.

the "epistemology of interpretation." But if we think of Davidson's discussions in this way, we must be clear about how Davidson understood this. At the time, Davidson was primarily interested in the epistemology of interpretation as this was seen from the perspective of the interpreter, with little or no attention to the epistemic perspective *of the interpretee*.[12] It is not that Davidson did not characterize the interpreter's perspective on the interpretee; of course he did. It is rather that his characterizations of the interpreter's perspective on the interpretee are primarily, if not entirely, in semantic terms. Absent is any explicit acknowledgment that the process of Radical Interpretation is one in which the interpreter must think of the interpretee as in the business of acquiring *knowledge* of the world. As Davidson described matters, it is as if the interpreter, H, simply regards the interpretee, S, as providing H with evidence for a theory H is constructing regarding S (S's language)—as if S is nothing other than another piece of furniture in H's world. True, this particular piece of furniture is a complicated one, in that at the very same time that S is in the world, S is also reacting to the world (that is, by producing utterances in the face of worldly events and conditions). Still, S remains a piece of furniture for all that—or so Davidson's early descriptions of the task of interpretation might encourage us to suppose.

It is interesting in this regard to contrast Davidson's early descriptions of the task of interpretation with his subsequent writings on the topic. These bring in a decidedly epistemological angle on the task—one that appears to acknowledge the epistemic perspective of the interpretee as well. Thus in his (1991) Davidson explicitly connects issues of interpretation with issues of knowledge. He writes that "the triangulation which is essential to thought requires that those in communication *recognize* that they occupy positions in a shared world" (Davidson 1991: 213; italics added). Since what holds for H when interpreting S also holds for S when interpreting H, and since this is something that both H and S can appreciate on reflecting on the process of interpretation itself, Davidson here has all the pieces he needs to recognize that, in the course of interpretation, the interpreter must regard the interpretee as herself in the business of acquiring and communicating knowledge.

I regard Davidson's move to a more encompassing orientation—one that has in its view how things are with the interpretee both semantically *and epistemically*—as a step in the right direction. Still, I think Davidson himself did not move quite far enough in this direction. For while he speaks of the interpreter and interpretee as needing to "recognize that they occupy positions in a shared world," he does not dwell on how this

---

(It should be kept in mind, however, that my aim in this chapter is not Davidson exegesis so much as it is to contribute to our understanding of the nature of language interpretation.)

[12] This is not entirely true. After all, Davidson famously made an analogy between the problem of Radical Interpretation, in which one has to break into the belief-meaning circle of another speaker, with the problem of "radical decision-theory," where one has to break into the belief-preference circle of another agent (Davidson 1974a, 1975). Still, so far as I can tell, in his early discussions he did not think systematically about how the task of interpretation might be affected by the fact that the interpretee is also an epistemic subject—one who aims to acquire (not just true belief but) knowledge.

might affect their epistemological characterization of one another. He does speak of the need, in the course of triangulation, for interpreters to regard interpretees as responding "knowingly and intentionally" to the relevant stimulation (1992/2001: 120–21). But he quickly moves on from his "hasty remarks" without indicating how the point at issue affects our understanding of the task of interpretation itself.

This is unfortunate. To see why, suppose that our conception of the task of interpretation acknowledges that an interpreter will have to think of her interpretee in distinctly epistemological terms: as an epistemic subject, one who aims to acquire knowledge of the world. In so doing we acknowledge that part of the explicit aim of interpretation is that of capturing of the interpretee's *distinctly epistemic perspective*. It is not enough to see the subject under interpretation as a creature with thoughts, who can give verbal expression to those thoughts. Rather, the interpretee is also to be seen as aiming (in her thought and speech) at knowledge. What emerges from this, I submit, is a deeper explanation of the value of intelligibility, and its role in the justification of this-or-that methodological principle of interpretation. For one of the payoffs of rendering another subject intelligible is that such a subject can then serve *as a potential source of worldly knowledge for the interpreter herself*. So far as I can tell, Davidson himself never explicitly considered how this role others play, or can play, for us—a role in which they are sources of knowledge, or at least epistemically high-quality belief, regarding a shared world—might bear on the methodological principles of interpretation themselves.

It is precisely this idea—the idea of regarding the task of interpretation as requiring the interpreter to capture the distinctly epistemic perspective of the subject under interpretation—that I aim to develop in what follows. I think that such an idea is best developed in terms of MMENA—the hypothesis that it is mutually manifest to parties to a speech exchange that assertion has an epistemic norm. The reason for this is straightforward. If the task of interpretation involves the interpreter's capturing the distinctly epistemic perspective of the interpretee, we can wonder how a hearer H comes to know, of a speaker S whom H aims to interpret, that S is an epistemic subject—that S is in the business of knowledge acquisition—in the first place. How does S "signal" to H that she, S, is in that business—or that she is manifesting the results of her inquiries? The answer, I think, is obvious: S makes assertions, and H apprehends this fact.

4.4 MMENA and the Epistemology and Methodology of Interpretation

It is at this point, of course, that we can begin to appreciate the role MMENA might play in an account of language interpretation. The main point of assertion is to present-as-true a given content, in such a way as to implicate one's own epistemic authority regarding the truth of the content so presented. In Chapters 2 and 3 I argued that it is by participating in the practice of assertion, understood to be a type of speech act regarding which it is mutually manifest that it is governed by a robustly epistemic norm, that a speaker implicates her epistemic authority in connection with the claim she is making. If this is correct, then it is by participating in this practice that a speaker can both manifest her role (for others) as a potential source of knowledge and present (to others) the results of her inquiries; and it is in correctly apprehending another's assertions that a hearer recognizes that the speaker has so presented herself (and her results). Assertions are not always warranted, of course; nor are they always sincere (in the sense characterized in Section 4.2). And hearers are not always entitled to accept the assertions they observe. But the central point remains: in making a sincere assertion a speaker has performed an act in which she manifests the role she plays as a potential source of epistemically high-grade information, and this is something that a hearer familiar with the practice of assertion is in a position to discern upon observing the assertoric act itself. For these reasons it seems that any attempt to derive methodological principles of interpretation from the role speakers play as potential sources of knowledge does well to start by focusing on cases involving the apprehension of sincere assertion. This is the focus of the remainder of this chapter.

Before proceeding further, however, a preliminary worry needs to be addressed. As Davidson conceived of it, the "methodological problem of interpretation" is "to see how, given the sentences a man accepts as true under given circumstances, to work out what his beliefs are and what his words mean" (Davidson 1975/1984a: 162). Given this minimalistic understanding of the task, it might be wondered how the situation of the Radical Interpreter can be illuminated by reflecting on cases in which the interpreter observes what she regards as a sincere assertion. The worry is that the identification of a sincere assertion already rests on knowledge of features of the interpretee's psychology—about whose contents the interpreter is supposed to be agnostic at the outset of interpretation.

This concern can be addressed by considering the role played in Davidson's own account by the interpreter's recognition of the interpretee's assent-manifesting behaviors. For Davidson, assent is the behavior by which a speaker manifests her attitude of holding-true, as directed at a given sentence (as used on an occasion). On that picture, a subject's assenting to a sentence under a given set of conditions is the basic sort of evidence for the theory of interpretation. Of course, assentings can serve this role only when they are sincere, that is, only when they are made under conditions in which the speaker does in fact hold-true the sentence-token in question.[13] What is more, Davidson's account appears committed to the further idea that, for her part, the interpreter is in a position to distinguish (sincere) assents, prior to being in a position to

---

[13] I note here that the notion of the sincerity of an assent would appear to be non-derivatively linked with the attitude of holding-true, in a way that the notion of the sincerity of an assertion need not be non-derivatively linked with the attitude of belief (for which see Section 4.2). So insofar as we want to do with the minimal evidential basis for interpretation, one might think that we would do well to focus, at least in the first instance, on the case of assertion. But given what Davidson has to say about our ability to discern when others hold-true given sentences (for which see the text above), we do not need to restrict ourselves in this way.

know the meaning of the sentence being assented to, and so prior to being in a position to know the belief being manifested in the assent. Davidson is very clear on this point:

> ... [W]e can tell when a speaker holds a sentence to be true without knowing what he means by the sentence, or what beliefs he holds about its unknown subject matter, or what detailed intentions do or might prompt him to utter it. (1974a; as reprinted in Davidson 1984a: 145)

Now, I submit that in all crucial respects we can treat (sincere) *assertions* as Davidson would have us treat (sincere) assentings. In particular, a hearer's discernment that a (sincere) assertion has been made is independent of the hearer's knowledge of what has been asserted, and so what belief is being manifested, in precisely the way that a Radical Interpreter's discernment that a speaker assents to (and so holds-true) a given sentence is independent of the interpreter's knowledge of what the speaker takes the sentence to mean, and so what belief it expresses. So, too, one can discern that a sincere assertion has been made without knowing "what detailed intentions do or might prompt" the speaker to have performed that speech act. To be sure, the interpreter must be able to tell that the interpretee is not merely play-acting, since speech acts performed under such conditions are not actually assertions; but this point has an analogue in the case of assenting behavior, since would-be assenting behavior exhibited while play-acting is not real assenting behavior. So it would seem that if Davidson is entitled to assume that interpreters can discern (sincere) assentings prior to knowing what has been (sincerely) assented to—and it is unclear how else one could hope to break into the "belief-meaning" circle—we are presently entitled to assume that interpreters can discern (sincere) assertions prior to knowing what has been (sincerely) asserted as well.

None of this is to deny that there are differences between assent and assertion. One such difference is obvious: assertion is a speech act, whereas assent is an attitude (of holding-true a given sentence). Still, it would seem that a Radical Interpreter is in a position to discern sincere assertions at roughly the same time that she (the interpreter) is in a position to discern the acts through which her interpretee manifests the sentences to which he assents. For one thing, another's assertion is often the best evidence we have for thinking that she holds-true a given sentence. What is more, even in those cases where the interpreter has another route to ascertaining the sentences that a speaker holds-true, in many, or perhaps even most, of the circumstances in which a speaker manifests her attitude of holding-true, she would (were she appropriately prompted) make the corresponding assertion.[14,15] And this, in turn, affords

---

[14] I say 'most,' not 'all': it may be that there are cases where someone believes something but does not take herself to have the requisite epistemic authority to flat-out assert it. This possibility raises interesting questions concerning the relationship between what some have called the norm of belief (which specifies the conditions under which it is appropriate to believe something) and the norm of assertion. I pursue these questions in Chapter 6.

[15] Of course, there are situations where a speaker who firmly believed something would refrain from asserting it, out of considerations of, for example, the desire for privacy, or politeness, and so on—but it would seem that in these circumstances she would *also* refrain from manifesting her attitude of holding-true.

the interpreter with materials—available at early stages of Radical Interpretation—with which to confirm hypotheses to the effect that a sincere assertion has been made.

Now, I do not insist that the Radical Interpreter must be able to discern sincere assertions right from the outset of the process of Radical Interpretation. This might well be asking for too much. After all, assent appears to have few attitudinal contrasts—dissent, agnosticism, and perhaps incomprehension—each of which is empirically associated with a distinctive behavioral marker, and these facts combine to make the hearer's task of discerning assent-behaviors that much easier. Not so for assertion: it has many speech act contrasts, and the behavioral markers of each can be quite subtle. Still, there are paradigm cases, even early on in the process of Radical Interpretation, in which the hypothesis that a sincere assertion has been made is itself likely true: consider a speech act made in the context in which the speaker appears to be making an observation about a salient feature of the perceptual environment. My assumption is that these cases, together with what the interpreter can learn from the interpretee's assent-behaviors, give the interpreter enough to go on so that she can begin to acquire a more general competence to discern the speaker's sincere assertions.

With this as a background defense of my focus on the case of (sincere) assertion, I now proceed to my positive proposal. The question I seek to answer is this: given a case in which a hearer is warranted in thinking that a speaker has made a sincere assertion, how does this fact alone affect the interpretation of the speaker's speech act?[16] My answer will be that MMENA provides us with the basis for imposing an epistemic constraint on interpretation. The constraint itself is an epistemicized version of the sort of methodological principle of interpretation that is more traditionally advanced in connection with Radical Interpretation: the Principle of Humanity (Grandy 1973).

Suppose MMENA is true. In that case it is mutually manifest that one must: assert p, only if one satisfies (robustly epistemic condition) E with respect to [p]. Then we obtain the following result: if a hearer H is warranted in regarding a speaker S as having made an assertion, then H is warranted in assuming that it is mutually manifest that S did something which was warranted only if S satisfied some substantial epistemic condition vis-à-vis the asserted proposition. Now let us designate as "the relevant epistemic authority" whatever is needed in order for S to satisfy epistemic condition E in a given case. In these terms, H is justified in assuming that it is mutually manifest that S did something which was warranted only if she (S) had the relevant epistemic authority. Of course, this alone does not entitle H to think that S *had* the relevant epistemic authority. What H is warranted in accepting, rather, is that either S had the relevant epistemic authority, *or else* S's assertion was unwarranted. Now suppose that hearers are in a position to tell more or less reliably when they are in the presence of a *sincere* assertion.[17] Confronted with something that H is justified in regarding as a sincere

---

[16] Later I will briefly discuss the complications that arise in connection with insincerity in assertion.

[17] It needs to be kept in mind that by 'sincere' assertion I mean one in which the speaker does in fact aim to satisfy the norm peculiar to assertion—*whether or not* she succeeds in doing so. I will return to the question regarding what sincerity in assertion comes to in Chapters 6, 10, and 11.

assertion by S, H would then be entitled to accept that the following is mutually manifest: in speaking as she did, S regarded herself (if only implicitly) as having the relevant epistemic authority. Of course S might not, in fact, have the relevant authority: perhaps her implicit self-regard in this respect was mistaken. But the point remains: sincere assertion manifests a speaker's *self-regard* as having the relevant authority, and a hearer who is justified in his judgment that another speaker's assertion was sincere is thereby justified in thinking that the speaker so regards herself (if only implicitly).

A word is in order regarding the idea of a speaker's (implicitly) regarding herself as being relevantly epistemically authoritative. This idea itself can be derived from MMENA, as follows. Take a case in which a speaker makes an assertion. And suppose (with MMENA) that it is mutually manifest to speaker and audience alike that a speaker who asserts has done something warranted only if she has the relevant epistemic authority. Then the speaker who asserts knows that her performance is so assessable. So insofar as she is sincere—insofar as she aimed to satisfy the norm of assertion—she must regard herself as relevantly epistemically authoritative. Of course, she might not have given the matter any explicit thought; she might simply have asserted what she did. Still, her so regarding herself would be discernible in her reactions to challenges to her assertion. She would regard a challenge to her assertion as legitimate if it legitimately challenged her epistemic authority, and she would regard herself as required to reply to any legitimate challenge. (Any speaker who did not act in this way would be considered deviant.) It is in this sense that we might say that her regarding herself as epistemically authoritative is implicit, even in those cases in which she gave it no thought prior to asserting as she did.

Still, it might be objected that there are people who assert who do not regard themselves, even in this implicit way, as relevantly authoritative. As an illustration, it might be urged that very young children are like this—at least at the early period in their participation in the practice of assertion.[18] In response I grant this, but suggest that we can accommodate the point by regarding very young asserters as not yet full participants in the practice. They only become full participants when they acquire the disposition to have the sort of reactive attitudes (to other speakers, and to themselves as speakers) that are characteristic of our assertoric practice. (For a discussion, see Chapter 3.) This move is not *ad hoc*: arguably, the basis for our recognition of them as making assertions at all is that they are performing an act which in most other respects is like the one we (cognitively mature) subjects perform when we assert. We can recognize their actions as having this significance, first, in that we can explain away their lacking the disposition to have the higher-order attitudes characteristic of mature assertoric practice, and second, in that we expect their performances to emerge into mature practice as time goes on (and they become more cognitively mature). In this way we can grant that very young children assert, even as we recognize that they lack

---

[18] At a minimum, very young children are limited in their capacity for higher-order thought, whether other-regarding, as is seen in the standard interpretation of the false belief test, or self-regarding, as here.

the full set of reactive attitudes, and so lack the implicit self-regard characteristic of mature assertion.[19]

Having just defended the claim that a sincere (cognitively mature and healthy) asserter will implicitly regard herself as having the relevant epistemic authority, I now want to appeal to this fact to characterize a thesis in the methodology of interpretation. The claim I want to defend is this ('AIP' for the 'Assertion-Interpretation Principle'):

> AIP   For any set of sincere assertions by another speaker, favor those interpretations which make the best sense of the speaker's regarding herself as having been in the relevantly epistemically authoritative position vis-à-vis the propositions in question.

Later I will address the grounds for thinking that AIP is well-motivated as a constraint on interpretation. Before doing so, however, I want to do two things. First, I want to say what is involved in "making the best sense of" a speaker's regarding herself as having the relevant epistemic authority. Second, I want to comment on the strength of the constraint imposed by AIP.

What is involved in making sense of a subject's self-regard as relevantly authoritative on an occasion of making an assertion? I assume that this can be done in one of two ways. We can make sense of this either in a *vindicatory* fashion, as when we so interpret her that she comes out having the very authority she takes herself to have, or in a *non-vindicatory* fashion, as when, although we interpret her in such a way that she comes out lacking this authority, we have a plausible (and charitable) explanation for why she so regarded herself. Thus understood, AIP enjoins us to minimize cases in which she lacks the authority but where there is no explanation of this fact. In other words, this is an epistemicized version of Grandy's Principle of Humanity.

How strong a constraint is this? I submit that, so understood, the strength of the constraint imposed by AIP will turn on two things: the precise content of the norm of assertion, and the degree to which we will tolerate radical forms of skepticism.

The strength of the constraint AIP imposes on interpretation will turn on the precise content of the norm of assertion. It is this that will determine how we understand "epistemically authoritative" in AIP: stronger, more demanding methodological principles of interpretation result from more demanding epistemological properties. So, for example, if the norm of assertion is knowledge, then an interpreter who recognizes a speaker to have produced a sincere assertion must treat the speaker as regarding

---

[19] It may be that there are others, beyond the very young, who lack even the implicit self-regard. Perhaps there are forms of cognitive illness whose characteristic manifestation is to destroy (or otherwise interrupt the natural course of) higher-order thought, or which otherwise interferes with self-regarding thought. This may be. But I want to suggest that insofar as we regard a subject who suffers from such a condition as asserting, it is only because we recognize what he or she is doing by reference to our ordinary standards of assertion. Of such a person we might say: she does not recognize herself as having done something for which she needs the relevant epistemic authority, but she ought to. This 'ought' claim is precisely what warrants our regarding her act as having the standing of an assertion.

herself as having spoken from knowledge.[20] If the norm is rational belief, then the interpreter must regard a sincere asserter as regarding herself (merely) as having suitable rational backing for her assertion. And so forth. However, I propose to bracket this matter, and work with the schematic AIP itself. (As we will see, though it is schematic, AIP suffices to enable us to see how assertion's norm constrains interpretation.)

But even after we fix on the precise content of the epistemic norm of assertion, we still have not fixed the strength of the constraint imposed by AIP. For the strength of this constraint also turns on the degree to which we will tolerate radical forms of skepticism. For even after we fix the precise content of the norm of assertion, we can ask what is involved in "making the best sense" of the speaker's epistemic self-regard. In insisting that we do so, does AIP merely require us to make sense of the fact that the speaker *regards herself* as having the relevant epistemic authority? Or does the satisfaction of this condition require instead that we render the speaker in such a way that she actually *has* this authority (for many or most occasions of sincere assertion)? It is here that we must confront the question of skepticism, since it is our attitude towards skepticism that will determine what we take to be required to satisfy the condition in question. Suppose (in a skeptical vein) that it is possible for an arbitrary speaker to fail radically in her attempts to conform to the norm of assertion: it regularly or perhaps even always happens that she makes sincere assertions without having the relevant epistemic authority. Here the speaker's own self-conception, as someone who possesses the relevant epistemic authority, is itself a delusion. In this case, AIP's demand—to "make the best sense of" the speaker's self-regard as having the relevant authority—would merely demand that we make sense of the hearer's delusion of being relevantly epistemically authoritative. To do so, we would have to come up with the best error theory (the one that minimizes the number of occasions on which we have no explanation for her failure to conform to the norm). On the other hand, if we do not countenance this skeptical possibility, AIP's demand will be more substantial. For in that case we would have to so interpret her sincere assertions, so that we regularly vindicate the hypothesis that she has the relevant epistemic authority she takes herself to have—or at least that we minimize the number of occasions on which she inexplicably lacks this authority.

Now, Davidson himself was famous for having argued that we have no choice but to see others as by and large speaking and believing truths—or at least what the interpreter herself regards as truths. Interestingly, given a very weak assumption, AIP itself would appear to yield an argument for an epistemicized version of this conclusion. The weak assumption is one Davidson himself endorsed: interpreters have no choice

---

[20] For an interesting argument in defense of a position in this vicinity, see Williamson (2000: 267). As noted previously, Williamson (2007: chapter 8) defends a knowledge-maximization approach to interpretation. Interestingly, this argument does not derive from the norm of assertion, so much as it does on the conditions on reference: Williamson's claim is that reference-assignments are guided by the methodological principle enjoining us to maximize the speaker's knowledge. See Williamson (2007: 264).

but to approach the task of interpretation from their own perspective—that is, from the perspective of what they themselves take to be true. (See Davidson 1973/1984a: 137; Davidson 1974a/1984a: 152; Davidson 1974b/1984a: 196.) With this assumption in mind, let us return to what is involved in the process of making sense of another's self-conception as someone who (on the various occasions of sincere assertion) has the relevant authority. Given our assumption, the hearer/interpreter H has no choice but to put herself into the speaker S's shoes, in order to discern what propositions are such that, so positioned, H would take himself to have the relevant epistemic authority regarding them. If all H has to go on here is his own background beliefs and the processes he uses to acquire information, it would appear that H has no choice but to see S as in a position to satisfy E with respect to the propositions H would take himself to be in a position to satisfy E, were he in S's shoes. It appears, then, that insofar as H aims to interpret S's assertions, he must regard S's self-conception—that she is relevantly authoritative, on the occasion of her sincere assertions—as broadly correct. The point here is not that S's self-conception must *be* correct; only that H himself has no choice but to *assume* this.

It might seem that this is too much to assume.[21] Cannot there be speakers who participate in the practice of assertion, yet who do not care one whit for conforming to the norm of assertion? And if there can be such speakers, do we not have to justify the move to assume (or the move to have the Radical Interpreter assume) that sincere speakers have the self-conception as relevantly epistemically authoritative? But this worry, while based on a truth, would seem not to touch the spirit of the proposal. A first, superficial reply to make is that an asserter who does not give a whit about conforming to the norm of assertion is not sincere in her assertion, and so the existence of such asserters is no counterexample to the thesis that sincere (cognitively mature and healthy) asserters will regard themselves as having the relevant epistemic authority. Still, this reply is superficial, as the existence of such asserters does raise the question of how the interpreter ought to *justify* his determination that a given assertion is sincere—that it was produced in an attempt to conform to assertion's norm. In response, I acknowledge that any particular judgment regarding a specific asserter, to the effect that she is sincere on a given occasion, is fallible: the interpreter might be wrong. Still, there is evidence that our interpreter can use. Presumably, this will include the sort of features of which Davidson spoke in connection with the discernment of sincere assent, and it will also include the sort of features by which we discern sincerity (facial expression, ability to look one in the eyes, and so on). Of course, even this sort of evidence is itself only a fallible guide to sincerity: an interpreter could have evidence of this sort, and so reach the verdict that the assertion is sincere, and yet it is false that the assertion is sincere. (Think of extremely talented liars and excellent bullshitters.) But this poses no in-principle problem for the Radical Interpreter, and this sort of fallibility

---

[21] I thank an anonymous referee for suggesting the need to respond to the objection that follows in this and the next paragraph.

will not be news to anyone who is not committed to a kind of verificationism regarding sincerity. (Of course, if an interpretee is systematically insincere, never giving a whit about conforming to the norm of assertion, it may well be that the Radical Interpreter has no choice but to turn to another speaker first. Do not start by trying to interpret a bullshitter!)

Perhaps a worry remains. Suppose that there can be whole communities in which it is standard practice to let others get away with assertoric unwarrantedness. Perhaps what is going on in such communities is that people assert, giving not one second's thought to their degree of epistemic authority, where this is perfectly in keeping with the loose social practices of the community. In such communities the Radical Interpreter will once again be wrong to start off with the assumption that sincere asserters regard themselves as relevantly epistemically authoritative. My reply is as previously: this objection, while based on a scenario that is (not merely possible but) actual in a variety of communities, does not touch the spirit of the proposal. To begin, we can note that the earliest sort of evidence available to the Radical Interpreter will be evidence from situations of observation: cases in which the interpretee is (by hypothesis) directly observing matters before her. The fact that she is a member of a community that only loosely enforces assertoric norms will be irrelevant to cases in which she is prompted by queries regarding simple perceptual matters, or in which she makes simple observation reports. Once the Radical Interpreter has managed to interpret a good deal of the terms she uses under such conditions, of course, the Radical Interpreter can then begin to develop an account on which he can make sense of the community's "looseness" in policing assertoric standards. So even here the Radical Interpreter can get by. Stronger, the only sense she can make of that looseness is precisely by relying on the distinctly epistemic orientation towards others' speech (as it is that orientation that enables him to interpret would-be observation sentences, the earliest evidence she has to go on).

My suggestion, then, is that when it comes to the interpretation of another's assertoric utterances, we have no choice but to approach these by remaining sensitive to the speaker's own epistemic perspective. In particular, the task of interpreting another's sincere assertions requires the interpreter to engage in a decidedly epistemic activity: the interpreter H must assess S's performances from the perspective of S's own self-conception as being relevantly epistemically authoritative. In doing so the interpreter regards the interpretee as involved in an activity that cannot be understood except in epistemic terms—as aiming at knowledge (or some other epistemically high-grade status). Where Davidson speaks of the need to "[assign] truth conditions to alien sentences that make native speakers right when plausibly possible, according . . . to our own view of what is right," I would suggest that we speak instead of the need to assign truth conditions to sentences so as to minimize the number of times in which the speaker inexplicably lacks the *relevant epistemic authority*—still by her (the interpretee's) own view of what is right. In short, we must see another's sincere assertions not merely as manifesting her self-conception as relevantly authoritative, but as manifesting that very authoritativeness itself (and as explicable when it fails to do so).

4.5 In Defense of the Norm-Based Account of Interpretation: AIP

But what reasons might be offered for thinking that AIP, interpreted in something like the foregoing fashion, is indeed a constraint on interpretation? I offer three reasons in defense of this claim. The proposed AIP-based constraint captures how interpretation *actually* proceeds, and how it *ought* to proceed (Section 4.5.1);[22] it is independently motivated, since it can see the imposition of the constraint on interpretation as deriving from features of assertion itself (Section 4.5.2); and it has a plausible account of the 'charitableness' that is required by successful interpretation (Section 4.5.3). At a minimum, in all three respects the AIP-based constraint is preferable to Davidson's truth-based Principle of Charity. I should add, as a fourth reason, that it avoids one of the objections recently put to Williamson's own (2000, 2007) epistemic constraint on interpretation (Section 4.5.4).[23]

4.5.1 AIP Captures How Interpretation Does and Should Proceed

The AIP-based methodology reflects the proper starting points of, and evidence for, language interpretation—both how it actually proceeds, and also how it ought to proceed.

It is uncontroversial that the process of interpretation will focus at the outset on observation sentences. This is a point Quine himself made, and Davidson followed him on this. But why is this? Davidson's own favored explanation was that in these cases the very conditions that prompted the subject's assent were the conditions that gave the truth conditions of the sentence assented to. Still, we can continue to ask why this is so. The answer is obvious: because in these cases the conditions that prompted the subject's assent are conditions whose obtaining the subject is (typically) in a position to know and about which she is in a position to make an epistemically authoritative report.

This point is so obvious that its full significance might easily be lost. That is, it might simply be supposed that the assigning of truth conditions to observation sentences is a straightforward affair—one that does not require any elaborate discussion. Indeed, the very use of the label '*observation* sentence' suggests how such sentences ought to be interpreted: their interpretation ought to capture *what is presently being observed* by the subject under interpretation. But how should the intepreter understand "what is presently being observed by the subject under interpretation"? Should she (the interpreter) consider all of the information that (if contemporary vision science is to be trusted) is registered by the subject's visual system? Or some more restricted part of the total information that is registered by that system? If the former, then we would

---

[22] For this point, and for the argument used to support it, I am indebted to an argument found in Williamson (2007: chapter 8).

[23] I refer to the objection in McGlynn (2012).

arrive at some rather curious interpretations of her speech, since a good deal of the information in question is registered and processed by *subpersonal* (and so *subdoxastic*) processes. Surely it would be curious indeed to think that an assertion prompted by a visual observation of the passing scene is to be interpreted in terms of intensity changes, illumination gradients, and the other items represented in "early vision." Yet changes in these features systematically affect the information that is registered at the personal (or doxastic) level, so we can ask: by what right do we interpret assertions by restricting our attention to person-level information?[24] It is here, of course, that the distinctly epistemic dimension of interpretation is seen: we interpret an assertion as pertaining to tables and chairs, and not to sets of intensity changes and illumination gradients, and so on, because tables and chairs constitute the sorts of thing regarding which the subject under interpretation is in a position to acquire knowledge or epistemically high-grade belief.

Let us say that a constraint on interpretation is semantic when the feature it enjoins us to maximize (alternatively: when the feature is such that the constraint enjoins us to minimize the lack of this feature[25]) is some purely semantic property such as *truth*, rather than some epistemic property such as *knowledge* or *justified belief*. Then our present point can be put in terms of a dilemma that must be faced by any approach to interpretation on which the constraints on interpretation are semantic. The dilemma focuses on how we should understand the notion of the observable in the claim that observation statements constitute the primary evidence for interpretation. Either we understand *what is observable* in epistemic terms, or we do not. If we do, then the game is over: we have in effect acknowledged an epistemic constraint on interpretation after all. But (taking the other horn) if we do not understand *what is observable* in epistemic terms, then we face the question of why interpreters should restrict themselves to considering only conceptualized contents—person-level information—when they consider candidate interpretations of another's assertions. It is clear that interpreters do so restrict themselves; but the question concerns why they should. After all, even Davidson himself noted that there are various kinds of information that are registered by the interpretee's visual system in the course of seeing the world; whence the restriction to a narrow range of this information? More specifically, why do we restrict ourselves to information that can be represented in conceptualized contents—the sort of contents that amount to something that the subject herself might entertain in thought? The answer appears to be straightforward: this is the sort of information that the subject herself might come to *know*, or *believe on the basis of the evidence* she currently has

---

[24] It will be true, of course, that further data from a subject's assertions will help us delimit further the possible interpretations of her speech. Thus, the fact that she uses 'chair' in this scenario and 'book' in that one might well be enough to rule out certain interpretations that assigned some subpersonal items to her words. But how can we be sure that we can always rule out all such assignments? This question becomes pressing if we do not appeal to the interpretee's perspective as an epistemic subject—one who aims to acquire knowledge (justified belief, rational belief, and so on).

[25] I will leave off this qualification in what follows.

before her. Of course, if this is correct—and I do not see how else to justify the interpreter's favored interpretations, involving these person-level conceptualized contents, when so much other information is registered by the interpretee's visual system—then once again it seems that we are treating *what is observable* as an epistemic notion after all. In short, any approach to interpretation on which constraints are purely semantic either has no justification for our actual practice, or else it is forced to acknowledge epistemic constraints after all.

Now, it may well be that Davidson himself never intended his own account of the method of interpretation to be fully semantic in this way. As I noted previously, his later work suggested a greater awareness of the need of the interpreter to regard the interpretee as a distinctly epistemic subject.[26] But this is so much grist for my mill, since in that case we are favoring epistemic constraints on interpretation. Stronger, the epistemic constraints in question are precisely those favored by the proposed AIP-based methodology: we ought to so interpret another's assertions so that we minimize the occasions on which she inexplicably lacks the relevant epistemic authority. It is this that justifies our favoring the person-level conceptualized contents that are typically ascribed in the course of interpreting another's language.

4.5.2 AIP and Assertion-Generated Constraints on Interpretation

A second reason in support of the AIP-based constraint on interpretation is that it enjoys independent motivation. The present proposal can be justified in terms of the very features of assertion—features that assertoric speech has, independent of considerations having to do with interpretation. Thus, anyone who concedes that assertion has a robustly epistemic norm will already have granted all that is required by the AIP-based proposal. On this score, the contrast with the Davidsonian approach involving the Principle of Charity is sharp. He tries to justify his imposition of the Principle of Charity by appeal to the need to render the speaker interpretable, but then leaves interpretability itself as an unjustified justifier. As a result, the move to accept his proposal comes at the cost of having to accept one or another strong claim about the interpretability of others—a claim that is obviously not motivated independent of considerations having to do with interpretation.

Consider the constraint imposed by AIP, which itself requires us to make sense of the speaker's self-conception as having been relevantly authoritative in the assertions she makes. This injunction will have us prefer interpretations on which either the speaker is authoritative with respect to that content or else we can explain her lack of authoritativeness. And this involves interpreting sincere assertions by asking ourselves what the speaker was then and there in a position to know (believe with justification, believe rationally, and so on)—and using this to constrain our interpretation. Reflecting on this, we can now see that the very feature that makes a speech act one of

---

[26] See my (2011), where I develop this point at length.

assertion—namely, its answerability to a robustly epistemic norm—is something that motivates a constraint on the interpretation of token assertions themselves.

To appreciate the significance of this point, return to Davidson's own justification for imposing a truth-maximizing Principle of Charity in the course of interpretation. His justificatory claim was that without doing so the subject under interpretation would be uninterpretable. Precisely why we should expect another subject to be interpretable—let alone why, even if others *are* interpretable, this fact should be the ultimate ground of the methodology of interpretation—are matters on which Davidson is silent. By contrast, the justification for imposing the AIP-based constraint appeals to nothing beyond our account of assertion itself. In conforming to this constraint, interpreters are thus doing no more than acknowledging the speaker's competent participation in the practice of assertion itself.

4.5.3 AIP and Charity in Interpretation

There is yet a third consideration in support of the AIP-based approach to the methodology of interpretation, as against Davidson's approach. The AIP-based methodology has a deeper account of the 'charitableness' that is required by successful interpretation.

Let us start with a question that is not often addressed in discussions of the methodology of interpretation: what is 'charitable' about this-or-that methodological principle of interpretation? Davidson regards the charitableness of his Principle of Charity to consist in the idea that it imposes a requirement to maximize others' *truths* (in belief and in speech).[27] The present proposal explains the charitableness of AIP as resting on two more fundamental points.

Davidson's view is that we are charitable when we attribute truths to a subject under interpretation. What makes this charitable? Well, it is certainly more charitable than attributing falsehoods to the subject, and more charitable still than regarding the subject as unintelligible. So it would seem that the charitableness of the interpretation scheme favored by Davidson consists in the comparison of truth with falsity and unintelligibility. I mention this since I think it makes clear that, though this *is* a sort of charity, it does not go very deep. For all Davidson's truth-based methodology has to say, the fact that we need to maximize the truths we attribute to the subject reflects no deeper fact about the interpretee herself—only that if she is to be interpretable at all, we must do so.

Contrast now the charitableness of the methodological principle deriving from AIP. This methodological principle enjoins us to make sense of the speaker's self-conception as relevantly authoritative in the claims she makes. In what way is this charitable? Well, to begin, following this methodological principle will have us interpret sincere assertions in such a way as to render them so that either they are authoritative or else

---

[27] In asking this question I am going to be bracketing skeptical scenarios in which the best that can be hoped for in interpretation is *agreement* between speaker and hearer, not the truth of the beliefs that constitute that agreement.

their lack of authoritativeness can be explained in a plausible fashion. What is more, I assume that, all else equal, an explanation that vindicates the interpretee's claim to authoritativeness is to be preferred to one that explains its lack of authoritativeness: the former is simpler (in not involving an error that needs to be "explained away"). If this is so, then following this rule of interpretation will put some pressure on interpreters to *vindicate the speaker's own self-conception* as a subject who succeeds at acquiring and communicating epistemically authoritative beliefs. This is doubly charitable, first, in vindicating her self-conception, but second, in representing her in such a way that her success in the way of asserting truths reflects a cognitive achievement of hers (the sort we dignify with 'knowledge' or 'justified belief'). But even in cases in which an interpretation in the spirit of AIP cannot vindicate the subject's self-conception as relevantly authoritative, still, the present proposal requires that the hearer render intelligible this aspect of the speaker's self-conception: if it cannot be vindicated, the hearer's self-conception as authoritative must still be respected insofar as failures must be explicable whenever possible. This respect for a speaker's self-conception as authoritative is itself a core part of the charitableness of the proposed method. What is more, where Davidson was satisfied to regard the charitableness of his Principle of Charity to consist in the idea that it imposes a requirement to maximize others' truths (in belief and in speech), the present proposal sees any truth-related implications of the method as deriving from its imposition of *epistemic* criteria—namely, those implicated in the epistemic norm of assertion.

4.5.4 *AIP and Williamson's "Knowledge-Maximization" Method*

Finally, the proposal to use AIP to motivate an epistemicized version of Grandy's Principle of Humanity will enable us to avoid an objection that McGlynn (2012) raised against Williamson's own knowledge-maximizing account of the method of interpretation (Williamson 2007).

I begin with Williamson's own proposal that we should replace Davidson's Principle of Charity, which would have us maximize the number of truths that we attribute to the interpretee, with a principle that would have us maximize the knowledge that we attribute to the interpretee. Williamson uses an example to show why this sort of method is to be preferred. Without entering into the details, the point of the example is to show that there are cases in which the Principle of Charity would deliver an unintuitive result, where the knowledge-maximizing principle would deliver the correct result, and where the latter appears to offer us an explanation of the correctness of the correct result (Williamson 2007: 263–64). The example involves a speaker who (looking at a particular woman) asserts 'She is F, G, H . . .,' where the woman at whom she is looking (W_1) only seems to be F, G, and H (when actually she is none), but where another woman whom the speaker has never before met (W_2) is F, G, and H. Williamson remarks that it would be wrong to interpret the speaker as saying of W_2 that she is F, G, and H, despite the fact that this would maximize the truths we attribute to the speaker; and intuitively the explanation for this is that the speaker did not know of W_2 that she is F, G, and H. (Williamson points out that a merely causal story about reference-fixation will not explain all that we want explained, and that in any case it will not be satisfactory for cases involving abstracta—whereas the knowledge account avoids both of these issues.)

In response, McGlynn (2012) argues that knowledge-maximization does not deliver the right verdicts in several different types of cases. Of these, the strongest is the case he calls 'Hallucinogen,' and which I quote at length here.

> Jane is taking part in a trial of a new drug with powerful hallucinogenic properties. Sitting in her cubicle, she appears to see a number of people in front of her. In fact, there is only one other person in the cubicle, Helen, who is standing several feet away from her. Helen appears to Jane to be no more flesh and blood than the other figures that appear to her in the cubicle. Despite knowing that she will experience hallucinations while in the cubicle, Jane judges, 'She is beautiful,' 'She is freckled,' 'She has green eyes,' and so on, keeping her attention firmly on Helen the whole time. Each of these judgments is correct. (McGlynn 2012: 398)

McGlynn argues that, given a plausible (methods-based) safety condition on knowledge, none of these judgments are knowledgeable, yet it is clear that the verbalizations should be interpreted as regarding Helen. I think this verdict is correct, and that it can be used to show that a simple 'knowledge maximization' principle of interpretation will not do. At the same time it fails to score points against the methodological principle of AIP. This is for the simple reason that AIP requires, not that we maximize the number of assertions that come out authoritative, but rather that we *make sense of* the speaker's self-conception as relevantly authoritative when she asserts. In cases like 'Hallucinogen' we do so by invoking auxiliary (independently justified) hypotheses about the speaker's perspective. It is in terms of these hypotheses that we make sense of her assertoric behavior under conditions in which, by (our representation of) her own lights, she regards herself as not in a position to know whereof she speaks. In doing so we are conforming to the requirements of AIP, not by maximizing the number of assertions that come out authoritative, but rather by explaining why this is not appropriate in the circumstance. AIP, then, is closer in spirit to the Principle of Humanity (enjoining us to minimize unexplained errors) than the Principle of Charity. In any case, it is not susceptible to worries arising from cases in which there is no knowledge: so long as we can continue to make sense of the subject's epistemic perspective on the proposition in question, including her self-conception of her epistemic standing, AIP will deliver the right verdicts.

With this in mind, we can see that AIP will only 'tend' to favor ascriptions that maximize the number of warranted assertions. It will favor such ascriptions in any case in which not doing so would leave unexplained the hearer's epistemic self-conception on the proposition at hand. However, what McGlynn's case shows is that there are situations in which making sense of the hearer's epistemic self-conception may require construing that self-conception as faulty, but where the faultiness can be explained away. In such cases, AIP will favor such ascriptions.

4.6 Interpretation, Comprehension, and the Epistemology of Testimony

There is one remaining issue that ought to be dealt with before concluding. How does the present chapter's conclusion, to the effect that

(*) (given a generally anti-skeptical outlook) a correct theory of interpretation will have us minimize the number of occasions on which sincere assertions come out as inexplicably lacking relevant epistemic authoritativeness

relate to the issue in the epistemology of testimony taken up in Chapter 2, regarding the conditions on a hearer's being entitled to accept what she is told? In particular, does something in the vicinity of (*) constitute a reason to favor a non-reductionist account of those conditions? Now, while no one has argued from anything as weak as (*) to a non-reductionist conclusion, some have tried to do so from a slightly stronger starting point, to the effect that

(**) (given a generally anti-skeptical outlook) a correct theory of interpretation will have us maximize the number of occasions on which sincere assertions come out as relevantly epistemically authoritative.[28]

I am not defending anything as strong as (**). But it is worth noting that even if something as strong as (**) were true, it would not support the argument described. By making this clear, I aim to clarify the weakness of the connection between the methodology of interpretation and the epistemology of testimony.

Suppose, with (**), that if interpretation is to proceed at all, we must maximize the cases in which assertions come out as relevantly authoritative. The argument I am presently examining purports to use this claim to support the view that hearers are presumptively (though defeasibly) entitled to accept another's say-so—that is, to support the non-reductionist position in the epistemology of testimony. In response, I submit that the argument contains a crucial lacuna. It is one thing to presume (in the course of interpretation) that a speaker who makes a sincere assertion is epistemically authoritative; it is quite another to be justified in accepting what that speaker (is represented on that interpretation as having) said. Even if it is true that as interpreters we have no choice but to presume relevant epistemic authoritativeness on the part of sincere asserters, this does not tell us how strong an epistemic position we need to occupy in order to be justified in accepting a proffered assertion in any given case. For all that a hearer/interpreter must presume in the course of interpreting another's assertion, this presumption, by itself, is not sufficient to justify the hearer/interpreter in accepting the assertion.

---

[28] See Coady (1992) (who attributes a view in this vicinity to Davidson) and Stevenson (1993). Graham (2000c) responds to Coady (1992).

The present point is not *ad hoc*. In order to be justified in accepting an assertion, one needs to be entitled to regard the assertion as trustworthy. Those who are reductionists in the epistemology of testimony hold that the entitlement in question requires one to have reasons to regard the observed assertion as credible. But note that the presumption an interpreter must make in the course of interpretation is generic: it flows directly from the methodology of interpretation itself. So even if it is granted that the generic presumption in question is in fact *a* reason to accept an assertion, reductionists have grounds to deny that this reason is *sufficiently strong* to entitle acceptance outright. If this generic presumption in question were strong enough, then any assertion, *insofar as it were interpretable at all*, would be such that the hearer is (at least presumptively) entitled to accept it so long as there are no reasons against doing so. Such a view is a non-reductionist view alright; in fact, it comes close to the view of Burge (1993). But I see no reason why the reductionist has to accept it. I repeat: the reductionist can allow that the presumption of authoritativeness granted to (sincere) assertions in the course of interpreting them provides *some* (minimal) reason in favor of acceptance, while still insisting that, because this presumption is not a sufficiently specific reason, by itself it does not justify acceptance outright. And this is enough to show that even something as strong as (**) can be squared with reductionism—the interpretation-based argument in Coady (1992) and Stevenson (1993) to the contrary notwithstanding.

In fact, the foregoing would appear to illustrate the subtle but important difference between the perspective we occupy as *interpreters* of others' assertions, as against the perspective we take as potential *consumers* of those assertions.[29] As interpreters, we hold fixed (what we take to be) our knowledge of the world around us, and use this knowledge to inform how we interpret another's assertion. Our attitude is something like this: what could the speaker have asserted, consistent with the hypothesis that the (sincere) assertion she made was epistemically authoritative? Here, something like the Principle of Humanity is appropriate: we are, after all, trying to render the speaker's perspective, and the cost of having access to that perspective is that we must work to minimize unexplained error. But it is far from clear that this sort of humanity-based charity is appropriate when it comes to the matter of whether to *accept* the assertion. There it is not the speaker's perspective, but our own, that is in play. This is reflected in our perspective as potential consumers of assertions. Insofar as we are consumers of assertions, we regard them as potential opportunities

---

[29] Of course, in speaking of our roles as interpreters and consumers of assertions, I am employing analytic categories for a process that is typically effortless, fast, and near-automatic. On most occasions we simply react to an observed assertion by accepting it or rejecting it; it is not all that common that we have to spend time having to think about how to interpret it. Yet even if my analytic categories—the hearer as interpreter vs. the hearer as consumer—do not typically straightforwardly correspond to distinct elements in the psychological reality of the audience, it is still important to distinguish them—if only to make clear that the sorts of assumptions that we have to make as interpreters of others' assertions do not settle the epistemological issues that arise in connection with us as consumers of those assertions.

for the acquisition of knowledge (justified belief; rational belief). To exploit these opportunities, we must react to them in ways that are epistemically proper. What such propriety demands of us is precisely what is at issue in the reductionism/anti-reductionism debate. My point here is simply that this matter is far from settled merely in virtue of the sort of humanity-based charity we need to extend as interpreters of others' assertions.

The picture we have arrived at, then, is this. In interpreting S's assertions, H will aim to make sense of S's (perhaps implicit) self-regard as relevantly authoritative on the matter at hand. This will involve either vindicating S's claim to relevant authority, or explaining it away (by showing that, while S lacked the authoritativeness she claimed, we can explain the failure of authority—typically, because we can explain why she thought she was relevantly authoritative). The requirement is to minimize those cases in which H can do neither—that is, neither vindicate the claimed authority nor explain it away. The interpretation that H settles on then constitutes how H has *comprehended* S's assertion. In comprehending S's assertion, H mentally represents it as having a certain content. This comprehension-constituting representation is epistemically appropriate so long as it was arrived at through a proper method of interpretation. Insofar as they are bound up with the correct method of interpretation/comprehension, the assumptions H makes as part of his attempt to make sense of S's self-conception as relevantly authoritative *do not stand in further need of justification*. However, once we turn our attention from the matter of H's interpreting and comprehending S's assertion, to the matter of H's acceptance of that assertion, it is a controversial matter whether H needs more in order to accept the content he has comprehended. This controversial matter is one of the core questions posed in the epistemology of testimony literature. In the context of debates in the epistemology of testimony, all sides can agree that if H is to come to know (or even to acquire justified belief) through accepting S's assertion, H must be justified in regarding S as relevantly authoritative. What is contestable is whether this justification—the sort of justification that would underwrite H's testimony-based knowledge that p—requires more than the sort of entitlement H has for making the presumptions bound up with interpretation. It would appear that, at a minimum, the sort of justification that would underwrite H's testimony-based knowledge that p requires that there be no relevant defeaters; and whether more than this is needed is precisely what is at issue in the debate between reductionists and anti-reductionists in the epistemology of testimony. (See Chapter 2 for a discussion.)

We are now in a position to make a point of more general interest, pertaining to what we might call the epistemology of comprehension in its relation to the epistemology of testimony.[30] The point is twofold. First, take a given assertoric speech act that can be

---

[30] The point I am making in this paragraph is indebted to Rysiew (2007a); and versions of it have also been made to me, in conversation, by Peter Graham. See also Graham (2010).

interpreted/comprehended in such a way as to preserve the hypothesis of the speaker's relevant epistemic authoritativeness. Call this *the fact of interpretability/comprehensibility*. This fact, by itself, provides some reason to suppose that the speaker is, in fact, relevantly authoritative, and so provides the hearer/interpreter with some reason to accept what the speaker (on that interpretation of her speech contribution) asserted. But second, when it comes to the ultimate acceptability of the assertion, the sort of reason one has in virtue of the interpretability of the assertion is (arguably) a relatively *weak* reason: while it does speak in favor of accepting the assertion, arguably it does not by itself provide anything like an all-things-considered justification for doing so.

These points correct what I regard as two faulty tendencies in the literature in the epistemology of testimony. On the one hand there are those who, noting that assertoric speech must be presumed reliable (epistemically authoritative) if it is to be so much as interpretable (comprehensible) in the first place, conclude from this that some form of non-reductionism is true.[31] This view gets one thing right: the very fact that a purported piece of testimony can be comprehended is itself a reason in favor of accepting the testimony. But at the same time it mischaracterizes the strength of this reason: it falsely assumes that this reason is sufficiently strong to provide an all-things-considered justification to the hearer to accept the testimony. On the other hand there are those who, rightly thinking that the bare comprehensibility of a piece of testimony, by itself, cannot justify one in accepting the testimony, conclude from this that the mere fact that something is a piece of testimony can have no epistemic significance—and typically conclude further that some form of reductionism is true.[32] This view gets one thing right: non-reductionism cannot be established merely on the basis of considerations having to do with interpretability or comprehensibility. But at the same time this view falsely assumes that comprehensibility considerations have no epistemic significance whatsoever. I believe that there is a middle ground between these two extremes: the fact that a piece of testimony (or an assertion) is comprehensible is epistemically significant in its own right, and constitutes something in favor of accepting the testimony (assertion), though it stops short of something that provides an all-things-considered justification for acceptance.[33] (See Chapter 2, Section 2.5, and Chapter 3, Section 3.7 for a discussion of the sort of considerations that, I think, might be used to establish such a non-reductionism.)

---

[31] In addition to Coady (1992) and Stevenson (1993), we might regard Burge (1993) as an even more explicit version of this sort of argument.

[32] Here I would locate standard internalist views in the epistemology of testimony (see Fumerton 2006). And it is arguable that ordinary evidentialist views (see Feldman and Conee 1985), and views on which testimonial belief is a species of belief based on inference to the best explanation (see Lipton 2007), should also be located here. I say it is 'arguable,' since such views have not been developed in sufficient detail for me to be able to tell whether these views deny any epistemic significance to the comprehensibility of a piece of testimony.

[33] Although I do not have time to argue for this, this "middle position" is itself compatible with a version of anti-reductionism. See Goldberg and Henderson (2006) for a version of an anti-reductionist thesis that can accept this "middle position."

4.7 Conclusion

In this chapter I have argued that the norm of assertion can be used to motivate an independently plausible account of the method of interpretation. After formulating the hypothesis as MMENA, I argued that the method of interpretation deriving from MMENA is to be preferred both to Davidson's own Principle of Charity and to Williamson's (2000, 2007) Principle of Knowledge-Maximization.

5
Assertion and Assertoric Content

5.1 A Role for MMENA in the Determination of Assertoric Content

The sort of picture I have been developing so far in this book centers on MMENA—the hypothesis that it is mutually manifest to participants to a speech exchange that assertion has a robustly epistemic norm. In Chapter 1 I argued that, of all the accounts on offer regarding the nature of assertion, MMENA best explains the battery of characteristics assertions have. The next seven chapters attempt to use MMENA to forge connections between the nature of assertion and various other issues of philosophical interest. So far, these issues have concerned epistemology and philosophy of language.[1] Thus I argued that MMENA itself best explains the epistemic significance of assertion—both its role in the spread of knowledge (Chapter 2) and its role in the generation of the epistemic expectations, and the corresponding responsibilities and entitlements, attending to assertoric speech (Chapter 3). And in Chapter 4 I argued that MMENA can be used to argue for an illuminating account of the nature and method of language interpretation. In this chapter I continue to explore MMENA's bearing on issues pertaining to the interpretation of assertions. By combining some of the results from the previous three chapters, I argue that MMENA can be used to impose further constraints on the content of assertions—constraints that go beyond those established in the previous chapter. The significance of this argument lies, in part, in the challenge that it poses to a view I call Internalism about Assertoric Content.

The argument I am about to give is not without precedence. Rather, it aims to correct what might be seen as a flaw in an argument I have presented previously (for which see Goldberg 2007a: chapter 3). The strategy of that argument was to bring considerations regarding an asserter's epistemic responsibilities to bear on the determination of the content of her assertion. It began by noting that a person who makes an assertion is standardly taken as blameworthy if the face-value interpretation of her words turns out to be false or otherwise unwarranted—whatever she meant by producing those words. And it took this consideration to establish two things: first, that the phenomenon of blameworthiness standardly tracks sentence meaning, not speaker meaning;

---

[1] In later chapters I will go on to discuss issues in philosophy of mind, ethics, social philosophy, and philosophical methodology.

and second, that sentence meaning is determined by the ordinary, face-value interpretation of the sentence in the context of utterance. From this I drew the conclusion that the face-value interpretations of one's assertions stand by default, where this default is overridden only under certain specific circumstances (described in some detail there). In drawing this conclusion, however, I relied on two key assumptions. The first was that the best explanation for why it is standard to regard the speaker as blameworthy in this way is that it is *proper* to do so; and the second was that it is proper to do so precisely because the face-value-determined content *just is* the content of her assertion. One or both of these assumptions can be doubted. We might doubt the first assumption by maintaining that, while it is standard to hold people to the face-value interpretation of their words, strictly speaking it is not *proper* to do so. Alternatively, we might doubt the second assumption by maintaining that a speaker can properly be held responsible for the falsity or unwarrantedness of the face-value-determined content even if that content was not the content of her assertion.

In this chapter I aim to present an argument in this spirit *without* relying on either of these controversial assumptions. Like the argument from Goldberg (2007a), the argument I will be presenting here appeals to the sort of epistemic responsibilities that are generated by the making of an assertion. But rather than *assuming* the connection between what a speaker can be held responsible for and the content of the assertion she made, I will be *arguing* for such a connection. I will proceed as follows. In Section 5.2 I appeal to MMENA to argue that if communicative exchanges involving assertions are to have some of the features I have been describing in the first several chapters of this book, then hearers are under some pressure to favor the "face-value" interpretations. (Here I will spend some time saying precisely what makes an interpretation count as "face-value.") Then, in Section 5.3, I will use this result to argue that at least in a certain subclass of cases there is some pressure on people to favor the face-value interpretations (on pain of assertion's not playing the knowledge-communicating role we take it to play in cases of this sort). In Section 5.4 I suggest that even if the idea of face-value interpretations is a fiction, it is a useful one, where its utility lies in making vivid the constraining role that the semantic rules of a public language have in the determination of semantic content. In Section 5.5 I go on to use this result as part of a *reductio* of the hypothesis that in the case under consideration the non-standard (or non-face-value) interpretation of the assertion is correct. Finally, in Section 5.6, I argue that this sort of consideration bears against, or at least raises challenges to, a variety of theories of assertoric content.

5.2 MMENA and the Hypothesis of Face-Value Interpretations

If MMENA is true, then when a speaker S makes an assertion, it is mutually manifest that what she did is warranted only if she possesses the relevant epistemic authority. If this sort of communicative exchange is to be fully successful, then there must be some way for S and H to agree on what it would take for S's speech contribution to have been warranted. Among other things, this means that speaker and hearer alike must each have a way to determine the responsibilities that are engendered and the expectations that are rationalized by the performance of the assertoric speech act; and their determinations must agree on what those responsibilities and expectations were. We can get at the scope of these responsibilities and expectations by considering the scope of the required epistemic authority—that is, the authority that would warrant S's assertion. H must comprehend this if he is to count as having understood S's assertion. But of course, the relevant authoritativeness is S's epistemic authoritativeness *regarding the content she asserted*.[2]

It will be helpful to come at the same point by considering how things stand from the different perspectives in a speech exchange. If a hearer H is to be entitled to regard a speaker S as having the relevant authoritativeness on an occasion on which S made an assertion—something H must be if he is to be justified in accepting S's assertion—then H must be in a position to appreciate (if only implicitly) the scope of the authoritativeness required to warrant that assertion.[3] What is more, if S is to anticipate what responsibilities her audience is likely to regard her as accruing in virtue of having made the assertion she did, she must have some way to anticipate how her assertion will be regarded by an arbitrary hearer. In particular, S must anticipate the scope of the authoritativeness an arbitrary hearer will take to be relevant to the issue of her assertion's warrantedness. Since it is the content of an assertion that determines the (minimum[4]) scope of the authoritativeness required to warrant the assertion, it appears that both S and H must be in a state of coordination with respect to the content that is to be assigned to S's assertion.

But now consider that this sort of coordination—H's determination of the scope of the authoritativeness needed to warrant S's assertion, S's anticipation of the scope of authoritativeness H will take to determine the conditions on the warrantedness of

---

[2] It is controversial whether this *exhausts* the scope of the relevant authoritativeness that warrants assertion: perhaps speakers must also be authoritative regarding the obvious implicatures or presuppositions of their assertions, if those assertions are to count as warranted. (See Goldberg 2007a: 87–92 for discussion.) But whether this is so or not, the relevant authoritativeness must cover *at least* the content of the assertion. And this is all that I need for my argument here.

[3] It is here that we must bear in mind the distinction I made at the end of Chapter 4, between the epistemology of comprehension and the epistemology of acceptance. Insofar as the matter is merely to comprehend an assertion, a hearer is (defeasibly) entitled to assume that the speaker is relevantly authoritative. Call this the *comprehension entitlement*. But insofar as the matter is whether to *accept* a comprehended assertion, the comprehension entitlement does not suffice to justify him in accepting the assertion. Call the claim that the comprehension entitlement is sufficient to justify acceptance (at least when no defeaters are present) the *sufficiency thesis*. Reductionism denies the sufficiency thesis; and even among anti-reductionists the sufficiency thesis is controversial. While some (such as Coady 1992, Stevenson 1993, and arguably Burge 1993) appear to accept it, many others (Graham 2000c and Goldberg 2007a) do not. (The latter hold that while acceptance is default-justified, its status as default-justified reflects more than the comprehension entitlement alone.)

[4] See fn. 2.

S's assertion—happens in real time. So if communication is to be (not merely successful but also) an efficient means for the near-effortless spread of knowledge (or epistemically high-quality information), then these determinations must be made in an efficient and nearly-effortless fashion. And we can ask: just how does S so easily and effortlessly anticipate the authoritativeness H will likely take to be relevant to the warrantedness of S's assertion? How does H come to be in a position from which he can determine the scope of the required authoritativeness—let alone determine whether S actually is relevantly authoritative—in such an easy and effortless fashion?

In this connection, it is worth considering the idea that when we observe the speech of our colinguals, we take their words "at face value." Let us suppose for the moment that doing so is a matter of endorsing the interpretation that the assertion wears "on its face," and hence the one that is mutually accessible to all parties to the speech exchange. Of course, it is a substantial hypothesis that assertions *have* such interpretations. It may well be that this hypothesis is nothing more than a useful fiction. But I want to argue that even if it is nothing more than a useful fiction, the notion of a face-value interpretation can be used to help us see how arbitrary speakers and hearers might solve the sort of coordination problem just described. In the remainder of this section I will continue to develop the idea of face-value interpretations as though there really are such interpretations. In the section to follow I will discuss how to modify these ideas even if the idea of face-value interpretations is a fiction.

Starting with the thought that there really are face-value interpretations, I note that in that case we appear to be in a position to answer our previous questions. In particular, the face-value hypothesis enables us to account for the near-effortless on-the-fly coordination that obtains in a good many speech exchanges, even when the parties to the speech exchange have not previously interacted with one another. In particular, if what is wanted is an interpretation on which these parties can solve the coordination problems I have been discussing, "face-value" interpretations are the natural answer. If they were typically the correct interpretation, we would then have an explanation for how communication succeeds in being what it is: the efficient and near-effortless way to spread epistemically high-quality information throughout a community. If they were not typically the correct interpretation, by contrast, we would be left without an explanation of the prevalence of successful communication.

Stepping back, we can now see that parties to a speech exchange are under some pressure to regard "face-value" interpretations as correct. It is in endorsing such interpretations that hearers solve the coordination problem they face; and it is in their deference to the prevailing linguistic norms and practices—factors which determine face-value interpretations (more on this later)—that speakers solve the coordination problem *they* face.

The time has come, then, to be a bit more explicit about the key notion I am employing here—that of a "face-value" interpretation. I will call an interpretation a *face-value* interpretation when it satisfies two conditions. First, it must conform to the following quasi-disquotational schema:

QD S assertorically uttered 'p', so S asserted that q, where q = F('p', L, C)

where F is some function taking us from sentences of a language L uttered in context C to the interpretation of that use of that sentence on that occasion. Second, the function F itself must assign its interpretation by recursively employing the semantic rules or standards of the prevailing linguistic community. An interpretation that meets these two conditions is "face value"—it wears its interpretation on its face—in the sense that it is determined by the words figuring in the utterance under interpretation, together with features that are public and accessible to all. These include the standards of the shared, public language, and whatever values context needs to supply (as called for by the rules of that language).

Several comments about this notion are in order. First, in using QD to characterize what makes an interpretation "face value," I do not assume that a hearer H consciously or explicitly entertains (an instance of) QD. The idea, rather, is that H is guided in interpretation by (his recognition of) the very words S used, together with his knowledge or grasp of the semantics of the shared public language, and his knowledge of how to determine the required contextual values to arrive at the interpretation. This can be the case even when (as is typical) H engages in no explicit or conscious use of QD itself.

Second, a comment is in order on the role played by the rules or standards of the public language. Suppose that H is guided in interpretation by (his recognition of) the very words S used in making her assertion. Suppose in addition that none of these words is context-sensitive, so that when stating what S asserted H can simply re-token the sentence-type S uttered, intending to be using these words to capture what S meant with them. These two suppositions ensure that, at least in successful cases, H means whatever S meant with these words—that H's and S's uses of these words express the same proposition. Still, this is not sufficient to prevent a scenario in which S's use of these words—and so, by extension, H's redeployment of these words—was itself idiosyncratic. But to interpret someone's words "at face value" involves holding them to the "common coin" meanings of their words. Hence the requirement on conformity to the standards of the public language: this requirement is motivated by the need to ensure against idiosyncratic interpretations whose idiosyncrasy is grounded in idiosyncratic usage by the source speaker herself.

What can be said to motivate the idea that hearers typically do hold their interlocutors to these "common coin" meanings? Once again, the explanation we seek can be found by reflecting on the situation of the hearer H. It will be helpful to focus in the first instance on cases of homophonic comprehension, where (in expressing how he has comprehended S's assertion) H can and does re-deploy a token of the very same sentence-type S herself had used. (Example: S assertorically utters "The cat is on the mat," and H expresses his comprehension of S's assertion by reproducing "The cat is on the mat.") We can get an easy entry into the utility of a "common coin" when we consider that in cases such as this, the very word-types that H (re)deploys in interpreting

S's speech contribution on this occasion are themselves (re)deployed yet again by H in various other settings: not only in H's interpretations of S's other speech contributions, but also in H's interpretations of *other* speakers, and in the claims H makes more generally as well. As a result, insofar as language is the vehicle enabling the communication of information between speakers, the coordination that must be attained is not merely that between H and S but also between H and other speakers (past and future) and with H's own usage (past and future). How can this massive coordination problem be solved? It is here that the hypothesis of a shared, public language earns its keep. In particular, as hearers we come to the scene presuming that our interlocutor's usage is in accord with the norms and practices of our shared linguistic community. This presumption is defeasible, of course, as there are cases in which a speaker uses an expression in an idiosyncratic fashion. Still, as hearers we presume conformity to prevailing linguistic norms and practices, and in the absence of evidence to the contrary, this presumption informs our interpretation.

Of course, not all cases of comprehension are homophonic: in some cases, the hearer must change the sentence he uses to capture his comprehension of S's assertion. This is most obvious in cases involving indexicals and other explicitly context-sensitive terms: if you assertorically utter "I am hungry now" at 12:15 pm, and you ask me at 12:30 pm what I understood you to have asserted, I will reply "You were hungry then," indicating the point in time at which you made the assertion. Still, in these cases interpretation is "face value" (and "common coin" meanings are utilized) in that interpretation remains under the explicit guidance of the semantic standards of the language we have in common, in obvious ways. In particular, I am guided by your use of "I" to pick you out as the reference (it being a rule of English that "I" refers to the subject who produced the token, and in context that subject is you), and I am guided by your use of "now" to pick out the time of your utterance (it being a rule of English that "now" refers to some more or less definite interval of time surrounding the production of the token, and in context I used "then" to pick up the reference anaphorically). Perhaps other types of context-sensitive expression can be handled in like fashion; one thinks here of such things as the so-called comparative adjectives such as "tall" (where the relevant comparison class is provided by context).

Of course, there are other varieties of context-sensitivity, and not all of them are such that the contextually-provided contribution to the proposition asserted is under the explicit guidance of the semantic rules of the language. Consider cases of disambiguation, as when "Sally's book" must be disambiguated in the context use to indicate whether it is a book *belonging to Sally*, or *currently in her possession*, or *of her authorship*, and so on. In addition there is what Bach (1997) calls the variety of *widely pragmatic* phenomena, where the contextually-supplied information is not under the guidance of semantic rules at all. Here we might locate what in pragmatics is known as *free enrichment*, as when "John has already eaten" is taken to mean that John has already eaten today, or has already eaten dinner, or ... In the previous paragraph we saw that cases in which the contextually-supplied values are under the strict control of the rules of the language pose no problem for the face-value hypothesis, since the proposition yielded by F('p,' L, C) is itself under the strict control of the "common coin" meanings (the semantic rules of the common language). But cases in which the contextually-supplied values are not under the strict control of the rules of the language are not recoverable in this fashion; they require *wide pragmatic processing* (Bach 1997). But even in such cases there will be a proposition yielded by F('p,' L, C), and while this proposition will not be the one "meant" by the speaker, it will be such that the one "meant" by the speaker must be recoverable from it through some widely pragmatic process. In that case I will describe the proposition "meant" by the speaker as Wide Pragmatic Enrichment, or WPE, of the face-value proposition. In such cases, the hearer still relies on the face-value interpretation in comprehension, if only as the material on which to arrive at the WPE proposition itself. And, as we will see later, this will be sufficient for the purposes of the argument to follow.

I have just been arguing that face-value interpretations play a central role in hearers' comprehension of assertions: these interpretations either constitute what the hearer takes the speaker to have asserted, or else they are required in the course of the hearers' recovery of what was asserted (where what was asserted is some WPE of the face-value interpretation). I now want to consider how the hypothesis of face-value interpretations can be used to explain how in typical cases hearers are in a position to discern the scope of the epistemic authoritativeness required to warrant the assertions they observe. Suppose that face-value interpretations are typically the interpretations that hearers favor (in one of the two ways just mentioned) in interpreting an apparent colingual's words. The result would be that insofar as the content of a given assertion just is the face-value-determined content, or some WPE of the face-value-determined content, a hearer who so interprets the assertion is in a position to discern the scope of the epistemic authoritativeness required to warrant the assertion. In the simple case, where the content asserted just is the one identified by the face-value interpretation, the hearer discerns the scope of the epistemic authoritativeness required to warrant the assertion in the very act of interpreting the assertion at face value. In the other case, where the content asserted is some WPE of the content identified by the face-value interpretation, the hearer discerns something that *substantially constrains* the scope of the required authoritativeness: it must be some content that is recoverable as a WPE of the face-value interpretation. In that case, insofar as both the speaker and the hearer are pragmatically competent, there should be no in-principle difficulty in coordination. Of course, precise coordination in this sort of case is more complicated, and harder to achieve; but perhaps this is to be expected (and so the fact that this little model predicts such complication is a feature, not a bug).

Of course, anyone who accepts this account of successful communication must face the question of how there can be "face-value" interpretations. What is it about our language communities, or our language, that enables speech acts to have "face-value" interpretations in the first place? This is a matter about which many others have written extensively elsewhere. Here I propose to be very brief.[5] Speech acts might have

---

[5] But see Goldberg (2007a) for a more detailed, Burge-inspired account.

"face-value" interpretations so long as these acts are executed by way of doing things with a shared, public language—one with standards of correct usage. These standards enable S and H to calibrate their reactions to and expectations of one another's speech behavior: it is in terms of these standards that S anticipates H's reaction to S's assertion; and it is in terms of these standards as well that H determines the scope of the authoritativeness required to warrant that assertion. I cannot claim to have offered a knock-down proof of the existence of such languages and their attendant norms; I can only say that in the absence of such language and their attendant norms we are owed an explanation of various of the core features that assertion-based communication appears to have.

5.3 The Idea of Face-Value Interpretations as a Useful Fiction

In the previous section I argued that we can account for various features of assertion-based communication on the assumption that the proper interpretation of an assertion is typically either the face-value interpretation or else some WPE of that interpretation. However, some may continue to doubt whether it is true that, for each assertoric utterance, there is always, or even typically, a single proposition that deserves to be described as *the* "face-value" interpretation of that assertion. Even those who endorse the Burge-inspired idea of public language standards of correct usage might recoil at the idea of a single proposition that deserves to be so described. In this section I will argue that even if such doubts are warranted, and so even if the idea of face-value interpretation is a fiction, still, the idea remains a useful one in the present context. In particular, it can still be used as part of an account of the features of assertion-based communication to which I have been drawing out attention in this chapter.

Recall the challenge. On the assumption of MMENA, there are mutually manifest normative expectations that hearers and speakers have of one other, centered on the scope of the epistemic authority required to warrant the speaker's assertion. The challenge is to account for the fact that in typical cases involving an arbitrary speaker–hearer combination of (apparent) colinguals, the speaker and hearer are able to align in a highly efficient and apparently effortless way on the scope of the relevant entitlements and responsibilities involved in the speaker's having asserted as she did. (These are the types of entitlements and responsibilities I discussed in Chapter 3.) If true, the hypothesis of face-value interpretations can explain how this is done. The explanation is as follows. The scope of the warranting authoritativeness just is (or at least centers on)[6] the asserted content. But now suppose that the correct interpretation is either the face-value interpretation itself, or else some interpretation that involves a WPE of the

---

[6] I speak of the scope of the authoritativeness "centering on" the asserted content if only to capture the idea that the scope can include obvious implicatures as well.

face-value interpretation. In the former case, all the materials needed to interpret the utterance, and hence to recover the asserted content, are publicly available, and involve only the participants' linguistic competence (including competence at identifying the relevant contextually-supplied values for expressions whose semantic rules call out for such values). And since the content for which the speaker requires relevant authority if her assertion is to be warranted just is the content identified in a correct interpretation of her speech act, the result would be that this sort of linguistic competence would suffice to enable the speaker and hearer to align on the entitlements and responsibilities attendant to the speaker's asserting as she has. In the latter case, where the correct interpretation is some WPE of the face-value interpretation, we need only complicate this picture a little by adding that (in addition to linguistic competence of the sort just described) wide pragmatic processing is also needed in the determination of the scope of the speaker's required authoritativeness. This will make such a determination a more complicated affair, with the result that a precise alignment will be more difficult to achieve; but this is precisely what we would expect in such cases. I now want to suggest that even if there is no single proposition that is ever singled out as *the* face-value interpretation of another's speech, even so, the materials employed by the face-value account can play a crucial role in helping us to address this challenge.

My idea is simply this. So long as there are public standards for the use of expressions, these standards can be used to constrain the scope of the speaker's required authoritativeness (when she makes an assertion by way of producing an utterance of a public language sentence). This is true whether or not these standards yield a unique proposition as *the* face-value interpretation of her sentence. And this constraining feature is crucial to how speakers and hearers align in particular cases. Of course, if there is no unique proposition singled out as the face-value interpretation, then somehow both the speaker and the hearer will need to determine which, of the propositions available as candidates for being the proposition asserted, is the proposition asserted. (Or perhaps there will be more than one proposition asserted, as in the speech act pluralism of Cappelen and Lepore 2005—in which case the scope of the speaker's required authoritativeness will extend to include all the propositions asserted.) In such a case, achieving a precise alignment will be correspondingly more difficult.[7] It will presumably involve all of the widely pragmatic processes mentioned previously (in connection with WPEs). And there remains the possibility that there is no definite answer to the question *Which proposition(s) was/were asserted?*, beyond pointing to some collection of propositions and being told that whichever it is (they are), it is (they are) among that collection. In this case, precise communication will be a much messier affair. But

---

[7] Or is it? One possible hypothesis is this: the selection of one proposition, from among the set of all candidate propositions in the mix (that is, those whose ascription to the assertion would conform to the standards of public usage of the shared language), is achieved simply in virtue of the hearer's intention to be using her words to express the same proposition as the speaker had expressed. It would be interesting to see what implications there would be for such a view. Space limitations prevent me from following up on this here, however.

still—and importantly—there is a crucial role being played by public standards of usage. For in effect, these standards narrow the field of possible candidates considerably. In effect, speakers and hearers do not approach one another blindly, having to arrive anew at an interpretation of each speaker as if performing Radical Interpretation each time. Rather, they approach one another *as colinguals*—that is, as sharing a public language whose standards for correct usage delimit the possible things that can be asserted by speakers using that language (at least in those cases in which the speakers themselves have no idiosyncratic intentions not to conform to standard usage; more on this in Section 5.4).

In short, I claim that a core part of what lies behind the idea of face-value interpretations—in particular, the idea of public languages with standards of correct usage—will be part of any plausible account of how speakers and hearers align in assertion-based speech. It is perhaps clear from the foregoing how such a proposed explanation would proceed. What is less clear is why we should think that any adequate explanation will have to take something like this form. It is to this issue that I now turn.

5.4 Against Idiosyncrasy

I have just argued that hearers (and speakers) are under some pressure to favor (one or another of) the face-value interpretation(s) of others' assertions. To be sure, things are not so simple: there are cases in which the correct interpretation is not the face-value interpretation itself, but rather some WPE of that interpretation; and it may even be the case that the very idea of face-value interpretations is itself a fiction, albeit a useful one. But at any rate, if hearers are to be in a position in which to determine the scope of the epistemic authoritativeness required to warrant an observed assertion, and if speakers are to be in a position in which to anticipate what their audience will take to be the scope of that authoritativeness, and if all of this is to happen (in real time) in an easy and efficient way, then hearers and speakers have little choice but to favor interpretations that conform to the standards of usage of the public language that they share. Any interpretation that conforms to such a set of constraints I will call a face-value* interpretation. Hearers should prefer these interpretations when it comes to how they comprehend an observed assertion; and speakers should prefer to be so understood when they make assertions. This line of reasoning is generic, in the sense that it yields a conclusion about how things are (or should be) in general. It is generic in another sense as well: it does not establish that the face-value* interpretation is true in any particular case. What is more, it is clear that people do sometimes use their words idiosyncratically, and in at least some of these cases the face-value* interpretation (or the WPE derived from it) would be an incorrect interpretation. What is wanted—what I hope to provide in this section—is an argument that enables us to draw conclusions in particular cases regarding the content of the assertions that were made.

What I will argue in this section is that *in an important subset of cases*, successful communication depends on the correctness of face-value* interpretations. The subset in question consists of cases involving what I call 'ordinary conditions': they are cases in ordinary conversational contexts involving participants who know little of each other beyond what they learn in the course of the conversation itself, and who defer to the prevailing norms and practices of their shared linguistic community. I will argue for this by way of *reductio*, showing that any non-standard interpretation of an assertion made under 'ordinary conditions' will lead to unacceptable results.

Let a content ascription be any ascription of the form (*Speech act*) *A had the propositional content that p*. Let a theory of assertoric content for a language L be any theory which is such that, given any assertion α that was performed by using a sentence of L, the theory yields a content ascription for α.[8] I offer the following as a recipe for bringing out the key point. Begin with a case in which the speaker makes an assertion under conditions in which she is epistemically authoritative regarding the face-value*-determined content.[9] Then vary background conditions so that, while she is still epistemically authoritative regarding that content, she is *not* epistemically authoritative regarding the content ascribed by the non-standard content ascription. My main contention is that in at least some of these cases, the assertion she made is nevertheless warranted. More explicitly:

> In at least some of the cases in which the speaker S is *not* relevantly epistemically authoritative regarding whether q, where [q] is the content ascribed by some non-standard ascription, but *is* relevantly epistemically authoritative regarding whether p, where [p] is the content ascribed by the face-value interpretation, the assertion S made is warranted.

(Call this 'The Contention.') The burden of the argument to follow is that The Contention is true in cases involving 'ordinary conditions.'

To illustrate, I offer the following variant on a familiar example from the literature. Sally is doing a research project on common but mistaken views about health. Being old-fashioned, she goes to the library and does research. Over the course of her research she reads a good many authoritative texts. In one of those texts she comes across a claim made by way of the following sentence: 'Arthritis affects children as well as adults.' Consequently, she comes to acquire a belief that she expresses by assertorically uttering 'Arthritis affects children as well as adults.' She does so on the basis of accepting the book's claim. (She knows that the book was written by one of the world's

---

[8] Slightly more formally: let C(α, L) be a content ascription for an assertion α of language L. Then C(α, L) is *face-value* when the following conditions hold: (i) ℓ is some public language, (ii) it is mutually manifest to the members of the speech exchange that L = ℓ, and (iii) C(α, L) = C(α, ℓ).

[9] If one favors the speech-act pluralism of Cappelen and Lepore (2005), then replace 'content' with 'contents', where this is taken to cover all and only the propositions that are asserted, according to that theory. I will not bother with this complication in what follows, but will pretend as though only one proposition is asserted in each act of assertion.

leading experts on the health topics that are discussed in the book.) The book in question went on at some length regarding the symptoms and prevalence of juvenile rheumatoid arthritis. On the basis of having accepted the expert's recorded views, it would seem that Sally is relevantly epistemically authoritative regarding whether arthritis affects children as well as adults.[10] Now imagine a theory of assertoric content on which Sally's assertion of 'Arthritis affects children as well as adults' does not have as its content the proposition *that arthritis affects children as well as adults*. For the sake of concreteness, suppose that this theory regards her assertion as having a metalinguistic content: *that the disease commonly known as 'arthritis' affects children as well as adults*. (This ascription is being chosen only for the sake of illustration; any non-standard content will do, as we shall see later.) Now, it is easy to imagine changes in the scenario so that, while Sally remains epistemically authoritative regarding whether arthritis affects children as well as adults (where *that arthritis affects children as well as adults* is the content of the proposition regarding whose truth she is epistemically authoritative), she is *not* epistemically authoritative regarding whether the disease commonly known as 'arthritis' affects children as well as adults (where *that the disease commonly known as 'arthritis' affects children as well as adults* is the content of the relevant proposition). So, suppose for example that—unbeknownst to Sally—very recent linguistic changes are afoot, and it is no longer so common for the condition involving inflammation of the joints to be known as 'arthritis'. (The expert's book, though not old, was written before these recent linguistic changes took place. Even so, the book remains perfectly authoritative regarding the properties and prevalence of the condition in question, even as it is somewhat out of date in calling this condition 'arthritis'.) In that case, Sally is *not* relevantly epistemically authoritative regarding whether the disease commonly known as 'arthritis' affects children as well as adults. But then, given MMENA, if the content of Sally's assertion is the non-standard (metalinguistic) content, her assertion is not warranted. And yet this seems wrong: why think that Sally's failure to be epistemically authoritative regarding recent linguistic changes in the designation of the condition have any bearing on the warrantedness of her assertion?

It might be replied that the lesson I am drawing from this case depends on a very specific metalinguistic content ascription, and so does not generalize well. For example, suppose that the metalinguistic content of Sally's claim was *that the condition which this particular author called 'arthritis' affects children as well as adults*. Then the counterfactual scenario I have described previously would not show that Sally fails to be relevantly epistemically authoritative, and so would not show that Sally's assertion is unwarranted. For even if the content of her assertion is this metalinguistic content,

---

[10] Keep in mind that the relevant sort of authoritativeness is the sort of authoritativeness needed to warrant assertion. Clearly, Sally is no expert regarding arthritis merely in virtue of having read about the condition; but this is acceptable, since expertise is not necessary for one to be warranted in making assertions about arthritis. It suffices if one is in a sufficiently good epistemic position regarding the particular claim in question; and for this, acquiring one's information from the testimony of an expert (under conditions in which one was entitled to accept her say-so) suffices.

and so the relevant authoritativeness concerns this, still, it would seem that she is relevantly authoritative: after all, Sally read a book in which the author referred to a disease as 'arthritis' and claimed of it that it affects children; simple inferences from this would appear to put Sally in a position in which she is authoritative regarding whether the condition which this particular author called 'arthritis' affects children as well as adults.

In response, it would be easy to imagine yet another scenario in which Sally remains epistemically authoritative regarding whether arthritis affects children as well as adults, but *not* epistemically authoritative regarding whether the condition which this particular author called 'arthritis' affects children as well as adults. Here is a case. The author of the book was one of the world's leading experts on arthritis, but he has a linguistic peculiarity: he called this condition by a name no one else had ever heard of. He persisted in doing this throughout his career. However, the editors at the press, knowing that this would lessen the book's utility for the general population, replaced the name the expert used with 'arthritis'. (Suppose that they told the author that they were merely going to make cosmetic changes to the manuscript to enable it to be better utilized by the public, and the author agreed, without knowing what changes were in store.) As a result, although the book on which Sally based her assertion used 'arthritis', it was not the author of that book who had used the term, but the editors. In this case, Sally is not relevantly epistemically authoritative regarding whether the condition which this particular author called 'arthritis' affects children as well as adults. In fact, Sally knows nothing about the author's use of 'arthritis'. Yet Sally (who is ignorant of the author's linguistic peculiarities, but knows of him that he is an expert regarding the health issues mentioned in his book) remains epistemically authoritative regarding whether arthritis affects children as well as adults.

This example should make clear that my point does not depend on the particular metalinguistic construal that I presented previously. On the contrary, it generalizes quite naturally: given MMENA, *any* non-standard content ascription (to an assertion made in ordinary contexts) will yield false predictions about the scope of the authoritativeness required to warrant the assertion. To bring this out we need only follow the previous recipe in a case not involving a metalinguistic content ascription. We can model such a case on examples familiar from the literature on semantic externalism and anti-individualism, in which a speaker S uses an expression regarding whose application conditions S has *false beliefs*. The most familiar case from the literature is Burge's Burt, who regularly makes assertions using the word-form 'arthritis' but who believes—falsely—that the condition in question occurs not only in the joints but also in the thigh. If asked, Burt might reply that 'arthritis' refers to an inflammatory condition affecting both the joints and the thigh. Now imagine a theory of assertoric content, N^*, that interpreted Burt's use of 'arthritis' to express a concept that was true of an inflammatory disease of the joints and thigh. So when Burt assertorically utters 'Arthritis is more common than cancer,' N^* assigns that assertion a content which is true only if there is an inflammatory condition affecting the joints and the thigh, which condition is more common than cancer; and when Burt assertorically utters, 'I have arthritis in my knees,' N^* assigns that assertion a content which is true if and only if (there is an inflammatory condition affecting the joints and the thigh, and this condition affects Burt's knees). Of course, there is no such condition; so on the content ascriptions yielded by N^*, these two 'arthritis'-assertions come out false. What is more, none of these interpretations will be face-value* interpretations, since the standards of English do not sanction applications of 'arthritis' to diseases of the ligaments. As Burge (1979) noted, this is already a strike against such a construal. But my present point is different from Burge's. My point is that N^*'s construals of Burt's 'arthritis'-assertions risk rendering Burt guilty (not merely of having said something false, but also) of having done something *unwarranted* in asserting as he did.[11]

We can reach this result by applying MMENA to the case of Burt's 'arthritis'-assertions. When we do so we get the result that those assertions are proper only if he had the relevant epistemic authority. But Burt *lacked* that authority with respect to the contents N^* ascribed to his assertions. After all, Burt is not a doctor; most of what he believes regarding the condition he calls 'arthritis' he learned from others—in which case he has the requisite authority only if they did. But surely those from whose testimonies Burt acquired his 'arthritis'-beliefs were not *themselves* using 'arthritis' to designate an inflammatory condition of the joints and the thigh. Nor did they have relevant expertise (or even epistemic authority) regarding such a condition. The result is that, insofar as we render Burt's 'arthritis'-assertions as pertaining to an inflammatory condition of the joints and the thigh, *Burt himself is not relevantly epistemically authoritative*. In this way we see that the combination of N^* and MMENA (together with prevailing background conditions) imply that Burt's assertions were unwarranted. But this result is unacceptable: intuitively, Burt *was* relevantly epistemically authoritative. Or we can easily tell the story so that this is the case. Thus assume that he was told both that arthritis is more common than cancer and that he has arthritis in his knee, by his local doctor (these were the contents of the doctor's assertions). What is more, assume that Burt knows that his doctor is highly reliable on health matters, and so was justified in accepting what the doctor told him. Then Burt's own 'arthritis'-assertions, based as they are on the doctor's authoritative word, were warranted. So N^*, which implied the contrary, should be rejected.

The example of Burt, as well as the example of Sally, involves assertions formed on the basis of another's testimony. But I want to re-emphasize that this is an inessential feature of the examples. What is driving my use of the examples of Burt and Sally is not the fact that their assertions are testimony-based, but the fact that the speaker

---

[11] It is worth noting that if knowledge (or any other truth-entailing epistemic status) is the norm of assertion, then it follows from Burt's having asserted falsely that Burt has asserted improperly. However, if the norm of assertion is a non-truth-entailing epistemic status, then false assertions will not be a subset of improper assertions. As I am remaining neutral on the particular content of assertion's norm, I am not entering this debate here; I write as I do only to emphasize that the implication regarding the impropriety of Burt's assertion holds *whatever the norm of assertion happens to be*.

lacks epistemic authority regarding the non-standard (non-face-value*-determined) contents. So long as this feature remains in place, it does not matter what grounds the epistemic authority regarding the face-value*-determined contents—that is, whether it is another's testimony, or the speaker's own proprietary evidence.

5.5 Against Internalism about Assertoric Content

In this chapter I have been appealing to MMENA in conjunction with humdrum facts about the prevalence of efficient and near-effortless knowledge communication through assertions. My aim in doing so has been to motivate the claim that there are constraints on a theory of assertoric content that go beyond what was discussed (in connection with the methodology of interpretation) in Chapter 4. In particular, my claim has been that we have reasons to favor content ascriptions that preserve the face-value* interpretation of sincere assertions made under 'ordinary conditions'. In this penultimate section I want to suggest how this constraint has bite. To do so I will be discussing several theories of semantic content which, I will claim, violate, or threaten to violate, this constraint. These theories have in common a shared assumption about the supervenience base for ascriptions of semantic content. It is because of this assumption, I will be arguing, that the theories themselves appear to run afoul of the face-value* constraint (FV*).

I begin with the shared assumption. I will label this assumption "Individualism about Assertoric Content," which I formulate as follows:

> IAC   For all speakers S and assertoric speech acts A, the propositional (assertoric) content of A does not depend for its individuation on anything beyond the internal states of S.

So formulated, IAC is programmatic: it does not tell us what constitutes the "internal states" of a subject. On some versions of IAC, S's internal states (henceforth, her 'I-states') are states of her physical body; on other versions, S's I-states are her phenomenal states.[12] But whichever way we go in spelling out I-states, IAC insists that the propositional content of an assertion of S's is fixed by facts *regarding S herself*—facts that do not involve or presuppose anything beyond S.

IAC is *not* a thesis about the methodology or epistemology of interpretation (comprehension); it is a thesis about content-individuation. This said, it has implications for the epistemology of comprehension. In particular, if IAC is true, then it is hard to see how face-value* interpretations will regularly be true in all cases of assertions made in 'ordinary circumstances.' The contours of the difficulty are not hard to discern, at least in outline form. Face-value* interpretations are interpretations that

---

[12] I take this, or something like it, to be the view of Loar (2003), Farkas (2007), Henderson and Horgan (2007), and Kriegel (2011, 2013).

respect the prevailing standards of usage within S's and H's shared speech community. But these standards of usage do not supervene on the I-states of either H or S. Hence the key difficulty facing the proponent of IAC, which is to ensure that (1) the I-states of the speaker S are such that S's assertion (made in 'ordinary circumstances') is to be ascribed the (or a) face-value*-determined content, and (2) the I-states of hearer H are such that H's comprehension of S's assertion ascribes to that assertion the (or a) face-value*-determined content. I will call the first of these, (1), the "speaker-FV* requirement," and the second of these, (2), the "hearer-FV* requirement". If a theory of assertoric content fails to ensure the satisfaction of (1), the speaker-FV* requirement, it will yield false predictions about the scope of the authoritativeness required to warrant S's assertion. If a theory of assertoric content fails to ensure (2), the hearer-FV* requirement, it will yield false predictions about what arbitrary hearers will regard as the scope of the authoritativeness required to warrant S's assertion. In either case, failure to ensure these things will render the theory susceptible to the sorts of objection presented in Section 5.5.

IAC, of course, is a general thesis about the supervenience base for ascriptions of assertoric content; it is not itself a theory of assertoric content. To derive such a theory we need to descend from the heights of IAC, to consider particular proposals that conform to IAC. In what follows I will consider three such proposals. I will discuss (i) Radical Holism (RH) about belief and meaning, (ii) Inferential-Role Semantics (IRS), and (iii) Foundationalist Phenomenalism (FP). (These do not exhaust the possibilities, of course, but are paradigms of IAC views; and I suggest that variations will be similar enough that my discussion here will carry over to them.) In the case of RH it is clear that the proposal will regularly fail to satisfy one or both of the FV* requirements. With respect to the other two theories, matters are more complicated. Perhaps they can satisfy the FV* requirements; but given the doubts that exist on this score, the burden is on proponents of these views to show that they can.

Let RH be the thesis that the meaning of an expression τ on an occasion of use O by a speaker S is determined by all τ-beliefs S has on O: these τ-beliefs individuate the meaning of τ on O.[13] And let a τ-belief be any belief in whose linguistic expression the word-type τ occurs (used rather than mentioned). RH implies that any difference in τ-beliefs is *ipso facto* a difference in meaning. It should be clear that such a view is a non-starter. In particular, it lacks the resources to ensure the satisfaction of either the speaker-FV* requirement or the hearer-FV* requirement. It lacks the resources to ensure the satisfaction of the speaker-FV* requirement, since there is nothing that ensures that the totality of τ-beliefs S has on O will match the relevant usage standards of S's speech community. Since face-value* interpretations are interpretations that respect the prevailing usage standards of that community, the result is that there is nothing to prevent the totality of τ-beliefs S has on O from determining some content

---

[13] This may be the view of Bilgrami (1992).

other than the (or a) face-value*-determined content. A similar point can be made in connection with RH's inability to ensure that the hearer-FV* requirement is satisfied. Thus it would be easy to describe cases in which, given the τ-beliefs of either S or H on O, either the speaker-FV* requirement or the hearer-FV* requirement (or both) fail(s) to be satisfied.

If the difficulty facing RH derives from the fact that it regards *all* of S's τ-beliefs on O as relevant to the individuation of the meaning S expresses with τ on O, Inferential-Role Semantics (IRS) is motivated by one lesson we might take from the difficulties facing RH on this score. The lesson is this. Suppose that it is true that the meaning of an expression τ (in a given speaker's idiolect) depends on the connections τ bears to other expressions in her idiolect, where these connections are seen in the set of sentences that the speaker would use to express the totality of her τ-beliefs. Even so, it will not do to think that *all* of these sentences are relevant. For if we include all of the sentences she accepts in determining what τ means, we obtain the following unhappy implication: if she forms new τ-beliefs (accepts a new τ-sentence) or gives up old ones (no longer accepts a τ-sentence she once accepted), the meaning of τ changes. To avoid this implication, there must be some principled way to distinguish those connections that are part of τ's meaning, so to speak, and those that are not. IRS addresses this matter as follows: τ's meaning consists in the *canonical inferences* in which τ figures. The notion of a canonical inference can be spelled out in a variety of ways: perhaps it is a matter of those inferences that the speaker accepts merely in virtue of her understanding of τ;[14] or those τ-involving inferences that the speaker would accept whatever empirical information about the world she has or could get; or those τ-involving inferences that the speaker finds primitively compelling; or those τ-involving inferences that the speaker, on reflection, endorses, and which she would not surrender come what may; or . . . The proposal, then, is that the meaning of τ is its inferential role.

The challenge facing IRS is straightforward. Because IRS regards meaning as determined by inferential role, and regards inferential role as determined by the canonical inferences that the subject herself accepts, the result is that IRS cannot guarantee that the inferential role a given word-form has for S and for H matches the inferential role that the word-form has *for the public language*. Suppose S is such that, for a good many of the word-types she uses in communication with others, she cannot produce, and in many cases cannot even recognize when produced, the standards of usage for that word-form that are prevalent in her community. Putnam's famous example of 'beech' and 'elm' illustrates. Putnam noted that he did not know the difference between beeches and elms: presented with various proposals regarding what the difference between beeches and elms might be, he was not in a position to discern the proposal that captures those differences. Now consider the implications of this for IRS. If the meaning of 'beech' in Putnam's idiolect is given by the canonical inferences (accepted

---

[14] This assumes that we have some prior and independent characterization of what is involved in understanding an expression.

by Putnam) in which 'beech' figures, these inferences might not discriminate between the meaning of 'beech' and the meaning of 'elm'. Thus they might include 'If something is a beech it is a tree', 'If something is a beech it is deciduous', and so forth. But he might also accept each of the sentences that results when we replace 'beech' with 'elm'. And there might be no difference, save inferences to conclusions about what the trees are called, that differentiate the sets of canonical inferences he accepts for each. The result, of course, would be that, by the lights of IRS, the only difference in meaning between 'beech' and 'elm' in Putnam's idiolect would consist in a difference in the metalinguistic inferences he drew: "If something is a beech then people in the US will typically refer to it with the word 'beech'", and so on. In that case, IRS will face the difficulties I presented previously in connection with metalinguistic construals of assertions. Besides, it will not sanction face-value* interpretations in these cases, and so will run afoul of one or both of the FV* requirements in such cases (whenever the assertions are produced under 'ordinary circumstances').

I would diagnose the problem facing the proponent of IRS as follows. Speakers are sometimes (and arguably often) ignorant of the public standards for correct use of word-forms that figure in their own idiolect. Such speakers will not latch onto the "canonical inferences" that will capture these criteria. The result is that IRS cannot ensure the satisfaction of the speaker-FV* requirement for such speakers; and so we can construct examples in which (by the lights of IRS) this requirement is not satisfied. The same point can made in connection with hearers who are ignorant of the public standards for correct use of word-forms that figure in the speaker's idiolect: IRS has no way to ensure that the hearer-FV* requirement is satisfied for such hearers, and so we can construct examples in which (by the lights of IRS) this requirement is not satisfied. In this way we see that IRS, like RH before it, will yield false predictions regarding the scope of the authoritativeness needed to warrant assertions, and/or false predictions regarding what arbitrary hearers take to be the scope of this authoritativeness.

One final theory of assertoric content that is in accord with IAC is what I will call Foundationalist Phenomenalism (FP).[15] The basic idea behind FP is that phenomenal content is the basis for mental content generally. If applied at the level of language, the thesis would be that each non-logical and non-indexical expression of a subject S's idiolect is equivalent in meaning to a complex expression that is a logical construction out of other expressions in S's idiolect, where each of these other expressions designate phenomenal feature-types. Such a view can be usefully regarded as a contemporary linguistic version of what at one time went under the name "phenomenalism." I want to raise two difficulties for FP in connection with assertion-based communication: the problem of idiosyncratic experience, and (as a special case of this first problem) the problem of expert assertion.

---

[15] Such a view appears to be endorsed by Henderson and Horgan (2007), Farkas (2007), Loar (2003), and Kriegel (2011, 2013).

The problem of idiosyncratic experience is based on the idea that if FP is true, then whether the meaning of an expression-form in S's idiolect is to be assigned its 'face-value' interpretation—the interpretation determined by the prevailing norms and practices of the speech community—will depend on the course of S's experiences. We can make the present point in a vivid albeit admittedly overly-simplified way, as follows. Let us speak of the meaning of an expression on an occasion of use as what that expression contributes to the proposition expressed by the use of that expression on that occasion. (Here I restrict this to expressions whose contributions are not determined in a token-sensitive fashion.) In these terms, FP holds that the meaning of an expression in S's idiolect is to be characterized in phenomenalist terms (which themselves refer to phenomenal feature-types exemplified in S's experiences). If this is correct, then whether a given word-form in S's idiolect is assigned the face-value* meaning will depend on whether the face-value* meaning is synonymous with the phenomenalist characterization in question, which in turn will depend on the course of S's relevant experiences.[16] Idiosyncratic experiences, then, threaten to have the result that the meaning a given word-form has in S's idiolect differs from the face-value* meaning of that word-form. Depending on how widespread are the differences across speakers in the phenomenal characterizations that each assigns to a given word-form, we might have a case where few if any word-forms of anyone's language are ever correctly interpreted in terms of the face-value* meaning. A wholesale violation of the speaker-FV* requirement looms. (And similar remarks are in place regarding the hearer in her attempt to comprehend a speaker.)

It is important to appreciate the extent of the difficulty here. No doubt, as a subject gains experience both of the world and of other speakers' use of the word-form in question, the differences between the phenomenal characterization that characterizes the meaning of the word-form in *her* idiolect and those that characterize the meaning of the word-form in other speakers' idiolects will be reduced. But what reasons do we have to expect that these differences will generally be eliminated? Or that at no time will the incidence of subjects with idiosyncratic experiences relative to a given word-form get in the way of successful communication, in cases in which the intuitive verdict would have been otherwise? It seems that we are owed much more before we can be sanguine about the risks FP is running with respect to both the speaker-FV* requirement and the hearer-FV* requirement.

A special case, or what we might see as a special case, of the problem of idiosyncratic experience is the problem of expert assertion. Consider an exchange between an expert and a non-expert, where the latter aims to learn from the former on some topic within her (the expert's) expertise. Presumably the two subjects will have very different relevant experiences (in the sense of 'relevant experiences' characterized in fn. 16). In that case, they will mean very different things by some of the

---

[16] Here, an experience is relevant when S's having that experience bears on the phenomenalist characterization of the meaning of the word-form.

word-forms each uses (the expert in her assertion, and the non-expert in his homophonic comprehension of the expert's assertion). We then get the result that the hearer (here, the non-expert) fails to recover the content of the speaker's (here, the expert's) assertion.

Whether the hearer's failure to recover the content of the assertion is owed to idiosyncratic experience or to the difference between his expertise and the speaker's, the result will be a further distancing from the natural picture of the linguistic communication that is suggested by MMENA. To see this, consider these matters from the perspective of the assertion-oriented communication of knowledge. Suppose a hearer's homophonic comprehension of a speaker's assertion does not succeed in capturing the propositional content of the assertion itself—whether because one or both of them had idiosyncratic relevant experiences, or because we have a case of an expert and a non-expert. Then once again we confront the following situation. Hearer H will regard speaker S as having made an assertion that is proper only if S is epistemically authoritative regarding what H has comprehended S as having asserted. Stronger, H will regard himself as *entitled* to so regard S. But in fact, since H has not preserved the content of S's assertion, what H regards as the relevant epistemic authoritativeness needed to warrant the assertion is not what in fact is the epistemic authoritativeness needed to warrant the assertion. Once again, we have a case in which a theory of assertoric content—here, FP—makes false predictions regarding the scope of the authoritativeness required to warrant the assertion, and/or false predictions regarding what an arbitrary hearer will regard as the relevant scope of that authoritativeness.

I have argued that any theory of assertoric content that conforms to IAC's internalist strictures will be hard-pressed to preserve the face-value* interpretations of assertions. We now see that the problem is more fundamental than this: particular internalist theories of assertoric content are hard-pressed to see how content can be so much as preserved across ordinary assertion-oriented communicative exchanges. This is a problem, since I have argued that content preservation generally, and content preservation that is underwritten by face-value* interpretations in particular, is part of the best explanation we have for the efficiency and near-effortlessness of assertion-based communication of knowledge (or epistemically high-quality information). To be sure, there are many more IAC accounts; but space limitations prevent me from covering all of them, and prevent me as well from entering into details about those I did cover. But I think I have said enough to warrant the following conclusion: several of the main IAC accounts face challenges in this connection, for reasons that appear to stem from the internalistic orientation of these accounts. We should expect that other IAC accounts will face similar difficulties. If I am correct about this, then to the extent that FV* really is a constraint on the interpretation of sincere assertion, internalist approaches to linguistic content will be hard-challenged to satisfy this constraint.

5.6 Conclusion

I want to conclude this chapter by returning to the comparison between the argument I have offered in this chapter, and a similar argument I presented in Chapter 3 of Goldberg (2007a), in which I argued that a person who testifies is standardly taken as blameworthy if the face-value interpretation of her words turns out to be false or otherwise unwarranted—whatever she meant by producing those words. As I noted at the outset of this chapter, the argument of Goldberg (2007a) supports the hypothesis that face-value interpretations are generally *correct* only by making two auxiliary assumptions: first, that the best explanation for why it is standard to regard the speaker as blameworthy in this way was that it is *proper* to do so, and second, that it is proper to do so precisely because the face-value-determined content *just is* the content of her testimony-constituting assertion. As I noted in Section 5.3, the argument of this chapter has no need for either of these assumptions. To see this, let us waive these assumptions; and let us waive as well any assumption to the effect that for any assertion there is a single proposition picked out as the "face-value" interpretation of the assertion. Even so, to the extent that one's favored theory of semantic content yields nonstandard (non-face-value*) content ascriptions to particular assertions, to just that extent one's theory risks yielding false predictions regarding the warrantedness of the assertions in question across a range of counterfactual circumstances. A proper appreciation of this, I argued, will have us favor face-value* interpretations, at least in those ("ordinary circumstances") cases in which the speaker herself aimed to be in conformity with prevailing linguistic standards. Since this result derives from the hypothesis that it is mutually manifest to participants to a speech exchange that assertion has an epistemic norm—MMENA—the result is that MMENA itself can be used to establish constraints on interpretation that extend beyond those noted in connection with the methodology of interpretation itself. This chapter thus adds a second way, in addition to that presented in Chapter 4, in which the hypothesis that assertion has a robustly epistemic norm bears on a correct account of the contents of (assertoric) speech acts.

6
Assertion and Belief

6.1 The Link between Assertion and Belief: Contingent or Essential?

This chapter concerns the relation between assertion and belief. Perhaps everyone can agree that assertions are apt vehicles for the expression of belief. But we might wonder whether this aptness is a merely contingent feature of assertions, as some (including perhaps G. E. Moore 1993: 210) appear to have thought, or whether the connection is not merely contingent but part of the very nature of the speech act itself.[1] Since it would be surprising indeed if the connection were merely contingent—after all, it would seem that assertion's epistemic significance would be mysterious if it were not intimately connected to assertion's role as manifesting belief;[2] what is more, belief would appear to be the sincerity condition on assertion—we might wonder what best accounts for the non-contingent connection. In this chapter I argue that MMENA, the hypothesis that it is mutually manifest that assertion has an epistemic norm, can be used to construct a plausible account of the relation between assertion and belief.

Our discussion of assertion's relation to belief might do well to begin, however, not with MMENA, but with the account of assertion which gives pride of place to its role in the expression of belief. I refer, of course, to the account offered by Bach and Harnish (1979). As we saw in Chapter 1, they write that one asserts that p in uttering e if in uttering e one expresses both (i) the belief that p and (ii) one's intention that one's audience come to believe that p (1979: 42). We do well to remember, too, that their use of "expresses" here is a technical one. They explain it as follows: "For S to *express* an attitude is for S to R-intend the hearer to take S's utterance as reason to think S has that attitude" (1979: 15). And one R-intends an effect if one intends to bring about this effect by means of the audience's recognition of this intention. In short, on the Bach–Harnish view, any speech act that fails to express belief (in their sense of 'express') is *ipso facto* not an assertion.

---

[1] Others, including Dummett and Jary (2010: 36), hold that the connection is non-contingent but that it runs in the other direction: rather than assertion's being characterized in terms of the expression of belief, they think that belief ought to be characterized in terms of assertion.

[2] Compare Baldwin (1990: 228–29, and 2007: 77–78).

A very similar view is endorsed by Bernard Williams, who discussed assertion at some length in his (2002). There he writes that

A asserts that *p* where *A* utters a sentence *S* which means that *p*, in doing which either he expresses his belief that *p*, or he intends the person addressed to take it that he believes that *p*. (2002: 74)

What is more, Williams thinks that sincerity in assertion just is the expression of belief: "... Sincerity consists in a disposition to make sure that one's assertion expresses what one actually believes" (2002: 96). Thus, on the Williams view, as on the Bach–Harnish view, any speech act that fails to express one's belief, or which is not intended to be taken as an expression of one's belief, is *ipso facto* not an assertion.

An interesting objection to such views, and indeed to any view that regards assertion as the expression of belief in either of these senses, comes in the form of bald-faced lies (Sorensen 2007).[3] As Sorensen characterizes these, they are speech acts in which one utters a declarative sentence whose content one disbelieves, albeit fully aware that one's audience recognizes that one does not believe the content in question, and without any intention to deceive them into believing that one believes it (or any intention to get them to believe it themselves). Sorensen's interest in the phenomenon of bald-faced lies was in the very possibility of lies without the intention to deceive, as well as in the wrongness of such lies (given that there was no deceptive intent). But it is worth noting that such lies also pose a problem for any account of assertion that characterizes the speech act in terms of the expression of belief. For it would seem that bald-faced lies are assertions, yet they do not express belief in either the Bach–Harnish sense or in the Williams sense. Indeed, the bald-faced lie is a challenge to most of the accounts of assertion.[4] (I will return to this matter later.)

Both the Bach–Harnish view and the Williams view would explain the aptness of assertion to express belief in terms of the very features that characterize the speech act of assertion itself. We might say that on their view, the connection between assertion and belief is constitutive: any speech act that did not express belief (in the Bach–Harnish sense) and was not intended to be taken as expressing belief could not count as an assertion. Despite the challenge presented by bald-faced lies, I regard it as a virtue of these accounts that they regard the connection between assertion and belief as non-contingent. But while I agree with these views that assertions' aptness to express belief is not merely a contingent feature of assertions, but instead is to be traced to the very nature of assertion itself, I disagree that the best account of this relation is the one

---

[3] I thank two referees for pointing out the relevance of this phenomenon to the present topic.
[4] Besides the norm-based view (whose account of the bald-faced lie I present in Section 6.3), the only other view that appears to accommodate this phenomenon is the view that characterizes assertion in terms of the declarative mood. To a rough first approximation, according to such a view assertion is the speech act that is typically performed when one utters a sentence in the declarative mood (where the act's status as an assertion stands by default, albeit the default is defeasible). Something like this was the view of Dummett (1981, 1993) and (more recently) of Jary (2010).

they propose. In this chapter I develop and explore an alternative account—one that derives from the hypothesis that it is mutually manifest to competent speakers that assertion has a robustly epistemic norm (MMENA). In particular, I will be arguing, first, that the fact that assertions are apt vehicles for the expression of belief is best explained in terms of MMENA, and second, that this account of the relation between assertion and belief has several other virtues as well.[5]

6.2 MMENA and the Assertion–Belief Connection

Let me begin with my proposed MMENA-based explanation of the relation between assertion and belief. MMENA itself consists of two claims: first, that assertion is answerable to a robustly epistemic norm (I dubbed this claim 'ENA'); and second, that this is mutually manifest to any competent speaker of a language exchange (this is the 'MM' part of 'MMENA'). With these claims in place, the explanation proceeds by noting that in asserting that p, a speaker S does something for which it is mutually manifest that what S did was warranted only if S was relevantly epistemically authoritative regarding whether p. My strategy will be to argue that whatever epistemic authoritativeness comes to, it is intimately linked with the subject's doxastic attitude towards the proposition asserted, and that this link, together with the mutually manifest nature of ENA, accounts for assertion's status as a vehicle for the manifestation of belief.

Now, ENA itself requires one not to assert that p unless one is relevantly epistemically authoritative with respect to the truth of [p]. There are a variety of candidates regarding what it is to be relevantly epistemically authoritative with respect to the truth of [p]. As noted in Chapter 1, these are the variety of candidates for the standard imposed by the norm of assertion. As I have been doing throughout this book, so too here I want to be officially neutral on which of these candidates gives the norm's standard. Instead I will be arguing that whichever it is, so long as it is robustly epistemic, we can derive conclusions about the subject's doxastic attitude from an observed assertion.

To do so, it will be helpful to have before us the leading candidates for the sort of epistemic authoritativeness relevant to the norm of assertion. The following are the leading eight candidates.[6] To be relevantly epistemically authoritative, it is necessary

---

[5] Compare the following to Reynolds (2002: 155–57). Reynolds is speaking of testimony, and the norm of testimony, though I think that what he says could be translated, *mutatis mutandis*, to the norm of assertion. (Indeed, he appears to use these two interchangeably.)

[6] The eight that follow are all instances of norm-based accounts of assertion on which there is a single invariant standard provided by the norm of assertion. The account I favor, which is presented in Part IV of this book (Chapters 9–11), does not endorse a single invariant standard, but rather holds that the standard is determined in a context-sensitive fashion. (Compare to Turri 2010a and McKinnon 2013.) (In Chapter 11 I will discuss how my context-sensitive account might nevertheless succeed in explaining all the things explained by MMENA.) Turri (2014) also notes that we might distinguish the *permissibility* of an assertion from its *goodness*: the phenomenon that he describes as "suberogatory assertion" (Turri 2014) involves cases in which the assertion is permissible (satisfying something like a reasonable belief standard) but not good (failing to satisfy something like a knowledge standard). Here I have not made that distinction; I am assuming that the standard is one for permissibility, period.

and sufficient that S (i) is epistemically certain that p; (ii) knows that p;[7] (iii) has a warranted belief that p; (iv) has a doxastically justified belief that p; (v) is (propositionally) justified in believing that p; (vi) has an epistemically rational belief that p; (vii) is in a position in which it would be (propositionally) rational to believe that p; (viii) is in a position to know that p.[8] Note that many, though not all, of (i)–(viii) involve believing p: belief is present in (i)–(iv) and (vi), though not (or at least not necessarily) in (v), (vii), and (viii). So suppose that one of (i)–(iv) or (vi) captures the norm of assertion. In that case, since each of these conditions requires that the subject believes that p, it would follow that an assertion that p is proper only if the subject believes that p. In this case, belief as a condition on appropriate assertion falls out directly from ENA itself. Suppose instead that one of (v), (vii), or (viii) captures the relevant notion of epistemic authoritativeness. None of these conditions require that the subject believe that p. But even so, there is something that can be said here to connect belief to assertion. Let us say that a proposition that p is *belief-worthy* relative to a subject S when, given S's epistemic perspective, it would be epistemically proper to believe that p. In that case we can say that if any of (v), (vii), or (viii) are true, then the asserted proposition is belief-worthy relative to the asserter.[9] In that case, we could say that, while it may not be true that belief is required for proper assertion, the belief-worthiness (relative to the would-be asserter) is required.

Given this, we can now bracket which of (i)–(viii) captures the relevant sort of authoritativeness. Instead, our strategy will be to reason from what is common in all of these cases, together with what is mutually known by speaker and hearer alike, in order to reach the conclusion that if a subject is both sincere and rational in asserting that p, then she believes that p. To begin, it is mutually manifest to all competent language users that an assertion that p is proper (warranted) only if the speaker is relevantly epistemically authoritative regarding whether p. Since this is mutually manifest, it is something that the speaker knows. At least in this respect a speaker who asserts that p must see herself as presenting as true a proposition in such a way that it is mutually manifest that she has done something warranted only if she has the requisite authority, where the requisite authority involves a status which would render belief rational. (It may require more than this, but it will require at least that much.) In this case it would seem mutually manifest that if she is both sincere and rational, she believes the content asserted. This is true no matter the standard itself, provided, of course, that it is robustly epistemic (in

---

[7] Following Turri (2011), we might want to distinguish the condition that S know that p, from the condition that S (know that p and) *express* her knowledge that p in the assertion. I will not attend to this difference here, even as I concede that the difference is real. For a sense of how this distinction might be used to introduce new variants on (i)–(viii) here, see Turri (2014: 560).

[8] There are also variants on these, such as the view that (ix) it is reasonable to believe that one knows that p (anticipated in Lackey 2007 and suggested in Neta 2009), and (x) one reasonably believes that p (for which see Hill and Schechter 2007; Kvanvig 2009). I will not bother with a separate treatment of these, since they can be handled in a manner similar to how one of (v), (vi), or (vii) is handled.

[9] I will return to the issue of the norm of belief later.

the manner of one of (i)–(viii). It would seem, then, that the proponent of MMENA can capture a non-contingent connection between assertion and belief.

In light of this, it is worth asking after the conception of insincerity that emerges out of this account of assertion's connection to belief. Whereas those standards whose satisfaction explicitly requires belief—as in (i)–(iv) and (vi)—can accept the straightforward characterization of assertoric insincerity as a matter of asserting what one does not believe (of which disbelief is a special case), what can be said if we assume one of the standards that are not belief-entailing—(v), (vii), or (viii)? Take a case in which S asserts that p, and so is aware that her assertion is proper only if she has such authority, yet who fails to believe that p. This is an ordinary case of insincerity. We have seen previously that those who endorse one of (v), (vii), or (viii) can say in such a case that the speaker ought rationally to believe that p. But irrationality is one thing, insincerity another. Can the proponent of MMENA who endorses one of (v), (vii), or (viii) acknowledge this as a case of insincerity?

She might be tempted to try to do so with the following proposal: insincerity is present whenever one asserts under conditions in which one recognizes that one lacks the requisite authority to be warranted in asserting. However, this will not work. For a speaker might recognize that she lacks the requisite authority to assert that p, and yet even so she might believe that p anyway. If such a speaker wanted to manifest her belief in speech, she might assert that p. But were she to do so, her assertion would not appear to be insincere (as the previous proposal would have it), so much as it would be *reckless*.[10] The proposal might be rectified so that insincerity is a case in which not only does the speaker recognize that she is not in a position to assert warrantedly, but, what is more, she does not believe, where her lack of belief reflects her recognition that she is not relevantly epistemically authoritative. But such a proposal, while enabling us to avoid having to call the reckless asserter insincere, achieves this result by fiat, and so fails in an important way: it *builds in* the lack of belief condition in insincerity, and so cannot be used to explain it.

I propose that the proponent of MMENA who endorses one of (v), (vii), or (viii) should simply allow that the reckless asserter does exhibit a sort of insincerity, albeit not a standard form. While such a view might initially appear *ad hoc*, it can be defended as follows. Start with the general characterization of speech-act insincerity as follows:

> INS S's speech act is insincere when S does not have the attitude that S's audience would be entitled to regard S as having, in virtue of the performance of S's speech act itself.

This is a general characterization, available to anyone. If it is used by the proponent of MMENA, we obtain the result that a speech act is insincere whenever the speaker fails to have the attitude which her audience is entitled to regard her as having, in

---

[10] I thank an anonymous referee both for this example and for this way of describing the example.

virtue of having performed a speech act characterized by a robustly epistemic norm. Now suppose further (to bring out the present problem) that the relevant standard is not belief-entailing; that is, that it is one of (v), (vii), or (viii). These standards require sufficient grounds for propositional justification, propositional rationality, and being in a position to know, respectively. Consequently, if one of these provides the correct standard for the norm of assertion, INS would yield the result that someone who asserts entitles others to regard her (the speaker) as representing herself as satisfying such a condition.[11] I submit that to represent oneself in this way when one does not regard oneself as satisfying such a condition does involve a form of insincerity. It is not a standard form of insincerity, but it is a form of insincerity for all that—it involves representing oneself as relevantly epistemically authoritative, despite knowing that one is not.

Why think of this as a form of *insincerity*? I can bring out the relevant intuition by way of the following dialogue:[12]

SMITH: It's going to rain tomorrow.
JONES: On what grounds do you say that?
SMITH: Well, I don't really have good grounds for saying this.
JONES: Then don't assert it!
SMITH: But I was just expressing my belief.
JONES: If that's what you wanted to do, then make it clear that's what you were doing!

It should be clear that Jones's criticism of Smith involves an objection to Smith's having asserted what she did. It should also be clear that Jones's criticism involves an objection to the form of words Smith chose to perform the (expressive) act she (Smith) wanted to perform: Jones thinks that, given Smith's desire to express her belief, she should have chosen different words for doing so (perhaps employing an explicit "I believe that" operator at the outset). But in addition to these criticisms I submit that Jones's criticism also involves an objection to the effect that Smith misrepresented herself to her audience. True, the misrepresentation is not the sort present in a lie: it is not a matter of Smith's representing herself as believing what she stated, when in fact she does not believe any such thing. Even so, there is misrepresentation in Smith's representing herself as suitably epistemically authoritative, when in fact she did not believe she was suitably epistemically authoritative. This, I want to say, is the sort of self-misrepresentation involved in reckless assertion.[13] Nor should one

---

[11] See Chapter 1, and also Section 6.4 in this chapter, for the mechanisms involved in this sort of 'self-representation'.
[12] The initial assertion in this dialogue was suggested to me by an anonymous referee, as an example of sincere but reckless assertion.
[13] Contrast the case where Smith *does* regard herself, albeit wrongly, as satisfying the norm of assertion. This would not be a case of insincerity, but only of unwarranted assertion. This highlights that if the example is to present a challenge on the present score, the challenge arises from the fact that the speaker believes she

think to argue that because she never intended her audience to believe that she *was* as she represented herself as being, this form of self-misrepresentation is not insincerity—any more than one should think to argue in the case of a bald-faced lie that because the speaker never intended her audience to believe that she was as she represented herself as being, the self-misrepresentation in a bald-faced lie is not insincerity. Both arguments fail. Both examples are cases in which there is insincerity in the self-representation, albeit without the intention to deceive. Of course, the reckless asserter *does* believe what she asserts, and so in this sense (and unlike the bald-faced liar) "stands behind" her speech contribution. But this is not the sort of "standing behind" that assertion promises (as it were), which is why we can call this a case of insincerity (albeit without the intention to deceive). To be sure, the intuition remains that the insincerity of the negligent asserter (if that is what it is) is importantly different from the insincerity of one who does not believe what one asserts to be the case. But we can capture this intuition as well: one who does not believe what she asserts to be the case is doubly self-misrepresenting (both along the dimension of what is believed, and of satisfying the norm of assertion), whereas the reckless asserter is only singly self-misrepresenting (only along the dimension of satisfying the norm of assertion). Any felt difference in cases is attributable to this difference.

And so we can conclude: whichever of (i)–(viii) captures the sort of epistemic authoritativeness relevant to the norm of assertion, the proponent of MMENA can provide a plausible account of the non-contingent relation between assertion and belief. If the proponent of MMENA endorses a standard of assertion which is belief-entailing (as in (i)–(iv) and (vi)), then her view entails that sincere assertion requires belief. If she endorses a standard of assertion which is not belief-entailing (as in (v), (vii), or (viii)), then her view entails that sincere assertion requires belief in those cases in which the subject is rational. And even there, the proponent of MMENA has a plausible account of insincerity in assertion, in the form of INS. We have seen that this characterization, together with MMENA, can handle the case of the reckless asserter, even on the assumption that the norm of assertion itself is not belief-entailing.

6.3 Does Warranted Assertion Require Belief?

Suppose one takes it as given that warranted assertion requires belief. On this basis might one try to argue against the candidates whose satisfaction does not imply belief—that is, (v), (vii), and (viii)? If successful, such an argument would be one way to whittle down the available candidates for the norm of assertion. Such an argument depends on

---

does not satisfy the norm of assertion. Only once that feature is in place does the case begin to appear as if it involves insincerity after all—albeit of a non-standard form (of the sort described above).

the claim that there can be no such thing as an assertion (properly so-called) that does not even aim to be taken as expressing the speaker's belief. But is this claim correct?

The idea that warranted assertion requires belief has been called into question in several papers by Jennifer Lackey. In particular, Lackey (1999, 2007b) has presented cases in which (it could be argued that) an assertion is warranted despite the fact that the speaker herself does not believe what she asserts. Lackey (1999) presents this in the form of the creationist teacher. There, the teacher asserts one of the claims of evolution, and does so on the basis of the class materials she was given by her school district (included among which were the materials on evolution); but as a creationist the teacher fails to believe what she asserts, since it is contrary to her creationist ideology. (As Lackey tells the story, the teacher asserts it out of her sense of duty as a teacher, given the curriculum.) And in her (2007b) Lackey explicitly argues for the possibility of proper assertion without belief in cases involving what Lackey herself calls "selfless assertion." In one of the cases, a doctor asserts something to one of her patients regarding the causes of autism, where what she asserts is both true and reliable, yet where the doctor herself fails to believe it, owing to her emotional condition on thinking about her own autistic child. (As Lackey tells the story, the doctor asserts this out of her sense of duty as a doctor.) Roughly put, in both of these cases the proposition is *highly belief-worthy*, though for idiosyncratic (and largely non-epistemic) reasons the speaker does not believe the proposition in question. If Lackey's description of these cases (as involving warranted assertion without belief) is sound, it is a virtue of a theory of assertion's norm to be able to square with cases of warranted assertion without belief.

One who wanted to defend the idea that warranted assertion requires belief, or must be intended to be taken (by the audience) to express belief, might respond to this use of Lackey's cases as follows. Consider the hearer's attitude towards the following hypothesis:

BELIEF Speaker S (who just made an assertion) believes what she asserted.

In the cases Lackey describes, the audience's attitude towards BELIEF is not so much as raised. But consider that if the audience were apprised of the fact that BELIEF is false, then the audience presumably would not believe what was (apparently) asserted. What is more, since the speaker could anticipate all of this in advance, and since presumably the speaker aims in her assertion at getting the hearer to form the relevant belief,[14] then at the very least she (the speaker) must have intended that her assertion be taken by the audience in such a way that if the audience raised the question regarding BELIEF, they would regard it as true. And if this is so, then the Lackey cases (as we might call them)

---

[14] The Creationist Teacher has this aim if only out of a sense of duty, and perhaps because her evaluation will depend on how well the students do on examinations—where it might be anticipated that they will do better to the extent that they come to endorse what she presents as true (rather than merely try to regurgitate it).

do not show that there can be warranted assertion in the absence of any intention that the audience regard the assertion as expressing her (the speaker's) belief.

However, this objection does not seem particularly compelling.[15] For one thing, in the case of the emotionally distressed doctor, the doctor intended to communicate the information that she (recognizes that she) herself *would* believe, were she to be less emotionally distraught. Relatedly, it would seem that insofar as assertion aims to be the vehicle for the communication of epistemically high-quality information, the relevance of belief is only indirect. That is, the speaker's belief is relevant in a particular case insofar as the epistemic quality of her assertion is determined by the epistemic features of the belief; but if there are cases in which the epistemic quality of an assertion is determined in some *other* way, we have no reason to care very much about the speaker's belief.[16] (In words I used previously, what matters in the first instance is the belief-*worthiness* of the asserted content, not whether in fact it is believed by the asserter.) Bringing this point to bear on the speaker's intentions, we can say this: asserters need not have the intention that the audience should regard her assertion as expressing her (the speaker's) belief. It would suffice that she (the speaker) intend to present the proposition as belief-*worthy*. If this is so, then the intention to express one's belief or to have one's assertion regarded as doing such is not essential to assertion.

Interestingly, something like this very point might be taken to be supported by an example that was originally used by Donnellan (1966) to make a point about the referential use of definite descriptions. Donnellan was addressing the question of whether the referential use of a definite description of the form 'the D' requires the speaker to believe (or to believe that the audience believes) that the object referred to is in fact D. He answered in the negative. Not only does the speaker not have to believe, nor intend that her audience believes that she believes, that 'the D' picks out an object which is D; what is more, the audience need not believe that the object is D in order to understand the speaker's assertion. Donnellan's example was of someone who referred to a particular person as 'the King,' under conditions in which it was mutually believed that the person in question was an illegitimate usurper of the throne (and hence not the King). Although Donnellan was interested in characterizing the referential use of definite descriptions, and not the nature of assertion, his case can be used to think about assertion as well. In particular, on the assumption that the person did, in fact, assert the proposition that the King is on the throne,[17] then here we have a case

---

[15] In this response I am indebted both to Lackey (2007b) and also to a conversation on this topic with Lackey herself.

[16] Indeed, we might take this to be one of the central lessons of Lackey (2008). It is a point that has also been emphasized, albeit in different ways, in Graham (2000a, 2000b).

[17] I should acknowledge that this is controversial, and goes to the heart of the sort of issues Donnellan was raising regarding the semantics and pragmatics of reference. See, for example, Kripke (1977) for an influential defense of the idea that the speaker does assert this, while simultaneously having made speaker reference to the (allegedly usurping) individual in question.

in which an assertion is made without any intention that the assertion express, or be taken to express, a belief on the part of the speaker.

This use of Donnellan's example depends on construing the assertion as having the content *that the King is on the throne*, and as this might be doubted. One thing that might be said against the claim that the speaker asserted the proposition *that the King is on the throne* is this. It is common knowledge (a) that the assertion was made on the basis of the speaker's having observed a particular individual on the throne, and (b) that the individual seen on the throne is taken by all parties involved not to be the King, but a usurper. Under these conditions, regarding the content of the assertion to be *that the King is on the throne* appears to have the implication that the assertion was not warranted (by the lights of ENA, whatever the particular norm happens to be). After all, the speaker has no evidence regarding the (actual) King's whereabouts, beyond the evidence that he is not on the throne (since the usurper is); were the speaker to be taken to have asserted something regarding the (actual) King, then, the assertion would be epistemically baseless. Yet surely it would be uncharitable to reach this 'unwarranted assertion' verdict on such grounds. Since such a verdict is in place so long as we construe the assertion as having that content, that construal is dubious. Indeed, I think something like this reasoning was used by Donnellan himself to conclude that the referential use of a definite description can affect the semantic value of that use of the description.

Might this reply be met by appeal to the distinction between speaker reference and semantic reference, in the manner of Kripke (1977)? The idea would be that the speaker was relevantly authoritative regarding the truth-value of the proposition she meant to express, but not regarding the truth-value of the proposition she did express. What is more, it was mutually clear in context that the speaker did not believe the proposition that was the literal content of his utterance, so in uttering what he did he ran no risk of confusing his audience. In this way we might explain away the intuition that the previous construal is dubious, as confusing the one proposition for the other. The difficulty, however, is that this reply does not seem to enable us to preserve the hypothesis that assertion can be warranted even in the absence of belief. For either the speaker asserted *that the King is on the throne*, or she did not assert this. If she did, her assertion is not warranted (as noted previously). But if she did not assert this, this is presumably because she asserted, regarding the usurper, that *he* is on the throne; only then she believes what she asserted, in which case this is not an example of a warranted assertion *without belief*.

I conclude that the issue regarding whether there can be warranted assertion without belief is vexed. Lackey's cases may be cases of warranted assertion without belief, though there would appear to be some difficulty in establishing the existence of such cases using Donnellan's distinction between the referential and attributive uses of descriptions. So it is not clear whether (a) belief is required by warranted assertion, nor is it clear whether (b) the intention to be regarded as expressing belief is itself a necessary condition on making an assertion. Of course, if (a) or (b) hold, then none of (v), (vii), and (viii) can capture the norm of assertion, since a speaker can satisfy both (a) and (b) without believing the content asserted. Of course, we might turn the tables if it turns out that neither (a) nor (b) holds. What we could conclude from this would depend on whether there could be cases of warranted assertion without belief. If there could be, this would be evidence against (i)–(iv) and (vi) as capturing the norm of assertion, and in favor of one of (v), (vii), and (viii). But if all cases of assertion in the absence of belief were unwarranted, then this would provide some support for one of (i)–(iv) and (vi) as capturing the norm of assertion.

In keeping with my neutrality on the candidate epistemic norm of assertion, I do not want to address this matter further here.[18]

Now let us ask: what might favor the MMENA-based account of the relation between assertion and belief, over an account like that of Bach–Harnish or Williams (characterized at the outset of the chapter)? One consideration was already suggested: if Lackey's (1999, 2007b) suggestion that there can be cases of proper assertion without belief is correct, then it is a virtue of an account not to require that the connection between the two is constitutive. (Indeed, Lackey herself uses the cases to say that even those who endorse the knowledge norm should really hold that *being in a position to know* is the norm.) But it is worth noting as well that Sorensen's case of the bald-faced lie would appear to support the norm-based account over the Bach–Harnish account or the Williams account. For the latter accounts appear to face difficulties even recognizing the bald-faced lie as an assertion, whereas the norm-based account of MMENA faces no such difficulty (on any version of this account, the bald-faced lie is an assertion, albeit an unwarranted one).

A second consideration favoring the norm-based account is related.[19] Most people will agree that the point of assertion, or at least a central point of this speech act, is to communicate epistemically high-grade information. But if it is to be successful in this way, then assertions must be recognized as having this point. Of course, one of the virtues of MMENA is that, given that ENA is mutually manifest, this fact can help explain why assertions are recognized (by all competent speakers) as apt for the communication of epistemically high-grade information. That MMENA can also be used to account for the connection between assertion and belief, using the very features of assertion that make it apt for this sort of communication, would then be a virtue, since in that case we have an explanation for belief's relation to assertion in terms of the very point of assertion. Such an explanation, I submit, should be more satisfying than one that purports to represent the expression of belief (in the Bach–Harnish sense) as necessary for assertion. For it would seem that such a view would then have to offer another independent explanation for how assertion manages to be universally recognized as apt for the communication of epistemically high-quality information. I do not say that such an explanation is not

---

[18] I will address it at some length in Chapters 10 and 11, when I discuss the sincerity condition further. There I will be arguing that there can be warranted assertion without belief—though my case for this is very different from the ones considered above.

[19] With thanks to Jennifer Lackey for emphasizing this point to me (in conversation).

forthcoming; presumably one could reason from the assumption of belief's being constitutive of assertion, together with assumptions about the epistemic standing of beliefs (in general), to conclusions about the communicative aptness of assertion (in general).[20] My claim is that such an explanation would be no better than the MMENA-based explanation—in which case the latter is to be preferred, on the grounds that it can be used to explain not only this phenomenon but also the host of others at issue in this book.

6.4 Belief-Worthiness, Assertion, and the Pragmatics of Epistemic Self-Representation

On the MMENA-based account of the relation between belief and assertion, we have obtained the following result ('WBW' for 'Warranted only if Belief-Worthy'):

WBW   When one asserts that p, one does something regarding which it is mutually manifest that what one did was proper only if the proposition that p was belief-worthy (where the relevant notion of belief-worthiness is to be unpacked in terms of the particular epistemic norm of assertion).

WBW holds no matter what the particular epistemic norm of assertion is; the choice of the particular norm only affects what belief-worthiness is to amount to. We can use WBW to explain several other aspects of the relation between assertion and belief. Here I take up the topic of the way one *represents oneself* when one makes an assertion.

The language of "self-representation" is not mine. On the contrary, it is common to hear philosophers who talk about assertion say such things as that

ARB   To assert that p is (among other things) to "represent oneself" as believing that p.[21]

Indeed, a good many authors who work on assertion hold the stronger view that

ARK   To assert that p is to represent oneself as *knowing* that p.[22]

This talk of "self-representation" in both ARB and ARK can be understood in terms of WBW.

---

[20] I consider (and reject) such a proposal in Chapter 1 of this book.
[21] For a recent explicit endorsement of this view, see Rysiew (2007b: 631).
[22] See Black (1952: 31), Unger (1975: 250–65), Slote (1979), Davidson (1984b), Williamson (1996: 498), DeRose (1991: 597–98) and (2002: 180), Reynolds (2002: 140), Hawthorne (2005), Stanley (2005), and Rysiew (2007b: 632). Other notions in the literature attempt to describe something in the neighborhood of this phenomenon: Searle (1969) speaks of the subject's *bearing responsibility for the satisfaction of the sincerity, preparatory, and essential conditions* (where one of the preparatory conditions on assertion is that the subject knows the proposition in question), Stalnaker (1974) speaks of the *pragmatic presuppositions* of an assertion, Brandom (1994) speaks of the subject's (assertion-generated) *discursive commitments*, and Alston (2000) speaks of the asserter's *taking responsibility* for the obtaining of certain conditions.

Before going to the explanation itself, it is worthwhile spending a little time seeing how MMENA can be used to make sense of the language of "self-representation." On the assumption that MMENA is true, all parties (speakers and hearers alike) know, and know that the others know, and so on, that assertion has a robustly epistemic norm. So all parties know, and know that the others know, and so on, that in the making of an assertion the asserter S is doing something warranted only if the norm is satisfied. From speaker S's perspective, things look thus: S is aware of having done something regarding which she could anticipate that the hearer H would regard her as having acted in a warranted fashion only if the norm was satisfied. From H's perspective, things look thus: H could anticipate that S would anticipate that H (having observed S's assertion) would so regard S—that is, would regard S as having acted warrantedly only if the norm was satisfied. In sum, both parties are aware of what in Chapters 2 and 3 I called the "epistemic significance of assertion." Now, since failure to live up to a standard is grounds for criticism and censure, and since people can be expected to want to avoid criticism and censure whenever possible, one who does something of one's own free will, regarding which it is common knowledge that a performance will be held against a standard, can be presumed to have aimed to satisfy that standard in acting as she did. From this we can say that the following will be known by all parties: one who asserts that p can be presumed to have aimed to satisfy the norm of assertion. We might say that it is a characteristic side-effect of assertion that it will generate this presumption. And since this side-effect is common knowledge—something that the speaker and hearer both know, and know that the other knows, and so on—it seems that the asserter can be said to have anticipated this outcome, and in this sense to acknowledge it. This is my reconstruction of the language of "self-representation": to the extent that the asserter can properly be said to represent herself as doing something in asserting that p, it is that she can be held to have acted so as to generate the presumption in her audience that she aimed to satisfy assertion's robustly epistemic norm.

With this explanation of the language of "self-representation" in place, we can now move on to ARK and ARB. Let us begin with the stronger claim: ARK. In what sense can it be true that to assert that p is to represent oneself as knowing that p? Suppose that knowledge is the norm of assertion. Then one who asserts that p does something regarding which it is common knowledge that what she did was warranted only if she knows that p. The claim that one who asserts that p represents oneself as knowing that p is then a special case of our previous claim, to the effect that the asserter can properly be said to represent herself as doing X in asserting that p, insofar as she can be held to have acted so as to generate the presumption in her audience that she aimed to satisfy assertion's norm (where X is that norm).

The proposed explanation of ARK depends on the knowledge account of assertion. Those who reject that knowledge is the norm of assertion will presumably reject ARK as well. (But see McKinnon and Simard Smith 2013, who argue that one does not need the knowledge account to be able to derive ARK.) But whatever one's take on ARK itself, virtually everyone—or at least everyone among those who thinks it makes sense to employ the language of "self-representation" in connection with assertion—will accept ARB in some form or other.[23] To explain it, we cannot depend on any particular norm of assertion. In what follows I want to argue that, no matter what the norm of assertion is, something in the vicinity of ARB will hold.

I have already argued in Section 6.3 that if any of (i)–(iv) or (vi) is the norm of assertion, then S's believing that p is a necessary condition on S's warrantedly asserting that p. In that case, one who asserts that p does something regarding which it is common knowledge that what she did was warranted only if she bears some happy epistemic relation to the proposition that p, where standing in such a relation requires minimally that she believe that p. The phrase "the asserter represents herself as believing" can be understood as a gloss on this. But what should be said if one of (v), (vii), or (viii) is the norm of assertion? These conditions can be satisfied in the absence of belief. Still, as I already argued, their satisfaction requires that the asserted proposition be "belief-worthy" relative to the speaker. The result is that insofar as the speaker is not divided against herself—insofar as she believes what she herself (implicitly) recognizes as worthy of belief—her assertion is warranted only if she believes it. So if any of (v), (vii), or (viii) gives the norm of assertion, then at the very least it will be common knowledge that one who asserts that p regards the proposition that p as belief-worthy. From this alone we can obtain the result that one who asserts that p represents herself as regarding [that p] as belief-worthy in the relevant sense. And while this does not amount to ARB, it does come close. (See Chapter 11 for further discussion.)

In short, no matter what the particular norm of assertion happens to be, something in the vicinity of ARB will come out true. And if one of (i)–(iv) or (vi) is the norm of assertion, then we can vindicate ARB itself.

6.5 Assertion and Moore's Paradox

These locutions—that the asserter "represents herself" as knowing (believing) what she asserts—are often invoked in the course of a proposed diagnosis of Moorean absurdity (Moore 1993), in one or more of its forms. So if my reconstruction of what these locutions amount to is correct, then insofar as the locutions themselves can be employed in a proper diagnosis of Moorean absurdity, to that extent we can conclude that the robustly epistemic norm of assertion can be used to diagnose this phenomenon.

The idea that the norm of assertion might be relevant to a proper diagnosis of the phenomenon of Moorean absurdity is not new, of course; the literature on Moore's paradox and assertion is substantial.[24] What I want to add to this discussion is the

---

[23] In Part IV of this book I defend something slightly weaker than ARB. When I do, I will be revisiting this talk of how one "represents oneself" in asserting that p (see especially Chapter 11).

[24] In part this is owing to Moore (1993) and Williamson (1996), who proposed that the norm of assertion might be used to explain the Moore-paradoxicality of Moorean assertion. Then again, since Moore-paradoxicality appears even at the level of belief itself, many have argued that a proper diagnosis

suggestion that a good deal of the virtues of the appeal to the norm of assertion in connection with a diagnosis of Moore-paradoxicality do not depend on any particular proposal regarding the norm of assertion, but instead can be obtained by appeal to the more general hypothesis, MMENA. (I should add that I will not be defending the categorical thesis that Moore-paradoxicality is best explained by appeal to the norm of assertion; instead I will be defending the conditional thesis that *if* Moore-paradoxicality is best explained by appeal to the norm of assertion, then—surprisingly—the explanation need not appeal to much beyond the generic ENA.)

Let us start with the phenomenon of Moore-paradoxicality itself. As Moore (1993) noted, the assertion of either of the following two appears absurd:

MPB1   p, but I do not believe that p

and

MPB2   p, but I believe that not-p.

The absurdity, however, is not that of logical inconsistency.[25] For as Moore pointed out, it is possible for the proposition that p to be true while one oneself does not believe that p (or even while one oneself believes that not-p). To assume otherwise is to assume that one oneself is omniscient or infallible. Still, absurdity results if one *states* that one oneself is currently in such a position. Hence the "paradox": there is a type of state of affairs which is quite common—a state of affairs in which it is the case that p, but subject S does not believe that p (alternatively: S believes that not-p)—yet it would be absurd for S herself to assert that this state of affairs has obtained. Whence the absurdity?

A natural diagnosis—one which has been offered by many people (though others have found it wanting[26])—treats this phenomenon as reflecting the norms of proper assertion. This diagnosis is natural on the assumption that the absurdity is generated by the act of *stating* or *asserting* that one oneself is in such a position.[27] Here I do not want to defend the categorical claim that this is the proper way to diagnose Moore-paradoxicality. Rather, I want to ask the following question: *assuming* that this is the best diagnosis, what specifically do we have to assume about the norm of assertion in order to provide the diagnosis? My answer is: less than one might think. If I am correct about this, then while the phenomenon of Moore-paradoxicality might be used to support the hypothesis that assertion has a robustly epistemic norm (ENA), this phenomenon cannot be used to help us distinguish precisely what that norm is.

must go beyond the level of speech. This raises issues regarding the relation between the norm of assertion and the norm of belief and judgment; I return to this in Section 6.6.

[25] Moore (1993) himself noted this; for a recent discussion, see Sorensen (1988).
[26] For a discussion of the various issues involved in diagnosing Moorean absurdity, see the various contributions in Green and Williams (2007).
[27] However, as noted previously, Moore-paradoxicality appears even at the level of belief itself. On this basis, many have argued that a proper diagnosis must go beyond the level of speech.

Let us start first, not with MPB1 and MPB2, but with another version of Moore's paradox that has been used recently by some as a reason to favor the knowledge norm of assertion (Williamson 1996, 2000). This involves the following:

MPK   p, but I do not know that p.[28]

Once again, it would appear absurd for one to assert MPK, yet the state of affairs it describes is common (for each of us there are lots of true propositions that one does not know). Williamson (2000) takes the Moorean absurdity of MPK to support the knowledge norm of assertion:

> What is wrong [with an assertion of MPK] can easily be understood on the hypothesis that only knowledge warrants assertion. For then to have warrant to assert the conjunction 'A and I do not know A' is to know that A and one does not know A. But one cannot know that A and one does not know A. One knows the conjunction only if one knows each conjunct, and therefore knows that A (the first conjunct); yet one knows the conjunction only it is true, so only if each conjunct is true, so only if one does not know that A (the second conjunct); thus the assumption that one knows the conjunction that A and one does not know that A yields a contradiction. Given that only knowledge warrants assertion, one therefore cannot have warrant to assert 'A and I do not know A'. In contrast, the hypothesis that not only knowledge warrants assertion makes it hard to understand what is wrong with an assertion of that form. One often has good evidence that A whilst knowing for sure that one does not know A; in such cases one has good evidence short of knowledge for the conjunction that A and one does not know that A. (Williamson 2000: 253)

(Williamson goes on to show how the knowledge norm also explains the absurdity of asserting MPB1.) If Williamson's argument is sound, then—contrary to my previous claim—considerations pertaining to Moore's paradox favor one particular candidate norm of assertion.

But it is not clear that proponents of other norms cannot explain the absurdity of asserting MPK.[29] Consider the scenario Williamson himself describes: "One often has good evidence that A whilst knowing for sure that one does not know A." Williamson holds that this scenario spells doom for any view on which warranted assertion does not require knowledge, since it would appear that by the lights of any such (not-knowledge-requiring) view it can be proper to assert MPK—an unhappy result. But, as defenders of, for example, the justification view have noted, this argument can be met in at least two different sorts of ways. One way involves showing that, contrary to what Williamson supposes, the justification rule does *not* imply that there are cases in which an assertion of MPK is permissible. This is a view defended by Kvanvig (2009: 149–54). He argues that the

---

[28] When it comes to the knowledge version of Moore's paradox, we do not need a version corresponding to MPB2, since 'p, but I know that not-p' is flat-out contradictory, given the factivity of knowledge.

[29] Many others have made this point. In addition to what I go on to cite later, see the recent defenses in, for example, Stone (2007), Littlejohn (2010), and McKinnon and Simard Smith (2013).

sort of justification needed to warrant knowledge is the sort that, given truth and the satisfaction of an anti-Gettier condition, turns a belief into knowledge. Clearly, one who knows that one does not know that p is not in this sense justified in believing that p: knowing that one does not know defeats the justification. (Kvanvig adds that one virtue of this justificationist view is that it gives the right results in lottery cases: one should not assert lottery propositions, since one's justification is not the sort that, when added to truth and the satisfaction of an anti-Gettier condition, yields knowledge.) But defenders of the justification view (or something close to it) have responded to Williamson's previous argument in a second way: namely, by maintaining that the impropriety of an assertion of MPK is to be traced to something other than the norm of assertion. Douven (2006: 473–76) defends a view of the latter sort (albeit in connection with the 'rational credibility' view of the norm of assertion). He argues that the "odd-soundingness" of asserting MPK can be traced to its being uncommon in everyday discourse to hear assertions of this sort, and to the fact that, since (part of) one's (typical) aim in asserting something is to get them to believe it, asserting MPK is in this sense self-defeating. This is because in stating that one does not know that p, one undermines the relevant effectiveness of one's asserting p: others will not be all that likely to accept that p on one's say-so when they are aware that one regards oneself as not knowing that p. In short, there appear to be ways of saving norms (iv), (v), and (vii)—the (doxastic and propositional) justification norms and the rational credibility norm—in the face of arguments that appeal to the Moore-paradoxicality of assertions of MPK.

Does the Moore-paradoxicality of asserting MPK give us a reason to favor a norm of assertion that requires belief for its satisfaction? If so, it would give us a reason to disfavor norms (v), (vii), and (viii). But even here we see that proponents of these norms have resources for dealing with the absurdity of asserting MPK.[30]

This is perhaps most obvious in the case of (viii), on which being-in-a-position-to-know is the norm of assertion.[31] By the lights of this norm, my assertion of MPK is proper only if I am in a position to know the following: p, and I do not know that p. I am in a position to know this only if I am in a position to know both disjuncts, and so only if I am in a position to know that p, and only if I am in a position to know that I do not know that p. But it is plausible to think that being in a position to know, like being (doxastically) justified in believing, can be defeated by the knowledge that one does not know. Stronger still, it is plausible to think that being in a position to know can be defeated by being in a position to know that one does not know. For being in a position to know is a matter of satisfying all of the conditions on knowledge save belief, in which case (since the knowledge here is to the effect that one does not know that p) one has the grounds for knowing a proposition which is such that, if believed, would defeat one's being in a position to know. And I submit that this is a normative defeater

---

[30] This point is also emphasized in McKinnon and Simard Smith (2013).
[31] Points similar to those I am about to make can be found in Lackey (2007b).

of one's being in a position to know that p.³² In this way we see that being in a position to know, both that p, and that one does not know that p, is not a stable position: being in a position to know the former requires not being in a position to know the latter. Hence any assertion of MPK would be improper by the lights of a being-in-a-position-to-know norm.

Moving next to (v), according to which propositional justification is the norm of assertion, we can say the following. If an assertion of MPK is to be proper, then I must have propositional justification for believing that: p, but I do not know that p. But propositional justification, like doxastic justification, can be defeated. And so once again considerations like those Kvanvig (2009) uses to defend the justification norm can be used to show that, by the lights of the propositional justification norm of belief, no assertion of MPK can be proper. And similar considerations bear on (vii), on which assertions are proper only if the speaker is in a position in which it would be (propositionally) rational to believe that p. So it appears that the Moorean absurdity of asserting MPK does not rule out any particular (epistemic) norm of assertion.

I will not here discuss how the hypothesis that assertion has a robustly epistemic norm might be used to provide an account of the 'standard' case of Moore-paradoxicality, involving MPB1 and MPB2; this is a matter that has been discussed at great length elsewhere, by other people.³³ Instead I will conclude that, at the very least, the case of Moore-paradoxicality that has been most saliently used to support a particular proposal regarding the norm of assertion—the case of MPK—fails to discriminate among the various epistemic norms. Insofar as an appeal to the norm of assertion is the proper way to diagnose the Moore-paradoxicality of 'p but I do not know that p,' the generic hypothesis that assertion has a robustly epistemic norm of some sort or another, ENA, appears to be sufficient to explain what needs to be explained.

Of course, not everyone accepts that we should appeal to the norm of assertion to deal with the phenomenon of Moore-paradoxicality in the first place. One of the grounds for skepticism on this score is that the phenomenon of Moore-paradoxicality arises at the level of judgment and belief as well (see, for example, Sorensen 1988 and Baldwin 2007). Simply put, it would be as absurd to believe or judge what is expressed by MPB1, MPB2, and MPK as it is to assert them. But perhaps this point merely pushes us to consider whether belief (alternatively: judgment) has a norm in terms of which we might account for the Moore-paradoxicality of believing (or judging) what is expressed by MPB1, MPB2, and MPK. Recently, many have become interested in the "norm of belief." This is an interesting topic in its own right. But since this book is

---

³² Here I am assuming the following: if you have information available—represented by your mind/brain—which is such that, were you to believe it, it would defeat your justification for believing that p, then you should not believe that p (on the grounds that this information constitutes a normative defeater).

³³ For recent discussions, see Baldwin (2007: 85–86) and Adler and Armour-Garb (2007: 146–51). See also Littlejohn (2010), where it is argued that the knowledge norm of belief is not supported by reflections on Moore-paradoxical sentences (and presumably Littlejohn would have similar things to say about the knowledge norm of assertion); and McKinnon and Simard Smith (2013).

focused, not on belief or judgment, but on assertion, I will restrict myself here to this issue pertaining to the norm of belief only insofar as it relates to the topic of assertion's norm. The question I will be pursuing is this: does belief, too, have a norm, and if so, *how does the norm of belief relate to the norm of assertion*? While such questions can be raised in connection with the phenomenon of Moore-paradoxicality, they are interesting in their own right. In the following section I will address them independently of the phenomenon of Moore-paradoxicality; I will return to that topic, briefly, at the end of the section.

6.6 The Norm of Assertion and the Norm of Belief

Does belief have a norm? To answer in the affirmative is to hold that there is a way to fill out the following schema so that it makes a true statement:

BEL   One must: believe that p only if …

That is, BEL states that it is proper to believe that p only if some further condition is met.[34] The question whether belief has a norm, then, boils down to the question whether there are conditions which specify, for each proposition, the conditions under which it is improper to believe that proposition.

It is tempting to think that anyone who distinguishes epistemic justification from knowledge ought to think that there is a way to make BEL true: what fills in the blank are the conditions on epistemic justification.[35] I say that this answer is tempting: what makes it so is the idea that a belief is (im)proper when it is *epistemically* (im)proper, together with the idea that, at least to a first approximation, the theory of epistemic justification *just is* the theory of epistemically proper belief.[36]

However, instead of starting from scratch with the norm of belief, it is worthwhile asking whether we can learn anything about the norm of belief from what we already know(!) about the norm of assertion.[37] One defense of this strategy is suggested by the thought, endorsed by many, that (in the words of Timothy Williamson) "believing p stands to asserting p as the inner stands to the outer" (Williamson 2000: 255–56).[38] If this is the right way to think about the relation between judgment, belief, and assertion, then the norm of belief should be precisely

---

[34] Spelling out the sense of the 'must' here is no easy task. See Gibbons (2013) for a detailed discussion.
[35] One might distinguish between propositional and doxastic justification, in which case there will be two distinct answers; but to keep things simple I will have doxastic justification in mind when I speak of justification in an unqualified way.
[36] I discuss this, and propose several modifications, in Goldberg (forthcoming a).
[37] Douven (2006) reverses the order of argument: he starts with the norm of belief, and uses this to establish claims about the norm of assertion.
[38] In this respect, Williamson seems to be endorsing a point that Dummett had endorsed several decades earlier, when he wrote that "judgment … is the interiorization of the external act of assertion" (Dummett 1973: 362). A version of this claim is endorsed by Jonathan Adler as well, under the label "the belief-assertion parallel" (Adler 2002: 74). Douven (2006) follows Adler.

the norm of assertion—and this, because the former is something like the inner version of the latter.

Are there additional things that can be said on behalf of identifying the standards provided by these two norms? I want to begin by reviewing a series of considerations that have been offered in support of the case for the identification. (After doing so, I will go on to offer a series of considerations for doubting this identification.)

A first way to defend the claim that the standard provided by the norm of belief and that provided by the norm of assertion are the same standard, is to try to show that neither standard can be stronger than the other—in which case they must be the same.

In this light, consider the claim that the norm of assertion can be no weaker (less demanding) than the norm of belief. Suppose the contrary—that is, that the norm of assertion *is* weaker than the norm of belief. Then there could be cases in which, while it is improper for S to believe that p, it is proper for S to assert that p. This sort of scenario seems patently unacceptable: surely one is not entitled to assert something one is not entitled to believe for oneself! After all, a hearer would be entitled to resent one who asserted something that was not even proper for her, the speaker, to believe.

I have just reviewed one reason for thinking that the norm of assertion should be no weaker than that of belief. Can we defend the claim that the norm of assertion should be no *stronger* than the norm of belief?

Such a view has been recently defended by Jonathan Sutton. Like Williamson (whose 'knowledge-first' approach to epistemology Sutton endorses), Sutton holds that the norm of assertion, and hence of belief, is knowledge. But here I am less interested in Sutton's defense of that particular norm, than I am in his argument bearing on the relation between the two norms. In defense of the claim that the norm of assertion should be no more demanding than that of belief, Sutton writes:

If beliefs so transmitted [through assertion] meet the primary standards governing good belief for both speaker and hearer—that is, they are justified in an evaluative sense—and meet standards of permissible belief . . . it would be mysterious if the assertions transmitting the beliefs failed to meet the standards governing good assertion. (Sutton 2007: 46)

Sutton's reasoning is this: if S's belief that p is proper from an epistemic point of view, then it should be proper or warranted from an epistemic point of view for S to manifest that belief by asserting that p. Assertion's norm should not demand more than belief's norm. A second sort of consideration supports the same conclusion. To see this, suppose (for the sake of *reductio*) that the norm of assertion is stronger than that of belief. In that case, one could have a justified belief in a content which one would not be warranted in asserting. That is not necessarily an objectionable outcome, until one realizes that there may be no way to express this belief in a warranted linguistic act. While one might think to do so by way of the hedge "I *think* that p" or "I *believe* that p," the difficulty is that in asserting "I think it is the case that p," it is often the case that one is properly taken to have asserted that p.[39] (A point very

---

[39] Does this point undermine my case in Chapter 4, in defense of the face-value presumption? It does not, since in assertorically uttering "I think that p" one is asserting the face-value content that one oneself thinks that p; my present claim is that one is (at least in some cases) *also* correctly taken to have asserted that p.

much in this vicinity is made in Maitra and Weatherson 2010: 104–5; and see also Cappelen and Lepore 2005.) If this is so, there will not be any simple, warranted assertoric act through which to express that belief. To avoid this, we reject the assumption that led to it—the assumption that the norm of assertion is stronger than that of belief.

I have just pointed out one way through which to try to establish the identity of the standards of the norm of assertion and that of belief: show that the former can be no weaker than, but also no stronger than, the latter. A second way to try to argue for the identification of the standards provided by the norm of assertion and that of belief is by linking both with judgment. The materials for this sort of argument are offered by Alexander Bird (2007). He writes:

If one is entitled to judge that p one should be entitled to assert that p to oneself... At the same time, what one is entitled to assert to others one is entitled to judge... This last argument... [shows] that the norms for judgment and assertion must be identical, whatever they are. (Bird 2007: 95)

While Bird himself focuses exclusively on judgment rather than belief, it is plausible to regard belief as the mental correlate of—or the mental state that correlates with—the act of judgment. Then, insofar as we can assume that one is entitled to believe that p iff one is entitled to judge that p, Bird's position implies that the two standards—the norm of assertion and the norm of belief—are identical. It does so by appeal to the following two conditionals: if one is entitled to believe that p then one is entitled to assert that p (to oneself); and if one is entitled to assert that p (to others) then one is entitled to believe that p (for oneself). So, one is entitled to assert that p iff one is entitled to believe that p.[40]

6.7 In Defense of Different Standards for Assertion and Belief

As noted, the normative standards for assertion are the same for that of belief only if the former can be no weaker (less demanding) than, but also no stronger (more demanding) than, the latter. But we can challenge both of these claims.

Consider first the claim that the normative standard for assertion should be no weaker (less demanding) than the norm of belief. One way to object to this claim is by way of an example from McKinnon (2013), who notes that a teacher might be warranted in asserting a proposition expressing the core claim of a scientific model, even as she knows that the model is only a close approximation to the truth, and so knows that the asserted proposition is literally false[41]—with the result that she herself does not

---

[40] For one final discussion of the identification of the standards of the norm of assertion and that of belief, albeit in the context of an endorsement of the knowledge norm, see Rysiew (2007b: 633). Others who argue that the norms of assertion and belief ought to be the same include Adler (2002) and Kvanvig (2009).

[41] This is something that has been emphasized in connection with education and philosophy of science by Kate Elgin. See Elgin (2004, 2007, 2009a, 2009b).

believe the proposition (and is warranted in her doxastic attitude). One might try to respond by claiming that the assertion is pedagogically warranted, but not warranted *simpliciter*, though this move begins to seem *ad hoc*, and calls into question whether there really is any clear sense to the idea of an assertion's being "warranted *simpliciter*."

Consider next the claim that the normative standard for assertion should be no stronger (more demanding) than the norm of belief. A first argument against this claim comes from Jason Stanley, who is interested in defending the idea that the conditions on entitled assertion are indeed more demanding than that on entitled belief. He writes:

> When someone asserts something, she takes on the commitment of transmitting her knowledge of it to her interlocutor. On the assumption that acquiring a belief via testimony results in having a weaker epistemic position towards the content of that belief than the one from whom one has acquired the warrant to believe it, it makes perfect sense that assertion would have a more demanding norm than full belief. (Stanley 2008: 52–53)

Stanley's argument has the right form, but it would appear to depend on a controversial assumption, to the effect that

> TWW "acquiring a belief via testimony results in having a weaker epistemic position towards the content of that belief than the one from whom one has acquired the warrant to believe it."

(I label this 'TWW' for 'Testimony Weakens Warrant.') TWW has itself been challenged in two (related) ways. First, there are those who would deny TWW because they endorse the view that testimony-based belief (typically) *preserves* the epistemic strength of the testimony. Burge (1993) defends a version of this thesis on broadly rationalistic grounds; and Goldberg (2010a) defends a version of it on broadly reliabilist grounds.[42] Second, there are those who would deny TWW because they endorse the view that there are times when the hearer's testimony-based belief enjoys a *superior* epistemic status relative to the speaker's epistemic position towards the same content. This, after all, is the upshot of various arguments against the idea that testimony only preserves knowledge, never generates it.[43] It would seem, then, that Stanley's objection cannot be sustained without addressing the substantial case that has been made for the idea that in at least a great many cases the hearer's epistemic position is at least as good as that of the speaker from whom she acquired the belief.

A second reason for calling into question whether the norm of assertion should be no stronger (more demanding) than the norm of belief is based on examples taken from MacFarlane (2010: 82).[44] It seems that there can be cases in which one retracts

---

[42] Bernecker (2009) appears to defend a version of this preservationist thesis regarding memory. He points out that doing so is compatible with the claim that there are occasions when a hearer is in a superior epistemic position vis-à-vis the content she believes on the basis of testimony than was the speaker herself. (He defends what he calls a *moderate preservationism*; see Bernecker (2009: 99–100).)

[43] See Lackey (1999, 2008), Graham (2000a, 2000b), and Goldberg (2005, 2007a, 2007b).

[44] But see also Kvanvig (2009), who makes a similar distinction between retracting an assertion and retracting a content.

an assertion, taking oneself not to have been in a position to defend it, yet properly continues to hold on to the belief in question. In fact, one might even avow the belief even as one retracts. MacFarlane writes: "Indeed, it is possible to retract [an] assertion while avowing the belief: 'I retract that, as I can't defend it. But I still believe it'" (82). Of course, the mere possibility that one might say this does not establish that the normative standard for assertion and that for belief ought to be distinguished. After all, one who wanted to defend the claim that the norm of assertion is no stronger than the norm of belief might reply that while a speaker might say this, she would be wrong to continue believing in such circumstances. But this is simply not obvious. I offer two cases in defense of the permissibility of believing that p even after one has retracted one's assertion that p.

The first is a testimony case. Consider any case in which H asserts something he believes on the basis of another's testimony, where the truth of the belief comes into question. If it is mutually known that the audience expects more than H's reasons for trusting the source speaker, then H, who is not in a position to give more than this, may well retract the assertion. Even so, if he continues to have reasons to trust his source, he may continue to believe with warrant.

The second is a case of dealing with the skeptic. It has been said of G. E. Moore's "proof" that, while he is entitled to believe its premises and its conclusion, still, when dealing with a skeptic he should not *assert* the premises and conclusion.[45] Suppose that this is right. Then in encounters with the skeptic, one is warranted in having beliefs whose contents one would not be warranted in asserting. One wants to say to Moore: "You cannot just *assert* that this is a hand! You are dealing with a skeptic, who baldly denies precisely what you assert!" But Moore would be right to reply: "Do you mean that I am not even warranted in believing this?" Insofar as both sides are right, as seems plausible, we need to distinguish between the standard of the norm of belief and that of assertion.

So far, I have presented several objections to the identification of the standard for proper belief with that for warranted assertion. These objections have all targeted one of the two claims: that the norm of assertion can be no weaker than the norm of belief, or that the norm of assertion can be no stronger than the norm of belief. But it is possible to directly challenge the identification itself.

One might think to challenge the identification directly by appeal to the idea that there is a risk-tolerance parameter in the standards for proper belief that is not present in the standards for warranted assertion. Many people (van Fraasen 2002; Adler 2002) have noted that insofar as we think of evidence as warranting belief, there will be a question regarding precisely how much evidence is required to do so, and that this leaves room for a risk-tolerance parameter on the standards for belief. Let us use the "payoff structure of a belief" to designate a way of representing the positive utility for

---

[45] Many people have held this view. For a relatively recent example, see Pritchard (2007).

the subject if the belief is true, as against the negative utility for her if the belief is false. The point regarding risk tolerance is this: it can be rational to tolerate a greater exposure to falsity in a case in which the payoff structure of a belief is great (one expects great things if the belief is true, and thinks this rather likely). But precisely how much risk one should be willing to tolerate may be a personal matter. If this is so, that one believes that p can reflect one's risk tolerance on the issue. Notice, though, that nothing parallel would appear to be present in the case of assertion. When one asserts that p, one presents p as true in a way that is backed by one's epistemic authority. It would seem that to do this is to present [p] as true, and hence belief-worthy, to one's audience, whatever their risk tolerance happens to be.

Still, this criticism of the belief–assertion parallel might strike some as objectionable on the grounds that the appeal to a risk parameter makes belief seem more voluntaristic than in fact it is. What we would like is a reason to doubt this parallel that does not make belief seem voluntaristic. This brings me to a second way that one might think to argue directly against the identification of the normative standards for belief and those for assertion. The basic point, which I will develop at greater length in Chapters 8 and 10, is simply this: assertion is a public act, whereas belief is neither an act nor a public matter, and there are reasons to think that both of these differences bear on the respective standards of each. I assume that the sense in which assertion is an act is clear. The sense in which it is public is simply twofold: the act of assertion is one that is (typically, normally) produced in a public setting, making the identity of the speaker, as producer of that act, a matter of public knowledge. (As we will see in Chapter 8, both of these aspects of assertion's publicness are crucial to its having the sort of features we take assertion to have.) After arguing that belief differs from assertion in both of these respects, I will go on to argue that these differences bear on the norms governing both.

It should not be controversial that belief is not an act. Decades of argumentation against the volitional account of belief would appear to make this clear. In fact, it is often taken as an embarrassment of one's account of belief, or of doxastic justification, if it implies doxastic voluntarism, the idea that belief is an act (or that it is something that is in our control). Even those who endorse versions of epistemic normativity on which belief is analogized to an act go out of their way to distance themselves from doxastic voluntarism. Consider Ernie Sosa's (2007, 2009) account of epistemic normativity as a species of performance normativity. Even though he speaks of beliefs as performances, he introduces this proposal with an immediate caveat:

> Some acts are performances . . . but so are some sustained states . . . Such performances can linger, and need not be constantly sustained through renewed conscious intentions. The performer's mind could wander, with little effect on the continuation or quality of the performance. Beliefs too might thus count as performances, long-sustained ones, with no more conscious or intentional an aim than that of a heartbeat. At a minimum, beliefs can be assessed for correctness independently of any competence that they may manifest . . . (2007: 23)

I take it as given that beliefs are not acts. But nor are they private in either of the senses associated with assertion. They are not (standardly, typically) produced in a public setting, nor for this reason is the believer's belief (standardly, typically) a matter of public knowledge. To be sure, one can manifest one's belief; and the standard way to do so is by way of making the corresponding assertion. But it is the assertion rather than the belief that is the public act.

One might think to challenge my claim that belief is not a public phenomenon by appeal to comments Clifford makes in his classic paper, "The Ethics of Belief." In fact, it seems that Clifford himself is a proponent of an identification of these standards precisely because he thinks belief is, in the relevant sense, a public matter. He notes that false belief can do serious damage to a community, precisely because it can get passed from person to person via testimony. Thus, he speaks of the "village rustic" as keeping "fatal superstitions" alive (Clifford 1999: 73), and he goes on to editorialize that beliefs are "common property":

Whoso would deserve well of his fellows in this matter will guard the purity of his beliefs with a very fanaticism of jealous care, lest any time it should rest on an unworthy object, and catch a stain which can never be wiped away ... That duty is to guard ourselves from such beliefs as from pestilence, which may shortly master our own body and then spread to the rest of the town. What would be thought of one who, for the sake of a sweet fruit, should deliberately run the risk of delivering a plague upon his family and his neighbors? (Clifford 1999: 74–76)

What is more, many contemporary authors appear to agree with Clifford that belief is public in this sense (Craig 1990: 11; Zagzebski 2003: 143; Grimm 2009: 259–60; Kusch 2009: 61). Now, while I agree that we do have duties to our fellows, and while I do think that this can constrain what we ought to believe, I think this has more to do with ethics than it does with epistemology. And while the ethics can put constraints on the epistemology, deriving these constraints is no simple matter. It is so complicated that I save my comments for the next chapter, where I take up the ethics of assertion and belief. For now, I will assume that belief is not public in the uncontentious sense that it does not offend against the nature of belief to hold one's beliefs privately.

I have just argued that belief is unlike assertion in being neither an act nor a public matter in these senses. I now want to argue that these differences are relevant to the norms that govern assertion and belief. Why think that these differences make a difference? One reason is this: as I suggested in Chapter 3, and as I will go on to argue at greater length in Chapters 8–11, we can think of the norm of assertion as essentially playing the role of a solution to a two- or multi-party coordination problem, having to do with the calibration and alignment of expectations among parties to speech exchanges involving the communication of information. But to see the norm of assertion in this light just is to see it in the light of assertion's status as a public act. (Chapters 9–11 develop the idea of the norm of assertion as a solution to a particular coordination problem, and Chapter 8 explores the breakdown of the practice when the publicness of assertion is no longer in play, as in the case of anonymous assertion.) Insofar as belief is neither an act nor a public matter in the relevant senses, we would anticipate that the norm that governs it is sensitive to different considerations. And indeed, in Chapters 8 and 11 I will argue that the evidential sensitivity of belief ensures that its standards diverge from those of assertion.

One might grant the difference but deny that it makes a difference in connection with the respective normative standards of belief and assertion. After all, one might think that to assert is to do something like what the assurance view of testimony thinks is going on in the act of testifying: it is to "give one's word," or to enable another to "take it from me."[46] Following up on this thought, one might think that to be in a position to perform this sort of act with warrant, one must occupy the relevant epistemic position vis-à-vis the asserted proposition. And if this is correct, it looks once again as if warranted assertion (assertion satisfying the norm of assertion) requires proper belief (and so requires satisfying the norm of belief). But this reply is too quick. In particular, it overlooks the possibility that there are speech exchanges in which information is needed and is exchanged, but where all parties recognize that, while one can be in a better or worse epistemic position on the information in question, knowledge (or doxastic justification or the other epistemically high-grade statuses) is practically impossible to come by.[47] If there is still point to presenting a proposition as true in such a way as to implicate one's own epistemic authority (whatever strength it might be), this would be a situation in which the norm of assertion would be less than that of belief. And indeed I will be arguing in Chapters 8 and 11 that this sort of situation arises with some regularity in everyday life. If this is correct, we need to distinguish the standard imposed by the norm of assertion from that imposed by the norm of belief.

How then should we respond to the arguments in favor of the belief–assertion parallel? To begin, we must reject the point (endorsed by both Dummett and Williamson) that assertion is the outer analogue of judgment and belief. But we have already seen a reason to do just this: assertion is a public act, and insofar as it offers the solution to a coordination problem, it is *not* the outer analogue of judgment and belief. For the very same reason we can reject Bird's claims that "If one is entitled to judge that p one should be entitled to assert that p to oneself . . . At the same time, what one is entitled to assert to others one is entitled to judge" (Bird 2007: 95). But what should be said about the first consideration offered in defense of the belief–assertion parallel—that it would be absurd to think that we are entitled to believe something we would not be

---

[46] For a discussion, see Chapter 2, Section 2.7, and Chapter 3, Section 3.4.

[47] As will emerge, I do not have in mind the sort of "train" cases discussed in Williamson (2000), in which one needs to respond quickly to a query lest one lose the opportunity to act on information. In that sort of case there are practical constraints on one's assertion. The cases I have in mind, to be described in later chapters, are not of this sort.

entitled to assert, or that we are entitled to assert something we would not be entitled to believe? While a full answer will have to await my discussion of the norm of assertion itself (Part IV), here I can highlight the reasons we have already seen for rejecting both of these claims. First, there were my two illustrations of MacFarlane's point about retraction; these give us examples of warranted belief without a corresponding entitlement to assert. In addition, there was the possibility envisaged previously, where there is a point to authority-invoking information exchanges under conditions in which it is mutually acknowledged that knowledge and justified belief are not to be had. Cases of this sort provide a schematic example of warranted assertion without an entitlement to believe. (I will present concrete examples of this phenomenon in Chapters 8 and 11.) Finally, there is McKinnon's (2013) case of the teacher who asserts something she herself recognizes to be only a close approximation to the truth.

I conclude, tentatively, that we should not assume that the standard provided by the norm of belief is the same as the standard provided by the norm of assertion. If this is correct, then even if an appeal to the norm of belief is needed for an account of Moore-paradoxicality, we should not think to conclude from this alone anything very substantial about the norm of assertion. (I will return to the phenomenon of Moore-paradoxicality, briefly, in Chapter 11, once I defend my own particular account of assertion's norm.)

6.8 Conclusion

In this chapter I have argued that, more than other theories of assertion, MMENA provides us with an attractive account of the non-contingent relation between assertion and belief. While some have thought to appeal to the norm of assertion to provide an account of Moore-paradoxicality, I have argued, first, that even if this were the right account of Moore-paradoxicality it would not distinguish the precise content of the norm of assertion; and second, that we have grounds for distinguishing the standard provided by the norm of assertion from that provided by the norm of belief. The significance of the latter point lies in part in this, that insofar as the norm of belief is needed to account for the phenomenon of Moore-paradoxicality in its full generality, we have reason to think that no account of the norm of assertion can be derived from a proper treatment of that phenomenon.

7
The Ethics of Assertion (and Belief)

7.1 MMENA and the Ethics of Assertion and Belief

This book has been a systematic exploration of MMENA—the hypothesis that it is mutually manifest to all competent speakers that assertion answers to a robustly epistemic norm. In Chapters 1–3 I argued that such a hypothesis explains the core features of our assertoric practice, pertaining to assertion's epistemic significance. Then, in Chapters 4–6 I used MMENA to explain assertion's connection to several phenomena in the philosophy of mind and language. I argued further that we need not take a position on the precise content of the norm in order to obtain the results I have claimed. In this and the next chapter my aim is to use MMENA itself to explain two other phenomena associated with assertion. Here I do so in the context of an interest in ethics. My thesis is that MMENA can be used to establish two claims in this connection: first, that there is such a thing as an 'ethics of assertion'; and second, that, given the connection between assertion and belief, the 'ethics of assertion' can be used to provide motivation for some (interpersonal) constraints bearing on what might go under the label 'the ethics of belief'.

Before proceeding to my discussion, I want to provide a little background on the connection between assertion and the ethics of belief. Investigations regarding the 'ethics of belief' typically speak about one's duty to believe in line with one's evidence. In virtue of what does one have such a duty? In this chapter I aim to suggest that we can see at least some doxastic duties as arising from the duties and responsibilities that we bear to one another as participants in speech exchanges. In arguing for this I will be drawing on some of the results for which I have argued in previous chapters. From Chapter 3 I will use the idea that, given MMENA, the act of asserting something gives rise to certain responsibilities—responsibilities which reflect the mutual expectations that speakers and hearers are entitled to have in situations involving observed assertions. Here I will expand on that discussion to make clear that both speakers and hearers are under normative pressure to the other(s) in the speech exchange. From Chapter 6 I borrow claims regarding the connections between assertion and belief. The aim will be to argue that the responsibilities and entitlements engendered by assertion, together with the connection between assertion and belief, enable us to derive some (admittedly minimal) constraints that we might collect under the label 'the ethics of belief'.

Since the constraints I will be deriving are somewhat minimal, a comment is in order regarding why they should be of interest. I submit that the manner in which I purport to derive them—from the norm governing assertion—is noteworthy, for it suggests that at least some of the duties and responsibilities that go under the label of the 'ethics of belief' are duties and responsibilities that one owes, not (or at least not merely) to oneself, but (also?) to others. Given that the phenomenon of belief is often regarded as a personal (individualistic) affair, I regard it is an interesting result that at least some of the 'ethics of belief' is motivated by interpersonal considerations—what we owe to one another as fellow communicators in a world in which we depend on others for much of what we take ourselves to know. In this respect I am developing a line of argument to which Clifford himself would have been sympathetic.

7.2 The Ethics of Assertion, Part I: What the Speaker Owes to the Hearer

This book has been oriented around the development and use of the hypothesis I have been labeling 'MMENA.' This is the hypothesis that it mutually manifest that assertion is governed by a robustly epistemic norm:

> ENA   S must: assert p, only if S satisfies epistemic condition E with respect to the proposition that p, that is, only if E(S, [p]).

As I argued in Chapter 3, if MMENA is true we would predict that the practice of assertion is rich with mutual expectations between speakers and hearers. These expectations are grounded in common knowledge of the fact that assertion has a robustly epistemic norm. In this section I want to revisit this point briefly. After doing so I will go on to argue (in the second half of this section and the whole of the next section) that the mutual expectations themselves reflect what we might call the 'ethics of assertion'.

I begin with the mutual expectations that arise in connection with assertion. Suppose that MMENA is true. Then, in asserting something, the speaker performs an act regarding which it is common knowledge that her act was warranted only if she had the relevant epistemic authority. We might then regard the act of asserting that p as conveying[1] that the speaker does, in fact, possess the relevant epistemic authority with respect to the truth of the proposition that p. (See Chapter 6, Section 6.4 for a full discussion.) Now, others have remarked that a common reaction elicited by assertion is to query how the speaker knows, or what her evidence is.[2] Employing MMENA, we

---

[1] By 'conveying' I have in mind something like 'communicating, as part of the conventional significance of the illocutionary force of the speech act.' Clearly, what is conveyed in this sense is not part of the content asserted.

[2] The "How do you know?" reaction is described in Williamson (2000). See also Stone (2007), Kvanvig (2009), Turri (2010b), and McKinnon (2012) for more recent discussions of the nature and significance of the characteristic reactions to assertions.

can describe such a case as one in which the hearer is requesting the speaker to vindicate the conveyed claim of relevant epistemic authority. The fact that such a response is ordinary highlights one class of expectations in play when assertions are made: hearers expect speakers who make an assertion to recognize that they are under some obligation to vindicate their relevant epistemic authority, if appropriately called upon to do so. But we might also note that speakers typically anticipate that hearers will have such expectations. (See Chapter 3, Sections 3.2 and 3.3 for discussion.) This is why it comes as no surprise to a speaker if, having made an assertion, she elicits one of these responses in a hearer. What is more, in such a situation the speaker herself will regard herself as under an obligation to respond (at least as long as she has no reason to regard the query as illegitimate). These expectations that speakers and hearers have of one another are part of our assertoric practice.

In Chapter 3 (especially Sections 3.2 and 3.3) I argued that we can describe these mutual expectations using the language of responsibility and entitlement. When a speaker makes an assertion, she does something regarding which it is common knowledge that what she did is proper only if she had the relevant epistemic authority. But in that case the hearer is entitled to believe that the speaker *acknowledges that she has the responsibility* to possess the relevant epistemic authority. The propriety of this talk of entitlements and responsibilities has as its source the norm (or rule) governing assertion.[3] In previous chapters I cited Angus Ross's comments in this connection:

It is a quite general feature of rule-governed life that the responsibility for ensuring that one's actions conform to the rules lies primarily with oneself and that others are in consequence entitled to assume, in the absence of definite reasons for supposing otherwise, that one's actions do so conform. Thus where the rules are such that one may perform a certain action only if a certain condition obtains ... then to perform the action is to entitle witnesses to assume that the corresponding condition obtains. If that assumption proves false and others act upon it with unfortunate consequences, at least part of the responsibility will lie with oneself for having entitled them to make that assumption. (Ross 1986: 77–78)

Ross's conclusion on this score[4] is in the vicinity of the claim I wish to make, though it is a little stronger. His conclusion is that if it is common knowledge that doing X is proper only if such-and-such is the case, then if subject S does X, others are entitled to assume that such-and-such *is* the case, with the result that they can blame S if it should turn out that such-and-such is *not* the case. Applied to the case of assertion, Ross's claim would be this: if you assert that p, others are entitled to assume (in the absence of definite reasons to the contrary) that the assertion was warranted, with the result that they can blame you if it should turn out that it was not warranted.

---

[3] I describe this sort of entitlement at greater length, and designate it as a "practice-generated entitlement," in my (forthcoming b).
[4] Interestingly, Ross makes the foregoing remark in connection with the rule-governed nature of language use.

Ross puts an epistemic gloss on a point that I think is better rendered in normative (but not epistemic) terms. Unlike Ross, who thinks that another's assertion provides the hearer with a defeasible entitlement to assume that the relevant assertoric standards are met, my claim is this: if you assert that p, others are entitled to assume that *you (acknowledge that you) are responsible* for having met the relevant assertoric standards (= for having had the relevant warranting authority). In one clear sense, my claim is weaker than Ross's. That a speaker has a certain responsibility, even that she acknowledges having this responsibility, does not imply (or give us reason to think) that she has fulfilled the responsibility. Consequently, an entitlement to assume that one has (acknowledges having) a certain responsibility, by itself, does not entitle one to assume that one has met the responsibility, nor does the former entitle one even to assume that the latter holds *absent reasons to think otherwise*. Compare: I am entitled to expect that my adolescent children will be home by 11 pm tonight, as this is the mutually acknowledged house rule; but, even though this entitlement would underwrite my holding them responsible if they violate this rule tonight, the entitlement does *not* provide me with an epistemic justification to believe that they *will* be home by the required time! (If it did, parenting might be much less stressful than it is.) As we will see, however, my weaker claim, to the effect that S's asserting that p entitles an audience to assume that S is (and acknowledges being) responsible for having the relevant warranting authority, is not without consequence.

Before getting to this, though, it is important to be clear about what makes it appropriate to speak of responsibility in connection with assertion. Assertion—at least in its paradigmatic instances—is a public act.[5] Its public nature is seen in the facts, first, that assertions are (typically) made to an audience, but second, that the distinctive significance of acts of this type—their aptness for spreading knowledge, but also their susceptibility to being exploited in lies or other forms of insincerity—reflects what is common knowledge regarding what we are entitled to expect of one another when acts of this type are performed. The responsibilities that arise in connection with assertion arise from this distinctive significance.

Some have tried to get at this distinctiveness by likening the act of asserting something to the act of promising something.[6] The idea that asserting is akin to promising (in some relevant respect(s)) has much to say for it.[7] As I see matters, the core similarity is this: the making of an assertion, like the making of a promise, generates a certain kind of *entitlement* for the relevant audience to form a certain expectation. To promise to X is (among other things) to entitle the person (or persons) to whom one made the promise to expect that one will X.[8] If one then fails to X, so that the audience's

---

[5] This point will be developed at great length in Chapter 8, when I discuss the phenomenon of anonymous assertion.

[6] See, for example, Ross (1986: 79), Watson (2004), Hinchman (2005), Owens (2006), and Moran (2006). I discussed the promising model of assertion, briefly, in Chapter 3, Section 3.6.

[7] This said, I think the analogy is likely to mislead in important respects. See Chapter 3, Section 3.6.

[8] It is also to incur the obligation to X, of course.

expectation is violated, the audience can *hold one responsible* for the unhappy state of affairs. In a similar way, to assert that p is to entitle the relevant audience to expect that one has the relevant epistemic authority with respect to the proposition that p.[9] However—to revisit the point I made in the previous paragraph—to say that H is entitled to expect S to have the relevant epistemic authority does not imply that H is *justified in believing* that S has the relevant epistemic authority.[10] The entitlement here is rather an entitlement to *hold S responsible* for having that authority (akin to my entitlement to expect my children to be home, and hence to hold them responsible for being home, by 11 pm tonight). The core of the parallel between promising and asserting, then, comes to this: in both cases the speaker (in performing the speech act she did) authorizes the hearer to form a certain expectation; this expectation reflects the mutually recognized, interpersonal nature of the expectations generated by speech acts of that kind (promise or assertion); and the relevant audience is entitled to hold the speaker responsible for the satisfaction of this expectation, so that if the expectation is violated (its content is false), that audience can blame the speaker and demand redress. Just as a person who promises "owes it" to the relevant audience (here, the addressee) to do what she promised, so too a person who asserts "owes it" to the relevant audience (here, those who observed the assertion) to have the relevant epistemic authority.

I have just defended the idea that it is appropriate to speak of responsibilities in connection with a speaker's making an assertion, and correlatively of a hearer's entitlement to hold a speaker responsible. Still, we are not quite at the point where we can speak of assertion's generating distinctly *moral* responsibilities. To see why this is, we will need to go beyond the similarities between asserting and promising, and say a few things about the particular content of the norm of assertion itself. My point here can be made in terms of the knowledge norm of assertion, so assume (for the purpose of illustration only) that knowledge is the norm of assertion:

KNA   S must: assert p, only if S knows that p.

(The idea of KNA is that an assertion is improper if it is not knowledgeable.) Now it would seem that there are ways of failing to know that p which are such that, were one to fail to know that p in one of these ways, then, while one's assertion that p would be unwarranted (for failing to satisfy the knowledge norm), one would be *blameless* in so doing. (And by 'blameless' here I mean to include any sense relevant to one's moral duties to others.) Consider, for example, Gettier cases: there, one believes that p, one's belief is both true and justified, yet one fails to know that p, owing to some sort of

---

[9] In Chapter 3, Section 3.6 I argued that the relevant audience should be seen to be, not just the person to whom the asserter addressed herself, but anyone who observed the assertion. This was a crucial difference between my view of assertion, and the assurance view of testimony (taken as an account of testimony-constituting assertion).

[10] Whether the entitlement to assume that S has the authority is sufficient for H to be justified in *believing* that S has the authority is a further question—one at the heart of much discussion in the epistemology of testimony. This point is missed by some who contribute to the literature; see Goldberg (2011) for a discussion.

knowledge-undermining epistemic luck (not reflecting any intellectual irresponsibility on one's own part). So it would seem that if knowledge is the norm of assertion, then not all unwarranted assertions are cases in which the speaker deserves moral blame. The further result would be that if the speaker can be held responsible in these cases, the responsibility at issue is not *moral* responsibility.[11]

I do not intend this to be a novel point. Indeed, proponents of KNA themselves have acknowledged as much. Thus it is standard for such proponents to distinguish between the primary and secondary senses of propriety, arguing that an assertion can be improper in the primary sense (for failing to satisfy KNA) while proper in the secondary sense (for being such that, given the speaker's epistemic position at the time, it was reasonable for her to suppose that she satisfied KNA). Versions of this distinction have been made by Williamson (1996) and DeRose (2002). Both of them note that the distinction itself can be independently motivated, since it will be needed in any domain in which the standards are objective, and where subjects' judgments regarding the satisfaction of those standards can be reasonable even when false.[12] What is more, many will think that it is plausible, and in any case it is open to defenders of KNA to accept, that moral responsibility goes with secondary propriety, not with primary propriety.[13] But, whether or not this analysis is accepted, and indeed whether or not we accommodate the present point in terms of a primary/secondary propriety distinction, the point remains that we cannot simply assume that the responsibility for satisfying the norm of assertion is a moral one, or that violating it warrants an allegation of moral blameworthiness.

So let it be agreed on all sides: if the norm of assertion is knowledge (or indeed any sort of 'externalist' epistemic standing), then not all cases of improper assertion are cases in which the speaker deserves moral blame. What, then, can we say about the connection between the responsibilities generated by assertions, and one's moral responsibilities more generally? Two initial things are worth highlighting in this connection. These points hold even on the assumption that knowledge (or some other 'externalist' epistemic standing) is the norm of assertion. Both have to do with the responsibilities generated by assertoric speech. First, it remains the case that one who asserts in violation of the norm of assertion, under conditions where it is reasonable to expect that she aimed to assert warrantedly,[14] "lets the hearer down"—even if it is sometimes the case that the speaker is not susceptible to moral blame for so doing.

---

[11] What sort of responsibility is it? I would say that it is the sort of responsibility that is bound up with our participation in a practice or rule-governed game, whereby participants are each responsible for participating in accord with the prevailing standards (playing by the rules). See Goldberg (forthcoming b) for more details.

[12] Not all have been happy with this distinction. See Lackey (2007b).

[13] Indeed, a point in this vicinity has been made by Gideon Rosen (2002: 74–79), in another context altogether. I cite and discuss the relevant passages later.

[14] This is meant to rule out cases of manifest irony, bald-faced lies, and other forms of obvious insincerity. Later I will defend the imposition of the "reasonable to expect" condition.

("Letting the hearer down" would then not be, or at least not always be, a moral failing.) And second, we can bring in the moral dimension here, albeit in a qualified way, by saying this: in any case in which the speaker "lets the hearer down," insofar as this "letting down" reflects a failure of the speaker to have lived up to her moral responsibilities, she deserves moral blame.[15]

We are now at the crux of the matter. When is a speaker's "letting the hearer down" a matter of her having failed to live up to her *moral* responsibilities? What is the hearer entitled to hold the speaker *morally* responsible for? I submit that, given MMENA (and the mutual knowledge that it engenders), the moral dimension of a speaker's responsibilities to a hearer boil down to this: a hearer is entitled to regard one who asserts as *having done what can reasonably be expected of her to ensure that her assertion satisfied assertion's norm*. This is a special case of a general point that many other authors have made in the ethical domain. The point concerns what people are entitled to expect of one when it is mutually manifest that one has a certain responsibility/obligation (or set of responsibilities/obligations). Gideon Rosen considers the case involving our moral obligations in general:

It is reasonable to expect a person to meet his epistemic obligations in coming to a view about what to do (provided he knows what they are and has the capacity to meet them). And it is reasonable to expect a person to do his best to act in light of his considered view about what he has most reason to do. (Rosen 2002: 79)

This comment comes only pages after Rosen has described what is *un*reasonable to expect in this regard:

It is unreasonable to expect people not to do what they blamelessly believe they are entitled to do, and it is unreasonable to subject people to sanctions when it would be unreasonable to expect them to have acted differently. (Rosen 2002: 74–75)

Putting the two points together, we can discern Rosen's view regarding what it is reasonable to expect of a person, S, who has a mutually manifest obligation or responsibility: it is reasonable to expect her to have (what by her lights are) reasonable views regarding what those obligations (responsibilities) are, and (what by her lights are) reasonable views regarding what would satisfy those obligations (responsibilities); and it is reasonable to expect that she has done her best to act in light of these (by her lights) reasonable views. Assuming MMENA, we would obtain the result that it is reasonable to expect that the speaker who asserts has done her best to act in light of the requirement to be epistemically authoritative. (Indeed, this provides a rationale for DeRose's and Williamson's notion of secondary propriety, discussed previously.)

It is worth acknowledging that when it comes to the question of what we are entitled to expect from others with responsibilities or obligations, Rosen's views are among the least demanding of the views one can find in the ethics literature.[16]

---

[15] See Goldberg (forthcoming b). [16] For one recent response, see E. Harman (2011).

Others would have us reasonably expect more. Some hold that our responsibilities go far beyond what Rosen would claim—with the result that others' reasonable expectations of us go far beyond this as well. The dispute here is helpfully cast in the debate in the literature on culpable ignorance. It is helpful to frame our present topic in this way, since in effect we are asking when a speaker's failure to satisfy the robustly epistemic norm of assertion is culpable, and when her failure to do so is blameless.[17] (This literature can also help us to pursue questions such as: what is a subject responsible for knowing when she asserts? What, epistemically speaking, can we hold an asserter as being responsible for?) On this score, it is interesting to consider those whose views on culpable ignorance are more demanding than Rosen's—that is, those who think that our responsibilities extend beyond what Rosen depicts. FitzPatrick writes that we will rightly regard a subject as responsible for her own ignorance when (s)he

could reasonably have been expected to take measures that would have corrected or avoided it, given his or her capabilities and the opportunities provided by the social context, but failed to do so either due to akrasia or due to the culpable, non-akratic exercise of such vices as overconfidence, arrogance, dismissiveness, laziness, dogmatism, incuriosity, self-indulgence, contempt, and so on. (FitzPatrick 2008: 609)

And for his part, James Montmarquet speaks about the "basic responsibility [we] bear for the exercise of certain kinds of traits of intellectual character" (Montmarquet 1992: 331). Clearly both FitzPatrick's view and Montmarquet's view would require more of an asserter than Rosen's view does. Where Rosen's view merely requires that the asserter have reasonable views and do what can reasonably be expected of her with respect to the requirement to be relevantly epistemically authoritative, FitzPatrick's view and Montmarquet's view would require an additional set of things: that the speaker have cultivated her intellectual character, and that she not have been ignorant (with respect to satisfying the requirement to be epistemically authoritative) out of any intellectual or character vice. Clearly, if FitzPatrick or Montmarquet is correct, then the claim, to the effect that hearers are entitled to expect that an asserter has done what can be reasonably expected of her in connection with having the relevant epistemic authority, is understood to involve having cultivated (and having asserted on the basis of) a proper intellectual character.

Now I do not want to get involved in the dispute over what we can "reasonably expect" of an asserter in connection with her having satisfied the norm of assertion. (This is an interesting issue, but pursuing it would take me too far afield from my present purposes.) Happily, I do not have to get involved in this dispute to make the point I want to make. In particular, all that I need is a point which is in common between these two sides. My point is simply that a hearer is entitled to regard one who asserts as

---

[17] The classical piece in this literature is H. Smith (1983). Other seminal papers include Adams (1985), Calhoun (1989), Moody-Adams (1994), Buss (1997), and A. Smith (2005).

having done what can reasonably be expected of her (whatever that is) to ensure that her assertion satisfied assertion's norm.

To return, then, to the main topic: even on the assumption that not all unwarranted assertion is morally blameworthy assertion, we still have discerned a significant connection between the norm of assertion and the moral responsibilities attendant to assertoric speech. The picture would be this: having asserted that p, S has the responsibility to have the relevant epistemic authority, whatever it is; assuming that such authority amounts to knowledge or some other 'externalist' epistemic standing, then S may fail to live up to her assertion-generated responsibility without being morally blameworthy; and whether a case of unwarranted assertion involves moral blame is determined by whether S did what could reasonably be expected of her to ensure that she had the relevant authority.

We are now in a position to speak about one aspect of what we might call the "ethics of assertion." We can speak of that aspect that pertains to what the speaker owes (morally speaking) to the hearer. At least, we are in a position to speak to *part* of the responsibilities we have as speakers: what I will call responsibilities that arise *when we make an assertion*. I will call these *responsibilities-for-having-asserted*. (In Section 7.4 I will go on to argue that there can be responsibilities-*to-assert*—that we can be under an obligation to make an assertion—as is seen in the fact that the allegation "But you should have told me so!" sometimes rings true.[18] I will call these *responsibilities-to-assert*.) The position we are now in enables us to address a speaker's responsibilities to a hearer that arise in virtue of her having made an assertion—her responsibilities-for-having-asserted.

I submit that a speaker's responsibilities-for-having-asserted come to this: she (the speaker) must have done what can reasonably be expected of her to ensure that she did, in fact, have the warranting epistemic authority. I regard it as an interesting and substantive question what we can reasonably expect of each other in this regard. I suspect that matter is very complicated; in particular, I suspect that an adequate account will have to accommodate facts regarding the various sorts of context in which we make assertions, the various interests that are (mutually known to be) in play, and the various interpersonal relations we have to those to whom we address our assertions. It is here, in connection with the ethics of assertion—and more specifically still, in connection with the responsibility-for-having-asserted—that I think the phenomenon of *second-person address* is significant: in making an assertion, what we owe, ethically speaking, to the person whom we are addressing typically differs from what we owe to someone who merely overhears us. But we should not confuse this point about the *ethics* of assertion for a point about the *epistemology* of assertion, as the "assurance view" of testimony is wont to do. (See Chapter 2, Section 2.7 and Chapter 3, Section 3.6 for more details.)

---

[18] These obligations arise when a speaker has, or takes herself to have, some information which the hearer wants or could use, and when certain other conditions obtain. Under these to-be-specified conditions, the speaker is under a moral obligation to say what she knows, or takes herself to know.

However, rather than trying to provide an account of precisely what a speaker owes to a hearer (in virtue of having asserted something), I want instead to move on to consider another part of the 'ethics of assertion.' I do so out of the conviction that what a speaker owes to a hearer (in virtue of having asserted) is only *part* of the content of the ethics of assertion. Another part involves responsibilities-to-assert, of course. But before I can get to that, I want to address yet another side entirely: the ethical responsibilities on the part of *the hearer*, what he owes to the speaker, as it were. This part has generated much less discussion in the philosophical literature on assertion, but thanks to such thinkers as Ted Hinchman, Richard Moran, and above all Miranda Fricker, it has recently been the subject of some interest.[19] It is an important part of our story; and I turn to it now, as my results here will subsequently be used to inform my account of the responsibility-to-assert (Section 7.4).

7.3 The Ethics of Assertion, Part II: What the Hearer Owes to the Speaker

I want to suggest that if MMENA is true—if it is mutually known by competent language users that assertion is answerable to some sort of epistemic norm—then the hearer has certain responsibilities to the speaker as well.

To obtain an initial sense of the idea that hearers might owe things to speakers, consider the following case. In the course of a joint activity between various people who are coordinating with one another, Samantha tells Harry that p. The speech act passes in silence: Harry neither confirms that he has accepted what Samantha has told him, nor says anything to indicate that he has rejected (or otherwise ignored) what she has told him. Soon thereafter, Samantha acts on the assumption that Harry accepted that p—only to find out that Harry does not accept that p. The question is: if Samantha's acting on the contrary assumption led to difficulties (for Samantha or for the joint activity), does Harry bear any responsibility for these difficulties? Does Samantha enjoy anything like an entitlement to assume that when her assertions pass in silence they have been accepted—so that Harry had a responsibility to indicate rejection? Is this case relevantly analogous to the responsibility Samantha would bear if Harry had accepted Samantha's statement under conditions in which Samantha did not in fact have the relevant epistemic authority?

Interestingly, it would appear that one need not endorse MMENA to hold that the hearer has responsibilities of some sort or other. Although I do not know whether Stalnaker would endorse the hypothesis of hearer responsibilities, his account of assertion does lend itself to arguing that there are such. In his original (1978) paper on assertion, he wrote:

To make an assertion is to reduce the context set in a particular way, *provided that there are no objections from the other participants in the conversation* . . . [T]he essential effect of an

---

[19] See Hinchman (2005), Miranda Fricker (2007), Moran (2006), and Wanderer (2011). A brief but (characteristically) highly suggestive and insightful discussion can be found in Anscombe (1979).

assertion is to change the presuppositions of the participants in the conversation by adding the content of what is asserted to what is presupposed. This effect is avoided *only if the assertion is rejected*. (Reprinted in Stalnaker 1999: 86; italics added)

As I say, it is not entirely clear from this whether Stalnaker would agree that all parties to the conversation are entitled to assume that an assertion has been accepted unless there is some public indication otherwise. However, such a reading is compatible with this passage. And it would be the proper reading if we assume that hearers who object to or otherwise reject an assertion have a duty to make this fact known. In certain circumstances, this assumption is plausible. Employing the notion of "reasonable expectation" developed previously, we might say that, at least in those cases where it is mutually manifest that the success of a joint activity depends on cooperation and coordination, a speaker has a reasonable expectation of being informed when a co-participant rejects her assertion. (Again, this is an expectation in the *normative* sense in which I hold my children responsible for being home by 11 pm, not in the *predictive* sense in which I would bet that they will.)

The case of Samantha and Harry enables us to get at questions that are in the ballpark of the sort of issue I want to raise in this section, but they do not get at the most general form of that issue. For one thing, the previous case is one in which Samantha and Harry are engaged in a joint activity; and it might be thought that this makes the case sufficiently special so as to preclude any general conclusions regarding hearers' responsibilities in the face of assertion as such. For another thing, even if there are responsibilities that hearers bear to speakers on observing them make an assertion, it is not obvious that these responsibilities take the form: either accept what the speaker says, or make clear that you do not do so. (In fact, it is very easy to imagine all sorts of cases where hearers are under no such obligation: cases of duress or pressure, cases involving threats, cases involving that lonely guy sitting next to you on the plane who will not stop talking, and so forth.) Again, we would like a more general way to get at the sorts of responsibilities a hearer owes a speaker on an occasion of assertion.

Still, I think that this initial case is instructive. I submit that it gets at a sort of *disrespect* Harry exhibits towards Samantha were Harry simply to disregard Samantha's assertion that p as having any bearing on the question whether p. Suppose that soon after Samantha asserts that p to Harry, a question arises which turns on whether p. If in response Harry reacts in such a way as to make clear he has no opinion regarding whether p, where this attitude does not rest on his having any reasons to be dubious of Samantha's assertion to that effect, it seems that Harry has not given Samantha's assertion its due. Simply put, in asserting that p Samantha presents p as true in such a way as to convey that she is relevantly epistemically authoritative; and in failing to regard Samantha's assertion as having any bearing on whether p, without having any reason to question whether Samantha actually does have the relevant epistemic authority,[20] Harry offends against Samantha's implicit claim to have relevant epistemic authority. This is precisely the sort of case that has led Miranda Fricker (2007) to coin the term "epistemic injustice": in disregarding her assertion, Harry has done Samantha an epistemic injustice.

In order to make clear that Harry is under some obligation here, and (more specifically) that it is appropriate to talk of the *(moral) responsibilities* that Harry in his role as a hearer has to Samantha in her role as a speaker, I want to develop the hypothesis that simple disregard of an assertion involves a kind of disrespect. I assume that to disrespect someone is to harm them in some morally relevant way; the question I want to raise concerns the nature of the disrespect involved in a case in which a hearer does not accord another speaker's assertion the status it deserves. Here I assume that simply disregarding an assertion is a paradigmatic way of not according the assertion the status it deserves. The first matter to be addressed, then, concerns the status that an assertion deserves to be accorded (from a moral point of view).

I submit that the status that an assertion deserves (from a moral point of view) to be accorded is the status of *being taken seriously*. The idea behind this notion can be developed in connection with MMENA itself. According to the MMENA-based account I have been developing, assertion is an act that conveys a speaker's claim to relevant epistemic authority on the matter. In light of this, I want to say that a hearer accords the proper status to assertions when he takes acts of this sort as conveying such a claim, and when he evaluates them in the manner appropriate to acts of that kind. When he does so, I will describe him as *having taken the assertion seriously*. Now, I do not suppose for a moment that taking an assertion seriously involves any substantial kind of inquiry. That would be a rather serious over-intellectualization; we are not always so self-conscious and deliberate in our responses to others' statements, and yet we are not for that reason disrespecting them. What is more, I do not intend that to take an assertion seriously, one has to adopt a serious demeanor and act the part. Often, we do not behave like this, and (usually) it is no form of disrespect when we do not. Rather, what I have in mind is this: when S asserts that p, H takes the act seriously when (1) H apprehends the act as one whereby S has conveyed her epistemic authoritativeness regarding p, and (2) H evaluates that act in ways proper to acts of this type. Conforming to (1) and (2) is often, perhaps even typically, a highly automatic affair. One does so, for example, whenever one reacts to an assertion by believing what was said (because it was said so); but one also does so when, whether or not one believes what was said, one implicitly or explicitly registers that the act of S's asserting that p offers the opportunity for belief in p. For that alone indicates that one takes the act to bear on the truth of what was asserted. By contrast, one violates

---

[20] Such a reason might be a reason to question whether p (say, H has evidence that he thinks S lacks, supporting the hypothesis that ~p); or it might be a reason to question whether S's evidence is good evidence for p (say, H has evidence that he thinks S lacks, which suggests that S's evidence for p is defeated, or weak, or misleading, or . . .); or it might be a reason to question whether S was sincere in her assertion that p. These alternatives need not be exhaustive.

the requirement to take assertion seriously when one fails to treat the act as bearing on the question whether p. Of course, to say that one ought to treat the act as bearing on whether p is not to say that one must accept that p, or hold that the act provides a decisive (or even a defeasible) reason to believe that p, only to recognize or register that the act purports to bear favorably on the truth of p.

Consider in this light the case of the man who regularly and systematically disregards what women say. To make my point vivid it will help if he is rendered as a cartoonishly egregious sexist. (Hopefully there are few who are actually like him!) Perhaps he systematically disregards what women say because he does not think any act of a woman *can* convey relevant epistemic authority (he takes what in fact are their assertions and regards them as mere expressions of emotion and unsubstantiated opinion, and does not regard these "expressive acts" as conveying any epistemic authority). If so, he violates (1). Alternatively, it may be that he systematically disregards what women say because, while he does regard them as asserting, and so regards them as acting so as to convey having the relevant authority, he thinks that in point of fact they never have such authority. Here, he may satisfy (1) but he fails to satisfy (2). (Regarding acts that convey one's having authority, it is not proper to acts of that sort to dismiss the relevant claims in the manner in which he does.) I assume, however, that most cases of sexism are not of this cartoonish sort. A less egregious, though perhaps no less noxious, form of sexism is found in those who regularly discount the authoritativeness of female speakers, thereby requiring more of them if they are to be seen as having the relevant authority than would be required of a male.[21] They, too, fail to satisfy (2), as they allow their sexism to get in the way of a proper evaluation of the acts.

My claim, then, is that observed assertions ought to be accorded the status that acts of this type deserve; and so, assuming MMENA, this means hearers ought to accord them the status of conveyers of epistemic authority regarding the asserted content, and ought to evaluate them in ways proper to acts of this kind. One might well agree that the case of the sexist is a case of disrespect, and so is a case in which the hearer mistreated the speaker, while simultaneously worrying about my analysis of the harm done. In particular, one might worry about the requirement that I would place on hearers, according to which they must *take assertions seriously* in the sense here characterized.[22] Consider the case of the garrulous taxi driver: he talks, and talks, and talks, oblivious to your utter lack of interest. Do you owe him or his assertions anything? It might seem not, and it might also seem that my proposal regarding what hearers owe speakers does not have the resources to avoid the contrary verdict.

In response, I want to distinguish two questions. First, what is the garrulous taxi driver owed merely in virtue of the fact that he has made an assertion (or actually a

---

[21] As I understand her, this was the sort of case that most occupied Miranda Fricker in her (2007).
[22] I thank Ernie Sosa, Mike Ridge, and Paul Bloomfield for making this point, separately, in conversation.

bunch of assertions)? Second, what is he owed *all things considered*—where all things include the facts that he is talking non-stop, that you did not ask to converse with him, that the topic is tedious to you, that you would rather be thinking about other things, that he is invading what limited privacy you have in the back seat of his cab, and so forth? My answer to the first question is this: he is owed being taken seriously. Insofar as you were presented with his assertion that p, you ought to satisfy (1) and (2), period. This can seem demanding—so demanding that it can seem to make the objection's case. But this is not so. I want to suggest that while you do have this responsibility, what it requires of you in any particular case depends on all sorts of things. Cases in which there is an ongoing conversation with two (or more) willing partners are one thing; uninvited monologues are another. As speakers go on and on, *they lose their claim on our attention*. This is not to say that they lose their claim to being taken seriously, however. I think these two claims can be made to cohere.

Let me explain. First, in the case of the garrulous taxi driver, we can distinguish between the attitude you ought to have right at the outset, and the attitude you are morally permitted to have as you acquire a sense of what is going on. At the outset I think you owe a degree of attentiveness. Given the sort of speech act that it is, an assertion by its very nature has some claim on our attention.[23] But this claim on our attention begins to evaporate when a string of assertions are made in ways like the garrulous taxi driver makes them: in a monologue, under conditions in which not all parties are mutually invested or willing participants, invading the privacy of the other person, and so forth. At a certain point you need not even attend to what he is saying. But this (I want to say) is compatible with your taking him seriously. You may well continue to regard him as performing acts that convey his epistemic authority, and you acknowledge the bearing of these acts on the truth of what is claimed; it is just that you simply have a reason to ignore the claimings (not being interested in the subject-matter, not participating willingly in the "conversation," and not having any reason to do so). To see how this can be, suppose that in the middle of otherwise tuning him out you happen to catch his statement to the effect that he and his friends were out late last night drinking at the local pub, The Oxford Bar (on Young Street). And suppose that later in the day (long after you are out of the taxi and breathing fresh air again!) the issue comes up whether The Oxford Bar is still open, serving

---

[23] Relevance theorists speak of statements as having an implicit claim to relevance (Sperber and Wilson 1986, 1990). This is supposed to explain the interest we should take in them, and the attentiveness we should give them. Of course, the "should" here is not a moral one, but a practical one—as in, it is in the hearer's interest to do so. Even so, I submit that the Relevance theorist, too, has a use for MMENA in this explanation. For consider. The relevance of a statement is partly a matter of the relevance of the content to the hearer's interests or practical aims. But a statement that is relevant in this sense is not worth anything at all from a practical point of view if it is no guide to how things are: if it is the expression of a deranged person's wild imagination, it is not in your interest to attend to it. It is the feature of assertion whereby assertion conveys the speaker's epistemic authority, that renders the resulting statement made by way of an assertion something that is worth attending to, from the hearer's perspective. That hearers implicitly know this, and know that speakers (implicitly) know this as well, is further support for MMENA itself.

drinks. You say that it is, and you know this—how?—by having taken his assertion seriously. You were under no obligation to attend to his ramblings, of course; but, given that you did, when the issue about which he had spoken came up, you gave his speech its due. To be sure, if you had a reason to suspect that the taxi driver was bullshitting throughout his monologue—speaking with an utter disregard for the truth—you might have disregarded his statement altogether, as giving you no reason to believe that The Oxford Bar was still open, serving drinks. But even here you would not have disrespected him so long as you had *good reason* to regard him as bullshitting. For in that way you would have acknowledged the *conveyed* claim of authority, and responded appropriately to it (rejection on the basis of good reasons). In this way we see that taking another seriously does not require accepting what they say, even when one attends to their assertions; it only requires that if one does not accept the assertions, that one has supporting reasons.[24] (How demanding these have to be will depend on one's epistemology of testimony—a matter I will not enter into further here.)

It is a very difficult question in this regard to state what sort of claim on another's attention any arbitrary asserter has on an occasion of assertion. I do not quite know how to answer this. But I will say this much: given that assertions are acts that convey epistemic authoritativeness, an assertion has at least this much claim on our attention, that we ought to recognize the person as having conveyed that much. In some cases, this is enough to warrant a claim on our attention—as when we were not in the middle of something else, the topic is one of mutual interest, we have no reason to regard the speaker as bullshitting, and so on. In other cases this will not be enough to warrant a claim on our attention: we were justifiably preoccupied with something else, it should have been clear that we had no time for discussion, and so on. Most cases are probably somewhere in between.

In order to focus the discussion a little more, let us assume that the context is an ordinary one, the case is not a monologue, and so there is a plausible claim on the hearer's attention. My claim is that in this case, a hearer owes it to the speaker to take the assertion seriously (in the sense characterized previously). To fail to do this is to morally

---

[24] It might be thought that in saying this I am taking sides here on the Positive Reasons Requirement (PRR), and on the reductionism/non-reductionism debate in the epistemology of testimony. (For discussion, see Chapter 2, Sections 2.4 and 2.5, and Chapter 3, Sections 3.3 and 3.4.) While I can see why one might think this, I deny the charge. One might think that the requirement of positive reasons to reject only makes sense in terms of PRR and reductionist approaches to testimony. But this is not so. As I noted in Chapter 2, Section 2.4, reductionists are fond of pointing out that every testimonial exchange is "informationally rich" (Kenyon 2012; see also Lackey 2008). If this is so, then it is a point that holds no matter one's epistemology of testimony—and so can be appealed to no matter one's position on this score. What is more, the current issue is a moral one—What do we owe as hearers to those who assert?—rather than an epistemic one. The reductionism/non-reductionism debate, by contrast, is a debate about the conditions on epistemically justified acceptance. (Moreover, one can acknowledge the informational richness of testimonial exchanges without regarding reasons as required for justified acceptance. This is a point that has been made by Peter Graham on many separate occasions; see, for example, Graham 2006b.)

harm the speaker: it is to disrespect her in a certain sort of way. But can we become clearer on the nature of the disrespect?

In addressing this, I find it helpful to begin with some remarks by several authors who have written in an illuminating way about things in this vicinity. I begin first with a terse but highly suggestive remark by Elizabeth Anscombe (1979), who attests to the moral nature of the wrong that is done to a hearer whose assertion is not believed:

> It is an insult and may be an injury not to be believed. At least it is an insult if one is oneself made aware of the refusal, and it may be an injury if others are.

Glossing Anscombe's point in a more recent paper, Richard Moran puts matters this way (and here he is expressing a view which he appears to endorse):

> ... [T]he offense remains even when the speaker's audience takes his having made the statement to count as evidence for its truth, just as ... he may take the speaker's having made [a] promise to make it more probable that he will do the thing in question. The offense lies in his refusing to accept what the speaker freely and explicitly offers him, in favor of privately attending to what the speaker's action passively reveals, just as someone might refuse an apology while still taking it in this case to be a reliable indication of remorse. What makes sense of such refusals is the fact that acceptance of an assertion or an apology brings with it certain vulnerabilities and responsibilities of its own. Accepting an apology, for instance, brings with it the responsibility to put away one's resentment, and makes one vulnerable to a particularly bruising possibility of deceit. These risks are avoided by simply taking the apology as more or less good evidence for remorse, and then making of it what one will. (Moran 2006: 301)

So, too, Ted Hinchman notes the "slight" that a hearer exhibits towards a speaker when the speaker's telling is not accorded its proper status:

> Imagine A manifestly looks as if he needs to learn the time, so S tells him it's noon, but A doesn't regard himself as having thereby acquired any entitlement to believe it's noon. Imagine not that A regards himself as having acquired an entitlement to believe it's noon that gets defeated by such background knowledge as that S's watch tends to run fast, but that A regards himself as not having acquired any entitlement, not even a (now defeated) *prima facie* entitlement, to believe it's noon... [Here] A is failing to acknowledge S—he is, as we say, 'slighting' S ... [T]he explanation of S's sense of having been slighted ... [is that] she has tendered an invitation to A to trust her and explicitly been rebuffed. (Hinchman 2005: 565)

Glossing this, Hinchman goes on to say this:

> We can now account for the nature of A's abuse when he fails to regard himself as coming to have an entitlement to believe that it's noon—when he fails, in effect, to take S's word for it ... In telling A that p, S offers him something, an entitlement to believe that p, which she conceives as his for the taking. In recognizing her intention to tell him that p, A satisfies that intention, and S thereby counts as telling him that p. But in refusing to acknowledge the entitlement, he refuses the offer she makes in telling him that p ... [W]hat's at stake for S when she tells A that p is his recognition of her as worthy of his trust. (Hinchman 2005: 568)

Miranda Fricker casts the matter in terms of the sort of "injustice" that the hearer does to the speaker. Characterizing "testimonial injustice" as involving situations in which "prejudice causes a hearer to give a deflated level of credibility to a speaker's word" (Fricker 2007: 1), she notes that in such cases

> a hearer wrongs a speaker in his capacity as a giver of knowledge, as an informant ... [T]he primary harm one incurs in being wronged in this way is an intrinsic injustice. Clearly, this harm may go more or less deep in the psychology of the subject, and ... where it goes deep, it can cramp self-development, so that a person may be, quite literally, prevented from becoming who they are. (Fricker 2007: 5)

Finally, picking up on Fricker's work, J. Wanderer has more recently spoken of the nature of the "testimonial insult" that a speaker can experience when her testimony is not accorded proper status:

> I experience testimonial insult when I perceive that your deliberation following my testimony reveals that you did not treat that act as a genuine input to the deliberative process. (Wanderer 2011: 16)

Wanderer goes on to distinguish between two ways that testimony is not treated as a "genuine input into the deliberative process" and two corresponding "harms" that the hearer does to the speaker. The first obtains when the hearer *ignores* the testimony, which generates the harm of "depriv[ing] the testifier of an active voice in public discourse" (17); and the second obtains when the hearer *rejects* the testimony, which does a distinctly "second-personal" sort of harm to the testifier—one which "violates" her "full status as testifier" (19). Here Wanderer remarks that, while Fricker appears to have characterized only the former sort of injustice, what is distinctive of the latter sort is that "the injustice is firmly rooted in a normatively significant second-person relation between two people, in which deliberators do an injustice *to testifiers* in rejecting them" (19).

Several things about these remarks are noteworthy. First, everyone appears to recognize that a hearer H can do harm to a speaker S—H can "insult" S, or cause "offense" to her, or "slight" her, or "violate" her status as a testifier—if H reacts in certain ways to S's testimony. (I am going to assume that these remarks carry over to S's assertions more generally.) Second, given the language that these theorists use to describe this infraction, it would appear that this harm is a distinctly moral harm, or at least has a distinctly moral dimension. And third and relatedly, it would appear that at least many, if not all, of the authors recognize that the harm in question is a sort of harm that one particular person does to another particular person.

I submit that my MMENA-based account makes sense of these aspects of the ethics of assertion. My core claim has been that an assertion ought to be ascribed a status that is appropriate to its nature as an act in which the speaker has invoked her own epistemic authority. (Indeed, it is for this reason that an assertion that p is, in Wanderer's apt phrase, "a genuine input to the deliberative process.") To ignore or dismiss an assertion on insufficient grounds, then, is to disrespect the speaker as an epistemic subject *by inappropriately repudiating her claim to relevant authoritativeness.*

This suggestion aims to capture what is in common in the remarks by Anscombe, Moran, Hinchman, Fricker, and Wanderer. However, I think we can go beyond what is in common in these remarks. That is, it is possible to say more about the nature of the moral harm one does in cases in which one ignores or dismisses another's assertion—at least in those cases in which the conversation was mutual, and the parties were engaged in an exchange of what each side thought would be information that was useful to the other side(s). Consider that in this sort of case the speaker is disrespected (and thereby harmed) not merely as an epistemic subject, but also as someone who aims to be offering help. Since this help pertains to the epistemic needs of the hearer H (at least as these are anticipated by S), and since S's aim in addressing H is to satisfy those needs, H's repudiation of S's assertion is a case of S's failing to accept H's role in something that is—or at least which H should regard S as taking to be—a *joint epistemic effort*.[25]

I should say that the harm of which we have been speaking need not exhaust the harm that a hearer H does to a speaker S when H does not accord S's assertion its due status. In particular, if this failure to accord S's assertion its due status is itself a public act—one that is observed by others, and recognized by them to be the act of disrespect that it is—then it is quite possible that H thereby harms S's reputation, her standing in the community. This would be the case when (i) others are aware of H's ignoring or rejection of S's assertion (on the basis of no present evidence), and (ii) on the basis of this awareness others conclude that S's word is not to be trusted. Of course, it will not always be true that others who observe H's ignoring or rejection of S's assertion will draw such a conclusion; perhaps they will conclude that H is inappropriately dismissing S. But it can sometimes happen that others draw this sort of conclusion; and when it does, H's failure to accord S's assertion its due status harms S (not only by disrespecting S in both her role as epistemic subject and her role as a helper in a would-be joint epistemic effort, but also) by affecting her standing as a potential contributor to information-sharing exchanges in the more general community.[26]

In sum, I submit that in addition to the speaker's having responsibilities—what she owes to the hearer—the hearer, too, has responsibilities—what he owes to the speaker. The principal responsibility is to give to the speaker's assertion its due, and in particular to recognize, and respond appropriately, to the asserter's implicit claim to have relevant epistemic authority. Precisely what this comes to is a difficult question; again, I suspect that a full accounting will have to take into account the various sorts

---

[25] I will return to this at greater length when discussing the connections between the ethics of assertion and the ethics of belief.
[26] This is the sort of harm explored at length in Fricker (2007).

of context in which assertions are made, the types of relations in which hearers and speakers stand to one another, and so forth. My claim here is the minimal one that the ethics of assertion require the hearer not to summarily dismiss the bearing of the speaker's assertion that p on the question whether p. Failure to live up to this responsibility harms the speaker, first, by disrespecting her status as an epistemic subject in her own right, second, as a participant in what should be seen as a joint epistemic activity, and third, by diminishing her reputation among her peers (in those cases in which the hearer's disrespectful attitude is recognized by others).

7.4 The Obligation to Assert: "You Should Have Told Me So!"

So far, I have used MMENA to derive two sorts of moral responsibility generated by the making of an assertion. On the one hand, there are the speaker's responsibilities to the hearer. In this connection I spoke about the speaker's responsibilities-for-having-asserted as amounting to having done what could reasonably be expected of her to live up to the robustly epistemic standard of assertion's norm. On the other hand, there are the hearer's responsibilities to the speaker who has asserted. In this connection I spoke about the hearer as required to "give the assertion its due," and I characterized this as requiring that he take the assertion seriously, in the twofold sense of (1) regarding is as an act which conveys that the speaker is relevantly authoritative, and (2) evaluating it in a manner proper to acts of that kind. (Matters here are complicated, I acknowledged, since garrulous, rude, or invasive speakers can lose their claim on a hearer's attention; but I argued that this is compatible with the hearer's owing due regard for the assertion.) In this section I use some of these points to argue for one final aspect of the "ethics of assertion." I will argue that it can happen that a speaker is under a moral obligation to assert what she knows, or what she takes herself to know. This obligation is a species of the obligations that we have to help others in need.[27]

It should be uncontroversial that others' needs give us reasons to help them.[28] These reasons are not all-things-considered reasons—they can be defeated. But they are reasons nonetheless. Suppose you see a person holding two large bags of groceries, standing in front of a door, where it is manifest that he is wondering how to get the door open. You are nearby, not in any hurry, with nothing in your hands, and you acknowledge that it would not be very hard for you to help by opening the door for him. Here, his clear need gives you a reason to help him by opening the door for him; and the fact that you have no other pressing obligations, together with the ease with which you

---

[27] Some authors speak of these as forming an "imperfect duty."
[28] I have been aided in this section by discussions with Kyla Ebels Duggan. (She is not responsible for any of the errors or infelicities of this section, however!)

could help him, ensure that this reason is not defeated or overridden by other considerations. You should help him by opening the door.

It is very hard to make explicit the principles that govern the generation of these sorts of reasons, and the considerations that can defeat or override them. For my purposes, however, I will assume that this much is uncontroversial: there are occasions on which the fact that another person is in need generates for you a reason to help her; and in situations in which you have such a reason, where it is also the case that you are in a position to help with relative ease, and where there are no other countervailing (defeating or overriding) considerations, provides you with an all-things-considered reason to help her. In putting things in this way, I do not assume that the fact of another's need *always* generates a reason for you to help: perhaps there are constraints deriving from the spatial proximity between you and the person in need, or the relationship that holds between the two of you, and so forth. And in generalizing over countervailing considerations, I only assume that there are cases in which these *prima facie* reasons amount to *ultima facie* reasons to help. This much, I hope, is uncontroversial. We might describe this as the ethics of helping those in need.

One sort of need that can generate reasons of this sort is the need for information. Suppose that a stranger approaches you and asks you for the time. You understand her, have no reason not to oblige her, and take yourself to be relevantly informed (having glimpsed at a clock no more than several moments ago, and recalling your watch's readout). In this sort of case, her clear need for information gives you a reason to help her by telling her the time; and since you have no other countervailing reasons, you should help her by telling her what time it is. In short: we sometimes have ethical obligations to others that are generated by their needs, and a special case of this obtains when their need is a need for information.

Assertion figures in this story as the kind of speech act that is uniquely apt for addressing this need. MMENA enables us to see why this is. To begin with, people speak out of all sorts of motives. As a result, a speaker who aims to help another person by providing him with the information he needs is confronted with the problem of settling on an act which makes this motive clear. In parallel fashion, a hearer who wants his informational needs met is confronted with the problem of determining when another's speech act aims to satisfy that need. Now, both hearer and speaker will recognize that the hearer's need is a need for *true* information.[29] And both will recognize as well that the hearer will judge the chances that a speaker is speaking truly by judging the chances that the speaker *has the relevant epistemic authority* in relation to the proposition presented as true. Given these as background, what is needed, if a speaker is to address a hearer's need for information in a way that the hearer will recognize as aimed at being helpful, is a speech act in which the speaker not only presents-as-true what she takes to be the case, but also conveys that she has the relevant epistemic authority regarding the very proposition she presents-as-true in her speech act. In short, what is needed is the speech act of assertion, governed (in a way that is mutually manifest) by ENA.

---

[29] On the mathematical understanding of 'information,' the phrase 'true information' is redundant. What I have in mind is 'true propositions,' though I will disregard such details in what follows.

I do not claim that assertion is the *only* type of speech act through which a speaker can pull off this trick. One can implicate, suggest, lead one to conclude, manifest a presupposition, or imply in some other way. However, I do claim that the speech act of assertion will typically have two distinctive advantages over these other ways: it will typically be the *most efficient* and the *least risky* way to do so. Most efficient, because it will involve the least effort on the part of the hearer to work out the relevant content; least risky because, since it involves the least effort on the hearer's part, it leaves less room for mistakes in the hearer's recovery of the relevant content. What is more, this fact—that assertion will typically be the most efficient and least risky way to do so—is itself a piece of common knowledge. The result is that when a speech act *other than* assertion is used in these sorts of situations, it can often generate questions in the hearer's mind—questions that might lead her to wonder whether the speaker meant to communicate something other than what she said. Now, I submit that a speaker who, acknowledging her ethical obligations in connection with addressing a hearer's informational needs, aims to satisfy those needs, ought to do so in a way that avoids unnecessary risks of confusions in the communication. But the risks of confusion that arise when a speaker addresses another's informational needs through some speech act *other than* assertion will often be unnecessary risks. This is for the simple reason that any competent speaker has, and will be presumed to have, recourse to the speech act of assertion itself—with the result that the use of a speech act other than assertion can be expected to generate in the hearer's mind the question noted previously. The result is that the speaker who ought to satisfy another's informational needs on a given occasion will typically be under some pressure to do so by way of making an assertion, rather than through the performance of some other type of speech act. And so we get what we might call a 'positive duty' in connection with the 'ethics of assertion': when one has a non-defeated and non-overridden reason to address another's informational needs, and one regards oneself as having the relevant information in question,[30] one ought to do so by way of making the relevant assertion.[31]

I do not regard this point as particularly controversial. In fact, the prevalence of the allegation "But you should have told me so!" attests to the prevalence of this phenomenon. Consider how natural the following dialogues are:

BARNES: I didn't know that Bus 26 no longer runs on Saturdays.
BLOOR: Sure, that line was recently cancelled on weekends.
BARNES: Well, you should have told me so! I wouldn't have waited in the rain for hours.

---

[30] It may be that one does not have a non-defeated and non-overriding reason to address another's informational needs unless one reasonably regards oneself as having the relevant information. However, I am not sure whether this is so, so I add this condition at the risk of possible redundancy.

[31] One might worry that a speaker has this obligation only if she *reasonably* regards herself as having the information needed. (Does someone who thinks he knows everything really have a reason, even a merely *prima facie* reason, to help anyone in need of information?) This may be; if so, the reasonability constraint should be added to what I say later. I will not explore this further here.

Now, whether Barnes is correct in the allegation against Bloor depends on a host of things. But we can imagine a scenario in which this allegation is warranted: Barnes and Bloor are good friends; it is mutual knowledge between them that Barnes regularly uses Bus 26 on the weekends; it is mutual knowledge that Barnes was waiting for the bus last Saturday; Bloor knew all along that the bus was recently cancelled on weekends; Bloor had an opportunity to mention this to Barnes prior to Barnes's waiting last Saturday; and Bloor had no reason to hide the fact from his friend. Here, there was an obligation to help address a need that Bloor ought to have anticipated;[32] Bloor ought to have addressed that need by telling Barnes what he knew; and (for the reasons mentioned previously) it would have been best, all things considered, for the telling to proceed by way of Bloor's making the relevant assertion.

This, of course, is not the end of the story. Perhaps Bloor had an excuse; perhaps he did not anticipate that Barnes would need the information, and his ignorance on this score was non-culpable;[33] perhaps he simply forgot to mention this. I will not dwell on these. My claim is simply that there are cases in which a subject (had the knowledge in question, and so) had an obligation to tell, and so to assert what she knew (or took herself to know; see the next section). This is compatible with the idea that there are also cases in which the allegation that a subject was under such an obligation can be met by one of a range of legitimate excuses.

7.5 Deriving (some) Ethics of Belief from the Obligation to Assert

The foregoing considerations pertaining to an obligation to assert provide one basis on which to approach the ethics of belief. The strategy will be to use the foregoing considerations regarding the ethics of assertion, and in particular the obligation to assert, together with the link between assertion and belief,[34] to derive some (admittedly weak) constraints that we might group under the "ethics of belief" label. Here my claim is this: one's beliefs ought to be such, that when another's need for information becomes manifest (and there are no countervailing considerations), one addresses this need (by way of making an assertion) iff one properly takes oneself to have the relevant information. If this is so, I will be arguing, the norm of assertion exerts an indirect constraint on what (from a moral perspective) one ought to believe.

One point needs to be made at the outset, to prevent needless confusion.[35] The claim I will be defending is a biconditional: in the restricted set of conditions just mentioned (including the condition where one has relevant information), one ought to assert *if and only if* one properly takes oneself to have the relevant information. This can seem to be

---

[32] For an account of the "should have known" phenomenon, see Goldberg (forthcoming b).

[33] See footnote 17, above, for various references to the literature on culpable ignorance. See also Goldberg (forthcoming b).

[34] See Chapter 6 for additional comments on the links between assertion and belief.

[35] I thank an anonymous referee for indicating the need to make this point.

an overly-strong requirement. After all, in the literature on the norm of assertion, virtually no one defends a biconditional norm,[36] and those who do, typically formulate the norm as a norm of *permission*.[37] But it is to be borne in mind that I am not here stating the norm of assertion; I am stating the conditions on being *morally required* to assert. If I am right that there are conditions in which one is required to assert if one has, or reasonably regards oneself as having, the relevant information, then, if one is under these conditions, one must assert. This is where the 'if' part comes in. The 'only if' part comes in when we consider what is involved in the condition stating "if one has, or reasonably regards oneself as having" the relevant information. Here I will be appealing to MMENA and the norm of assertion itself: in particular, one ought (morally) to assert only if in so doing one would satisfy what I previously called the responsibility-for-having-asserted. Put together, we obtain a biconditional. This biconditional is a claim, not about when it is proper to assert (period), but when it is morally incumbent on one to do so (where failure to do so will warrant the accusation of "You should have told me so!").

In what follows I want to defend two claims, each corresponding to a dimension on which, given the connection between assertion and belief, the ethics of assertion constrains the ethics of belief. The first claim concerns the would-be speaker's *higher-order* beliefs—in particular, her beliefs regarding her epistemic position on the matter regarding which the other subject's need for information has become mutually manifest. To a first approximation, I will be arguing that insofar as a speaker S is a cognitively mature subject who has a *prima facie* reason to address another's informational need regarding whether p, then whatever second-order beliefs S has (concerning her own epistemic position regarding whether p) ought to be reasonable. (It is only in this way that, were she to assert, she would satisfy the responsibility-for-having-asserted.) I will develop this line of argument in Section 7.5.1. The second claim for which I will be arguing regards S's *first-order* beliefs—in particular, her beliefs on the very subject-matter regarding which the other subject's need for information has become manifest. To a first approximation I will be arguing that if (i) S is epistemically rational, (ii) S has a *prima facie* reason to address H's informational need regarding whether p, and (iii) there are no countervailing considerations that defeat this reason (save perhaps S's lacking the information sought), S ought to address this need by asserting that p if and only if she is relevantly informed as to whether p. As I develop this line of argument in Section 7.5.2 it will become clear how the norm of assertion (understood in terms of MMENA) exerts constraints on the ethics of (first-order) belief.

7.5.1 Assertion-Generated Ethical Constraints on the Speaker's Higher-Order Belief

Suppose that it is mutually manifest to S and H that H is in need of information regarding whether p, that S is nearby, and that it would not be particularly difficult or costly

---

[36] Leite (2007) criticizes DeRose (2002) as implicitly smuggling in the biconditional.
[37] See, for example, Blome-Tilman (2013) and Montminy (2013).

for S to provide that information to H were she (S) to have it. S should do so (by way of making the relevant assertion) if and only if she is relevantly informed regarding whether p.[38] To wit: if S is relevantly informed but does not share this information with H, she fails to help one in need, under conditions in which she was in a position to do so (and where there were no countervailing considerations). If S aims to help H by addressing his need for information regarding whether p, but is not herself relevantly informed, S's attempt will not succeed at being helpful, and may even be harmful (as when S's assertion is false and H, believing S, comes to act on the false belief, with bad consequences). As a result, if S is to determine whether she should help H on this occasion, she must determine whether she is relevantly informed.

Now let us restrict our attention to those cases in which this determination takes the form of S's forming higher-order beliefs regarding her state of informedness on the matter at hand. Insofar as these beliefs will determine whether she takes herself to be relevantly informed, and so will determine whether she regards herself as under an obligation to address H's need for information, ideally these beliefs ought to represent herself as relevantly informed if and only if she is relevantly informed. Of course, one's own state of informedness is not something that is transparent to one: there are cases in which one believes that p on the basis of good (but not infallible) evidence, where it turns out that it is not the case that p; and there are cases in which one believes that p on the basis of good (but not infallible) evidence, where it turns out that one's belief is true, but the truth of the belief is a matter of luck (Gettier cases). Presumably, one is not always, or perhaps even ever, in a position to rule out these kinds of scenario, while at the same time responding in a timely fashion to another's need for information. With these sorts of possibility in mind, we might say this: insofar as S determines whether she is relevantly informed whether p, and does so by way of forming higher-order beliefs about her state of informedness, she has a moral duty to be reasonable in the higher-order beliefs she forms.

To appreciate the basis of this duty, and to see what the demand of "reasonableness" amounts to, consider a case in which S forms higher-order beliefs about her informedness, where these higher-order beliefs fly in the face of the evidence she herself has. We can consider two cases. In one, she regards herself as relevantly informed when in fact she is not (the "false positive" case); in the other, she regards herself as not informed when in fact she is (the "false negative" case).

Taking the false positive case first, assume that S wrongly regards herself as in a position to be helpful in addressing H's need for information, where as a result S's assertion is either false or unwarranted. If H acts on the information S provides, only to find out that S was actually uninformed on the matter, I submit that H is in a position to resent S so long as S's state of actual uninformedness was something S ought to have discerned at the time. Harkening back to something I argued in Section 7.2, we can speak

---

[38] To be relevantly informed is to mentally represent how things are in a way that is both correct and *epistemically satisfactory*. More on the notion of epistemic satisfactoriness later.

in terms of what H can reasonably have expected of S: H is entitled to regard S as having done what can reasonably be expected of her in connection with satisfying the norm of assertion. Given this, H is entitled to suppose that any higher-order beliefs S formed in this connection captured all that H could reasonably have expected of S in this regard. While it is hard to say precisely what this comes to, it is clear how S might come up short. For example, if it was mutually manifest that a particular not-p scenario, α, was "live" in the context in which H was in need of information, then insofar as S (believing herself to be relevantly informed) asserts that p, H is entitled to regard S's epistemic position as being such as to be able to rule out α. To illustrate, suppose that it is mutually manifest to Samantha and Harry that there is some question as to whether last night's Yankees game was rained out. If, on the basis of her prior knowledge of the Yankees' schedule, *but lacking any special knowledge of last night's weather or of any details of the game itself*, Sally asserts that the Yankees played last night, then she was wrong to have taken herself to be relevantly informed. In such a case, Harry will be entitled to resent her for this if he were to find out the basis of her assertion. More importantly, he will be entitled to tell her that she should not have asserted *because she should not have regarded herself as relevantly informed*. The harms that befall Harry when he acted on the information Samantha gave him were owed to Samantha's epistemic negligence. That this epistemic negligence informed her actions, which in turn led to those harms, underscores the moral dimension of the act. In this way we see that the false positive case involves a moral failure in one's higher-order beliefs.

Next, taking the false negative condition, assume that S wrongly regards herself as uninformed, under conditions in which in fact she is informed. To make sense of this case, let us imagine that S regards herself as uninformed in the following sense: she regards herself as not having belief-warranting grounds for assertion either in [p] or its negation, and so she is agnostic regarding whether p. (In fact, however, she has strong, belief-warranting grounds for believing that p. If she had only thought about it for a moment or two, she would have realized this.) Then, even though it is mutually manifest that H needs information regarding whether p, S does not tell H that p. We can think of two cases here: S might remain silent, not saying anything at all; or S might say that she does not know whether p. Although both of these sorts of cases can be handled in the same way, it will be easier to discuss the silence case first.

If S is silent, saying nothing on the issue whether p, I submit that H is entitled to resent S ("You should have told me so!") so long as S's higher-order beliefs regarding her own state of informedness failed to capture something H could reasonably have expected of S in this regard. So, suppose that it was mutually manifest both that H's need was acute, and that S was the person in the best position to weigh in. Under these conditions, H was entitled to regard S's silence as indicating that there was no relevant information to be had. To the extent that it was unreasonable for S to regard her p-related evidence as insufficient to warrant assertion (had she just thought about it for a minute, she would have realized she *did* have warranting evidence), H is entitled to resent her for not speaking up. If this evidence was sufficiently good as to render assertion proper, H is entitled to resent S for not having informed him that p, and so is entitled to resent S for her having formed false higher-order beliefs regarding her own state of (un)informedness. (H to S: "Why didn't you tell me that p?" S to H: "Because I did not know that p." H to S: "But you should have known! Look at the evidence you had!")

What should we say of those cases in which S's evidence is clearly assertion-warranting, but where S, having false higher-order beliefs on this matter, merely says that she does not know whether p? Again, if we imagine a case in which S's epistemic position on p was so good that it was unreasonable for her to take herself not to know, then clearly H is entitled to resent her for not helping under these conditions; after all, it was unreasonable of S to have taken herself not to be in a position to do so. Of course, matters shade off from here, according to how clear it was that S's evidence was such as to render assertion proper.

Let me try to formulate more carefully the conclusion for which I have been gesturing. The thesis I have been gesturing towards is this (the 'Ethics of Higher-Order Belief'):

> EHOB Given two subjects S and H and circumstances in which (a) it is mutually manifest that H is in need of information regarding whether p, (b) (bracketing whether S has the relevant information) there are no considerations that defeat or override the reason S has to help H in this regard, and (c) S is a cognitively mature agent who has the capacity for higher-order belief, any higher-order beliefs S forms regarding her state of informedness on whether p ought to capture what H can reasonably expect of S in this regard.

My case for this has been as follows. First, when (a)–(c) are true, then S ought to provide H with that information (by making the relevant assertion) iff S is relevantly informed. But to determine whether she is in this position, S must have some sense of her epistemic position on the question of whether p. This is a matter of performing a reasonable self-assessment of her state of informedness. And given (c), this will take the form of higher-order beliefs regarding her epistemic position on p. In particular, she ought to determine whether she is in a position to make a warranted assertion on this topic (where this is a matter of satisfying the norm of assertion). And so we see that under conditions (a)–(c), S ought to form reasonable higher-order beliefs in connection with the question whether she is in a position to make a warranted assertion on the question of whether p.

7.5.2 Assertion-Generated Ethical Constraints on the Speaker's First-Order Belief

It is perhaps not particularly controversial that, given that assertions can be made in an attempt to help others in their informational needs, the 'ethics of assertion' might bear on one's higher-order beliefs concerning whether one is in a position to assert warrantedly. More surprising, perhaps, is that the ethics of assertion may constrain what one ought to believe *on first-order questions*. Although I am not in a position to argue for a strong conclusion in this connection, what I can do is argue for a conditional thesis: given a currently popular (though by no means uncontroversial!) assumption about the conditions under which evidence warrants belief, the ethics of assertion constrain the ethics of belief even on first-order belief contents. I will introduce the relevant assumption about epistemic rationality later. With it, I will argue for the following conclusion ('ABL' for 'Assertion–Belief Link'):

ABL Given two subjects S and H and circumstances in which (i) it is mutually manifest that H is in need of information regarding whether p, (ii) (bracketing whether S has the relevant information) there are no considerations that defeat or override the reason S has to help H in this regard, and (iii) S is epistemically rational, then S ought (morally) to address H's need for information (regarding whether p) by asserting that p iff S's evidence warrants the belief that p.[39]

Once I establish ABL, I will then use it to show how the ethics of assertion bears on the ethics of belief.

In order to establish that ABL holds, I need to establish that if (i)–(iii) hold, then the following Assertion–Belief biconditional holds:

AB≡ S ought (morally) to address H's need for information (regarding whether p) by asserting that p iff S's evidence warrants the belief that p.[40]

In order to establish this I will need to appeal to *another* biconditional regarding the ethics of assertion. I will call this biconditional the 'Ethics of Assertion biconditional':

EA≡ S ought (morally) to address H's informational needs (regarding whether p) by asserting that p iff S occupies an epistemic position in which she can rule out all relevant alternatives to [p].

My claim will be that the Ethics of Assertion biconditional, EA≡, holds whenever (i)–(iii) hold. Once I establish this, I will appeal to EA≡ as part of an argument to the effect that if (i)–(iii) hold, AB≡ holds.

---

[39] In effect, ABL amounts to a claim that (given (i)–(iii)) one should assert iff one should believe. For this reason it might be wondered how ABL squares with my argument in Chapter 6, where I presented the case *against* the thesis that the norm of belief and that of assertion are the same (the "symmetry thesis"). Simply put, ABL can be seen as a limiting case in which the norms are the same. The soundness of my case against the symmetry thesis depends on the claim that there are situations that do not satisfy (i)–(iii) (in which the norms diverge). See Part IV for an extended discussion of this.

[40] I distribute the 'ought' here so that this principle can be read as follows: if S ought (morally) to address H's informational needs (regarding whether p) by asserting that p, then S's evidence warrants the belief that p; if it is not the case that S ought (morally) to address H's informational needs (regarding whether p) by asserting that p, then it is not the case that S's evidence warrants the belief that p.

To see that EA≡ holds whenever (i)–(iii) hold, assume that (i)–(iii) hold. We can now break our task in two, corresponding to the left-to-right and the right-to-left direction of EA≡.

For the left-to-right direction, assume that the left-hand side (LHS) of EA≡ holds: S ought (morally) to address H's informational needs by asserting that p. Now we can note the following truism about what one ought to do when one ought to help another person: when one ought to help H in respect R, one ought to do so by way of φing *only if* φing helps H in respect R.[41] (If you should help an elderly person cross the street, then you should do so by way of gently guiding the person by the arm only if gently guiding the person by the arm helps the person cross the street.) Applied to the present 'ought,' we obtain: S ought (morally) to address H's informational needs by asserting that p, only if S's asserting that p addresses H's informational needs. But it is also clear, in turn, that S's asserting that p addresses H's informational needs only if it is also true that S can rule out all relevant alternatives to [p]. If this is *not* so—if S *cannot* rule out all relevant alternatives to [p]—then her asserting that p in this context is not helpful, for the simple reason that in such a case S's asserting that p would unduly expose H to epistemic risks. In particular, it would expose H to the risk of a situation involving the relevant alternative(s) which, by hypothesis, S cannot rule out. Were such a situation to obtain, S's asserting that p, far from being helpful to H, would be positively harmful to H—for H might well have proceeded, reasonably enough, to assume that S's having asserted that p authorizes H to regard all relevant alternatives as ruled out. And so we see that if S's assertion that p is to be helpful, she must be in a position to rule out all relevant not-[p] alternatives. If she is not in such a position, her assertion would not be helpful (and so she ought not to assert).[42] By contraposition we reach the desired conclusion: (under conditions in which (i)–(iii) hold) if S ought (morally) to address H's informational needs by asserting that p, then S occupies an epistemic position in which she can rule out all relevant alternatives to [p].

Now, to establish the right-to-left direction of EA≡, assume that the right-hand side (RHS) of EA≡ holds: S occupies an epistemic position in which she can rule out all relevant alternatives to [p]. But then, since by (i)–(iii) she is under an obligation to meet the informational needs of H if she has the relevant information, she ought to assert that p. But she *does* have the relevant information, since she can rule out all relevant not-[p] alternatives. And so we see that the right-to-left direction holds as well, and with this completes the argument that EA≡ holds whenever (i)–(iii) hold.

---

[41] Two caveats here. First, this truism should probably be relativized to circumstances, but I will not bother doing so here. Second, we might constrain the obligations in terms of what S *can reasonably expect* will help H in respect R. Thus constrained, the principle would read: when one ought to help H in respect R, one ought to do so by way of φing *only if* one can reasonably expect φing will help H in respect R. I believe that the present argument can be run on this reasonableness-constrained principle, but I will not present that version of the argument here.

[42] Recall here that the 'ought' in question is a moral 'ought.'

THE ETHICS OF ASSERTION (AND BELIEF) 199

I will now appeal to this fact in order to argue for ABL. In particular, my claim is that if (i)–(iii) hold, then, given a plausible (but by no means uncontroversial!) assumption regarding epistemic rationality, AB≡ holds.

Assume that (i)–(iii) hold, and that the LHS of AB≡ holds as well: S ought (morally) to address H's informational needs by asserting that p. Since S ought to assert that p, we obtain the result (from EA≡) that S occupies an epistemic position in which she can rule out all relevant alternatives to [p]. To occupy this position is to have an epistemic standing which warrants belief. But in such a case it would be *irrational* for S herself not to believe that p: having any attitude other than belief that p would fly in the face of the evidence that she has—evidence that enables her to rule out all relevant not-[p] alternatives. So we see that, on the assumption of (i)–(iii), if S ought (morally) to address H's informational needs by asserting that p, then S's evidence warrants the belief that p.

Now (to obtain the right-to-left direction of the rule in AB≡), we assume again that (i)–(iii) hold. However, rather than assume the RHS of AB≡ in order to derive the LHS, I will instead assume that the LHS of AB≡ does *not* hold, in order to derive that the RHS does not hold either (which is equivalent to what is wanted). So, assume that the LSH of AB≡ does not hold: it is not the case that S ought (morally) to address H's informational needs by asserting that p. Since this is also the denial of the LHS of EA≡, the RHS of EA≡ is false as well: it is not the case that S occupies an epistemic position in which she can rule out all relevant alternatives to [p]. Now consider the following assumption regarding the Evidence that Warrants Belief:

EWB   If S's evidence does not rule out all relevant not-p alternatives, S's evidence does not warrant the belief that p.

If we add EWB to what we have already derived, we reach the conclusion we want: S's evidence does not warrant the belief that p. (This is the negation of the RHS of EA≡, and thus we will have shown that if the LHS of EA≡ is false, so is the RHS.)

As I say, EWB is not uncontroversial.[43] Still, it does have something going for it. Here it is worth bearing in mind that EWB does not require that one's evidence rule out *all* not-p alternatives, only all *relevant* not-p alternatives. A central point of belief is to guide action (for example, by providing premises for practical syllogisms),[44] and all else equal it would seem unwise to employ [p] in a practical syllogism (or to act on the assumption of p) if one's evidence does not rule out all relevant not-p alternatives. Still, rather than argue for EWB, I will regard my conclusion as conditional on the assumption of EWB. In short: if EWB is true, then, given (i)–(iii) and the negation of the LHS of AB≡, we obtain the negation of the RHS of AB≡, which is the desired conclusion.

---

[43] Some will hold that lottery propositions (for a sufficiently large lottery) falsify ER: it is not epistemically irresponsible for a subject to believe that her ticket is a loser even when her evidence does not rule out that her ticket is a winner, but instead merely makes it very improbable that she will win.

[44] On this point, see Fantl and McGrath (2009).

Putting our two results together, we obtain the following: assuming that EWB is true, then in any situation in which (i)–(iii) hold, S ought morally to address H's informational needs by asserting that p iff S's evidence warrants the belief that p. But this is just to say that, given EWB, the Assertion–Belief biconditional holds whenever (i)–(iii) hold. So concludes my case for the assertion–belief link, ABL.

The time has come to show how, given ABL, the ethics of assertion, and especially the obligation to assert, imposes some (weak) ethical constraints on first-order belief. Suppose that ABL is true and that conditions (i)–(iii) hold. Then if S's evidence warrants the belief that p, S ought (morally) to address H's need for information (regarding whether p) by asserting that p; but if S's evidence does *not* warrant the belief that p, then S ought *not* to address H's need in this way. This gives us a way of determining, independently of what S actually believes, whether she ought to address H's informational needs by asserting that p: we simply assess S's epistemic standing on the question whether p. Now consider the two possibilities: either we determine that (given her informational state) she ought to address H's informational needs by asserting that p, or else we determine that (given her informational state) she ought *not* to address H's informational needs by asserting that p.

Taking the first possibility, suppose that we determine, independently of what S actually believes, that she ought to address H's informational needs by asserting that p. But if S ought to address H's informational needs by asserting that p, S herself *ought to believe* that p. She ought to believe that p, first, because her evidence rules out all relevant not-p alternatives (and one ought rationally to believe that p under such circumstances), and second, because if she does not believe that p, then her assertion would be insincere (and she ought not to be insincere).[45] Here is a case in which what S ought to believe is determined by what S ought to assert (in order to address a hearer's informational need).[46]

Next, consider the second possibility: that we determine, independently of what S actually believes, that she ought *not* address H's informational needs by asserting that p. In this case, S herself ought *not* to believe that p. This verdict reflects an assumption regarding an empirical connection between belief and assertion, whereby it is human nature to have a strong disposition to express one's beliefs in (assertoric) speech.[47] For this reason, if one is

---

[45] In Chapter 11 I revisit the issue of assertoric sincerity. My claim there is that there can be sincere assertion even when one does not believe what one asserts. However, that will be a special case. In cases in which it is mutually manifest that the audience is in need of information, the special case discussed there does not obtain. In such cases, sincerity requires belief.

[46] Does this falsify my core conclusion in Chapter 6, Sections 6.6 and 6.7, to the effect that the standards on belief come apart from the standards on assertion? No, it does not. There are two reasons for this. First, my claim here is restricted to those conditions involving the satisfaction of (i)–(iii)—roughly, to cases in which the issue of another's informational need has arisen, where one is in a position to help. This is compatible with saying that in cases that are not like this, standards for belief and assertion come apart. But second, as we will see later, the result I obtain here derives from moral principles of not subjecting others to the undue risk of harm; this has nothing to do with the norm of assertion or the norm of belief. Thus it can still be that the two norms swing apart even under conditions (i)–(iii). In that case, it would just be that there are further moral considerations bearing on belief and assertion, beyond what is present in the norms themselves.

[47] This point is emphasized by Zagzebski (2003: 143).

under conditions in which one's epistemic standing does not warrant the assertion that p, then to believe that p is to unduly risk exposing others to the risk of unwarranted—and so unhelpful—assertion. Thus, one should not believe that p in these circumstances, since one should not unduly risk exposing others to such risks. We might add: on the assumption that (*ceteris paribus*) one acts on what one believes, in believing that p under these circumstances S thereby unduly risks exposing others to liability in any joint effort in which the question whether to act on p is involved. (One ought not to unduly risk exposing others in this way.)

In effect, the foregoing argument appeals to that part of the ethics of assertion I have called the responsibility-for-having-asserted, together with links between belief and assertion, in order to argue that one ought not to believe what one would not be warranted in asserting. Failure to comply would put one in a situation in which one would not be in a position to be helpful, and would unduly expose another to the risk of harms, were the occasion to address another's need for information to arise. Seen from one angle, our result is not that surprising. After all, we systematically depend on one another for information, and since each of us is guided in our information-sharing practices by what we take to be true—that is, by our beliefs—we ought to believe only what would be helpful to provide to those seeking information. Seen from another angle, however, our result is surprising: what one believes is typically thought to be both a "private" affair as well as an affair over which subjects have little control, whereas what one asserts is a public affair in which the speaker is responsible for her actions. How can the norms of the latter generate ethical constraints on the former?

There are big questions here that I cannot claim to have addressed. Still, at least this much seems right: assertions have a collection of properties which make them a plausible candidate for grounding some ethical constraints on belief. In particular, assertions are the standard way by which to address others' need for information, they are the standard way by which linguistic creatures express our beliefs, and human beings have a strong disposition to express what we believe in this way. For this reason, the core thesis of this chapter—that the norm of assertion constrains the ethics of belief—is not much more surprising than is the claim that there are ethical constraints on how we ought to help others who seek information.

7.5.3 *Assertion-Generated Ethical Constraints on the Hearer's Beliefs*

I now turn to the last issue I will discuss: how what the hearer owes to the speaker (Section 7.3) constrains the ethics of belief. Happily, here I can be brief. Given MMENA and what is mutually known in a context of an observed assertion, the hearer owes the speaker the respect that is her due—respect that acknowledges her as someone who has invoked her own epistemic authority on the matter at hand. In Section 7.3 I framed this in terms of the hearer's responsibility to ascribe to the assertion its due—to take it as an act in which a speaker presents a proposition as true in such a way as to invoke her own relevant epistemic authority, and to treat it accordingly. To fail to do this is to treat the speaker with disrespect.

What does any of this tell us about the ethics of belief? More specifically, how can the mere fact that one must accord another speaker's assertion its due constrain what one oneself ought to believe? I submit that the obligations here are only indirect, but nevertheless real. They involve the attitudes we as hearers should have towards any observed assertion: they are not to be regarded as mere evidence, but rather as a claim to truth that purports to be backed by another epistemic subject's relevant authority. Since this might seem more controversial than I intend it to be, I will conclude by stating in programmatic terms the view I mean to be endorsing.

As I emphasized throughout Chapters 1–3, a hearer can come to know all sorts of things from another's assertion. In hearing S assert that it is cold outside, H can come to know: that S would like the heat turned up, that S has a cold (her voice is scratchy), that S is anxious (H knows that S only comments on the weather when she is anxious), that S speaks English, that an assertion was made, and so forth.[48] In none of these cases does H's knowledge depend on S's relevant epistemic authority. Indeed, in none of these cases does H even need to assume that S takes responsibility for having that authority. It is when H does assume that—roughly: when H accepts what S asserts, because S so asserted—that H takes on the sort of attitude that is appropriate to proper assertion. My claim, then, is this: when S asserts that p, H cannot simply regard the event as one of S's producing noise, regarding which H can then ask what sort of evidence S's having done so provides H.[49] Rather, H must regard S's assertion for what it is: an act whereby S presents a particular proposition as true, in such a way as to convey that she has the relevant epistemic authority on the matter. In the same way that a theorist would mischaracterize the role of assertion in the spread of knowledge if she were to regard assertion merely as evidence (in the manner of Chapter 2's Strong Evidentialist), so too a hearer would mischaracterize her moral duties to the asserter if she regards the assertion as but one more piece of evidence she has.

I rather doubt that this amounts to a requirement that H explicitly *believe* something of this sort. (Few of us ever do form such beliefs.) Rather, the obligation is this: one must so regard assertions that one manifests that one ascribes to them something like the status just described. One can do this without forming an explicit belief. Perhaps it is manifested in how one would defend oneself were one to refrain from accepting the assertion (one would recognize the need to have reasons for skepticism); perhaps it is clear in how one would defend oneself were one to accept the assertion (one would recognize one's dependence on the speaker's authority). The point is simply that one cannot simply ignore or reject an assertion on no grounds whatsoever. One must guide oneself in testimonial belief-formation so as to manifest one's sensitivity to other speakers as epistemic subjects in their own right.

---

[48] This point is also emphasized by Stalnaker (1978).
[49] As we have seen, this point is emphasized in Ross (1986), Hinchman (2006), and Moran (2006).

7.6 Conclusion

In this chapter I have appealed to MMENA—a thesis regarding the norm of assertion—in order to establish, both that there are ethical constraints on the practice of assertion, and that these constraints can be used to derive some (weak) constraints on what one ought to believe. The connection comes in the way that assertion answers to the informational needs of others. Insofar as there is an ethics of helping others in need, it seems reasonable to think that the norm of assertion can be used to derive constraints on what one ought to believe (regarding whether one ought to assert, and what one ought to assert). I cannot pretend to be fully confident that I have articulated a sound route from the norm of assertion to the ethics of belief. I hope instead that what I have presented here is suggestive. In particular, I hope it encourages others to consider the route from the norm of assertion to the ethics of belief, where the connecting link comes in the form of the ethics of addressing others' (informational) needs. If the foregoing argument merely succeeds in attracting attention to the prospects for an argument of this sort, I would be satisfied—even if the argument as I have presented it fails to convince.

8

Anonymous Assertion

8.1 Paradigmatically, Assertion Is a Public Act

The first seven chapters of this book have developed, defended, and explored MMENA—the hypothesis that it is mutually manifest to all competent speakers that assertion is governed by a robustly epistemic norm. In this chapter I employ MMENA to illuminate the public nature of assertion. In particular, I aim to address how the absence of a certain kind of publicness affects assertoric practice. In so doing I will be using MMENA to characterize how the anonymity of assertions affects the epistemological dimension of their production by speakers, and their reception by hearers. After arguing that anonymity does have implications in both respects, I go on to argue that at least some of these implications derive from a warranted diminishment in speakers' and hearers' mutual expectations of one another when there are few mechanisms for enforcing the responsibilities attendant to speech (for which see Chapters 3 and 7). As a result, I argue, there is a sense in which anonymous assertions do not carry the same "promise" of the speaker's relevant epistemic authoritativeness that ordinary assertions do. If this is correct, the phenomenon of anonymity provides us with a lesson regarding ordinary assertions: their aptness for engendering belief in others, and so for communicating knowledge, depends in general on *the very publicness of the act of assertion itself*.

I begin this discussion by remarking on the fact that many commentators have noted the poor quality of much of the commentary to be found on the Internet (websites, blog posts and comments, and so on). It is perhaps not particularly controversial to think that the *anonymity* that the online world provides is partially responsible for the lamentable quality here.[1] If you can say something under conditions in which no one knows who is saying so, then your tongue might be a bit freer in what you say. No doubt this phenomenon is not new. (Males of a certain age will recognize the venerable tradition of graffiti on the walls of the stalls in public restrooms for men.) But given the prevalence of the Internet in our lives, the role websites and blogs have come to play in many of our discussions, and the fact that most sites are accessible to everyone in the

---

[1] Recently, an app called Secret has been developed. Secret is like Facebook and Twitter in that it is a microblogging application, but it is unlike them in that it allows for anonymous posting. The results are perhaps what one would expect. See "Anonymous Social App Offers A Hotbet of Silicon Valley Gossip," *New York Times*, March 19, 2014.

world, it is plausible to think that the phenomenon of anonymous assertion is much more widespread these days. (So widespread, in fact, that we now have adopted an old word for a new use, as a way to single out the sort of person who abuses the anonymity (s)he is afforded in online contributions: (s)he is a "troll.") My aim in this chapter is both to characterize, and to offer a partial explanation of, the link between anonymity and the epistemic quality of assertions. To that end I will be appealing not only to MMENA itself, but also to several of the results I have obtained in previous chapters—results which themselves I obtained by appeal to MMENA.

My claims will be these. First, the fact of anonymity—the fact that one's assertion was anonymous—has implications for the warranted expectations that speakers have of their audience, and that the audience has regarding the speaker. In general, when it is mutually known by all parties that a claim was made under conditions of anonymity, this has a diminishing effect on the sort of (assertion-generated) expectations that speakers and hearers are entitled to have of one another.[2]

Second, this diminishment of warranted expectations under conditions of anonymity can be explained by appeal to MMENA. Throughout the book I have been arguing that, on the assumption that it is mutually manifest to all competent speakers that assertion has an epistemic norm, we would predict that some of the expectations generated by the making of an assertion will have an epistemic content: they are expectations pertaining to the epistemic position of the speaker. Here I will argue that when assertions are anonymous, most or all of the mechanisms that exist for the "policing" of assertions—for ensuring that speakers are living up to the responsibilities associated with asserting—do not apply, and both the speaker and hearer are aware of this (if only implicitly). It is for this reason, I will argue, that we see a diminishment in the warranted expectations that hearers and audiences have towards one another, when an assertion is made anonymously.

These claims, I think, point to one cost associated with the privacy or secrecy that the online world affords us. In particular, insofar as the Internet provides the opportunity to make claims while keeping one's identity a secret, this "opportunity" militates against the sort of conditions on which quality (assertion-involving) speech exchanges depend.

8.2 Anonymity

Throughout this chapter I will be speaking of anonymity, and of anonymous assertion. My general approach to anonymity is epistemic. To a very rough first approximation, a speaker or writer S is anonymous relative to a group of people G in a given (spoken or written) assertion when no one in G can knowledgeably connect S to the

---

[2] There are exceptions to this, of course. As I note in the penultimate section of this chapter, certain kinds of information can *only* come in a reliable way if the folks who have the information are accorded anonymity. (One thinks here of the contributions to the blog *What It's Like to Be a Woman in Philosophy*.)

assertion—more colloquially, when no one in G knows who produced the assertion. I acknowledge that the locution 'knows who' is a tricky one, and that as a result my characterization will inherit all of this trickiness. But to a first approximation we can say that no one in G knows who the speaker or writer is, in the sense relevant to anonymity, when no one in G has identificatory knowledge of the speaker or writer that would enable the reidentification of S *as* the speaker or writer.

This first approximation requires immediate modification, in that it is too weak: it allows as cases of anonymity cases we should want to rule out. It is easy to imagine cases in which, as a matter of fact, no one in a given group knows who the speaker or writer is, but not because the speaker or writer has hidden her identity in any way. Imagine that Sally writes a book, publishes it herself (her own vanity press), puts her name on the cover (she is hiding nothing), but as a matter of fact everyone who reads the book fails to observe the cover, and so as a matter of fact no one among the readers of the book (presently) knows who wrote the book. This is hardly a case of anonymity, yet it satisfies the previous characterization.

To rectify this situation, I would propose the following slight modification. (I do not pretend that the proposed characterization of anonymity is counterexample-proof, but it will be good enough to use for the purpose of this chapter.) The characterization is this:

> ANON   Given a speaker/writer S who produces a message *m*, S is anonymous (with respect to *m*) relative to an audience A when (i) no one among the members of A is currently in a position to acquire knowledge to the effect that S produced *m*, (ii) it is reasonable (for S) to expect that no one among the members of A will come to know something to this effect, and (iii) the explanation for both of the foregoing is that S's identity, *qua* producer of *m*, is in some way "hidden" from the members of A.

Note that ANON offers only a sufficient condition, not a necessary condition, on S's being anonymous (relative to A) with respect to *m*.

ANON calls for some commentary. First, instead of characterizing anonymity in terms of a lack of "knowing who," ANON's condition (i) characterizes it in terms of a lack of knowledge "to the effect that S produced *m*." I intend for the latter as a stand-in for the former. (Clearly, S is not anonymous merely in virtue of people failing to know her *as S*, since they may be able to identify her in other relevant ways. Which ways of identification are relevant to anonymity? That anyone can denote her as "the writer of this message" does not suffice to show that S is not anonymous. But this is a hard question to which I do not have anything more to say.) Second, the reason behind ANON's (ii) is this: an author S who posts under a pseudonym, under conditions in which only S herself (and perhaps her Internet provider) knows of S that she is the one posting under this pseudonym, can be said to be posting anonymously (to those in the relevant audience), even though there might be ingenious hackers who, given enough time and resources, could come to know, of S, that she is the one posting under this pseudonym.

The point about anonymity here is simply that it was reasonable for S to assume that no one among her audience will come to acquire this knowledge. Third, the idea behind ANON's (iii) is this: the facts (i) that no one among those in A is in a position to acquire knowledge to the effect that S produced m, and (ii) that it is reasonable for S to suppose that no one among A will acquire such knowledge, are themselves to be explained by the further fact that S's identity is in some way "hidden" from the members of A. This is to rule out a case like the one just mentioned, where condition (ii) is satisfied in virtue of Sally's recognition that the readers of her book are systematically uninterested in learning who wrote the book. In such a case, Sally is not anonymous even relative to a readership that is systematically uninterested in (and so ignorant of) her identity as author, even though ANON's conditions (i) and (ii) are satisfied.

Again, I cannot claim that ANON is counterexample-proof; I highly doubt that it is. Still, it is good enough to proceed for my purposes at hand: to explore the epistemic implications of anonymity in assertion. (My hope would be that whatever rectifications are needed to render ANON adequate, these could be made in such a way as to not undermine any of the arguments I am going on to be presenting.)

8.3 The Gap: Reductionism and Non-Reductionism Revisited

As in previous chapters, so too here I will be assuming MMENA—the hypothesis to the effect that it is mutually manifest that assertion is governed by an epistemic norm:

ENA   S must: assert p, only if S satisfies epistemic condition E with respect to the proposition that p; that is, only if $E(S, [p])$.

As in previous chapters, so too here I make no assumptions regarding the content of E, beyond that it is robustly epistemic. For whatever the norm of assertion is—whether it is as demanding as knowledge, or something that requires only an adequate degree of evidence—it should be agreed that in asserting something, the speaker performs an act regarding which it is common knowledge that her act was warranted only if she had the relevant epistemic authority. Throughout this book I have been arguing that it is this piece of common knowledge that provides the content of the sorts of expectations that characterize ordinary face-to-face communicative exchanges. We should be able to agree on this much even if we disagree over what the precise content of the norm is.

In Chapters 3 and 7 I argued that if MMENA is true, we would predict that the practice of assertion is rich with mutual expectations between a speaker and her audience.[3] Rather than reproduce the relevant arguments, here I merely summarize the results I obtained. First, some of the expectations one has in contexts of observed assertions

---

[3] In this chapter I will use 'speaker' to designate the producer of an assertion, whether spoken or written. Context will make it clear whether the case is one involving a speech act or a written communication.

will be expectations to which one is entitled. At a minimum, hearers will be entitled to regard asserters as being responsible for satisfying the norm. Some theorists—so-called non-reductionists regarding testimony (see Chapter 2, Sections 2.5 and 2.6)—will hold that a hearer is entitled to more than this. Such theorists will hold that, in the absence of reasons to think otherwise, hearers are entitled to regard speakers (not merely as *responsible for* satisfying the norm of assertion but) as *actually satisfying* that norm (see, for example, Ross 1986: 77–78). Other theorists—so-called reductionists—will deny this, maintaining that, while hearers may be entitled to regard speakers as *responsible* for satisfying that norm, hearers need positive reasons to regard it as actually satisfied in any given case. Which of these views is correct depends on the correct account of the epistemology of testimony (for which see Chapters 2 and 3). Both reductionists and non-reductionists can agree, however, that a hearer A is justified in accepting what she is told only if A is entitled to regard the speaker as having been relevantly epistemically authoritative. Where they disagree is over the conditions on being so entitled. Happily, we need not enter into this debate here, since the point I wish to make can be made whatever one's views on the debate between reductionists and anti-reductionists. The point I wish to make here is this: there is a gap that needs to be bridged, from what an audience is entitled to believe on observing an assertion, to an audience's being entitled *full-stop* to believe—to being *ultima facie* justified in believing—what was asserted.

To see this, suppose that reductionism is true. Then, on observing an assertion that p, an audience is entitled at most to believe that the speaker recognizes that she is under an obligation to have the relevant authority regarding the truth of [p].[4] Clearly, such an entitlement is not sufficient to justify the audience in believing that p (on the basis of the speaker's having said so). The audience will also need to be justified in thinking that the speaker *has* the relevant authority; for it is only *then* that the audience will be justified in accepting that p (on the basis of the speaker's having said so).

Now suppose that non-reductionism is true. Then, on observing an assertion that p, an audience is (presumptively but defeasibly) entitled to believe that the speaker has the relevant authority regarding the truth of [p]. Still, this entitlement is only presumptive; in order for it to hold, it must be the case that *there are no relevant defeaters*. From this we see that the absence of defeaters is a *further* condition on the audience's being entitled (full-stop) to regard the speaker as having been relevantly epistemically authoritative, and so is a further condition on the audience's being *ultima facie* justified in believing that p (on the basis of the speaker's having said so). Nor is this the only further condition. In particular, the mere lack of defeaters does not suffice to turn the presumptive entitlement (to regard the speaker as authoritative) into an

---

[4] 'At most': this depends on whether the reductionist accepts MMENA. If she does, she should allow that hearers are entitled to regard speakers as recognizing the responsibility for having the relevant authority. In this chapter I will be assuming MMENA, so will be assuming that the reductionist assumes it as well. With this understood throughout, in what follows I will skip the 'at most' qualification.

entitlement *full-stop*, and so does not suffice to render the audience *ultima facie* justified in believing that p (on the basis of the speaker's having said so). For suppose we have an audience who suffers from extreme gullibility: he would have been oblivious to the presence of defeaters had they obtained, and so would have believed whatever he was told. The mere fact that there were no defeaters—the speaker spoke in a way that would have struck an ordinary person as competent and sincere, her claim would have struck an ordinary person as not implausible on its face—does not seem sufficient, by itself, to entitle the audience to regard the speaker as relevantly authoritative.[5] Now it might be too much to require hearers to have *positive evidence* that there were no defeaters, in order for them to enjoy an entitlement to regard the speaker as relevantly authoritative. Even so, the following seems reasonable: a hearer is not entitled to regard the speaker in this way unless the hearer herself is counterfactually sensitive to the presence of defeaters, such that, had there been any relevant defeaters, she would have attended to them, and so would have refrained from so regarding the speaker.[6]

In this way we see that, whether we accept reductionism or non-reductionism, the following point holds: what an audience is entitled to believe on observing an assertion, by itself, does not suffice to provide *ultima facie* justification for the audience's belief in what was asserted. This is what I mean when I say that there is a gap that needs to be bridged, from the former to the latter. The existence of this gap is important. I am now going to argue that, when we consider how this gap is actually spanned, we will be appealing to considerations that are (typically) largely absent in cases in which an assertion is made anonymously.

8.4 Minding the Gap: Assessing Assertions

The question before us is this: how is it that, from what you are entitled to assume merely in virtue of having observed someone else make an assertion you understood, you come to be (*ultima facie*) justified in accepting the assertion? Here I go over the various factors that bear on this question. (I will return, briefly, to the debate between reductionism and non-reductionism.) This will pave the way for the next section, where I argue that many—though not all!—of these things are absent in cases in which an assertion is made anonymously.

First, some background. As consumers of others' speech, audiences have various ways of assessing the credibility of an assertion.[7] Some of these pertain to the audience's assessment of *the speaker*, others pertain to the audience's assessment of *the act of assertion itself*, still others pertain to the plausibility of *the content asserted*, and yet

---

[5] This is a point that Elizabeth Fricker has made; see Fricker (1994).
[6] For a defense of this sort of view within the framework of an anti-reductionist account in the epistemology of testimony, see Goldberg and Henderson (2006).
[7] Or perhaps we should say *the cognitive systems* of audiences have various ways of assessing the credibility of an assertion.

still others pertain to the *context of the communication*. What is more, many of these assessments are broadly subcognitive,[8] while some others are the result of conscious deliberation. In what follows I will use "assessment" broadly, to cover any of the (subcognitive or cognitive) resources that a subject (or her cognitive system) brings to the task of discerning the credibility of an assertion.

Consider first the audience's assessment of the speaker and her assertion. The audience will typically assess such things as how sincere and confident the speaker seemed in the assertion; how well-placed she was to have the knowledge in question, relative to what she is presently asserting (including her relevant background, if it is known by the audience); and what sort of motives she might have had in speaking as she did. In the latter respect, the audience might assess such things as whether the speaker had any present motive for insincerity, as well as what "pressures" there are on the speaker to speak responsibly.

Since the topic of the "pressures" bearing on a speaker to speak responsibly will loom large in my subsequent discussion, I want to dwell on this topic a little here. These "pressures" derive from what I will describe as the mechanisms for the "policing" of assertoric responsibility. By this I include all the practices and institutions that encourage speakers to live up to their assertoric responsibilities and/or enforce the repercussions for those who do not do so. These "pressures" can take many forms, but I will focus primarily on those that involve negative consequences the speaker would (likely) face if she is found to be speaking irresponsibly.[9] Such pressure on a speaker increases in proportion to (a) the severity of the consequence, as well as (b) the chances of her being "found out." Of course, these pressures work only if (a) and (b) are not negligible, and the speaker herself is aware of this; and so whatever knowledge an audience has of these pressures on the speaker is relevant to the assessment at hand only insofar as the audience regards the speaker as aware of these pressures, and as sensitive to them.

Considerations of this "outside pressure" sort are particularly important when it comes to an audience's assessment of written testimony. You do not know the journalist who wrote the article you just read in the *New York Times*; yet you probably regard her, if only implicitly, as highly reliable. This sense of yours is backed, at least in large part, by your (perhaps only implicit) awareness that the *New York Times* has a reputation to protect, and that it will go to great lengths to do so, especially when it comes to hiring and exerting editorial control over their journalists. (It is because these practices

---

[8] To the extent that we rely on subcognitive processes in our credibility judgments, there are real questions regarding how reliable those processes are; social psychology appears full of evidence that women and members of minority groups have their credibility systematically discounted. In this connection, see Fricker (2007) for a very robust defense of the idea that this constitutes an epistemic injustice to those who are the victims of this prejudice-based diminution in the credibility their words are assigned.

[9] Let us understand *speaking irresponsibly* as amounting to *violating the norm of assertion*. One can quibble with this identification—as I noted in Chapter 7, if the norm is knowledge, it would seem that not all forms of violating this norm are cases of irresponsible assertion (consider Gettier cases)—but these differences, though real, are not germane to the present discussion.

enforce a higher degree of reliability among its writers that the *New York Times* has a greater claim on our attention, epistemically speaking, than does the *National Enquirer*.[10]) There can be little doubt but that a system of very extensive social relations, perhaps together with our (merely implicit) awareness of these relations, warrants the credibility we assign to a good deal of the written reports we encounter. Of course, professional sanctions are not the only form of potential pressure that is brought to bear on speakers. There are all sorts of other pressures that can be brought to bear against an irresponsible asserter. These include a diminishment in the trust which such a speaker is accorded, the consequent diminishment in the roles that are open to her to play in the deliberations of the various communities of which she is a member, other forms of loss of status (and perhaps loss of friends and partners), and the moral disapproval of one's peers.

I have just spoken of the audience's assessment of the speaker and her assertion (with particular attention to the pressures that can be brought to bear on the speaker for asserting irresponsibly). Moving on, let us consider next the audience's assessment of the plausibility of the content of the assertion. Obviously, the audience is better positioned on this dimension to the extent that he himself has ample background knowledge on which to draw. If you are an expert in radiation, then you are in a good position to assess the plausibility of the latest claim made regarding radiation levels near various sites at the Fukushima nuclear reactor in Japan; if you are not an expert, you are more helpless in this regard. Still, it would seem that common sense itself often suffices to enable an audience to make at least some assessment of the plausibility of an asserted content. And this, together with other background knowledge that the hearer brings to bear in the assessment, is what he has to go on.

The purpose of these sorts of assessment is to bridge the gap I identified in Section 8.3. Let us use 'E' to designate the proposition that, according to one's favored theory, the hearer is (perhaps merely presumptively) entitled to believe merely in virtue of observing the speaker's assertion;[11] and let us use 'P' to designate the proposition asserted by the speaker. The gap, then, is that between the audience's (perhaps merely presumptive) entitlement to E, which she enjoys in virtue of having apprehended the speaker's assertion, and the materials that determine the (*ultima facie*) justification of her belief that P, formed on the basis of that assertion. The schema for bridging this gap will depend on whether one's epistemology is internalist or externalist. If one's epistemology is internalist, the gap will be regarded as to-be-bridged by the audience's reasons or evidence: her reasons or evidence, together with her observation of the assertion and her (perhaps merely presumptive) entitlement to E, must rationalize

---

[10] Of course, even such a respectable newspaper as the *New York Times* is not immune to journalistic lapses—indeed, even to occasional substantial journalistic lapses (the case of Jason Blair).

[11] According to non-reductionist positions, E is the proposition that the speaker is relevantly authoritative regarding P. According to reductionist positions, E is the proposition that the speaker acknowledges that she is responsible for being relevantly authoritative regarding P. (But see fn. 2.)

the transition to the belief that P. If one's epistemology is externalist, the gap will be regarded as to-be-bridged by factors which render the transition, from her observation of the assertion that P, to her coming to believe that P, one that typically results in belief that satisfies one's favored externalist condition. (Presumably, these factors involve but are not exhausted by the audience's background beliefs and her counterfactual sensitivity to things "not appearing right" in the way of assertion.)

To see how this works in a concrete case, let us assume that we want an account, not just of the hearer's justified belief that p, but her knowledge that p, formed through her acceptance of the speaker's assertion that p. In presenting such an account I will assume the non-reductionist's account of the assertion-generated entitlement, as well as an externalist account of epistemology. Both of these assumptions are made for the purpose of illustration only: together they place the *weakest* demands on a hearer, and so render the gap more easily bridgeable than on other assumptions. Consequently, if we can show that even here bridging the gap is a non-trivial affair, the point will be all the stronger on any epistemological view that places even greater requirements on knowledge and justified belief. So imagine that S, aiming to communicate that p to H, asserts that p in H's presence, and that H apprehends (and understands) this assertion. That is, H knows that S has asserted that p. Then, from the non-reductionist model, H is presumptively entitled to regard S as relevantly authoritative regarding the truth of the proposition that p. Clearly, H is not thereby in a position, merely in virtue of this presumptive entitlement and the other facts of the case, to know that p through accepting S's assertion. For one thing, S's assertion might be false. For another, even if S's assertion is true, this might be a matter of luck. Let us suppose, though, that neither of these things are true: S's assertion was knowledgeable. This still does not suffice for H to be in a position to come to know that p through accepting S's assertion to that effect. As noted previously, if H's acceptance is to be justified, it would seem that H cannot simply depend on the knowledgeableness of S's assertion; H needs to protect himself by being counterfactually sensitive to signs of incompetence or insincerity. That is, H must be such that, were S's assertion to have been incompetent (unreliable) or otherwise insincere, H would (likely) have picked up on this, and would not have accepted this assertion. How does H attain this sort of counterfactual sensitivity? Well, assertions that are insincere or incompetent often (though not always) exhibit features that give this away: the speaker did not look her audience in the eyes; the speaker seemed nervous; what she said just did not make sense; and so on. In other cases, while the assertions may not have those tell-tale signs of incompetence or insincerity, the hearer has background knowledge which, applied to the case at hand, sets off bells in his mind. This is precisely the job that is done by the two sorts of assessment I have mentioned previously.

It should not be particularly controversial to say that this sort of "counterfactual sensitivity" is a large part of our dealings with other speakers' assertions. But it is worth noting that the fact of an audience's counterfactual sensitivity reverberates for speakers as well. This is for a simple reason. Speech acts are performed with practical aims in mind. The speech act of assertion is typically performed with the aim of getting one's audience to believe what one asserts to be the case.[12] When this is one's aim, one is well-served to have in mind how the candidate audience is likely to react to one's assertion. Insofar as one anticipates that one's audience will be counterfactually sensitive in this way, one will adjust one's assertions accordingly: if one is aware that one cannot get away with just anything, presumably this will have a rather constraining effect on one's linguistic behavior.

In sum, the practice of assertion is informed by the rich stock of mutual expectations that hold between speaker and audience, and these expectations bear on the audience's acceptance of assertions, as well as the speaker's making of assertions.

8.5 Anonymity and the Impoverished Mechanisms for Policing and Assessing Assertoric Responsibility

I have been developing the idea that the practice of assertion—both the making of assertions by speakers, and their acceptance by audiences—is shaped in large part by the mutual expectations between speaker and audience, as well as the background knowledge the various parties bring to the communicative exchange. I now want to argue that a good deal of the expectations in play regarding ordinary assertions are epistemically unwarranted, and much of the background knowledge needed for the purpose of assessment will be unavailable, when it comes to assertions that are made anonymously.

The first point I wish to make is straightforward: when assertions are anonymous, there is little that the audience has to go on in assessing the assertion for credibility. (As a result, the audience's "counterfactual sensitivity" to defeaters will be correspondingly diminished.) To see this, let us consider how the anonymity of an assertion bears on the conditions for credibility-assessment.

Consider (what was noted previously) the four types of information that the hearer might bring to bear to the task of assessing assertions for reliability. These include (1) information regarding the speaker; (2) information regarding the act of communication (or assertion) itself; (3) information regarding the content of the communicated message; and (4) information regarding the context of the communication.[13] Cases can be found in which the hearer has ample information in each of these categories: consider, for example, a case of face-to-face speech with a good friend on a topic that is mutually familiar to speaker and hearer alike. What is more, it is easy to think of cases in which the hearer has significant information from some but not all of these categories. Cases of "stranger testimony" on a topic that is unfamiliar to the hearer—cases

---

[12] That is, this is what Austin would have called the "perlocutionary aim."
[13] These sorts of information are not separate, of course: sometimes the assessment is made on the basis of knowledge of the speaker's relation to the subject-matter of her testimony, connecting at least (1) and (3).

which are common in the literature in the epistemology of testimony—are cases in which the hearer typically enters with little or no background information to bring to the task of assessment;[14] but when the exchange is face-to-face, the hearer can acquire some information regarding both (1) and (2) from the exchange itself, and this is often enough to enable her to reach an assessment. (The speaker appeared normal, and spoke with apparent confidence on a topic regarding which people typically can be expected to be both sincere and competent, and so on.) Cases of reading newspaper articles are typically cases in which the hearer/reader has ample information in (4), and from this she can often draw relevant inferences regarding (1) from the fact that the speaker's/writer's article is published in a high-reputation newspaper. And so forth.

But now consider assertions made under conditions in which the speaker/writer is anonymous relative to the hearer. As in "stranger cases," so here too the hearer will start out with minimal background information with which to assess the speaker; but unlike stranger cases, the anonymity of the exchange ensures that there is significantly less information to be gleaned from the exchange itself with which to perform the assessment. Since the speaker/writer is unknown to the hearer/reader, the latter has no background information from categories (1) or (2). To be sure, if the message comes across as curious in any way—it exhibits emotional volatility, or anger, or incoherence; the sentences are ungrammatical, or otherwise unintelligible; or something else just does not seem right—then the audience, having come across the message, can draw inferences regarding the speaker's competence and/or sincerity. But if what is written gives no basis for an inference of this kind to be drawn, then the audience is left with little in the way to go on regarding (1) and (2). What is more, anonymity may obscure the context in which the communicative act itself was produced, and/or may obscure what the speaker/writer anticipated in the way of the context in which the message would be encountered by the hearer/reader. In such cases, the hearer has little information from (4) either. In such cases where background information from (1), (2), and (4) is minimal even after the hearer has observed the message, the only information that the hearer has to go on is the background information she has on the subject-matter of the message. To be sure, if the message is on a topic on which the hearer has ample background knowledge, she may have enough background information to assess the reliability of the message: perhaps the message is on a topic on which the hearer can draw on her expertise, and so can discern attempts to "fake" such expertise; perhaps the message is on a topic in which the hearer knows that saying something that even achieved *prima facie* plausibility was something that likely could come only from someone who knew what she was talking about; and so forth. What is more, insofar as the message is extended (involving lots of individual assertions constituting a whole report), it can be assessed for internal coherence, and there will be an increasing number of points

---

[14] But again see Kenyon (2012) for an argument that even here testimonial exchanges are informationally rich.

at which the hearer's general background information can be brought to bear on the report's overall plausibility. But there can also be cases in which the hearer has little or no relevant expertise on which to draw, and the report offers too little information from which to draw any substantial inferences regarding its internal coherence or its overall plausibility. Such cases represent the sorts of cases in which the hearer's background information is the least helpful in the task of assessment, with the result that, were the hearer to accept the report, she would be *most epistemically dependent* on the speaker/writer.[15]

It is clear that the epistemological perspective of the audience in such a case is seriously diminished, relative to the credibility-assessment task. For this very reason, it would appear that the audience's counterfactual sensitivity to defeaters would be diminished as well. To see this, imagine that, randomly surfing the web one day, you come across a site that presents several pieces of information about a place—or a person, or a time period—about which you know virtually nothing. Nothing on the site gives you pause—the sentences do not ramble, there would appear to be no vested interest that you can discern, it appears to be internally consistent and coherent, there are no claims that clash with your common sense and the little relevant background knowledge that you bring to bear. Still, you do not know who wrote this, you have no idea whether this site is monitored (and if so by whom), and so forth. How confident are you that, were the information on the site simply made up, you would recognize this, and would refrain from believing any of it? It would seem that your "counterfactual sensitivity" is seriously diminished.

In short, from the epistemic perspective of the audience, it is clear that anonymous assertions present a challenge: most of the ordinary ways of assessing reliability are not available. This alone might lead epistemologists to conclude that anonymous assertions are epistemically perilous creatures: since one does not have much to go on in making a credibility-assessment, one's counterfactual sensitivity to defeaters is diminished, and one is limited in the background information one might cite in any effort to render rational the move to accept the assertion. What is more, the hearer is aware (and the speaker can be presumed to be aware that the hearer is aware) that the various social practices that we have for "policing" assertions—the mechanisms whereby one's community encourages (enforces?) speakers to live up to their assertion-generated responsibilities—are inapplicable. In these contexts it is far from clear how any belief formed through such acceptance might

---

[15] It is interesting in this respect that the cases used in the literature for highlighting maximum (epistemic) dependence of a hearer on speaker are "stranger cases" rather than cases of anonymity. If the point is merely to highlight hearer epistemic dependence on speaker, the use of stranger cases is curious, since all else equal, hearer dependence is typically greater in anonymity cases than in "stranger cases." Later I will be suggesting something that can explain the focus on "stranger cases" in this connection: we think of assertion as a public act, where the publicity of the act is not merely in the fact that it is an act produced in such a way that others can observe it, but also in the fact that the speaker herself is public in a sense to be identified—and this latter sort of publicness *is central to assertion's playing the knowledge- and information-spreading role that in fact it plays.* Or so I will be arguing.

be doxastically justified (let alone knowledgeable when true). I will return to this point shortly.

8.6 Effects of Anonymity: Mutually Diminished Expectations

In this penultimate section, however, I want to begin by focusing on a dimension of anonymity that standard positions in the epistemology of testimony might well overlook: the perspective of the speaker, the producer of assertions. It is here, in connection with what I will call the pragmatics of anonymous assertion, that the implications of anonymity are most profound; and it is here, too, that we can begin to appreciate the sense in which it is the very publicity of ordinary (non-anonymous) assertions that renders this speech act apt for the communication of knowledge.

As noted previously, ordinary speakers recognize the various mechanisms that might be brought to bear on them, were it to be discovered that they asserted unwarrantedly. A speaker who asserts anonymously will recognize that no such mechanisms can bear against her—or at any rate that it is highly unlikely that any such mechanisms will bear against her—for the simple reason that no one (for whom the assertion was anonymous) will be in a position to warrantedly connect her to the assertion she made anonymously. This will enable her to evade having to take responsibility for any unwarranted assertions. At a minimum, even otherwise scrupulous speakers might lose some of the enthusiasm they have for self-scrutiny and self-policing; such speakers might give in to occasional tendencies to exaggerate or otherwise speak in self-serving ways (after all, no one will be checking up on them). To be sure, a speaker who goes too far—her tales are too tall, her exaggerations too big, her claims too implausible on their face—might well fail to get others to believe what she says. But while such an outcome might fail to advance her interests, still, it is no skin off of her back, so to speak, since it would not affect the trust she is accorded when she speaks in plain daylight. In short, such a speaker will quickly recognize that she is asserting in a context involving few or no mechanisms available for the encouragement (or enforcement) of assertoric responsibility.

It should be equally clear that conditions of anonymity affect not only what the speaker can expect from an audience, but also what an audience can expect from a speaker. This is because any reasonable audience will recognize the situation confronting the anonymous speaker. Such an audience will see that when mechanisms for the enforcement and encouragement of assertoric responsibility are minimal or non-existent, the speaker has less to worry about in making unwarranted assumptions—her doing so will not adversely affect her self-interest in any significant way. An audience who recognizes this will also be aware that it is reasonable to assume that the speaker herself recognizes this. Such an audience, I submit, has, and appreciates that he has, generic grounds for skepticism regarding the truth of assertions presented anonymously. To be sure, these generic grounds for skepticism do not ensure that it is never warranted for an audience to accept an anonymous assertion. If an audience has some independent way to confirm that a particular anonymous assertion is credible—say, it concerns a topic on which he (the audience) has extensive background knowledge; the assertion's content is plausible relative to that background knowledge, and he (the audience) recognizes that it is unlikely that one could simply lock on to such a plausible claim unless one really knew what one was talking about; or there are other social mechanisms in play that police the anonymous assertions (more on which later)—then it can be reasonable for him to accept the anonymous assertion. (Here the generic grounds he has for skepticism are trumped by his specific grounds for regarding this particular anonymous assertion as credible.) Still, he is left with generic grounds for skepticism regarding anonymous assertions as a class.

Of course, the speaker, too, is in a position in which to anticipate that the audience, reasoning in this fashion, will come to have diminished epistemic expectations regarding anonymous assertions as a class. Stronger, both speaker and audience alike are in a position to appreciate that the other will probably reason in this way. But for this very reason, these diminished expectations on both sides are likely to be *mutually acknowledged*. And this strikes me as an interesting outcome. For if I am right that it is the warranted mutual expectations of speakers and audiences that frame the epistemology of assertion, in the manner I aimed to describe in Chapters 2 and 3, then to the extent that assertions made anonymously constitute a class of assertions regarding which there is a diminishment in the mutual expectations that are warranted, to just this extent the *purport of belief-worthiness* of these assertions is diminished.

I just noted that an audience has *pro tanto* grounds for generic skepticism regarding the whole class of anonymous assertions, and that this point is mutually familiar to any competent speaker and audience. But for precisely this reason, the epistemic threshold for warranted acceptance of an assertion is systematically harder to meet in cases in which the assertion was anonymous than it is in cases of "ordinary" assertion. More specifically, I submit that the following is a possibility:

DIF   Two hearers who are exactly alike with respect to their relevant degree of informedness, their competences relating to the comprehension and assessment of testimonies, and the background information they bring to the scene may nevertheless be such that the hearer who observes an "ordinary" (face-to-face) assertion, by S, to the effect that p is warranted in accepting it, whereas the hearer who observes an anonymous assertion that p (by S, albeit unbeknownst to the hearer) is *not* warranted in accepting the anonymous assertion.

What might explain this? Since the speaker and the asserted content are the same in both cases, the epistemic difference in DIF cannot be chalked up to any difference in S's epistemic position regarding the proposition she asserted (= the proposition that p). Nor can we explain the epistemic difference in DIF by appeal to a difference in the hearers' epistemic perspective on the proposition asserted, since by hypothesis both hearers have the same relevant degree of informedness and bring the same background information to the scene. The epistemic difference in DIF, rather, lies in the audiences' epistemic position regarding the credibility assessment of *the speaker* and *the asserting* of the content. But we must also keep in mind that the audience's overall epistemic inferiority in assessing cases of anonymous assertion is mutually familiar to speaker and hearer alike. So a speaker who asserts anonymously should expect that a hearer who encounters her anonymous assertion will recognize his (the hearer's) own epistemic inferiority relative to the position he is in with respect to "ordinary" assertions. And this, I think, means that one who asserts anonymously should not expect— is not warranted in expecting—that the audience's assertion-generated expectations will be the same as in cases of ordinary assertion. Whereas in ordinary cases the hearer expects the speaker to recognize both the responsibilities attendant to the making of an assertion and the various mechanisms in place for "encouraging" speakers to live up to those responsibilities, the hearer who observes an anonymous assertion has grounds for thinking that there is little or no external "encouragement" putting any pressure on the speaker. It is in this way rational for the hearer to adjust her confidence in the trustworthiness of the assertion, absent reasons that address these concerns (of the sort just suggested, for instance).

I have been arguing, in effect, that *anonymity saps assertion of some of "the promise" of epistemic authoritativeness that ordinary (non-anonymous) assertion conveys.* How might we square this with MMENA itself—that is, with the hypothesis that it is mutually manifest that assertion answers to a robustly epistemic norm? I think the answer is this: the fact of anonymity itself provides a hearer with a generic reason for skepticism about the reliability of the assertion, with the result that, absent reasons with which to address this sort of skepticism (of the sort just discussed, for instance), the hearer is unwarranted in thinking that the speaker satisfied the norm of assertion. On such an account, it is by serving as this sort of reason that anonymity saps assertion of some of "the promise" of epistemic authoritativeness that ordinary assertion conveys.

However we decide to model the phenomenon, though, we can say this: insofar as there is a diminishment in the mutual expectations that are warranted in connection with anonymous assertion, the assertions themselves no longer convey that the speaker has the sort of epistemic authority that would be needed to warrant outright belief. I think that this point tells us something interesting about ordinary assertions: much of the epistemico-pragmatic potential of assertion as a speech-act type—much of what makes assertions apt to generate belief in hearers, and so apt for the transmission of knowledge—derives precisely from the fact that assertion is a *public act*. By speaking of assertion as a public act I have in mind two features of our ordinary assertoric practices. First, assertions are acts that are made "in public" by one whose identity can be known and tracked over time. Second, assertions are acts that are addressed to an audience of other epistemic subjects, who can be expected to have certain expectations regarding the asserter's epistemic perspective on the asserted content, who will rely on the mechanisms for ensuring general conformity with these expectations, and who can be expected to hold the speaker to her assertoric responsibilities. Insofar as assertions are anonymous, the basis of this "publicness" no longer exists; and my hypothesis is that the result is that the class of anonymous assertions do not have the belief-worthiness potential of ordinary assertions.

8.7 Relativized Anonymity and Anonymity-Policing Regimes

Even if I am correct in thinking that anonymous assertions do not have the belief-worthiness potential of ordinary assertions, still, it is worth noting that this fact need not doom anonymous assertion from ever being usefully employed. Clearly, there are all sorts of motives one might have for remaining anonymous in one's assertion, not all of which are nefarious. (Perhaps the most common non-nefarious motive is the fear of retribution when what is asserted goes against the interests of the strong or the influential.) What is more, there are even cases where anonymity can be an epistemic good. Here one thinks of the phenomenon of anonymous refereeing(!), the use that newspaper reports make of anonymous sources (although non-anonymous sources are preferred, when possible), and also the anonymity that allows claims to be made under conditions in which if there were no anonymity at all, then no claims, or highly unreliable ones, would be made. It is in the latter respect that one thinks these days of the role of anonymous postings for whistleblowers in industry, or on blogs such as *What It's Like to Be a Woman in Philosophy*. In the former case, insidious and unlawful business practices have been revealed which might never have come to light were it not for the anonymity provided to the whistleblower; and in the latter case, explicit and implicit forms of sexism and sexist practices have been revealed which would not have been revealed at all, or as reliably discussed, without such an anonymous forum. These are important points that must be accommodated by an adequate account of anonymity in assertion. I propose to do so here in this section.

If my argument is correct, how can it be that there are cases in which there are whole domains involving anonymous assertions, yet where the assertions themselves are reliable, truthworthy, and so on? I want to provide two complementary answers to this. First: in some cases the anonymity is "relative" in the sense that while the speaker is anonymous to the audience, nevertheless the anonymity is not total, and there are mechanisms for doing at least some of the sort of policing that I discussed in Section 8.4. Second: in some cases the anonymity is total or near-total, but these cases will tend not to be the best examples of anonymous assertions that nevertheless remain belief-worthy. I will take these up in turn.

I begin with the claim that regimes are imaginable which allow for (some) anonymity while still preserving the belief-worthiness of the anonymous assertions.

One such regime would be the "security wall" model. On this model, someone or some group is authorized to serve as a both a security wall (behind which the speaker's anonymity is preserved), but also as a filter (allowing only worthy asserters or worthy assertions to pass, and so to see the light of day). Insofar as the assertions that pass through the filter are seen as "backed" by the authoritativeness of the person or group who constitutes the security wall, and insofar as members of that group can be held responsible for the warrantedness of assertions that so pass, the security wall model might preserve the belief-worthiness potential of anonymous assertion. Blogs whose comments sections are monitored are in some respects like this. At the very least, the most irresponsible comments—those whose irresponsibility is obvious, and whose likely inflammatory effects are clear—are weeded out. Spokespersons for groups, corporations, or governments can play a similar role, speaking on behalf of their group, business, or government while leaving the informant anonymous.

Another regime might follow the Wikipedia model: we develop practices whereby all assertions made on a particular website (for example) are anonymous, so the barrier to entry remains low; but anyone is entitled to anonymously correct any assertion that is made, so the "cost" of correction is low; and constant or at least regular vigilance by the anonymous masses holds out the hope that errors are soon corrected. Since the Wikipedia phenomenon has been extensively studied already,[16] we might well learn about the conditions under which this sort of regime produces reliable information, and the conditions under which it does not. My present point is only that it offers a model in which anonymity is compatible with the sort of belief-worthiness potential associated with ordinary (public) assertion.

Yet a third regime is the communal shunning regime. Blogs whose bloggers (those who can make blog posts, as opposed to merely comment on posts) themselves are anonymous can exhibit a kind of self-policing of this sort. If one of the bloggers is seen to take advantage of his or her anonymity, he or she might be called out—not by name, of course, but as the source of the offending blog post. Of course, no one will know who was called out. But if the calling out makes clear to everyone that there are standards to follow, where it will be clear that when these are not followed the blogger will lose her claim to the community's attention, this can have the desired effect. What is more, insofar as there is an (anonymized) name associated with the blogger, that blogger can be tracked over time. Of course, this regime has the obvious disadvantage that insofar as acquiring new anonymized names is easy, an offending speaker can always shed old names for new ones. This might be addressed by a policy not to give out any new names, though of course there will be obvious limits to how far one can take this policy.

I do not claim that these are the only regimes imaginable; I am sure that there are others, and still others that do not presently exist but which will be developed in time. Still, we might wonder: can there be cases of anonymous assertion in which there is no

---

[16] See, for example, Fallis (2008).

regime for policing assertoric responsibility, yet where the assertion remains belief-worthy, or at least retains its promise of belief-worthiness, for all that? It is hard to see that these will be examples in which an audience will be able to put a good deal of stock. If an assertion is truly anonymous—no one (besides the speaker) is or can be in a position to know who the speaker is—to that extent hearers' counterfactual sensitivity will be correspondingly diminished. To be sure, there may be enough to go on along the other dimensions of assessment mentioned in Section 8.3—the context in which the assertion was produced might be known, or the content might be a sufficiently arcane subject-matter that there is expertise in the area that can be brought to bear on how plausible it is, and so on—there may be enough materials of this sort that there will be people who remain counterfactually sensitive with respect to the assertion. But in cases where this is not so, it is hard to see how hearers, by themselves, could be sufficiently counterfactually sensitive to the presence of defeaters. To be sure, if a great deal hangs on the truth of the matter on which the assertion is made, and the hearer has no other route to reasonable belief, it may well be that the hearer will accept what is asserted in a fully anonymous assertion. Alternatively, the speaker might simply hope to be trusted. But in both of these cases it is hard to see how the hearer can avoid having the sort of diminished epistemic expectations that follow on the heel of the sort of skeptical defeater I discussed in Section 8.5. So these are not the best cases with which to illustrate the worry of anonymous but credible assertions.

8.8 Conclusion

This chapter was intended as yet another instance in which the schematic hypothesis of MMENA—that it is mutually manifest that assertion is governed by an epistemic norm—can be used to shed light on the connections between the speech act of assertion and other phenomena of philosophical interest.

Here I have used MMENA to bear on the phenomenon of anonymous assertion, in order to argue that part of assertion's promise of belief-worthiness, and so part of what enables assertion to play the knowledge-communicating role that it plays, is grounded in the publicness of the act of assertion. We can bring this out whatever we regard the content of the norm's epistemic standard to be—so long as we take it to be robustly epistemic.

PART IV

A Case for Context-Sensitivity in the Norm of Assertion

In this part I enter the fray regarding the standard of the norm of assertion, defending an account on which the standard is set in a context-sensitive fashion, by reference to what it is reasonable to suppose is mutually believed in context.

9
Assertion and Disagreement

9.1 The Problem: The Persistence of Assertions under Conditions of Systematic Disagreement

This book aims to develop and defend an account of assertion on which assertion is constitutively governed by an epistemic norm. After presenting this proposal and offering an initial defense of it against competitor accounts of assertion (Chapter 1), I argued that the hypothesis that assertion has a robustly epistemic norm provides an illuminating account of the features that constitute the "epistemic significance" of assertion (Chapters 2 and 3). Then, in the subsequent five chapters (4–8), I appealed to the epistemic norm of assertion to account for those features of assertion that connect this speech-act type with various phenomena of philosophical interest—phenomena in the philosophy of language, philosophy of mind, ethics, and social philosophy. In all of these discussions, I have been neutral as to the content of the norm; I have been assuming only that the standard required by the norm is a robustly epistemic one. In this chapter I descend from the heights of neutrality to argue for what I will be calling a context-sensitive norm, according to which what is required to warrant an assertion depends on features of the conversational context in which the assertion is made. I believe that such an account is both independently motivated, and that it solves a problem that otherwise dogs the hypothesis that assertion has an epistemic norm. In this chapter I present the problem, and in the next chapter I suggest that the hypothesis that assertion has a context-sensitive norm both solves the problem and enjoys independent support. In the final chapter of the book I acknowledge the costs of endorsing a context-sensitive account of the norm of assertion, but argue that these costs are outweighed by the benefits.

The problem I will be developing in this chapter arises when we think about certain contexts in which assertoric practice continues despite the existence of what I will call systematic peer disagreement. I believe these contexts are a relatively common phenomenon: we see them in many areas of theoretical inquiry (including but not limited to philosophy,[1] politics, the more theoretical parts of the natural and social sciences,

---

[1] The topic of disagreement within philosophy has recently begun to receive more attention, not only in the literature on disagreement, but also (on occasion) in the literature on philosophical methodology. To see the literature focused on disagreement and philosophical practice, see Frances (2005), Goldberg (2008), Kornblith (2010), and Fumerton (2010).

and arguably religion as well).[2] More generally, such contexts obtain when dialogue turns to topics regarding which (i) the practice of advancing claims continues to have a point (perhaps because the need or desire for information persists), despite the fact that (ii) it is mutually acknowledged that practical challenges render the attaining of knowledge or another epistemically high-grade standing unlikely at present (or, in the worst case, even practically impossible). The problem is that it is hard to make sense of the legitimacy of our practice of assertion in these contexts. The aim of this chapter is to develop this problem, thereby paving the way for the two subsequent chapters in which I argue that a context-sensitive norm of assertion can answer this problem.

There are two caveats before I go on to develop the problem itself. First, unlike other chapters in this book, whose main focus is directly on assertion and assertoric practice, this chapter focuses in the whole on a topic in epistemology—the epistemology of disagreement—with only an occasional discussion of assertion. I believe that such a tangent is justified for the light that it will ultimately cast on the nature of assertion itself (Chapter 10). However, I think that the problem itself is interesting enough, and the light it ultimately sheds on assertion is strong enough, to warrant an extended discussion of the problem on its own. Second, the main example I will use to illustrate the phenomenon of systematic peer disagreements is the example of philosophy. I do so for a simple reason: philosophical practice offers the best (clearest and most robust) example of the phenomenon I have in mind, in which both conditions (i) and (ii) hold. Philosophical practice at its core involves the advancing and defending of claims in the face of pervasive disputation and disagreement. This is about as clear a case as we can have of a highly-regulated and (by all outward appearances) legitimate practice in which parties persist in making assertions even in the face of systematic peer disagreement. (I will defend this characterization later.) But philosophy is not the only example of this, and on occasion I will be suggesting how topics other than philosophy can be used to exemplify the phenomenon as well.

The problem that will occupy my attention in this chapter can be represented by the following MASTER ARGUMENT. In it, three propositions are each independently plausible, but they jointly imply an intolerable conclusion. The argument is as follows:

1. In cases in which S believes that p in the face of (what I will call) *systematic p-relevant peer disagreement*, there are (undefeated doxastic or normative) defeaters with respect to the doxastic justification of S's belief that p—with the result that S is not doxastically justified in believing that p.
2. If S is not doxastically justified in believing that p, then S is not warranted in asserting that p.

---

[2] 'Arguably': the question arises whether (some or most) religious disagreements are peer disagreements. I will not have anything to say about that here. See Lackey (forthcoming) for a discussion.

3. Some cases of disagreement regarding whether p are cases of systematic p-relevant peer disagreement.
4. (Therefore) In such cases, S is not warranted in asserting that p.

So framed, the conclusion of the MASTER ARGUMENT is that no assertion made under conditions of systematic peer disagreement is warranted.[3]

It is not hard to see why one might think that this conclusion is intolerable. The difficulty arises from the fact—or what I will argue is a fact—that it is common practice in certain domains to assert claims, including the conclusions of our philosophical arguments, even under conditions in which there is systematic peer disagreement in those domains. The result is that the conclusion of the MASTER ARGUMENT is a skeptical one: at least sometimes, and arguably often, standard assertoric practice results in unwarranted assertions. Since premise (2) is relatively uncontroversial—it would appear to be a direct implication of the core thesis of Chapters 1–8, to the effect that assertion is governed by a robustly epistemic norm—my focus will be on (1) and (3). After defending them, I go on to defend the idea that there are cases of ordinary assertoric practice in which assertions are made under conditions of systematic relevant peer disagreement. Hence our difficulty: three premises, each enjoying some independent plausibility, results in an unacceptable (because skeptical) conclusion.

9.2 Preliminaries

I regard (1) as the most controversial of the claims in the MASTER ARGUMENT. To argue for it, I first need to introduce the relevant key notions of *systematic p-relevant peer disagreement*, and of a *defeater*.

For the purpose of the following discussion, a *defeater* is a proposition[4] that bears against the positive epistemic status(es) enjoyed by a given belief. I will take defeaters to be of one of three types: *doxastic* defeaters, which are propositions that function as defeaters in virtue of being believed; *normative* defeaters, which are propositions that function as defeaters by being such that the subject ought (from the epistemic point of view) to believe them; and *factual* defeaters, which are propositions that function as defeaters by being true. Along with tradition, I will assume that rational belief and doxastically justified belief are susceptible to doxastic and normative defeaters, but not to factual defeaters;[5] whereas knowledge is susceptible to all three kinds of defeaters.

---

[3] As I have been doing throughout this book, I use 'unwarranted' to designate the property *being in violation of the norm of assertion*, and 'warranted' to designate the property of *satisfying that norm*.
[4] There is some disagreement over whether cognitive states can count as defeaters as well. For a very nice discussion, see Bergmann (2006: chapter 6). Ignoring this possible complication will not affect the treatment of disagreement, so I will do so.
[5] At least not unless the factual defeater is at the same time a normative or doxastic defeater. For a nice example of a defeater that is at one and the same time factual and normative, see Gibbons (2006).

The 'no defeaters' condition in epistemology—whether in the theory of rational belief, doxastic justification, or knowledge—can be motivated in a variety of different ways. In the theory of rational belief and in the theory of doxastic justification, the move to impose a 'no defeaters' condition can be motivated by appeal to the normativity of rational and justified belief. Two points are relevant here. First, S's belief that p is not rationally held or doxastically justified if S should not (from the epistemic point of view) believe that p. Second, S should not (from the epistemic point of view) believe that p if any of the following three conditions hold: (i) S's other beliefs are such that they are inconsistent with (or render sufficiently improbable the truth of) the proposition that p, where this sort of inconsistency is the sort that subjects are expected to discern and (subsequently) to avoid;[6] (ii) S's other beliefs call into question the goodness of S's grounds for believing that p; or (iii) there is a proposition that S should (from the epistemic point of view) believe, and were she to believe this proposition at least one (i) or (ii) would hold. Here conditions (i) and (ii) identify doxastic defeaters (those propositions the subject believes, belief in which makes (i) or (ii) true), whereas condition (iii) identifies normative defeaters (those propositions belief in which would make (i) or (ii) true).[7] Since the topic in which I will be interested concerns the bearing of a certain kind of disagreement on rational or justified belief, I will be focusing attention only on doxastic and normative defeaters, not on factual defeaters.

The notion of *peer disagreement* I have in mind is the notion of a disagreement among parties who are roughly equivalent in cognitive competence and intelligence (at least insofar as these bear on the matter at hand), in judgment bearing on the matter at hand, and in the relevant evidence they have. I will be focusing only on cases in which both of the parties not only are, but also do (or should) regard each other as, peers in this sense. Next, we can say that a peer disagreement is *p-relevant* when either (a) the disagreement is over whether p, or else (b) whether p is true turns on the outcome of what is being debated. The notion of a *systematic* p-relevant peer disagreement can now be introduced by way of a distinction between two types of disagreement. (These two "types" are really extreme points on a multi-dimensional continuum, but it will be easiest to idealize them and so treat them as two distinct kinds of disagreement.) Let us say that a peer disagreement regarding whether p is *one-off* when it concerns just the issue regarding whether p itself, and nothing more.[8]

---

[6] The part following 'where' is meant to distinguish the cases in question from the sort of case in play in a preface-paradox-type situation, where the subject reasonably regards herself as having inconsistent beliefs, but where this fact alone does not show her to be irrational. I will not attempt a characterization of when a discerned inconsistency is the sort that subjects are expected to avoid, and when it is not. I assume that we have an intuitive grip on the difference. (With thanks to David Christensen.)

[7] The status of normative defeaters is somewhat vexed, owing perhaps to the unclarity of the epistemic 'should believe' as well as unclarity about the motivation that various theories in epistemology might have for postulating such epistemic oughts. To the extent that I rely on normative defeaters in the argument to follow, I will do so only in contexts where I anticipate a broad consensus in the relevant claims of epistemic oughts.

[8] Both Elga (2007) and Kornblith (2010: 33) speak of "isolated disagreement," which is a sort of disagreement that (in Kornblith's words) does not "threaten to force [participants] to suspend judgment very widely."

To be sure, disagreements over whether p typically bleed into other areas: if I disagree with you (whom I regard as my peer) over whether p, I may well also disagree with you regarding which of us is more likely to have misjudged the relevant evidence, and so forth. But this bleeding can be more or less localized; one-off cases are cases in which the issue regards only whether p and those (few) localized matters that bear on this disagreement. A paradigmatic case of one-off peer disagreement would be the Check-Splitting case in Christensen (2007).[9] Peer disagreement regarding whether p is *systematic*, on the other hand, when three conditions hold. First, the disagreement is not localized around the question whether p—that is, the disagreement regarding whether p is part of a much wider disagreement, with lots of other related matters in dispute. (When a peer disagreement has this property I will call it *non-localized*.) Second, the disagreement is *widespread*, in the sense that at least two of the positions endorsed by the disagreeing parties have attracted, or are capable of attracting, a substantial and dedicated following. Thus it is not just a disagreement between two people, but between two (or more) *groups* of people, each of which is to some degree committed to its claims in the face of the disagreement. Third, and finally, the disagreement is *entrenched*, in the sense that the disagreement has persisted for at least some time, with both sides continuing to defend and advance their side, in the face of persistent challenges from the other side, where the defenses in question remain responsive to the relevant evidence and arguments.[10] Obviously, these three features are a matter of degree—a disagreement can be more or less non-localized, more or less widespread, and more or less entrenched. For this reason it would be best to speak of disagreements as more or less systematic (according to the degrees of each of these three characteristics they exhibit), but I will continue to speak of systematic disagreement *simpliciter*.

Claim (1) states that in cases in which a subject S believes that p in the face of systematic p-relevant peer disagreement, there are (undefeated) doxastic and normative defeaters with respect to the doxastic justification enjoyed by S's belief that p. One immediate objection that might be raised against (1) is this: the proposition that there is systematic p-relevant disagreement is not a defeater of one's doxastic justification unless there is some *independence* in the way the various disagreeing parties reached their views. To illustrate, suppose that views, for example, in philosophy are effectively passed down from teacher to student in the course of PhD training. In that case one might think that the fact that one's opponent believes as she does (in a given systematic philosophical disagreement) reflects more on where she trained than it does on the probative force of the mutually-possessed evidence—thereby decreasing the distinctly *epistemic* significance

---

[9] In this case, a group of diners aim to split the check evenly between themselves, but when two among them do the mental math involved, they arrive at slightly different answers. Christensen notes that at the point at which they discover that they have arrived at slightly different answers, both ought to be less confident in their particular answer.

[10] The point of the 'responsiveness' condition is to exclude cases in which allegiance to one or both of the positions is based on non-epistemic considerations.

of the disagreement.¹¹ Now this point must be acknowledged to be of great importance in assessing the probative force of evidence, and so is crucial to any discussion of disagreement that is formulated in evidentialist terms. However, it is of less importance in connection with the issue of whether systematic peer disagreement constitutes a *defeater*. This is for a simple reason. Later I will be arguing that the "mechanism" by which systematic peer disagreement constitutes a defeater is by way of making salient the possibility that at least one of the disputing parties to the debate is unreliable on the matter at hand. In light of this, suppose (with the objection) that the transmission of views in philosophy is not a rational process of sifting through the evidence, but instead is a matter of one's being influenced (via non-rational mechanisms) by one's teachers in graduate school. This fact will only make the possibility of unreliability on these matters even more salient—and so will only *enhance* the case for thinking that systematic peer disagreement in philosophy generates a relevant defeater. (After all, what goes for one's opponent equally goes for one oneself!¹²) On the other hand, if the acquisition of one's views in philosophy remains a rational process even in graduate school—the influence of graduate training in philosophy remains a rational influence, in which the student remains sensitive to the probative force of the evidence—then the fact that a person's views in philosophy are best predicted by where she went to graduate school, even if true, is irrelevant to the issue of whether systematic disagreement in philosophy generates a defeater. For in that case one cannot downgrade one's opponent merely because of where she went to graduate school, and so the argument to be given later, in defense of the claim that systematic peer disagreement in philosophy generates a defeater, will be untouched.

With this initial objection dismissed, I want to develop the case for (1)—that is, for thinking that systematic peer disagreement generates a defeater.¹³ The case I will be presenting is intended to be independent of one's views on the epistemic significance of peer disagreement more generally: the case aims to be compelling whether one favors a 'Conformist' or a 'Non-Conformist' position.¹⁴ What I will be highlighting is the distinctive epistemic situation that arises in cases in which the disagreement is systematic. My claim will be that in such cases one has good reason to think that *there is a serious chance that one of the parties to the dispute is unreliable regarding whether p*, under conditions in which one does *not* know that *one oneself is not among the unreliable parties to this dispute*.¹⁵ What is more, the rational pressure to accept this combination

---

¹¹ This is based on reflections in Kelly (2010: 145–50). Kelly himself does not speak of defeaters, but instead of the extent to which something like systematic disagreement threatens widespread skepticism. Still, I can imagine someone taking the spirit of his points and making claims regarding the extent to which systematic disagreement constitutes a defeater, in the manner suggested previously.

¹² See Section 9.4 for a development of the reasoning behind this symmetry claim in this context.

¹³ Interestingly, it is only in the last few years that the literature on disagreement has addressed the question of defeaters in any systematic way. For "early" discussions of this topic, see Frances (2005), Goldberg (2008), Bergmann (2009), Matheson (2009), Lackey (2010), and Thune (2010). More recent discussions can be found in Kotzen (2013), Littlejohn (2013), Hawthorne and Srinivasan (2013), and Rotondo (2013).

¹⁴ I borrow these terms from Lackey (2010).

¹⁵ With thanks to Jennifer Lackey for this way of putting the point.

of claims rises in proportion to the increased systematicity of the disagreement. This point holds, I will argue, even if we assume, with the Non-Conformist, that it can be rational to preserve one's pre-disagreement doxastic attitude towards p even in the face of p-relevant peer disagreement. (The thrust of my argument will be that matters are otherwise when the disagreement is systematic.)

9.3 Systematic Peer Disagreements as Evidence of Unreliability

In this and the following section I will be defending premise (1). I will divide my argument into two parts. In the first (in this section) I argue that, in cases of systematic disagreement, we have reason to prefer an explanation of the disagreement that calls into question the reliability of at least some of the disputing parties on the matter at hand. I will then go on to argue, in Section 9.4, that in these cases none of the disputing parties is in a position to rule out the hypothesis that she herself is among those who are unreliable. Finally, I will bring these considerations to bear on our conclusion, (1), in Section 9.5.

Let us say that a subject who has no reason to question her reliability on a given matter has an "epistemically clean bill of health" in making the judgment (or forming or sustaining the belief) in question. Now, if one has a compelling reason to doubt one's reliability in a particular judgment one makes, then one does not have an epistemically clean bill of health. In that case, one ought to refrain—it is rationally required that one refrain—from making the judgment (or at least have a lower degree of credence in the proposition in question). Now I submit that, when it comes to peer disagreement, the claim that a given subject has an epistemically clean bill of health on the matter would appear to be most plausible in a one-off case of peer disagreement, such as the Split-the-Bill case in Christensen 2007 (see fn. 9 for a description of the case). Here the fact that this is a one-off case of peer disagreement, on a topic on which it is mutually recognized that all parties have been reliable on related matters in the past, makes it plausible to suppose that this disagreement is the result of a temporary (one-time) problem with one (or perhaps both) of the disagreeing parties. This sort of disagreement is not something that ought to lead either of the disagreeing parties to question whether she is *generally* reliable on the matter at hand. Indeed, Non-Conformist positions on peer disagreement, according to which the fact of peer disagreement *per se* does not rationally require one to modify one's doxastic attitude in any way, insist on this point. On such a view, the fact of peer disagreement (taken by itself) does not give one any reason to question one's reliability on the matter at hand on the present occasion. I take this to be uncontroversial.

But now consider cases of *systematic* peer disagreement. Whereas in the one-off case it seems likely that we can explain the disagreement without postulating general unreliability in any of the disputing parties, the explanatory challenge is different when we consider peer disagreements that are systematic. For here we need to explain not only the *present* case of disagreement, but also the various other disagreements that go into making this an instance of a disagreement that is *non-local, widespread,* and *entrenched*. Given these features of the disagreement, it becomes increasingly plausible to suppose that at least one, and possibly many or all, of the parties to the dispute is/are unreliable on the topic at hand. Or so I contend.

My argument on this score takes the form of an inference to the best explanation. When we seek to explain the systematic nature of the disagreement regarding whether p, there are various hypotheses to consider. For present purposes, there are two key choice points. One is whether or not an explanation will need to advert to the unreliability of one or more of the parties to the dispute. The other is whether an explanation will need to treat all of the parties in like manner (or whether there is room to distinguish those "in the right" from those not "in the right"). With this in mind, I highlight the following four candidate explanatory hypotheses:[16]

H1: All of the parties are unreliable on the question whether p.
H2: Some but not all of the parties are unreliable on the question whether p.
H3: None of the parties is unreliable on the question whether p; someone is *merely wrong* regarding whether p.[17]
H4: None of the parties is unreliable on the question whether p; it is just that no one is right regarding whether p (that is, *everyone* is merely wrong).

H1 and H2 both allege unreliability on the part of at least one of the disputing parties; H3 and H4 chalk up the disagreement to errors that do not call into question the reliability of any of the disputing parties. My contention is this: when disagreement is systematic, we have evidence that at least one of the parties, and perhaps many or all, is/are unreliable on the matter at hand; it is simply not credible to suppose that this sort of disagreement can be explained by *mere mistakes*. So to the extent that a disagreement is systematic, we have reason to favor H1 or H2 over both H3 and H4.[18]

To begin, the sort of explanation that would leave unchallenged the reliability of the various disputing parties in a case of systematic disagreement would leave us with a mystery. Let us say that a subject S makes a *mere mistake* in her judgment that p when (one) S forms the judgment that p through the process φ, (two) it is false that p, and yet (three) even so φ is a reliable process, in the sense that a preponderance of φ's outputs

---

[16] I am indebted to Jennifer Lackey for the formulations in H1–H4.

[17] Let us say that S is "merely wrong" that p when (i) S judges that p, (ii) it is false that p, and (iii) S's judgment that p was formed in a way that does not call into question S's competence or general reliability on the question whether p. An example would be the check-splitting case: the fact that S got it wrong does not call into question her general reliability in matters of arithmetic. (Her being wrong is chalked up, rather, to a momentary condition—one which she herself could address if given enough time, paper and pencil, and so on.)

[18] Objection: if one (but not all) of the parties is not reliable on the topic at hand, this jeopardizes the claim that the dispute is a *peer* disagreement. Reply: this is correct, but does not undermine the epistemic significance I want to ascribe to systematic peer disagreements. Later, I return to this matter at length.

are (would be) true.[19] Now, if all parties to a systematic disagreement reach their own view by employing a process (or processes) that is (are) reliable in this sense, so that the disagreement is to be chalked up to *mere mistake(s)* on the part of one (or more) of the parties, why then is it that the disagreements are *systematic*? If it really were a matter of one or both sides making a mere mistake but still employing a reliable process on the issue at hand, we might expect to see far fewer disagreements, and certainly far fewer *systematic* disagreements. To see why, return to Christensen's check-splitting case. Here we do not think to question the reliability of the process used by the participating parties because (we can imagine) all parties have a track record of success on a wide variety of questions that call upon their arithmetic competence. In this mass of cases, they agree, or would agree, with one another. And furthermore, if we were to consider the parties' verdicts in future cases of mental math, we would predict much more agreement than disagreement. It is against this background that we do not think to question the competence (general reliability) of either party in the present case. The disagreement in the check-splitting case is thus seen as a relatively rare exception to the rule—a case of a *mere mistake* (or perhaps mistakes: maybe both parties are wrong).

Of course, matters are otherwise in the sorts of discussions on topics that (typically) give rise to systematic disagreements. Take the case of philosophy itself: we positively *expect* widespread disagreement, at least regarding a good number of topics (more on which later). Consider in this context the claim that systematic disagreements in philosophy are to be explained by the hypothesis of *mere errors* on the part of one or more parties to the dispute (where the parties are all assumed to be employing reliable processes on the topic at hand). Such a claim faces an obvious challenge. Why is it that the disagreement remains even after full mutual disclosure of the evidence, even after all of the parties continue to give the matter thought, and even after we avail ourselves of all manner of opportunities to discover our errors? Perhaps it will be said: because philosophy is just very hard. I do not disagree; but this, I submit, is a reason to think that at least some party to the dispute, and perhaps many or even all, is/are not employing a reliable process on the topic at hand. The contrast with the check-splitting case could not be clearer: in that case we do not think to question the arithmetic competence (the general reliability) of either participant precisely because we imagine that, were the disputing parties to do the math on a napkin and discuss it with each other, *they would reach agreement*. If they did not, we *would* think to question the relevant reliability of one or both of them. This suggests that hypotheses H3 and H4 become implausible to the extent that a peer disagreement is systematic.

It might be thought that one might resist this conclusion by being careful to disaggregate the various processes (process-types) involved in arriving at a philosophical conclusion.[20] These will include processes of reasoning, but also whatever processes

---

[19] This notion of reliability is meant to reflect the sort of reliability at issue in reliabilist theories of justification.
[20] I thank an anonymous referee for indicating the need to address this here.

provide us with the premises for our arguments as well. The thought is that once we disaggregate all of these process-types, we will be in a position to see how it can be that the processes involved are reliable—with the further result that we will be able to account for the fact of disagreement itself as a case in which one (or both) sides have made mere errors. (Perhaps the thought is that when various reliable process-types are employed in a long chain of reasoning, we would expect there to be a significantly higher chance of error in the conclusion, than in any particular premise.) For reasons I have discussed at length elsewhere (Goldberg 2009c), I am dubious that this reply will enable us to avoid the conclusion that systematic disagreement constitutes a defeater. But it is worthwhile making two key points here. The first is that, even if it works, this response does not bear on those cases in which there is disagreement over claims that are backed, not by argument or chains of reasoning, but by something epistemically basic (such as intuition). Second, there is clear reason to think that this response does not work even in the case in which the disputed claim is defended by reasoning on both sides. On this score, the chief difficulty for this reply is this. Even if it should turn out that one or both sides is employing reliable process-types throughout the chain of reasoning, the very fact that there is systematic disagreement on the issue whether p constitutes grounds to question one's judgment *at least on the matter at issue* (= whether p). For in that case there are grounds for thinking that one's reliance on *de facto* reliable processes does not protect one against a significant chance of error *at least in the present case*.[21] I will defend this claim at some length later. But if I am right about this, then the move to disaggregate processes in this fashion, in the hope that in so doing one will be able to avoid the conclusion that systematic disagreement generates a defeater, fails.

The core idea that systematic disagreement itself might generate a defeater can be reinforced by reflecting on a case in which you are a mere observer seeking to explain the distribution of doxastic attitudes among a certain group of people engaged in a discussion. Suppose that you present a series of quizzes on some topic (about which you know very little) to this population (about whom you are largely ignorant). In particular, you do not know the right answer to the questions on the quiz; and you do not know how well the participants know the topic in question, but you do have some reason to think that they are roughly "equals" in their degree of competence and reliability. Examining the results of the quiz you administered, you discover that there is prevalent disagreement among them as to the correct answers. Further, you discover that this disagreement remains, and in some cases expands, even after full mutual disclosure of the evidence—even as neither of the sides is disposed to charge the other side with ignoring evidence, or with being less intelligent, and so on. I submit that it would be more reasonable—indeed, much more reasonable—for you to conclude that the reliability of at least someone's judgment is at issue, than it would be to look for

---

[21] In Goldberg (2009c) I spoke about these as "dangerous contexts" for the use of reliable processes.

explanations that continue to assume that all parties are reliable on the topic in question. If unreliability is not at issue, it would appear just a strange coincidence that there is such widespread disagreement on the topic, across a variety of different questions, even after full mutual disclosure. Our conclusion would appear to be this: to the extent that peer disagreement is systematic, we have reason to favor H1 or H2—that is, we have reason to question the reliability of at least some of the parties to the dispute—over both H3 and H4—that is, over assuming that their reliability is intact (and that the disagreement is a matter of one or both sides' being merely wrong, occasion after occasion).[22]

This analogy is limited.[23] For one thing, there is a difference between being an observer to and a participant in a discussion. For another, participants in a systematic disagreement are unlike the observer I have described in that participants can be expected to have familiarity, both with their interlocutors, and with the subject-matter about which they are disagreeing. Still, the analogy is suggestive, since it makes clear that there are cases of an observed systematic disagreement in which we will explain the disagreement by hypothesizing that at least one side is unreliable on the topic at hand.

What is more, further support can be offered for my contention that we have reason to favor an explanation of systematic disagreement which calls at least one party's reliability into question, over an explanation which insists that none of the disputing parties' reliability is at issue. On any topic on which there is reliability (if perhaps only reliability *among the experts*) in a given domain or on a given topic, we would expect a high degree of unanimity in the judgments that are made within the domain (or on the topic at hand). Insofar as no one's reliability is in question, we would then expect that, once we restrict our attention to the relevant "experts," we will find at least some agreement on foundational matters. Or, at a minimum, we might expect that as time goes on, there will be some coalescing around the positions (truth wins out in the end). Yet in cases of disagreement in philosophy (to stick with our example), this is not what we find: the disagreement is systematic, and it persists. If ordinary epistemic explanations of the fact of disagreement are not to the point—we cannot downgrade our opponents for being ignorant of relevant evidence, or lacking in intelligence—some other explanation is needed. The ascription of unreliability to one (or more) of the disputing parties begins to seem a more reasonable explanation.

It might be objected: in the case of philosophy, there *is* some agreement over such matters as proper methods and which papers (and authors) are the ones to be read on a given topic. For this reason (the objection continues) things are not as bad as the (would-be) explanation in terms of unreliability would lead us to believe. But this objection can be met in two ways. First, it is not clear how substantial the agreement

---

[22] Later I will consider an argument that purports to show that if we must choose between H1 and H2 on the basis of considerations like those I have just put forward, then we ought to choose H1.
[23] With thanks to Peter Ludlow for a helpful conversation on this point.

is: the topic of philosophical methodology has become a particularly hot topic these days, but it is also one that generates a good deal of disagreement in its own right. Consider in this light of recent debates over the epistemic status of intuitions, the utility of conceptual analysis, the status of "experimental philosophy," the role of linguistic analysis in philosophical disputation, the proper status to accord to common sense (and to "common-sense propositions"), and so on. Consider also relevant concerns regarding implicit bias, which threaten to call into question the reliability of a whole range of judgments—including some of those regarding proper method and "the (contemporary) philosophical canon".[24] Second, even if it is granted for the sake of argument that there is agreement both over methodology and over the authors to be read on a given topic, this agreement is swamped by the tremendous disagreement over which (first-order) views on the topic are correct or most reasonable, and over how to weigh the various considerations in play. The persistence of this first-order disagreement would seem a little strange if in fact all parties are reliable on the topic.

Still, those unconvinced by the plausibility of the hypothesis of unreliability—those who think that any particular case of systematic disagreement in philosophy will be best explained without calling into question the reliability of any of the disputing parties—can respond with a challenge of their own. How can it be, they will ask, that we philosophers are unreliable in (some or perhaps many of) the philosophical judgments we make? What is wanted is a concrete proposal regarding how it could come to pass that a practice like philosophy could flourish, despite its occasional (regular?) lapse into topics in which its practitioners are unreliable in their judgments.

This is a large question—one that I am in no position to answer in anything like the detailed way it deserves. Still, I can make a few relevant remarks. One possibility is this: while there are reliable belief-forming processes or methods that can be brought to bear on the philosophical topics in question, it turns out that these processes/methods can be expected to be significantly less reliable in the philosophical domain in question (the reliability of those processes/methods being established in other contexts where they are more ordinarily employed).[25] Another, more radical possibility is that *no one is reliable* on the matter at hand because *there are* no reliable belief-forming processes or methods that can be brought to bear on these matters. A possibility which is more radical still is that in many of the areas of systematic peer disagreement in philosophy, *there simply are no facts of the matter*, hence no getting things right. And there are other possibilities as well.[26] Here is not the place for me to endorse one or another

---

[24] Of course, the hypothesis of implicit bias is relevant far beyond philosophy. For a discussion of the epistemic costs of implicit bias, see Gendler (2011).
[25] It was this idea that I developed, at some length, under the label of "dangerous contexts" in Goldberg (2009c).
[26] In conversation, my colleague Sean Ebels-Duggan has raised another possible explanation—but one which would preserve the hypothesis that all sides are reliable. It is this: the various sides are simply talking past one another, arguing over different things. If so, all sides can be both reliable and right, and are merely confused in thinking that they are disagreeing when they are not. I agree that this is a possibility; and I even concede for the sake of argument that this sometimes is the best explanation of what is going on in particular

possibility as the proper explanation—I offer them only to give a sense of the range of options one has for deepening one's explanation, once one comes to think that the proper explanation for the systematic disagreements in philosophy will involve appeal to the unreliability of one or more of the disputing parties.

9.4 Systematic Peer Disagreements and Grounds for Self-Doubt

I have just completed the first part of my argument for premise (1). I have been arguing that in cases of systematic peer disagreement, we have reason to prefer explanatory hypotheses H1 or H2 over both H3 and H4—that is, that we have reason to think that one or more of the parties to the dispute are unreliable on the matter at hand. But for all my argument so far has shown, there can exist parties to the dispute that not only have it right but *who are in fact reliable on the matter at hand*. What is more, if there is a side that is reliable on the topic at hand, it would appear to be under no rational pressure to regard as "live" the hypothesis of its own unreliability.[27] Or so we might think if we endorse something like the "Right Reasons" view of Kelly (2005), or some other version of a Non-Conformist view. Since I am trying to make a case for premise (1)— the premise that systematic peer disagreement generates a defeater—that is strong no matter one's approach to the epistemic significance of disagreement, more needs to be done. The present task is this: to get from the claim that *at least some party* is unreliable on the topic at hand, to the claim that *all* parties to the dispute have reason to question their own reliability. Since such a reason would in fact be a defeater, we would then have concluded our case for premise (1).

Before addressing this task, it is important to have in mind the difference between the present discussion and standard discussions of the epistemology of disagreement. In standard discussions of peer disagreement, including the discussion in Kelly (2005), the question is framed as one regarding the epistemic effects of the *present* case of peer disagreement. Should the fact that you *presently* disagree with someone you recognize as a peer lead you to revise your doxastic attitude towards the disputed proposition? The claim that I am making, and which I will continue to defend later, is addressed to a slightly different sort of case. The sort of case I am addressing is one in which the parties recognize that the disagreement is *systematic*. How should your recognition of the existence of *systematic peer disagreement* on some topic affect your views (if any) on the topic? Better yet, how should such recognition affect your attitude towards the prospect of having or arriving at reliable judgments on the topic? My claim has been

---

cases of philosophical disagreement. What I deny is that this will always, or even usually, be the best explanation of what is going on in cases of philosophical disagreement. (For a discussion of this move in the context of the internalism/externalism dispute in epistemology, see Goldberg forthcoming a.)

[27] I thank Cian Dorr, Jennifer Lackey, and Tim Williamson, each of whom pointed out something in this vicinity (in conversation).

that once one recognizes the existence of systematic peer disagreement on some topic, it is reasonable for one to endorse an hypothesis which questions the reliability of at least some of the disputing parties. In such a context it may well be that the epistemic effects of finding *yet another* peer who presently disagrees with one will be negligible; but this is because the recognition of the systematic nature of the peer disagreement should already have had substantial epistemic effects. This is a point that even the proponent of the "Right Reasons" view itself should accept.

Consider, then, the sort of evidence one has when one has evidence of a *systematic* peer disagreement. It is not merely evidence of a present disagreement. It is much more than that: it is evidence of a disagreement among peers that is entrenched, non-local, and persistent. We skew the significance of this evidence if we focus on the question regarding what one ought doxastically to do given only the *present* disagreement with an acknowledged peer. I mention this to dispel the idea that, assuming that Kelly's (2005) "Right Reasons" view is correct, the Right Reasoner is under no rational obligation whatsoever to take seriously the hypothesis that she herself is unreliable on the topic at hand. This may be so in a case of one-off disagreement, but it strains credibility to think that this is so in cases of systematic disagreement. Simply put, the two cases are not analogous in a crucial respect: to have evidence that the dispute in which one is engaged is a *systematic* peer disagreement is already to have evidence that puts rational pressure on one to call into question one's own reliability—*even if in point of fact one is reliable on the matter at hand*. Or so I want to argue in what follows.

Suppose that two disputing parties, S_1 and S_2, disagree over whether p, and that this is a case of systematic peer disagreement: the dispute over whether p is bound up in a much larger (and long-lasting) controversy that persists even after full disclosure. Suppose further that in point of fact S_1 *is* reliable on the matter, whereas S_2 is not. Is it reasonable for S_1 to regard herself as reliable on the matter?

One consideration suggesting that it would not be reasonable for S_1 to maintain her belief in her own reliability is this. I have argued previously that when it comes to systematic peer disagreements, neither H_3 nor H_4—the hypotheses that assume that all parties are reliable on the matter at hand—can provide a plausible explanation of the facts of the disagreement. That leaves us with H_1 and H_2. Now, H_2—the hypothesis that some *but not all* of the parties to the dispute are unreliable on the topic at hand—is consistent with S_1's being reliable on the topic at hand. But there would appear to be a reason why S_1 should reject this hypothesis in favor of H_1 (according to which *all* parties to the dispute are unreliable on the topic at hand). For consider: insofar as there is a reliability difference between the disputing parties, the disagreement is not a *peer* disagreement in the sense defined at the outset. So if S_1 regards this as a case of peer disagreement, she has reason to think that the disputing parties are *roughly equally reliable*. So if I am correct in thinking that systematic peer disagreements call into question the reliability of at least some of the disputing parties, it would seem that S_1 faces a forced choice between (on the one hand) her belief that her interlocutors are her peers, and (on the other) her belief in her own reliability on the matter at hand. If it remains reasonable for her to continue to regard her opponent(s) as her peer(s), she should conclude that (there is a serious chance that) she herself is unreliable on the matter at hand.[28]

My contention, that S1 should call into question her own reliability on the topic at hand, can be reinforced from another perspective. Let us start with a more general question: how should one address queries as to the reliability with which one has arrived at a belief or a judgment on a given occasion? Take an ordinary case of perceptual belief or judgment. If subject S relies on her perceptual faculties in an ordinary situation, it is downright unreasonable to think that S needs anything very substantial in order to rule out the hypothesis that she has arrived at her belief in an unreliable way. On the contrary, to rule out this hypothesis in an ordinary case of perceptual belief, it seems sufficient that circumstances are, or perhaps merely seem to S to be, ordinary. (After all, we typically assume that subjects are entitled to rely on their basic belief-forming processes. See Chapter 2, Section 2.5.) Matters are otherwise, however, if S has evidence of the possible unreliability of her perceptual faculties on a given occasion on which she is relying on them. Thus, imagine that S obtains testimony from a doctor whom she has independent reason to trust, to the effect that, unbeknownst to S herself, she has ingested a pill that will make her faculties unreliable (albeit in ways that would escape her unaided detection). Here, it does *not* seem unreasonable to think that S would need more in the way of supporting reasons, if she is to rule out the possibility of unreliability in perception. (The demands on her are greater even if in point of fact the doctor's testimony is false, and so S is reliable on this occasion.) But this is precisely the situation that, for her part, a subject participating in a systematic (apparently) peer disagreement is in. After all, I have been arguing that cases of systematic (apparently) peer disagreement in philosophy are cases in which all parties have a reason to think that at least *some* party to the dispute is unreliable. In this context, then, where one oneself is a party to the dispute in question, the hypothesis that *one oneself* is unreliable is sufficiently "live" that it requires being addressed. In other words, this is not like the case of perception, where one is entitled to rely on the process(es) that lead one to one's belief. In this case, it is not unreasonable to think that one needs reasons to think that it is not one oneself who is unreliable.

Turning to the case at hand, then, what reasons could S1 offer in defense of the claim that she is not unreliable on the matter at hand? This is not a one-off case, where S1 might appeal to her long (and independently confirmable) track-record on related matters. There is no independent access to the truth of the matter, so S1, like S2, has to go on whatever it is that she goes on in order to reach a judgment on the disputed

[28] Does this mean that the fact of systematic peer disagreement gives us reason to suspect that *all of us* are unreliable on the topic at hand? In general, I think that the answer is "Yes." Still, I think that the point I defend in the following two paragraphs is a better way to put the point: the fact of disagreement gives me (you) a reason to think that at least one of the disputing parties is unreliable on the matter at hand, and I (you) do not know that it is not me (you). (Again, I thank Jennifer Lackey for suggesting this formulation. I do not, however, claim that she endorses it!)

matter. In light of this, consider the situation as it strikes (or should strike) S1. Given that this is a case of systematic disagreement (and that S1, like S2, recognizes this), S1 (like S2) should conclude that chances are good that at least some party to this dispute is unreliable. In addition, S1 (like S2) should also appreciate that, given the entrenched nature of the disagreement, the unreliable party (whoever it is) is not in a position to discern her or his own unreliability; otherwise she or he would have done so, and the disagreement would have dissipated. Since both S1 and S2 regard the other as a peer, both S1 and S2 recognize the other as (roughly) equally smart, (roughly) equally knowledgeable of the arguments and evidence bearing on the question at hand, and so (roughly) equally likely to be right on the issue at hand. Suppose now that S1 thinks that it is not she herself, but S2, who is unreliable. In that case S1 would have to acknowledge that someone equally smart, equally knowledgeable of the arguments and evidence, equally attentive and motivated to get things right, and *who would be highly motivated to discern her own unreliability if she could*, nevertheless failed to do so, even having been given a good deal of time in which to do so. (Here I have in mind the length of time S2 has spent arguing and thinking about these matters.) But more than this: S1 must acknowledge that it is not only in the present case, but *in the entire history of the dispute*, that none of those who are among the unreliable parties have discerned their own unreliability. And this conclusion, in turn, should tell S1 something about the nature of the unreliability that is at issue here: this unreliability *is not discernible by very many people as smart as she is, as knowledgeable of the relevant arguments and evidence, who have had a good deal of time thinking about the relevant issues, who work in a manner that is at least somewhat independent of others, and so on.* But if it is in the nature of the unreliability at issue here that it is not discernible under such conditions, then this should temper S1's confidence in her own assessment that it is not she (S1) who is unreliable. (The same reasoning goes for S2, of course.)

Might S1 try to rule out that she herself is unreliable by proposing a psychological explanation of the intransigence of the opposition? To do so she might appeal to the self-interest we each have to defend our own views, and to have it seem that one's own views are the best. But this candidate explanation faces an obvious difficulty: it threatens to explain too much. For one thing, we might wonder why it does not apply to one oneself as well, to explain why one is "sticking to one's guns" in the dispute—hardly a happy epistemic situation to be in. For another, if it is the self-interestedness, for example, of philosophers, and in particular our need to have it seem (if only to ourselves) that our views are right, that explains the fact of systematic peer disagreements in philosophy, then we would expect that we would be likely to find such disagreements wherever people had a vested interest in having it seem that their views are right. Yet this is not what we find. So, for example, while it is hardly less true of, for instance, empirical (experimentally-minded) scientists that they have a vested interest in defending their views, even so, we find decidedly less systematic disagreement, and decidedly more agreement on the basic topics, in the empirical sciences than we do in philosophy. From this I infer that self-interestedness alone cannot explain the pervasiveness of systematic disagreements in philosophy; it seems that the fact of such disagreement tells us more about the epistemically inhospitable nature of the subject-matter of philosophy, than about the psychology of the folks who are rendering judgments regarding that subject-matter. So S1 would be left with the question of what explains the disagreement.

9.5 Systematic Peer Disagreements and Epistemic Defeat

The lesson here is generic. In cases of recognized systematic p-relevant peer disagreement, each of the parties has reason to endorse the following proposition:

> DEF   (There is a serious chance that) at least one of the disputing parties is unreliable regarding whether p, and I do not know that it is not me.

I submit that the rational pressure to endorse the hypothesis that someone or other is unreliable, as the best explanation of the disagreement itself, increases in direct proportion to the extent, prevalence, and duration of the peer disagreement itself.[29] This hypothesis becomes a better explanation as the disagreement appears not to be resolvable (anytime soon, or perhaps ever). Once we have drawn this conclusion, though, symmetry considerations of the sort I discussed in Section 9.4 appear to put each of the disputing parties in a position in which she cannot rule out the hypothesis that *she herself* is among the unreliable ones. It is this, I submit, that constitutes a defeater regarding each of the parties' respective beliefs regarding whether p.[30] Simply put, systematic peer disagreement provides excellent evidence for DEF, and DEF itself provides a reason to doubt the reliability of one's own belief that p. The result is that if one believes DEF, one has such a reason, and so defeater condition (ii) is satisfied; and since one who is a participant in a systematic peer disagreement ought to believe DEF, the

---

[29] Discussing whether "counterbalanced" attitudes might cancel out each other, and thus support the conclusion that the original first-order evidence alone determines what it is rational to believe, Kelly (2010) responds that "The addition of counterbalanced psychological evidence *does* make a difference to what it is reasonable for us to believe. For, once the counterbalanced evidence is added to our original evidence, a greater proportion of our total evidence supports an attitude of agnosticism than was previously the case..." (2010: 143). Although I am putting my point in terms of defeaters, rather than evidence, a related point could be made in terms of evidence: namely, that under conditions of systematic p-relevant peer disagreement, there is an increase in the evidence in favor of the hypothesis that at least some side is (undetectably) unreliable in the matter whether p, and this evidence can reach the point where agnosticism is the only doxastically justified attitude. (While Kelly himself appears to come to much the same conclusion in a schematically-described case at p. 144, he goes on to argue that this will not have such skeptical consequences as one might suppose, pp. 145–50. I am not as sanguine as he is on this score.)

[30] Compare as well the foregoing treatment of when disagreement gives rise to defeaters with the treatment in Bergmann (2009: 343–50). The view Bergmann defends is that "If in response to recognizing that S disagrees with you about p (which you believe), you either do or epistemically should disbelieve or seriously question or doubt the claim that you are, on this occasion, more trustworthy than S with respect to p, then your belief that p is defeated by this recognition; otherwise, not" (343).

result is that defeater condition (iii) is satisfied. Either way, one has a defeater. And this defeater is present even in cases in which one's belief that p is in point of fact reliably formed. (In such a case the disagreement would still be evidence for one's own unreliability, only it would be misleading. But since it is irrational to ignore the evidence, it would be irrational to ignore this evidence when, unbeknownst to one, it is misleading.)

In sum, I claim that (1) is true whatever one thinks on the question of the epistemic significance of peer disagreement in one-off cases. This is because the case for (1) proceeds by way of an inference-to-the-best explanation of the fact of disagreement in cases in which the disagreement is systematic—and the argument for this does not assume anything that even the most steadfast (Non-Conformist) view in the epistemology of disagreement should want to deny.[31]

9.6 Philosophical Disputes as Systematic Peer Disagreements

Let us now move on to (3) of the MASTER ARGUMENT. This is a claim regarding peer disagreements, to the following effect:

3. Some cases of disagreement regarding whether p are cases of systematic p-relevant peer disagreement.

I do not merely want to establish (3); my goal will be to establish that (3) holds in contexts in which the practice of assertion continues unabated, where despite the systematic disagreement it is plausible to think that at least some of the assertions made under these conditions are warranted. To do so, I will continue to focus on the case of philosophy. Thus I will be defending (3) by defending the special case of

3*. Some cases of *philosophical* disagreement regarding whether p are cases of systematic p-relevant peer disagreement.

Since (3*) entails (3), my case for (3) will consist of establishing (3*). To establish (3*), then, I need to establish that some philosophical disputes are cases of peer disagreement in which the disagreement itself is *non-local, widespread,* and *entrenched.* Consider in

---

[31] Objection: insofar as the truth-value of (1) itself is in dispute, and is part of a systematic peer disagreement, the result would be that my argument is self-defeating—since in that case we would have (from the very argument I have given for (1)) a defeater for belief in (1). (With thanks to Nick Leonard, Baron Reed, and Russ Shafer-Landau, each of whom—independently of one another—raised a version of this objection with me in conversation.) Although this objection merits an extended reply, it is possible to make clear the contours of my response. If it is true that the disagreement over (1) is part of a systematic peer disagreement, then the proper response, I submit, would be one of adopting a sort of Pyrrhonian skepticism regarding both (1) and the issue(s) regarding which there is systematic peer disagreement. In that case, the argument I am offering here would be akin to the ladder of the *Tractatus*—something that one must kick away once one ascends to appreciate the point that is being made. I hope to develop this idea in the future.

this light such long-standing disputes as that between internalists and externalists in epistemology,[32] realists and anti-realists, presentists and four-dimensionalists, cognitivists and non-cognitivists in ethics, or proponents of and skeptics regarding the *a priori*. Consider as well disputes which, though of a more recent vintage, still appear to be systematic (as they are becoming entrenched): the debate over the source(s) of normativity; between proponents and critics of an invariantist semantics for 'knows'; between individualists and anti-individualists regarding attitude individuation; between proponents and critics of intuition as a source of basic knowledge; between motivational internalists and motivational externalists in ethics; or between those who endorse, and those who deny, representationalism regarding sensory content. With a little more thought, more examples could be found.

The foregoing are topics on which there has been very active debate. But disagreement in philosophy is not limited to those topics that have been actively debated. On the contrary, there have been disagreements on topics which, though perhaps not always rising to the level of active debate, nevertheless are areas on which there is nothing close to consensus on many fundamental issues. Consider recent discussions on the epistemology of modality, or in metaethical discussions of the semantics of 'ought', or regarding the legitimacy of John Rawls' use of the veil of ignorance, or of the conceivability of zombies, or of the proper understanding of or rationale for secularism. I suspect it will be uncontroversial that these are controversial matters. Indeed, I suspect that one is hard-pressed to come up with many examples of substantial philosophical claims about which there is broad (if not unanimous) agreement.[33]

There can be little doubt but that most or all of these debates can be framed so as to bring out their status as peer disagreements. It is true that there are those philosophers who are a bit smarter, or more capable, or more widely read in philosophy than the rest of us. But it is dubious whether very many of the long-standing debates in philosophy are such that the smarter, more competent, better-read folk are entirely or even disproportionately represented on one side of the disagreement. Most of us would regard our adversaries as our peers, at least to a rough first approximation. In addition, it would

---

[32] This is the example discussed in Kornblith (2010). According to the recent Philosophical Papers survey (carried out in 2009), if we restrict ourselves to philosophers who claim an AOS in Epistemology, almost an equal number of people endorse or lean towards internalism as endorse or lean towards externalism (36.8% to 35%), and a slightly lesser percentage choose "other" (28.1%). See <http://philpapers.org/surveys/results.pl?affil=Target+faculty&areaso=11&areas_max=1&grain=coarse>.

[33] It is interesting to note that in the 2009 Philosophical Papers survey mentioned previously (see <http://philpapers.org/surveys/results.pl>), of the thirty questions posed to philosophers in the category of "target faculty," *only two* of these questions were such that one of the answers received at least 75% endorsement. In addition, *only thirteen* of the thirty questions were such that one of the answers received *even 50% endorsement*. This means that for the other seventeen questions, no single answer even achieved a majority—a fact that becomes even more impressive when we remember that endorsing an answer included not only those who were active proponents but also those who were "leaning towards" endorsing the view! This does paint a picture of widespread disagreement among "target faculty" in philosophy. A more serious examination of these data would see how (avowed) expertise in a subfield does, or does not, increase disagreement in that subfield.

appear that we have good reason to do so: there is some agreement, at least at a very general level, on the sorts of methods we use in philosophy (although there is disagreement regarding the legitimacy of some methods); we are roughly equally competent in logic and other more formal philosophical tools; we even agree, at least in a good many cases, on what pieces constitute "the" pieces to be reckoned with in a given area; and so forth.[34] It seems that we regard one another, and have reason to regard one another, as peers, despite our disagreements. In this way peer disagreement in philosophy would appear rampant.

Next, consider the claim that peer disagreements in philosophy are non-localized. It is of the nature of some (and perhaps most or even all) philosophical topics that they intersect with many other topics, creating a vast nexus of interconnections. This is certainly true of most or all of the previous topics. If you are an individualist about attitude individuation, this will probably help shape your views in many of the topics in philosophy of mind, philosophy of language, and perhaps epistemology; but so too your anti-individualist opponent will probably disagree with you on those topics as well. If you are a motivational externalist, this will probably affect your favored account of moral psychology, perhaps your account of the conceptual content of 'ought', and perhaps your philosophy of mind as well; though of course your internalist opponents will probably resist your views on most or all of these points. More generally, if you disagree with a colleague over a given philosophical topic on which you regard her as roughly your peer, you will also disagree about the weight to assign to a good many, if not all, of the considerations and arguments each side adduces as it attempts to make the case for its favored view. And these disagreements in turn may reflect still further disagreements about proper methodology: fans of zombie arguments typically endorse appeals to intuition and accept a straightforward connection between conceivability and possibility, whereas foes of such arguments often question the "data" of intuition and question as well the alleged link between conceivability and possibility. Thus it would seem that peer disagreements on such topics are non-localized.

Now consider the claim that peer disagreements in philosophy are widespread. I take this to be more or less obvious: the debates noted previously are not between a few individuals. Indeed, one might think that there is a positive correlation between those debates that have labels associated with the various "sides" and those peer disagreements that are widespread.

Finally, the debates are more or less entrenched. In fact, this appears to be a characteristic of all of the major debates in philosophy: they persist, with no side ever acquiring the right to say that it has triumphed over the other. I do not deny that there are debates that can be settled once and for all. Nor do I deny that debates that at one time are entrenched might nevertheless be settled once and for all. But the track record of philosophy is not particularly encouraging on this score.

---

[34] I thank Matthew Mullins for making this suggestion.

In short, it would seem that we have strong reasons to think that at least some, and arguably many, philosophical disagreements are systematic peer disagreements, and with this my case for (3) is complete.

9.7 The Persistence of Assertions in Systematic Peer Disagreements

So far I have argued, first, that systematic peer disagreement constitutes a defeater, and second, that the practice of philosophy often (typically?) takes places under conditions of systematic disagreement. Of course, these two points, by themselves, do not tell us very much about the nature of assertion—not even in the restricted context of doing philosophy—unless we assume as well that the practice of assertion continues even under these conditions. I will label this the assumption that there are Philosophical Assertions in cases of Systematic Disagreement:

PASD   It is common (ordinary; part of standard practice) for philosophers who recognize that they are party to a systematic p-relevant peer disagreement in philosophy nevertheless to persist in asserting that p.

It is worth noting that the problem I seek to raise regarding assertoric practice in philosophy (and by extension regarding assertoric practice more generally[35]) holds if but only if PASD is true. Suppose PASD is false. In that case it is not part of ordinary practice for philosophers to assert anything when in contexts of systematic peer disagreement. Then even if the conclusion of the MASTER ARGUMENT is true—assertions made under conditions of systematic peer disagreement are (all of them) unwarranted—this has no implications for the practice or assessment of assertions within philosophy. Of course, if PASD is true, philosophical practice does involve the assertion of propositions which, by the lights of the MASTER ARGUMENT's conclusion, are (all of them) unwarranted. This is the unhappy result of which I spoke at the outset of this chapter. In light of the role of PASD in securing the unhappiness of the MASTER ARGUMENT's conclusion, I want to spend some time discussing its plausibility.

Let me begin with what I regard as a misguided reason to think that PASD is false. One might think that PASD is false on the grounds that in philosophy we typically *argue* for our views (rather than assert them). There are two points I would like to make in reaction to this misguided objection to PASD.

First, the reaction is based on a contrast which, as stated, is confused. It assumes, confusedly, that one does not assert what one argues for. If this were true, then one would never count as asserting the conclusion of one's arguments. But surely one *does* assert the conclusion of one's argument (at least when one makes that conclusion explicit).

---

[35] And it is important to keep in mind that philosophical practice is supposed to be the best example of a more general phenomenon, whereby assertoric practice continues unabated even under conditions of systematic disagreement.

What is correct is that in arguing for a conclusion, as we do in philosophy, one's assertion is not *bald*: one is not encouraging one's interlocutor to accept the claim in question *merely on the basis of one's having said so*. Even so, a non-bald (argument-backed) assertion remains an assertion. Once this is clear, a related point becomes obvious. Take a case in which S asserts that p, where it is mutually manifest that this assertion was made on the basis of an argument S just gave. Even so, these facts do not ensure that S's assertion of p is warranted. On the contrary, the point of S's argument is precisely to make manifest the basis on which she asserts that p; her assertion that p is warranted only if this basis (the argument) is such as to render her assertion normatively acceptable (as satisfying the norm of assertion). So even though it is true that claims in philosophy are typically backed by argument, this does not show that such claims are not asserted, nor does it show that such claims (when asserted) are warranted.

But there is another point to be made on this score. Even if it is *often* true that in philosophy we argue for our views, it is not *universally* true. No one can possibly argue for all the claims she makes; some claims must be starting points for argumentation. My point here concerns, not the nature or structure of justification, but a limit on the presentation of one's views *in speech*. I mention this if only to forestall the thought that this point can be resisted, for example, by endorsing a coherentist epistemology. According to coherentism, there are no epistemic (justificatory) starting points. Even if this is true (which I doubt), it does not bear on my point about the limitations of argumentation in speech. Indeed, it is not hard to think of the sorts of assertions which at least some of us philosophers make at the outset of our arguments, and for which we offer little, if anything, in the way of an argument. These are typically the claims we find "intuitive." To be sure, some of these claims are no longer particularly controversial: that the Gettiered subject does not know is not something regarding which one expects to find disagreement (but see Weatherson 2003). However, some of the claims we make in philosophy are made despite the facts that (a) we have no argument to back them up, and (b) they remain controversial. Indeed, it is hard to see how it could be otherwise. Suppose you are trying to convince a philosopher of what you regard as the exorbitant costs of her view, and after doing so she remains unimpressed. "But do not you see?" you exclaim, "These implications of your view are absurd!" But she denies this; she maintains that they are not absurd, and questions you on this. At a certain point, the dispute is left with the familiar table-thumping. Alas, this is hardly an uncommon phenomenon in philosophy. It seems that the two sides are trading assertions about the relative implausibility of each other's implications.

Nor are philosophical assertions (made under conditions of systematic peer disagreement) limited to claims regarding the plausibility of (the implications of) our first-order views. On the contrary, they include claims of philosophical substance. The following situation should be familiar (and examples could be multiplied). A proponent of motivational externalism is at a conference at which she gives a paper. In the paper she advances a new argument. The argument itself appeals to some familiar claims, and some not-so-familiar claims. But among the familiar claims are some claims of substance. She is aware that some of these claims are controversial, and will be rejected by some in her audience. Still, she asserts them nevertheless. For how else could she advance her argument? Must she wait until all relevant systematic peer disagreements have been settled before asserting the premises of her argument? That appears to be a recipe for philosophical paralysis.

I have sometimes heard it said (in conversation) that there really are no straight (first-order) assertions of controversial matters in philosophy, only speculations and conditional (or otherwise hedged) claims.[36] A characteristic claim in this vicinity is that philosophers do not flat-out assert their claims, but instead suggest them tentatively, or with something like a "we have some reason to think that" operator in front of them.[37] I agree that this is sometimes the case. But I find it dubious in the extreme to think that *all* cases of apparent assertions made in philosophy under conditions of systematic peer disagreement are like this. Surely there are *some* cases in which a philosopher continues to assert that p, despite the systematic p-relevant peer disagreement.[38] Here, two points of support can be made. First, it should be obvious to anyone who has participated in or observed philosophical practice that there are (some, and arguably many) occasions on which a claim is advanced under conditions of systematic peer disagreement without any *explicit* hedge or "there are reasons to think" operator in play. For this reason, if the hedging proposal is to work, it must postulate an *implicit* (linguistically unmarked) hedge or "there are reasons to think" operator in play in all such cases. But such a global postulation would appear to be fully theory-driven, and so *ad hoc*. What is more (and this is my second point), there are independent reasons to think that such a postulation is not warranted. In particular, the suggestion—that philosophical practice under conditions of systematic peer disagreement always involves hedged rather than straight assertion—appears to be belied by other aspects of our practice. Why the vehemence with which some (apparently first-order, categorical) philosophical claims are made, even under conditions of systematic peer disagreement? Why so much heat, if all we are doing is entering hedged claims? Why do we go to such great lengths to try to defend our claims in the face of challenge? Why not shrug off such challenges to our claim that p, with the remark that, after all, we were merely claiming that there are reasons supporting that p? Relatedly: why is it that the typical response to challenges is to try to defend the claim that p, not the (weaker) claim that there are reasons to believe that p? Finally, if all we are doing in philosophy is entering hedged claims, why is talk of our philosophical "commitments" so prevalent? Reflecting on this practice, I conclude that assertions are made in philosophy, even in the face of systematic peer disagreement. PASD is true.

---

[36] Peter Ludlow (among many others) has suggested this to me (in conversation).
[37] This point was suggested to me by Cian Dorr. (I do not know whether he endorses this view.)
[38] Indeed, some philosophers have even conceded as much in their own case.

9.8 Conclusion

And so concludes my case for thinking that the MASTER ARGUMENT presents us with a problem. In a nutshell: we appear to make assertions in philosophy, even in the face of systematic peer disagreement; yet a valid, apparently sound argument would lead us to conclude that these assertions are, each and every one of them, unwarranted. To be sure, this argument depends on one further assumption which I have not explicitly defended here, to the effect that if S neither knows, nor is doxastically justified in believing, that p, then it is not warranted for S to assert that p. But this assumption holds if the norm of assertion is a robustly epistemic one—something that is a thesis at the heart of Chapters 1–8.

Some might think that we should simply accept the conclusion. Recently, several people (myself included) have argued that insofar as we believe our philosophical claims in the face of systematic peer disagreement, these beliefs are by and large doxastically unjustified.[39] If such a view is correct, one might think that it is not really that much further to hold that our *assertions* of these believed claims are unwarranted one and all. If (contrary to what I argued in Chapter 6) assertion is the outer manifestation of belief, perhaps we should expect that our philosophical assertions (made under conditions of relevant peer disagreement) are systematically unwarranted.

Since I find the MASTER ARGUMENT's conclusion unhappy, I find this reaction unhappy. I might put the matter as follows. Philosophizing as an activity flourishes (only?) in the context of dialogue and debate. If the practice is to flourish,[40] we should want it to include a speech act by which one can present a proposition as true in such a way as to implicate one's own epistemic authority on the matter. In short, we have reason to want the practice of philosophizing to include assertions. At the same time, philosophy is a subject-matter in which epistemically high-quality belief is hard to come by, perhaps (in certain domains) even practically impossible. The result is that the activity of philosophizing itself is something of a strange bird: it is a practice whose flourishing requires the performance of a speech act whose norm we appear systematically to violate in engaging in that practice. It may well be that one can decrease the strangeness of this practice by noting that, since we are all aware of the contours of this situation (if perhaps only implicitly), we allow each other to "get away with" making assertions under conditions when, strictly speaking, such assertions are unwarranted. But to my mind this move only makes things seem worse, since in that case, not only do we philosophers systematically violate speech-act norms, we fail to enforce those

---

[39] This is a view that has been advocated recently in Goldberg (2008) and Kornblith (2010). Frances (2005) appears to be broadly sympathetic to this view, as a special case of a much more general sort of skepticism that is generated by disagreement.

[40] Might it be objected that insofar as philosophical belief is doxastically unjustified (in the face of systematic peer disagreement), philosophical practice ought not to flourish? I think not. The value of philosophy might well lie in its production of some non-epistemic good. This is a theme to which I hope to return in subsequent work.

norms as well! This makes a mockery of the practice of assertion. It also makes a mockery of the activity of philosophizing. Is philosophy really such a shady activity that it requires us to allow each other to "get away with" systematic violations of speech-act norms? On the contrary, there is something slightly paradoxical, even offensive, in the thought that the flourishing of philosophical practice comes at the cost of systematically unwarranted assertions. This is a conclusion we ought to avoid if at all possible. In the next chapter, I suggest how we can do just this.

10

Mutuality and Assertion

10.1 The Challenge of Disagreement: Some *Desiderata* Regarding an Answer

In the previous chapter I argued that conditions of systematic peer disagreement (of the sort we find paradigmatically in philosophy, but also in politics, religion, and the more theoretical parts of the social and natural sciences) provide defeaters, with the result that there is no justified belief (and so no knowledge) under such conditions. This is a challenge to the hypothesis that there is a robustly epistemic norm of assertion: insofar as assertions continue to be made in these circumstances, the cost of insisting on a robustly epistemic norm of assertion would appear to be that we are forced to regard as unwarranted each and every assertion made in such contexts. In this chapter I argue that this problem can be resolved by appeal to the hypothesis that the standard set by assertion's norm is fixed in part in terms of what is mutually believed by the speaker and her audience in the context in which the assertion is made. What is more, such a "context-sensitive" account of the norm of assertion enjoys strong independent support. I argue that it can be motivated by appeal to Grice's guiding idea that conversation is a cooperative and rational activity between agents, where the rationality of speech contributions is to be understood by reference to how they contribute to the mutually acknowledged aims. In accord with this, the aim of this chapter is twofold: to solve the problem of disagreement (as we might call it); and to show how the proposed solution enjoys strong independent support.

It will help to begin by characterizing the nature of the problem of disagreement itself, at least in broad outline. In so doing I will be presenting in a schematic fashion the difficulty developed at length in the previous chapter. In the current presentation I aim to draw out a set of *desiderata*—conditions that we hope to meet with our ultimate "solution" to the problem.

The problem of disagreement is usefully understood as an apparently inconsistent triad of propositions, each of which enjoys some independent plausibility. The first captures the idea that assertion answers to an epistemic norm, which I have been formulating as

    ENA   S must: assert p, only if S satisfies epistemic condition E with respect to p; that is, only if E(S, [p]).

The second captures the Epistemic Significance of Systematic Peer Disagreement:

ESSPD Under conditions of systematic peer disagreement regarding the proposition that p, no party to the dispute satisfies E with respect to [p].

The final captures the claim that some Assertions are Warranted even under conditions of Systematic Peer Disagreement:

AWSPD It is sometimes the case that S asserts that p under conditions of a systematic p-relevant peer disagreement, and yet S's assertion is warranted.

That ENA, ESSPD, and AWSPD form an inconsistent triad is easily seen. Failure to satisfy ENA results in the unwarrantedness of an assertion. But if no assertion made under conditions of (relevant) systematic peer disagreement satisfies the norm of assertion, as ESSPD has it, no such assertion is warranted—contrary to what AWSPD says. The problem is that all three of these claims enjoy some plausibility, yet they cannot all be true.

All three enjoy plausibility. ENA is the core hypothesis of Chapters 1–8 of this book. If the argumentation of those chapters is sound, ENA enjoys tremendous explanatory virtues: it enables us to provide a unified account of a number of the features that characterize assertoric practice, and in so doing it enables us to see these features as reflecting the nature of assertion itself. ESSPD appears motivated by the argument from Chapter 9. There, I argued that conditions of systematic p-relevant peer disagreement constitute a defeater of the justification of one's belief that p, with the result that under such conditions there is no knowledge, doxastically justified belief, or even rational belief that p. On the assumption that the epistemic standard provided by assertion's norm is at least as demanding as rational belief—and if it is a robustly epistemic norm, as I have been assuming throughout, then the standard will be at least this demanding—the result would be that no one under conditions of systematic disagreement has the epistemic credentials to warrant assertion—precisely as ESSPD would have it. Finally, I spent some time in Chapter 9 arguing that nevertheless AWSPD is true: some assertions made under conditions of systematic disagreement are warranted. My illustration focused on assertoric practice in philosophy: not only is it the case that claims continue to be made even under conditions of systematic disagreement, what is more, we might think that the practice of philosophy depends on this feature. And, while philosophy is the paradigmatic example of the phenomenon, it is not alone. I suggested that we will see examples of warranted assertion under such conditions whenever claim-making persists under what we might call *diminished epistemic hopes* (where the prospects for epistemically high-grade belief are remote or non-existent[1]). Taken together, ENA, ESSPD, and AWSPD provide us with a

---

[1] By 'epistemically high-grade belief' I mean belief that amounts to knowledge or else is based on a knowledge-sufficient justification.

problem: to describe assertoric practice under conditions of diminished epistemic hope. To do so, we will need to reject one of these three propositions.

I suspect the first temptation will be to reject AWSPD. One might think to suggest that—appearances to the contrary notwithstanding—there really are no warranted assertions under conditions of systematic disagreement. One might explain away the appearances in one of at least two ways. (These are not incompatible, but can be combined.)

One way would be to hold that what appear to be assertions made in contexts of systematic disagreement *are not really assertions after all*. Perhaps they are hedged or qualified assertions; or perhaps they are a different speech act altogether. The difficulty with this reaction is that it seems seriously revisionary: although there surely *are* hedged or qualified assertions made in conditions of diminished epistemic hope, it is also the case that (to all outward appearances) there are many examples of *straight assertions* in these conditions as well.[2] To think otherwise is to embrace a rather seriously revisionary description of the practice. I do not claim that this is unacceptable; only that, since it is seriously revisionary, it would be better to see if we can address the problem without having to go this route.

The other way would be to hold that insofar as there are assertions made in these contexts they are, one and all, unwarranted—*appearances to the contrary notwithstanding*. An interesting comparison in this respect is the treatment given to predictions by a recent defender of the knowledge account, Matthew Benton.[3] In his (2012), Benton defends the knowledge account of assertion against the objection that such an account implies that all (asserted) predictions are unwarranted. He replies:

[P]redictions only *seem* permissible because they are naturally and normally made in contexts of acknowledged practical urgency wherein it is recognized that knowledge won't be had, yet predictions still must be made. Given such urgent contexts, it is understandable why we often enough don't enforce the knowledge requirement with predictions. (Benton 2012: 104–5; italics in original)

One might think to apply Benton's suggestion to the case of assertions made under conditions of systematic peer disagreement—conditions, that is, of epistemically diminished hope. The idea would be that, since we all know (and know that we all know) that knowledge is not to be had in these circumstances, and yet despite this we still find that there is a point to trading claims, the result is that "it is understandable why we often enough don't enforce" the requirement that assertions answer to a robustly epistemic standard in such cases.

---

[2] For what it is worth, I have a good deal of anecdotal evidence from fellow philosophers that they take themselves to be making assertions in their philosophical work. To be sure, not everyone says this, but a good many do—leading me to think that the move to redescribe apparently assertoric speech is rather seriously revisionary. As I say, it does happen that philosophers offer hedged or qualified assertions; but it also happens that philosophers make assertions.

[3] I thank an anonymous referee for suggesting that I consider this analogy.

This is an interesting suggestion, but I think it does not survive scrutiny. For one thing, the proposal as it stands is incomplete, and when we complete it the result suffers from a lack of motivation. We can see this even in the case of predictions. To see this, let us assume the knowledge norm, and let us grant that the knowledge requirement is not enforced with predictions. Even so, we *still* need a standard for warranted (prediction-constituting) assertions in these cases. After all, it is not as if, once we have agreed to waive the knowledge requirement when it comes to predictions, it is *anything goes*. On the contrary, there are warranted predictions, and there are unwarranted ones. (If, on the basis of good but not knowledge-sufficient evidence that the Yankees will win, you predict that the Yankees will lose, your prediction is unwarranted—albeit not because you did not know.) As a result, Benton must further complicate his story so as to include standards that are in place when we (assert so as to) make predictions. Benton might think to deny that these are standards of assertion (insisting that the norm of assertion is knowledge); but at this point, the proposal begins to seem unmotivated. (I will return to this Section 10.4.)

Relatedly, if Benton's treatment of predictions is extended to the case discussed in the previous chapter—the case of philosophical assertion—this would have unhappy implications for the practice of philosophy. If I am right that the practice of philosophy depends on the continued making of assertions under conditions of diminished epistemic hope, then we would reach the unhappy conclusion that the practice of philosophy is itself suspect to this extent. Perhaps (in the spirit of Benton's treatment of predictions) it might be replied that, though the assertions in question are strictly speaking unwarranted, we let each other "get away with" them anyway, out of an interest in continuing the practice of trading claims under these epistemically perilous circumstances. But this suggestion is not really helpful: why would we think any higher of philosophy merely because we let each other get away with what after all are shoddy assertions? After all, we do not even have the excuse Benton offers in the case of predictions: for most philosophical issues, there is no practical urgency to make claims! In this respect, applying Benton's proposal to the case of philosophical assertion would seem to condemn philosophical practice twice over: first, for unwarranted assertions, and second, for a refusal to police this lack of warrant without any compelling reason (such as practical urgency). And what goes for philosophy presumably goes for other areas in which the practice of assertion continues even under conditions of diminished epistemic hopes.

I conclude, then, that Benton's (2012) proposal regarding predictions does not offer a compelling basis on which to reject the claim, AWSPD, that there can be warranted assertions even in the face of systematic peer disagreement. Of course, if the costs of rejecting AWSPD are too much, another option would be to reject ENA itself—the guiding hypothesis of this book. This will be attractive to (some of) those who argue that assertion has no norm at all,[4] as well as to those who

---

[4] See Pagin (2011). See also MacFarlane (2011) for an inventory of the sort of views one can take about the nature of assertion. (Chapter 1 of the present book followed MacFarlane's inventory.)

argue that while assertion has a norm, the norm is not epistemic.[5] Still, the vast majority of people who work on assertion seem to regard it as having an epistemic norm of some sort or other. What is more, in the earlier chapters of this book I have argued that ENA itself has a variety of explanatory virtues. All of this should lead us to wonder whether we can preserve ENA and still allow that philosophical assertions can be warranted even when made under conditions of systematic disagreement.

This leads us to the option of rejecting ESSPD—the claim that no speaker who asserts that p under conditions of systematic (p-relevant) peer disagreement has the epistemic credentials to satisfy the norm of assertion. Here I note that one might think to respond by modifying the epistemic standard required by the norm of assertion: whereas ENA regards that standard as something *robustly* epistemic, perhaps we can weaken the standard so that, while it is still epistemic, it is not *robustly* so. (That is, we can allow that satisfying the standard requires an epistemic status that is weaker than doxastic or propositional justification—a status that is not sufficient to turn true unGettiered belief into knowledge.) But in that case the cost of maintaining that there is warranted assertion appears prohibitive: we will be forced to weaken the epistemic norm of assertion so as not to require anything like knowledge, justification, or rationality. This seems deeply implausible. For if the norm of assertion is weakened to the point where it demands something weaker than justified (or rational) belief, the result would be an obviously overly-permissive norm—one that sanctions a good deal of assertions we would want to regard as unwarranted. This seems to be a non-starter.

With this as our understanding of the nature of the problem to be solved, we can discern several conditions we would like to be able to satisfy in a solution. In particular, a solution will be a position which denies one (or more) of the three previous claims—ENA, ESSPD, or AWSPD—while nevertheless satisfying the following three conditions:

(1) It does not weaken E—the epistemic standard provided by the norm of assertion—to the point of irrelevance or insignificance.
(2) It recognizes the strengths of the arguments made on behalf of thinking that E is *knowledge*, or some other robustly epistemic property (such as knowledge-sufficient justification).
(3) It enables us to regard the relevant class of assertions as broadly warranted despite the fact that few if any speakers have any substantial epistemic credentials to make assertions in these areas.

---

[5] See Weiner (2005), where a truth norm is defended. Weiner does allow that there is a *secondary* sense in which the norm of assertion is epistemic: if we are to do our best in trying to conform to a truth norm, we must do so on the basis of considerations suggesting that our assertions are true—in other words, on the basis of something like good evidence or good reasons. In this respect, Weiner's views employ the primary/secondary propriety distinction that proponents of the knowledge norm themselves have used.

Now, it might be thought that there is no solution that satisfies all of (1)–(3). If this thought were true, then we would need to revisit the options of denying one (or more) of our three structuring assumptions (ENA, ESSPD, AWSPD) in one of the ways suggested previously. However, in what follows I will argue that there is a solution that satisfies all three *desiderata*, (1)–(3); and I will argue as well that this solution enjoys strong support independent of its offering a solution to the present problem.

10.2 Cooperativity, Mutual Belief, and the Fixation of Standards of Assertoric Warrant

The problem we are considering pertains to any domain in which the making of assertions continues despite diminished epistemic hopes. I have been focusing on one such domain—that of philosophy, where it is an ordinary part of the practice to make assertions under these conditions. I noted previously that some might be tempted to describe this part of philosophical practice by saying that participants in philosophical conversations regularly let each other "get away with" the assertions in question. Again, if this is merely a matter of letting one another "get away with" what in fact are unwarranted assertions, this is doubly bad for the practice. But we might well wonder whether this is the most perspicuous description of the practice. Perhaps it is not a matter of letting each other "get away with" anything; perhaps the assertions in question are warranted after all.

Of course, anyone who would like to try to make out such a view, and so who aims to satisfy *desideratum* (3) in the previous section, must face an immediate question of how to square the hypothesis that these assertions are warranted after all, with the claim that few if any speakers in these areas enjoy any substantial epistemic standing with respect to the propositions they are asserting. In short, it can seem that the move to satisfy (3) will come at the cost of having to weaken the norm's standard to the point of irrelevance, and hence at the cost of failing to satisfy *desideratum* (2). I should emphasize as well that this difficulty has nothing in particular to do with assertoric practice in philosophy: it is a problem facing *any* discourse in which assertions continue to be made (as an ordinary part of the discourse) under conditions of diminished epistemic hopes.

In this section I argue that the difficulty can be met. I propose to do so by developing an account of assertion on which the standard provided by assertion's norm is set in a context-sensitive way. I motivate such an account by appeal to broadly Gricean considerations, and in the next section I argue that the account delivers the desired outcome, satisfying *desiderata* (1)–(3).

An account of assertion is an account of a type of speech act, and as such it should be presented against the background of our best understanding of speech acts. Paul Grice (1968b/1989) has provided an important grounding principle for such an understanding. Regarding speech as a rational, cooperative activity, Grice formulated the familiar

Cooperative Principle as capturing a core part of the rationality which is distinctive of acts of this sort:

Cooperative Principle (CP) Make your contribution such as it is required, at the stage at which it occurs, by the accepted purpose or direction of the talk exchange in which you are engaged. (Grice 1968b/1989: 26)

Now most people who have employed Grice's CP (or the other elements of Grice's picture) have done so with an eye on characterizing the *content* dimension of communication. That is, they use Grice's framework to provide an account of how speakers manage to communicate more than they (strictly and literally) say, and of how hearers manage to recover what is communicated when this goes beyond what is (strictly and literally) said. But I see no reason why we cannot use Grice's insight to shed light on the dimension of (illocutionary) *force*. This is what I propose to do.

One might wonder how Grice's CP can shed any light on the dimension of illocutionary force in general, and on assertion in particular. But this suggestion is not as outlandish as one might suppose. On the contrary, it is a natural one. To see this, consider that Grice went on to present various maxims that he regarded as falling out of CP. Of these, the one which is most directly relevant to the speech act of assertion is the maxim he labeled 'Quality', which I repeat here:

Quality (Q) Do not say what you believe to be false. Do not say that for which you lack adequate evidence. (Grice 1968b/1989: 27)

Now, it is true that Grice's maxims are explicitly aimed at characterizing the notion of *saying* something. Still, when it comes to Q itself, it is not a far stretch to regard the maxim as contributing to our understanding of the more specific speech act of assertion. Indeed, we might well think that the 'quality' dimension of Grice's notion of saying just is a proposed characterization of the norm of assertion. On this picture, the speech act of assertion is governed by two rules: you should not assert what you believe to be false, and you should not assert that for which you lack adequate evidence. But precisely when is one's evidence "adequate"? I submit that we should answer this question by appeal to the CP itself: the standards for adequacy of evidence are determined, at least in part, by "the accepted purpose or direction of the talk exchange in which you are engaged." If this is correct, then we have characterized a feature of the illocutionary force of an assertion by appeal to CP.

Still, we need an account of how "the accepted purpose or direction of the talk exchange in which you are engaged" might serve to fix the standards of evidential adequacy. I propose that we can develop such an account in terms of Bach and Harnish's useful (1979) notion of *mutual belief*. The following is their gloss on the role that mutual belief plays in the sort of inferences that are made in the course of the production and comprehension of speech:

Mutual Belief If p is mutually believed between S and H, then (1) not only do S and H believe p, but (2) each believes that the other takes it into account in his thinking, and (3) each, supposing the other to take *p* into account, supposes the other to take him to take it into account. (Bach and Harnish 1979: 6)

I submit that the task of determining adequacy of evidence (and hence of determining the standards imposed by the maxim of Quality) is itself a special case of the sort of phenomenon of which Bach and Harnish are speaking. In particular, if there is mutual belief that the hearer faces a practical task in which she is in need of information, and that she is relying on the speaker to provide this information, then adequate evidence would be the sort of evidence for a proposition which would render it reasonable for the hearer to act on the assumption that the proposition is true. If there is mutual belief to the effect that the hearer needs information of which she can be certain, then adequate evidence would be the sort of evidence that would support certainty.

The point I am presently making can be formulated in terms of the norm of assertion. Return to my formulation of the hypothesis that (it is mutually manifest to all competent speakers that) assertion has an epistemic norm. Throughout the book, I have been formulating the hypothesis asserting an Epistemic Norm of Assertion as the claim that

ENA   S must: assert p, only if S satisfies epistemic condition E with respect to p; that is, only if E(S, [p]).

My present claim employs the notion of mutual belief to address the matter of what epistemic standards one must satisfy if one is to count as satisfying E with respect to p. Let us say that when a speaker S satisfies those standards, she has the *relevant warranting authority* regarding p. To a first approximation (to be modified in Section 10.5), the hypothesis is this ('MBS' for 'Mutual Belief Standard'):

MBS   When it comes to a particular assertion that p, the relevant warranting authority regarding p depends in part on what is mutually believed by speaker and audience (regarding such things as the participants' interests and informational needs, and the prospects for high-quality information in the domain in question).[6]

It is perhaps worth underscoring that, with its appeal to what is mutually believed in context, MBS utilizes a core component of my account of assertion: namely, the background of what is mutually manifest to the participants in given conversations. We might say that the 'MM' of 'MMENA' captures what is invariantly mutually manifest— that is, mutually manifest to any competent language user, no matter the context. But surely there can be other things that are mutually manifest in context to the participants of the conversation. MBS appeals to the entirety of what is mutually manifest, in the form of what is mutually believed by participants in a conversation. Later I will be

---

[6] My main modification will be that it is not mutual belief *per se*, but *what would be reasonably regarded as mutually believed*, that fixes the standard.

arguing that (a slightly modified version of) MBS's mutual belief model can address the problem of disagreement. My only claim here is that the model itself enjoys independent support: it can be seen as deriving from a broadly Grice-inspired approach to speech exchanges.

This last point is worth dwelling on in a little more detail. The model I am offering here is a special case of a more general picture of speech exchanges—one having nothing in particular to do with philosophy (or with disagreement, for that matter). On this picture, speech is a cooperative activity, and assertion is to be understood in these terms, as governed by rules of the sort Grice articulated in his principle of Quality. Insofar as these rules are themselves an object of (perhaps merely implicit) mutual belief, they determine a set of mutual expectations of speaker and hearer. That these expectations are (in part) epistemic, demanding adequacy of evidence, is precisely what makes assertion apt for playing the very important role it does: that of serving as the vehicle for the transmission of information. This point is familiar from my arguments in Chapters 2 and 3, but perhaps we can revisit it briefly here. A hearer who observes a speaker make an assertion, under conditions in which the rules governing assertion are objects of mutual belief, will expect that the speaker acknowledges these rules, and so will expect the speaker to acknowledge the responsibility for having had adequate evidence. Insofar as the hearer regards the speaker as having succeeded at following the rules, then, the hearer regards the speaker as having adequate evidence; and when the hearer's so regarding the speaker is rational, this rationalizes the hearer's move to accept the information the speaker presented in her assertion, on the basis of her having so asserted.[7] In sum, it is because of the rules governing assertion that this speech act is apt for rationalizing hearers' beliefs in what is asserted—and precisely this renders assertion apt for the transmission of information.

All of this is a familiar part of a broadly Grice-inspired picture of assertion. I am only introducing two wrinkles to this story. First, I am proposing that the determination of when evidence is "adequate" to render an assertion warranted is a matter of "the accepted purpose or direction of the talk exchange." Second, I am proposing to model the process by which this determination is made in terms of the notion of mutual belief. Both of these wrinkles (I have contended) are Gricean in spirit: they can be motivated as spelling out the picture of conversation Grice himself first introduced.[8] I now want to put this picture to work in addressing the problem of disagreement—the problem with which I began this chapter. In what follows, my claim will be that what is mutually believed on a speech occasion sometimes includes information regarding not only (some subset of) the interests and informational needs of one's audience,

---

[7] Of course, if the hearer were irrational in regarding the speaker as having conformed to the rules—the speaker asserted something regarding which it is common knowledge that no one has any evidence, or she had obvious vested interests in getting the hearer to believe what she said, and so on—then the hearer's acceptance is itself rationally flawed.

[8] But see Benton (forthcoming) for some reasons to worry about whether this proposal is truly Gricean in spirit.

but also the difficulties of acquiring epistemically high-quality information in a given domain in which the parties seek information. Insofar as this is the case, this body of mutual belief will affect the mutual expectations that speaker and hearer have of one another in the speech exchange. And it is this, I will go on to argue, that enables us to use the model to answer our original difficulty regarding philosophical assertion while simultaneously satisfying the three *desiderata* from the previous section.[9] The basic idea is that, while ESSPD is false (so that there are cases in which speakers do satisfy the epistemic norm of assertion even under conditions of systematic peer disagreement), the falsity of ESSPD does not result in a wholesale weakening of the standards, but is only a local (and fully predictable) effect of context.

10.3 Epistemic Groups and Assertoric Practice

Let us suppose that my two "wrinkles" are correct: what counts as adequate evidence (sufficient to warrant assertion) is a matter of "the accepted purpose or direction of the talk exchange"; and the purpose or direction of the talk exchange determined this through what is mutually believed in context. These two claims, by themselves, are not sufficient to address the problem of accounting for the practice of assertion in the face of diminished epistemic hopes. The key point is easy to appreciate in connection with assertoric practice within philosophy. Insofar as it is mutual belief that sets the standard of the norm of assertion in a given context, then what standard is in play in a given context will depend on what is mutually believed in that context. But so far we have no guarantee that what is mutually believed in any arbitrary philosophy context will be such as to establish standards that are satisfied in those cases in which, intuitively, we want to say that the philosophical assertions are warranted. In short, unless there is a way to ensure that there is the relevant sort of mutual belief among philosophers, the standards that prevail in a given speech exchange between philosophers will be hostage to doxastic idiosyncrasies of the speech participants. As noted, the problem here has nothing in particular to do with philosophy: the same sort of problem can be raised in any situation in which assertoric practice continues in the face of diminished epistemic hopes. If that practice is to be (broadly) warranted, we will need a way to ensure that in each of the cases what is mutually believed in context sets the appropriate standard. How to ensure this? I believe that the answer lies in the notion of an *epistemic group*. After introducing this notion I go on to show that if a collection of people constitute an epistemic group, then this can be expected to have an effect on assertoric practice among them—and the resulting model of assertion will be able to satisfy *desiderata* (1)–(3).

---

[9] I should make clear that while my proposed model has happy implications for the problem with which I began this chapter—the problem of warranted assertions made under conditions of systematic disagreement—it is proposed as modeling assertion as such.

I begin, then, with the notion of an epistemic group. It is sometimes mutual belief among participants to a conversation that they are speaking to one another *as neighbors*, or *as birdwatchers*, or *as philosophers*, or *as scientists*, or *as politicians*, or *as colleagues*, or . . . Being in such a group is sometimes associated with having certain kinds of knowledge (or at least belief). Such belief might regard the relevant subject-matter, the likely sources of further subject-matter information, the practices whereby such information is extracted, the ease of obtaining high-quality subject-matter information, and so forth. What is more, the existence of such knowledge or belief among the group's members can itself become a matter of mutual belief: the members of the group believe of themselves that each has the relevant subject-matter and procedural knowledge (or beliefs). When this is so, the members of such a group will use this mass of mutual belief to form mutual expectations: they will form expectations regarding what they can expect from each other, and what their group-interlocutors are likely to expect from them in turn, as they engage in communication and other forms of cooperative inquiry. When a group has such mutual (epistemic) expectations regarding each other as epistemic (knowledge-seeking) agents, I will call the group an *epistemic group*.

It is in the context of epistemic groups that we can reconsider the challenge to ensure that relevant mutual belief will prevail in any case involving philosophical assertion. In general, epistemic groups are the repository of mutual (subject-matter and inquiry-related) beliefs—and this background of mutual belief shapes assertoric practice within the group. The case of philosophy is a useful example.

Suppose that, in the course of making an argument for some controversial conclusion regarding (say) the nature of knowledge, Yang advances various claims—she asserts various propositions—as premises in her argument. She herself is well aware that with respect to each of the claims (assertions) she is making here, there will be those in the audience who will disagree with her. She could try to address all of their concerns, of course. But she knows, and anticipates that they know, that doing so would quickly spiral out of control: in order to vindicate each claim (assertion) in her main argument, showing each to be the conclusion of a further argument, she would need to make still further claims (assertions), and she anticipates that for at least some of these (and perhaps many or all of them) there would be further disagreement. She takes all of this as mutually known by herself and her audience; in any case she takes it as reasonable to suppose that any well-trained philosopher will be aware of all of this, and aware that the others are aware of it too. Accordingly, she anticipates that her audience will appreciate the position she is in. She recognizes, of course, that one cannot simply assert anything, willy-nilly, in philosophical contexts. But in light of what she reasonably regards as mutually believed among philosophers working in epistemology, she anticipates that her audience will expect that for any assertion she makes, she will be in a position to provide a defense of the assertion in question satisfying the standards for epistemology. Which is to say that the argument need not be knock-down, nor need it even persuade the other side (they can remain rational even as they deny her assertion); it need merely conform to professional standards (of rigor, clarity, responsiveness to prevailing reasons, and so on). This, then, is what informs her assertoric behavior.

What sort of evidence do we expect of one another when engaging in a speech exchange on some philosophical topic? It is not clear that there is one set standard for all of philosophy. On the contrary, it seems plausible to suppose that the expected standard can vary according to subject-matter: what we expect from a speaker who is advancing what she presents to be a theorem in logic is one thing; what we expect from a speaker who is advancing a claim in ethics (for example) is another still. I submit that this is because of what it is reasonable to assume is mutually believed among academically trained philosophers. It is reasonable to assume mutual belief among philosophers to the effect that (incompleteness aside) propositions in logic can be established or refuted by proof. This is why we will expect one advancing such a claim (by way of making an assertion) to have evidence that amounts to, approximates, or stands in for a proof. It is also reasonable to assume mutual belief among philosophers to the effect that propositions in ethics cannot (typically) be established in this way. This is why we will not expect anything approximating a proof of someone advancing a claim in ethics. Rather, what we will expect in the way of evidence in ethics turns on what is mutually believed—better, what it is *reasonable to assume* is mutually believed[10]—regarding the nature of the subject-matter in ethics: the sorts of considerations that can support such claims, the difficulty of synthesizing all of the considerations bearing on a given ethical question, the nature of the sorts of methods we use in doing so, the main considerations that have been presented to date, and so forth. If it is mutually acknowledged that a certain claim in ethics is part of a systematic disagreement, participants to the speech exchange will—or at any rate, should—adjust their evidence-related expectations accordingly. In particular, they should not expect the evidence to be decisive and clear; rather, they should expect that the evidence suffices to place the speaker in a position where she can "make a case for" the claim in question. (Precisely what this amounts to is difficult to put into words, though I assume that philosophers will recognize the phenomenon.) And what goes for contested ethical propositions, goes more generally for contested philosophical propositions—at least insofar as the participants to the speech exchange have the sort of mutual belief I have described.

Of course, examples like that of Yang, in which what is mutually believed among participants in a conversation helps to shape assertoric practice, can be found outside philosophy as well. For one thing, the case of philosophy is a special case of the phenomenon of epistemic groups; there are other epistemic groups, and so we should expect other examples in which mutually recognized membership in a relevant epistemic group will delimit the assertion-generated expectations that speakers and hearers have towards one another. For another thing, cases of discussions between members of an epistemic group are themselves special cases in their own right: many,

---

[10] I will return to this in Section 10.5, where I will use the "reasonable to assume" condition to modify the MBS principle itself.

and perhaps most, of our conversations are not as members of an epistemic group. In those cases, mutual belief shared among participants will either be *ad hoc* (formed in context) or formed in some other way; but if my hypothesis is correct, these will still be cases in which what is mutually believed in context sets the standard of the norm of assertion.

In fact, it is with these sorts of case in mind, where there is no relevant epistemic group in play, that we can reconsider *desideratum* (2). Earlier I claimed that a norm of assertion built around MBS can satisfy this *desideratum*, and so can accommodate the strength of the arguments made on behalf of thinking that the norm's standard is *knowledge* (or some other robustly epistemic property). I am now in a position to defend this claim, as follows. Having endorsed the Gricean claim that one should not assert that for which one lacks adequate evidence, my suggestion has been that adequacy of evidence ought to be determined in conjunction with the "purpose of the talk exchange" itself. One way to understand this is that speakers ought to make their contributions ones that are helpful to their audience. Insofar as the audience's needs and interests are matters of mutual belief between speaker and hearer, these needs and interests help to determine both what information would be helpful to the hearer, and what sort of evidence would be needed to warrant an assertion of the relevant content. This is the case in the example of Yang, in which two people speak to one another as members of a given epistemic group (academically trained philosophers). But now consider cases in which mutual belief is minimal: there is no relevant epistemic group in play, and no other basis for substantial mutual belief among participants in a speech exchange. In such cases, the speaker will not be in a position to tell either what information would be useful to the hearer, or what the hearer wants to do with it. In such circumstances, I submit, there will be upward pressure on the standard for warranted assertion. This is for the simple reason that, in these circumstances, the speaker will have to make assertions which are such that, *no matter the hearer's informational needs*, the speaker's epistemic standing on the content asserted will satisfy whatever (reasonable) epistemic demands the hearer might have. But this means that the speech contribution will have to be helpful in this way even if the hearer's (reasonable) needs require a high epistemic standard to be met.[11] Under these conditions, knowledge would appear to be required. We might model this point by saying that knowledge is the norm's "default setting"—its setting when what is mutually believed is not robust enough to adjust the standard in any particular way. But whether we choose to model the point in this way, my present claim is simply that the context-sensitive account I am offering has the resources to accept that (and to explain why) knowledge is the relevant standard for assertion in a good number of the conversations in which we make assertions. The account thus can claim to capture much of what motivates the

---

[11] Here I assume simply that there are many reasonable needs a hearer might have that would require a high degree of epistemic authoritativeness on the part of the speaker.

knowledge norm,[12] and can indeed accept knowledge as the relevant standard in many, perhaps even most, contexts.

I have just suggested that it is the interlocutors' respective lack of knowledge of each others' interests and needs that exerts upward pressure on the standard, with the result that knowledge is the standard required. But it is possible to present the present proposal (to the effect that knowledge is the norm's "default setting") from the reverse direction.[13] To do so, we might start by noting that the typical case of assertoric speech exchange is one in which what interlocutors want from each others' assertions is knowledge. If this much is correct, then knowledge would be required unless particular expectations were somehow to affect this default. The suggestion here is that knowledge is the default standard from the outset, and is adjusted lower (or higher) only if there are overriding expectations in the context.

I confess that I am uncertain as to which is the better explanation. But this need not deter us here, since, in either case, we have an account on which knowledge is the "default setting" of the norm of assertion. And this is all that we need to see how MBS itself, together with the hypothesis that philosophers constitute an epistemic group, can be used to respond to our original problem in a way that satisfies *desiderata* (1) and (3) as well.

Take *desideratum* (1) first, which is the desire not to weaken the epistemic norm of assertion to the point of practical irrelevance. I have just argued that, by the lights of MBS, we would predict that in contexts of minimal or no mutual belief, the prevailing standard will be as demanding as knowledge. In fact, MBS would predict that this standard will prevail in *any* context in which what is mutually believed is minimal.[14] In addition, in any case in which it is mutually acknowledged that the hearer is in need of knowledge, this will be the prevailing standard. To the extent that these cases are prevalent in ordinary, everyday life, MBS will not weaken the epistemic norm of assertion to the point of irrelevance; to the contrary, it will hold it up high.

Still, it might be wondered whether cases of minimal relevant mutual belief are prevalent in ordinary, everyday life. And here one might think that my position faces a dilemma. Either such cases of minimal mutual belief are prevalent, in which case my account can satisfy *desideratum* (1) (and so will keep the epistemic standard on assertion, E, substantial) but will fail to satisfy *desideratum* (3) (and so will fail to sanction the assertions that, intuitively, are warranted); or else such cases are not prevalent, in which case my account can satisfy *desideratum* (3) but not *desideratum* (1). In response, I want to highlight the context-sensitivity of MBS, together with the idea

---

[12] Much, but not all. For example, one might wonder how a context-sensitive account can handle the data from Moorean paradoxicality, introduced in Chapter 6, Section 6.5. I will return to this in Chapter 11.
[13] With thanks to Miranda Fricker for the suggestion that follows.
[14] Here I am silent as between the two explanations offered previously for the phenomenon whereby knowledge is the norm whenever mutual belief is minimal—the one being that minimal mutuality exerts upward pressure on the standard, and the other being that minimal mutuality is not a sufficiently robust basis for adjusting an already-in-place default of knowledge.

that assertoric practice within philosophy really is far from the standard instance of the production and consumption of assertion. One of the most common uses for the speech act of assertion is in satisfying others' informational needs; and the most common sort of need is a need (not just for information backed by good arguments and reasonable defenses, but rather) for *knowledge*. In this respect, what philosophers expect of one who advances a claim—namely, dialectically substantial reasons that are sensitive to the force of prevailing objections—is far from the standard expectations we have of assertions generally. In most cases it suffices to establish the warrant of one's assertion that one has the corresponding piece of knowledge; and further, it is sufficient to establish that one has the knowledge by citing a sanctioned source (such as perception, or understanding, or trust of a trustworthy speaker, or . . .) as the source from which one obtained the information. In such cases, warranted assertion need not require being in possession of substantial reasons on behalf of what was asserted, nor need it require having anticipated (and being prepared to reply to) a host of objections. In this respect at least, assertions in philosophical contexts are far from ordinary.[15] But insofar as academically trained philosophers are an epistemic group, they will have a rich stock of mutual belief as setting their mutual expectations, and in this sort of context the standards do adjust. In this way, MBS satisfies (3); and since it takes a good deal of mutual belief among participants to adjust the standards in this way, and since in other cases the standards remain high (unless adjusted by still further mutual belief), MBS satisfies (1) as well.

I conclude, then, that MBS offers the prospects for replying to our original difficulty, in a way that satisfies all of the *desiderata* (1)–(3). I now want to argue that it is not MBS as it stands, but a slightly modified version, that is defensible.

10.4 Objections and Replies: What Is Reasonably Regarded as Mutually Believed

I have been arguing for MBS, according to which the standard for warranted assertion is fixed in a context-sensitive fashion, by way of what is mutually believed in context. I have been trying to motivate this claim by appeal to a Gricean orientation on speech exchanges: the suggestion is that MBS can be seen as a special case of the Cooperative Principle, applied to the "adequate evidence" condition in the submaxim of Quality. It is important to me that the proposal can be motivated in this way: it provides support that is independent of the support provided by the fact (if it is a fact) that MBS enables us to respond to our original difficulty while simultaneously satisfying *desiderata* (1)–(3). Still, I recognize that, as a thesis about the norm of assertion, MBS will not be uncontroversial. In this section I aim to address several objections that might be leveled against it. I will argue that, while several of them do point out some costs of the

---

[15] With thanks to Michael Brady for indicating the need for this comment.

proposal, none of them succeeds in undermining it. Or rather, none of them succeeds in undermining a slight variant on MBS, the motivation for which will be apparent as we deal with the objections.

I begin first with an objection based on the contention that parties to a discussion cannot always tell whether there is a background of mutual belief. By itself, this contention need not amount to an objection: insofar as participants to a speech exchange are uncertain whether there is mutual belief, they will not be warranted in proceeding on the assumption that there is mutual belief, in which case the "default setting" for the norm will prevail. Still, one might try to work this contention into an objection by considering cases in which there is (not merely uncertainty but) disagreement in the respective parties' beliefs regarding what is mutually believed. Cases of this sort might be thought to raise an objection to MBS, on the grounds that MBS can offer no plausible verdict on such cases.

In reaction I submit that, far from constituting an objection to MBS, such cases can actually be used to support MBS: not only does MBS offer verdicts in such cases, what is more, the verdicts it yields are independently plausible. Take a situation in which one or more parties to a discussion has/have false beliefs regarding what is mutually believed in context. In such cases the two sides will not be calibrated in their respective expectations regarding the assertions being made by the other side. It will be helpful to have a schematic case before us. Suppose that speaker S, taking herself to be speaking to fellow philosophers on a topic which (she thinks) all will acknowledge as deeply controversial, holds that the standards in play will be those governing philosophical exchanges. Accordingly, S assumes that her assertions are governed by a "reasonable by philosophical standards" norm; and accordingly, S expects that H's expectations regarding S's assertions will be adjusted accordingly. However, audience H's expectations have not been calibrated to S's. On the contrary, H regards the context as one in which there is little or no relevant mutual belief. Consequently, H expects that, given the minimal mutual belief, S's assertions must meet suitably high epistemic standards (knowledge perhaps). (Assume that H cannot tell, merely from S's assertion, that the context is one of philosophy.) Clearly, S's and H's mutual expectations are not aligned; this is a case involving a failure of calibration.

Now let us ask: supposing S to assert that p under conditions of this sort of calibration failure, is S's assertion warranted or not? The objection we are presently considering holds that the proponent of MBS has nothing plausible to say in answering this question. But this is not so. I submit that, in cases of calibration failure, the question 'Warranted or not?' cannot be answered prior to determining the epistemic status of the beliefs that generated S's and H's respective expectations—and this will depend, in turn, on the prevalence and salience of the relevant groups and group practices. For example, suppose that S and H are at a philosophy convention, and that S's assertions are of propositions which anyone educated in philosophy would be aware are philosophical in nature. Then it would seem that S's underwriting beliefs—the beliefs underwriting S's expectations regarding H—are reasonable, whereas H's underwriting beliefs—the beliefs underwriting H's expectations regarding S—are not. In that case, we can say this: while S's beliefs regarding what was mutually believed were false, still, they were reasonable; whereas H's beliefs regarding what was mutually believed were not only false but unreasonable; and so, regarding the standard to apply to the case, we favor what S took to be mutually believed. To be sure, endorsing this verdict means replacing MBS with a view according to which what it is *reasonable* to regard as mutually believed is what sets the standard, as follows:

> RMBS   When it comes to a particular assertion that p, the relevant warranting authority regarding p depends in part on *what it would be reasonable for all parties to believe* is mutually believed among them (regarding such things as the participants' interests and informational needs, and the prospects for high-quality information in the domain in question).[16]

Given RMBS's standard, S's assertion was warranted (supposing of course that it met the threshold of philosophical defensibility). Of course, if the situation were otherwise—S and H do not know each other, they meet on the street, there are no grounds to assume that they share a philosophical background, and so on—then it would be H's underwriting beliefs that are reasonable, not S's. In this case we should conclude that the standard of assertion's norm is fixed by what H took to be mutually believed, and so S's assertion was unwarranted.

It is worth noting that, as a modification of MBS, RMBS can be motivated in Gricean terms in precisely the way that MBS itself was. Insofar as speech is a rational, cooperative activity, it stands to reason that the standards ought to be those that reasonable practitioners follow. In saying this, we abstract away from what speech participants actually believe regarding what is mutually believed in context, to what they *ought* (reasonably) to believe is mutually believed in context.[17] One might wonder how to determine what ought to be believed in this respect. This is a fair question. But this should be no more concerning to us than is the question when "evidence" counts as "adequate"—a question that any Gricean will have to face in any case. In this manner we can see that, while the move from MBS to RMBS does involve a modification, it is no departure from the Gricean picture itself.[18]

Still, the move to endorse RMBS raises a question: what should be said of cases in which both sides' underwriting beliefs are (not merely false) but equally reasonable (alternatively: equally unreasonable)? For surely there can be such cases. Simply imagine that, though they are in the lobby of a hotel that is currently hosting

---

[16] Compare RMBS's "reasonableness" standard to that in Lawlor (2013). (Lawlor's interest is not in assertion *per se*, but rather in those assertions of the form 'I know that p.' Still, despite this difference in focus, Lawlor's account motivates a "reasonableness" standard in a way for which I have some sympathy.)

[17] For the sort of "ought" that is in play here, see my (forthcoming b).

[18] I am indebted to Miranda Fricker for the suggestion that I make the present point. (In addition, once again I refer the reader to Benton (forthcoming) for some reasons to think that the proposal is not as Gricean in spirit as I am laying out here.)

a philosophy conference, still, there are many people other than philosophers mingling there; neither S nor H dress in any way that identifies them as philosopher or non-philosopher; H is not aware that there is a philosophy conference going on, and this ignorance is not unreasonable; and so forth. Then if S, taking H to be a philosopher, starts talking philosophy, it seems that their case is one in which both sides' underwriting beliefs are both false and equally reasonable. Here I think that the proponent of RMBS should simply acknowledge that there may be no fact of the matter regarding the warrantedness of the assertion. Nor do I regard this as an unhappy thing to have to say; I think that it captures a real fact: namely, that under conditions in which two sides err regarding what they mutually believe, where both sides' underwriting beliefs are equally reasonable, it seems simply wrong to think that there is some fact of the matter that determines the relevant standard to apply to the speaker's assertion.

Still, a related objection remains. This objection—better, this bundle of objections—derives from the fact that in many conversations there are multiple epistemic groups with which individual participants might identify in a given case. The point can be made about speakers, audiences, or both. Thus a speaker might be addressing her audience as a politician, as a citizen of this town or this region, and so on, and/or as a member of a particular profession; and there might be different possible candidate mutual beliefs corresponding to each of these groups. What is more, her audience might identify themselves in any of these or other ways, again with different possible candidate mutual beliefs corresponding to each. But there is still more: audiences often include many people, where there is no single epistemic group with which all identify, and where most in the audience identify with many different epistemic groups. In such complicated cases, what determines the mutual belief that sets the norm of assertion? Again, this turns from a question into an objection if the proponent of RMBS has no plausible answer to this question.

But I think that we already have the basis for a reply. Consider first a case of multiple-member audiences. There are at least two variants of this case. In the first, the speaker aims to be addressing a particular epistemic group; in the second, she does not. The first variant can be treated as a special case of the situation discussed at the end of the previous subsection: if the salience of the group she meant to be addressing is great enough, so that it was reasonable to form the underwriting beliefs she did, and reasonable to expect that at least the relevant members of her audience would discern this, then the corresponding standard is in play; and if not, then the case can be treated as previously discussed (so that there may be no fact of the matter regarding the prevailing standard). The second variant, in which the speaker does not aim to be addressing any particular group in the multi-member audience, can be assimilated into a case of no substantial mutual belief—the standard will be the "default" high standard. Note that this gives us a sense of how to handle the sort of case in which the speaker herself identifies with several groups. Again, if one identification is salient, then this group's standards prevail; if not, there may be no fact of the matter regarding the prevailing standard; or, if it is clear that she aimed to be speaking to everyone, the standard will be the "default" high standard.[19]

To be sure, these accounts would need to be developed in greater detail; my point here is only that nothing in this sort of objection presents an in-principle difficulty for the proponent of RMBS.

I turn, finally, to an objection which, if successful, *does* present an in-principle difficulty for the proponent of RMBS. This objection focuses on RMBS's implications for what we might call 'epistemically degenerate groups' (such as conspiracy theory groups of all sorts). If RMBS is correct, the objection holds, then there are cases in which assertions are warranted on virtually no grounds whatsoever. To see this, consider the possibility of a group of conspiracy theorists who have (underwriting beliefs generating) undemanding epistemic expectations of one another. Call this group The Conspirators. Imagine that the members of The Conspirators have all sorts of mutual beliefs about what counts as adequate evidence, when conspiracy hypotheses are warranted, and so forth (where these standards are, by our lights, very poor); and assume as well that they share (and recognize that they share) any number of assumptions about conspiracies they take to be real. Then if RMBS is true, these mutual beliefs shape assertoric practice among members of the group; and insofar as assertions conform to the standard that their underwriting beliefs pick out, their assertions are (by the lights of RMBS) warranted. But (the objection contends) this seems just wrong: if they make assertions regarding such-and-such a conspiracy, where the evidence behind these assertions is (we think) objectively weak, surely an account of the norm of assertion should return the verdict that these assertions are unwarranted. RMBS appears to lack the resources to deliver this verdict.

In response, I want to say that even if RMBS is guilty as charged, the charge is not as bad as it seems. For even if RMBS is guilty as charged, we can still level a variety of criticisms against the assertoric practices of The Conspirators. To see this, suppose that RMBS *is* guilty as charged: when speaking with each other, The Conspirators' assertions about this-or-that conspiracy are warranted whenever these assertions meet the group's (by our lights, poor) epistemic standards. Those of us who reject their epistemic standards are not without recourse to criticizing the group and its assertoric practice (albeit not by way of criticizing the assertions they make to one another).

For one thing, since we do not share The Conspirators' standards, The Conspirators cannot appeal to their own standards to warrant assertions when the assertions are made in contexts in which *non*-Conspirators are in the audience. In such cases, assuming that there is minimal mutual belief, RMBS will set the standard at "default" and so will deliver the verdict that such assertions are unwarranted. I do not assume that audiences can fix standards however high they like (a recipe for disaster, given the perpetual

---

[19] This point would lead us to predict that assertions made in print, where one cannot be certain of one's audience or the purposes to which they will put the information they come to endorse, will typically answer to the default standard.

possibility of philosophical skeptics amongst our audiences). I assume, rather, that any *reasonable* interest an audience has can contribute to the fixing of standards in conversations in which they are participants. To be sure, we would need an independent account of reasonableness here. While I cannot pretend to have such an account, my hope is that it is intuitive to think that the informational interests of the philosophical skeptic are not reasonable conversational starting points—at least when we are outside philosophical contexts themselves. If this much is true, then we can say that The Conspirators' conspiracy assertions are warranted only when speaking to one another, not when engaging the world at large. And I, for one, find this a tolerable implication: we might describe this as a case where they have a very non-standard (by our lights, degenerate) assertoric practice in place. (We might even go on to predict that groups with very non-standard assertoric practices will not last very long, unless they can convince many others outside their group to "join in"—hence such groups will be the exception rather than the norm.)

Still, one might wonder whether this is a tolerable implication. The key question is this: why think that (in cases in which co-Conspirators are speaking to one another) we need to accept their standards, rather than impose our own on them? If we impose our own standards on them, we might well acknowledge that they are making assertions, but we will say that these assertions are systematically unwarranted (no matter who the audience is, and no matter what epistemic expectations that audience has).

Let us consider, then, what can be said on behalf of an account of their assertoric practice that regards the proper standards (at least in cases of within-group assertion) as set by what The Conspirators themselves mutually believe in context. For one thing, such an account squares with the fact that the expectations they have of one another are deeply out of synch with our own. True, one might recoil at the idea that their within-group assertions are warranted. But—and this is the second point I wish to make in response to the objection—we can still criticize their standards, and with it the assertoric practice governed by those standards, *even after we acknowledge that the practice has its own internal coherence* (when the practice is restricted to members of that community).

Consider how we might criticize The Conspirators' assertions: we might criticize their standards themselves. We can do so even as we allow that, by the lights of those standards, their assertions pass muster when restricted to within-group contexts. To be sure, we will regard their assertions as unwarranted. But recall that this point is compatible with RMBS: it is only *within-group* assertions that RMBS must regard as warranted (when they meet The Conspirators' standards). So long as we are thinking of their assertions as assertions made *to us*—that is, to non-Conspirators who do not share their epistemic standards—their assertions are unwarranted. It is only when we are describing the practice of their making assertions to one another that RMBS delivers the verdict that their assertions are warranted. Of course, even this might be too much for some. But three points should mitigate the concerns here.

First, given that assertions are "public" in the sense I characterized in Chapter 8, there will be some pressure on any Conspirator to satisfy a more demanding norm—at least if he is to have any hope of relevance beyond the narrow conspiratorial world in which he lives. For insofar as The Conspirators' assertoric practices are themselves informed by what most everyone else will regard as a degenerate epistemic standard, the Conspirator who makes a within-group assertion can have no hope of anything other than being dismissed by the world at large. This suggests that epistemic groups with degenerate standards are not likely to have much influence, and so are not likely to persist in the greater world.[20] In any case, the acknowledgment that their within-group assertions are warranted will not have such negative effects on the speech community at large.

But there is a second consideration we can use to mitigate the badness of RMBS's implication that within-group assertions of The Conspirators are warranted. Consider how we would describe the situation if we assume that knowledge (or some other demanding but invariant standard) is the norm of assertion. We will say that The Conspirators' conspiratorial assertions are systematically unwarranted (a plus); but we will still need to explain the relative stability of their practice, the fact that they all appear to have calibrated their standards with one another, that they have very similar warrantedness judgments regarding their assertions. To be sure, the explanation is near to hand: The Conspirators have many (implicit) mutual beliefs regarding prevailing standards; only (the knowledge-norm proponent will add) those beliefs are *systematically false*. Here I only note that, once it is an open question whether there is one standard governing any assertion made at any time and in any place, this construal of their practice is no longer the only one. Nor is it a particularly charitable one. It seems decidedly more charitable to explain the stability and systematic nature of their practice as a matter of their embracing different standards, and then to register our disapproval of those standards themselves. At the very least, such a position is far less objectionable than we might have thought, on first confronting this objection.

This last point is reinforced by a third sort of criticism one might level at The Conspirators even after one acknowledges that their conspiracy assertions to one another are (sometimes) warranted. There is a distinction to be drawn between an assertion itself (an instantiation of a speech-act type) and the proposition asserted on a given occasion. RMBS bears on the question regarding the warrantedness of the former; it says nothing of the warrantedness of the latter. But for this very reason, we might direct our attention to the propositions that The Conspirators assert, and we can criticize the basis for believing that these propositions are true. We can do so even if, as proponents of RMBS, we allow that their within-group assertions are warranted. We might speak amongst ourselves, saying: "Well, of course that is what a Conspirator

---

[20] Interestingly, philosophical practice here is not in the same boat: whereas The Conspirators are operating in a domain in which there is a good deal of evidence, philosophy takes place in a context of diminished epistemic hopes. When this fact of diminished epistemic hopes becomes the object of mutual belief, it affects *everyone's* expectations about assertoric practice in this domain. The Conspirators are not in the same position.

would say, they have seriously impoverished standards for their assertions!" In saying this, we are criticizing their epistemic standards: we reject their standards (and so might reject their assertoric practices, informed as they are by those standards). But it is one thing to say that we reject their standards, and another to say that there is no assertoric practice correctly describable in terms of those standards. The present objection requires the latter, stronger claim. In light of the facts, first, that this stronger claim is in effect committed to what I called previously the uncharitable construal of their practice, and second, that even after we reject this stronger claim we can still criticize The Conspirators in all sorts of ways, I submit that it is best, all things considered, to regard The Conspirators' assertoric practice as RMBS would. I concede that this is at a cost; but, all things considered, this cost is outweighed by the other benefits of RMBS.

I conclude, then, that while the objections suggest the need to replace MBS with RMBS, there is no objection which undermines RMBS itself. This said, I acknowledge that the objections considered here, and in particular the objection from epistemically degenerate groups, do make clear that RMBS does have some striking implications (and comes at some cost). But given what RMBS has going for it, and given that these costs are not as great as one might have initially feared, the case for RMBS remains strong.

10.5 Conclusion

I believe that there are several lessons to be drawn from the foregoing reflections. First, even if assertions continue to be made in the face of systematic disagreement, and even if under these circumstances there can be little hope for knowledge or even doxastically justified belief, this does not establish that such assertions are systematically unwarranted. This is because the norm of assertion may well reflect the standing expectations that hearers have of speakers, and that speakers have of hearers, when there is mutual belief between them in a given speech exchange. Such a context-sensitive account of the standard fixed by the norm of assertion receives independent support from a broadly Gricean approach to speech. Such an approach, together with the hypothesis that (academically trained) philosophers form an epistemic group whose epistemic expectations of one another are highly calibrated, enables us to see how philosophical assertions can be warranted even when made under conditions of systematic disagreement—without at the same time lowering the norm of assertion to an unacceptably low standard.

11
The Costs of Context-Sensitivity

11.1 Implications of Context-Sensitivity in the Standard for Warranted Assertion

This book has explored, developed, and defended MMENA—the hypothesis that it is mutually manifest to competent speakers that assertion is governed by an epistemic norm. In the first eight chapters I developed the explanatory power of MMENA without saying anything more specific about the precise content of the norm itself, beyond assuming that the standard of the norm itself was robustly epistemic. The advantage of this way of proceeding is that it enabled me to explore the explanatory virtues of the hypothesis that assertion is governed by a norm, without becoming bogged down in squabbles over what the norm is—a matter on which a good deal of ink has already been spilled. In this way I hope to be articulating virtues upon which all proponents of the norm-based approach to assertion can agree.[1] In the previous two chapters, by contrast, I defended the ideas that the norm's standard is fixed in a context-sensitive way, and that the mechanism for the fixation of the standard is what is mutually believed in context by the parties to the speech exchange. To be sure, the conclusion for which I argued in the previous chapter implies that there are contexts in which the contextually fixed standard, while still epistemic, is not *robustly* so—and this is a modification of the assumption framing the first eight chapters. But even so, these two theses—MMENA, and the thesis articulating my context-sensitive (mutual belief) account of the norm's standard—amount to the full picture of assertion on offer. Still, it might be wondered how these two theses fit together. In particular, how do the arguments that I have offered on behalf of MMENA, as well as the various explanations I used MMENA to provide, comport with the idea that the requirement imposed by the norm of assertion is fixed in a context-sensitive fashion? On this score, there are a variety of questions that arise. My aim in this concluding chapter is to address these matters.

The questions I will be discussing—questions regarding the coherence of my two core theses—can be raised in connection with the provocative claim at the heart of the previous two chapters. That claim, which was the conclusion of my discussion of

---

[1] At least those proponents who agree that the norm's content is epistemic. Proponents of the truth norm, for example, are not among the beneficiaries. Proponents of the belief norm may be, according to whether they also endorse an epistemic norm on belief (on the model of Bach 2008).

systematic peer disagreement, was that an assertion can be warranted even under conditions in which the speaker *is not justified in believing what she asserts*. I have no doubt but that this claim will strike many as deeply contentious. I did my best to try to defend the claim against various objections in Chapter 10. In this chapter, however, I address objections (not to this claim taken by itself, but rather) to the coherence of this claim with one or more of the claims I have made on behalf of MMENA. For one thing, we might wonder about its coherence with what I have had to say about the epistemic significance of assertion: how does the provocative claim (that it can be warranted to assert what one would not be justified in believing) square with the role that assertion plays in the spread of knowledge, or the role of assertion in generating speaker responsibilities and hearer entitlements? We can note as well that if assertion can be warranted even under conditions in which the speaker is not justified in believing what she asserts, then it is false that all warranted assertion is belief-worthy; and so we can ask how to understand what in earlier chapters I called the *belief-worthiness purport* of assertion. Finally, if it can be warranted to assert what one would not be justified in believing, we appear forced to say that there can be cases of warranted assertion in which the speaker is either *irrational* (believing what she ought not to) or *insincere* (not believing what she asserts). Neither option seems particularly attractive; and so we might wonder whether the provocative claim itself might be unacceptable after all.

In this chapter I aim to address these concerns. To do so I will trace out the implications of my context-sensitive approach to assertion. And I will go on to argue that, in most cases, these implications, far from being objectionable, are plausible on independent grounds—features rather than bugs, as it were. In 'most' cases, though not all: there are some costs to going context-sensitive. My claim will be merely that these costs are outweighed by the benefits.

11.2 The Significance of Speech Context

I want to begin this chapter by characterizing the scope of the problems that I will be addressing. To do so, it will be helpful to have a simple version of my account of assertion before us. As noted, that account involves two claims. The first is MMENA—a claim to the effect that the following is mutually manifest to all competent language speakers:

ENA S must: assert p, only if S satisfies epistemic condition E with respect to p; that is, only if E(S, [p]).

The second is the hypothesis that the standard is fixed in a context-sensitive fashion, in terms of what is reasonably regarded as mutually believed in context:

RMBS When it comes to a particular assertion that p, the relevant warranting authority regarding p depends in part on what it would be reasonable for all parties to believe is mutually believed among them (regarding such things as the participants' interests and informational needs, and the prospects for high-quality information in the domain in question).

The resulting picture, I argued, is this. Absent reasons to think that there is anything special in play, the "default" standard is knowledge. In Chapter 10 I argued that the hypothesis that there is such a default standard, and that it is knowledge, can be motivated in either of two ways. The first is to note that knowledge is what we standardly expect of one another in ordinary circumstances. On this motivation, the default stands unless there is substantial mutual belief which adjusts the standard. The second motivation for the hypothesis that knowledge is the default standard is to note that if an assertion is to be helpful under conditions of minimal mutual belief, then having the relevant authority will need to satisfy the hearer's needs *whatever* she might reasonably expect in the way of the speaker's epistemic standing on the asserted content—and, since her expectations might demand knowledge, this will exert upward pressure on the standard. On this motivation, mutual belief is required if the standard is to be less than knowledge, since in the absence of substantial mutual belief the upward pressure will fix the standard as knowledge.

Suppose something like this picture is correct. The result is that cases in which the standard requires something less than knowledge will be those in which mutual belief is sufficiently robust to affect this change. There is some reason to suppose that these cases will be the exception to the rule.

An initial point that can be made on this score is that not all cases in which mutual belief is substantial are cases in which the standards will be affected. Often it is the case that what is mutually believed in context supports a demanding standard such as knowledge. Consider what one expects when one asks for directions, or for the time; when one inquires about the details of a commercial transaction; when one asks what is on the menu today. In each of these types of case and many more, one expects nothing less than a knowledgeable reply; or, failing that, some explicit hedge indicating the speaker's less-than-full confidence. What is more, there are many other types of circumstance in which nothing but knowledge will do—as when it is mutually believed that the stakes are high (there is a huge disutility for being wrong), or that the hearer is placing his full trust in the speaker (expecting that she will not let him down). Given this wide variety of cases in which what is mutually believed supports a standard of knowledge—and the foregoing list was not meant to be exhaustive—the result is that the requirements on warranted assertion weaken only under very restricted circumstances: not only is there substantial mutual belief, but this mutual belief includes beliefs regarding, for example, the difficulty or practical impossibility of acquiring epistemically high-grade information, as well as a continued mutual desire for informational exchange despite the epistemically inhospitable circumstance. In virtually any other circumstance, the "default" setting will be in place, and so there will be no worries of the sort described previously.

I have been minimizing the prevalence of the phenomenon whereby mutual belief will adjust the standard for warranted assertion so that it is weaker than knowledge. While the point of my doing so might be easily anticipated—later I will argue that the sorts of explanation I have offered in Chapters 2 and 3 regarding the epistemic significance of assertion are still widely in place, even after we accept RMBS—still, this move to minimize the prevalence of the phenomenon raises a challenge of its own. For now we might well wonder: if situations in which standards vary from the default are exceptional, why should we bother to endorse the hypothesis of context-sensitivity in the first place? Why should we not rather accept an invariant norm (such as knowledge) and explain away these exceptional cases as needed? What is to be achieved by going context-sensitive? This is a fair question.[2] But it is based on a misunderstanding of the motivation for the move to endorsing a context-sensitive account of the standard. My main motivation for this move is not to be able to account for the exceptional cases (which would be a bad methodology in any case). Rather, my main motivation is that I think it emerges naturally out of a Gricean picture of speech exchanges. Once one sees such exchanges as a rational, cooperative activity, one is already seeing these exchanges as taking place against a rich background of mutual belief and mutual expectation. Grice himself was clear about the phenomenon of mutuality when it comes to the production and apprehension of conversational implicatures. What I have added was the idea that a very similar thing can be seen to be in play when it comes to discerning the adequacy of one's epistemic position on a given proposition (see Chapter 10). Cooperativeness requires that (absent overriding reason not to do so) one provide one's audience with what is wanted in the way of information, in such a way that it is clear that this is what one is doing. When it is mutually manifest that the conversation is taking place under conditions of epistemically diminished hopes, and mutually manifest as well that both parties want to continue the conversational exchange, the very picture of Gricean cooperativeness would predict that both speaker and hearer adjust their epistemic expectations accordingly. It is this that motivates the context-sensitivity in my account. That the resulting picture can accommodate the phenomenon of assertion in cases of systematic disagreement is a bonus.

With this understood, I can now move on to see how context-sensitivity affects such things as the epistemic significance of assertion (its role in the spread of knowledge; its generation of speaker responsibilities and hearer entitlements; the beliefworthiness of assertion), as well as the nature of assertoric sincerity. While the implications of context-sensitivity on these matters will be far-reaching, they will be defensible for all that.

---

[2] Indeed, variants of this objection have been posed to me, in conversation, by Jennifer Lackey and Tim Williamson.

11.3 The Epistemic Significance of Assertion, Reconsidered

Suppose, then, that assertoric practice is governed by a context-sensitive (epistemic) norm whose default is knowledge, where it is only under very specific circumstances, in which the relevant mutually possessed attitudes are in place, that this default is overridden. (Here, mutual attitudes will be "relevant" when they include a continued desire for informational exchange and a recognition of the need for less demanding epistemic expectations from speakers.) In that case it is easy to appreciate the characteristic epistemic significance of assertion: its role in the spread of knowledge, its generating the characteristic entitlements and responsibilities associated with testimony, and its characteristic of belief-worthiness.

Consider first assertion's role in the spread of knowledge. Whenever the default is in place, an assertion is warranted only if knowledgeable. In such cases, the sort of account I offered in Chapter 2 is in place. What is more, since deviations from the default are cases in which it would be reasonable for the speech participants to regard the relevant mutual attitudes as in play, deviations from the default should not fool any reasonable participant into misevaluating the situation. Thus we might see the role of assertion in the spread of knowledge as emerging quite naturally out of the mutual-belief-based norm which I have proposed: hearers are entitled to regard assertions as answering to a robustly epistemic norm unless it would be reasonable to suppose otherwise, where this would be a matter of what is reasonable to suppose is mutually believed in context. While this picture does amount to a tweaking of the account offered in Chapter 2, the core of the picture I offered there remains in place.

Indeed, the picture on offer would appear to be confirmed by a prediction which, while surprising, turns out to be true. Our picture would predict that there are cases in which hearers are not entitled to expect knowledgeableness on the part of a speaker who has just asserted that p. This rather surprising prediction, though, turns out to be true (or so I submit). For this is precisely what we find in contexts like that mentioned in Benton (2012), where one speaker is offering a prediction; and we would also expect it when an assertion is made under conditions in which epistemically diminished hopes are mutually manifest. In the latter respect, philosophical assertions offer a case in point. No reasonable philosopher would move to accept another philosopher's assertion merely on the strength of their say-so! On the contrary, the reasonable philosopher will recognize his philosophical interlocutor's assertion for what it is: something backed by her relevant authority, but where the promise of that authority is recognized as that merely of being able to defend the claim advanced to some threshold of philosophical adequacy. (After all, that is the standard that is in place given what is mutually believed in context.) It is striking in this regard to appreciate that the reaction "How do you know that?" is typically *not* a proper response to a claim advanced in a recognizably philosophical setting.[3]

---

[3] But see McKinnon (2012), where it is suggested that "How do you know?" queries do not actually query one's knowledge so much as they query one's epistemic grounds.

To confirm this, one need only spend time at a philosophy conference.[4] What we find is that the standard reactions to philosophical assertions are "What is your argument for that?" or "On what basis do you say that?"

It is also easy to appreciate how to accommodate context-sensitivity in the account offered in Chapter 3 regarding assertion's role in generating the characteristic entitlements and responsibilities associated with testimony. Because knowledge is the default, and because the mechanism by which this default can be adjusted is provided by (what it is reasonable to assume is) mutual belief, the result is that assertions will generate speaker responsibilities and hearer entitlements. In any situation in which it is not reasonable to think that standards have been adjusted, a speaker who asserts that p will inherit the responsibility for knowing that p, and the hearer will inherit the entitlement to regard the speaker as (responsible for) knowing that p—precisely as in the account offered in Chapter 3. But when it is reasonable in context to suppose that there are relevant mutual attitudes affecting the standards, the corresponding responsibilities and entitlements will be adjusted so as to match the standards in play. Indeed, it is precisely this that we see when we recognize that philosophers do not expect knowledge from other philosophers' philosophical assertions. When I advance my philosophical claim that p, my philosophical interlocutors hold me responsible for being in a position to be able to defend this claim to a level of philosophical adequacy. Again, this is the sort of authoritativeness that is promised by an assertion made in such a context.

From this it should be clear, too, how to adjust the account I offered for assertion's purport of belief-worthiness. Again, in settings in which the default standard is in place, assertion purports to be belief-worthy as it answers to a demanding standard (knowledge). In settings in which mutual belief adjusts the standard, assertion's purport of belief-worthiness is correspondingly affected—since assertions purport to be belief-worthy only to the extent that the standards in play make belief reasonable. Again, this picture would lead us to predict that, when standards have been affected owing to mutual expectations of epistemically diminished hope, assertions made in such contexts will not even *purport* to be belief-worthy. But, while one might think it is surprising to learn that there can be assertions that are not (and that do not even promise to be) belief-worthy, in fact we find just this: as I noted previously, no philosopher accepts what another philosopher says merely because she said so. In fact, no philosopher regards p as belief-worthy merely because it is the conclusion of an interlocutor's apparently compelling argument. Rather, philosophers regard the assertion of the conclusion as belief-worthy only to the degree that its argumentative backing warrants belief in the conclusion proposition. But the assertion can be warranted for

---

[4] One might respond: the reason "How do you know that?" is not apt in response to an assertion made in a philosophical setting is precisely that assertions made in philosophical settings are made on the basis of arguments which precede the assertion. (Thus the speaker has already made clear the basis on which she is advancing the claim in question.) But this response fails to apply in cases in which a claim is advanced without any argumentative backing. As I noted in Chapters 9 and 10, this is an unavoidable part of philosophical practice.

all that—for this, all that is required is that the assertion satisfies the dialectical standards of philosophical practice. Again, what appears to be a surprising prediction of the model turns out to have confirming examples.

I submit, then, that the move to endorse a context-sensitive account of the standard of assertion's norm does not force us to repudiate the account I have offered of the epistemic significance of assertion. While some small adjustments in that account will need to be made, in each case these adjustments would seem to be independently motivated.

11.4 Sincerity in Assertion, Reconsidered

I turn now to the challenge of squaring the context-sensitive picture with a motivated understanding of assertoric sincerity. The challenge was this. On my context-sensitive picture of the norm of assertion there can be cases in which an assertion that p is warranted despite the fact that the speaker is not justified in believing that p. Thus it can seem that my account must endorse one of two unhappy verdicts in this case: either that there can be cases of warranted assertion of an irrational (unjustified) belief, or that there can be cases of warranted assertion in which the speaker does not believe what she asserted (hence is insincere). In response I want to use the context-sensitive account to argue that sincerity in assertion is not (always) a matter of believing what one asserts;[5] it is rather a matter of having the attitude that (given what is mutually believed in context) is required by the standard in play—since this is the attitude that one's audience is entitled to regard one as having (given that one performed the speech act one did). After defending this, I go on to argue that this rather significant adjustment in our conception of assertoric sincerity can be used to shed light on the practice of assertion in contexts of mutually acknowledged diminished epistemic hope. Once again, we will find confirming instances of what initially might have seemed to be a false prediction.

The point I wish to make on this score requires some digression into the nature of the attitude that is appropriate under conditions of diminished epistemic hope. To set up the digression, let us suppose (as I argued in Chapter 9) that it is not reasonable to believe propositions on matters regarding which there is systematic disagreement. (Call any such proposition a 'contested' proposition.) If our supposition is correct, then any belief in a contested proposition is unreasonable. Let us also suppose (as I argued in Chapter 10) that there are cases in which the assertion of a contested proposition is warranted. Putting these two suppositions together, we can conclude that there are cases in which it is warranted to assert a proposition which it would be unreasonable to believe. Unless we want to condemn everyone who asserts a contested proposition to unreasonableness—and if I am right, this would mean condemning any philosopher

---

[5] I am not the first person to have suggested this; see also Ridge (2006).

who persists in making philosophical claims in the face of systematic peer disagreement—we must allow that their doxastic attitude towards contested propositions is, or at any rate can be, something other than that of belief. But once we have agreed that belief in contested propositions is unreasonable, we immediately face the question whether *there is* a doxastic attitude which it would be reasonable to have towards such propositions. I want to answer this question in the affirmative; the attitude in question is that of *regarding-as-defensible*. In this section I develop this idea. As in the previous two chapters I will do so in connection with the philosophical practice of making claims under conditions of systematic disagreement; but the points I make in connection here will generalize to other cases of assertions made under conditions of diminished epistemic hope.

It will help to proceed at this point with a few uncontroversial comments about the nature of belief.[6] It is normatively inappropriate for a subject S to take an attitude of belief towards the proposition that p if S believes that the balance of evidence favors the hypothesis that not-p. Stronger still: taking an attitude of belief towards [p] is normatively inappropriate if S believes that the balance of evidence does not strongly support *either* that p, *or* that not-p. And even more strongly still: taking an attitude of belief towards [p] is normatively inappropriate if, given the state of the evidence, S *should* believe that the balance of evidence does not strongly support *either* that p, *or* that not-p. I take all of this as obvious.

Next, consider what is involved in having a view on a matter regarding which there is (acknowledged) systematic peer disagreement. (Since I discussed this at length in Chapter 9, here I will be brief.) Again, we will focus on the case of philosophy. So, let Ramirez be a philosopher who holds some view under conditions she recognizes as a systematic peer disagreement regarding the topic in question. If she is reasonable, Ramirez will recognize that the arguments on her side are not decisive; she will recognize that there are arguments on the other side that she is not in a position to refute. To be sure, she will regard the weight of the considerations supporting the opposition to be less than the weight of the considerations supporting her own view: if not, she is unreasonable in holding on to her view. But at the same time, she will acknowledge that her opponents do not agree with her on her weighting of the evidence. So even as Ramirez continues to hold on to and argue for her views in the face of this disagreement, she will acknowledge—or at any rate, she ought to acknowledge—that there are others who are equally smart, equally knowledgeable of the arguments and evidence, equally attentive and motivated to get things right, and who would be highly motivated to discern their errors if they could, but who nevertheless failed to do so, even having given the matter a good deal of their time and effort. But more than this: Ramirez will acknowledge—or at any rate she ought to acknowledge—that it is not only in the present case, but *in the entire history of the dispute*, that those who are in the wrong have not been brought to

---

[6] These comments are not intended as analyses of "belief," but rather as truisms to help us fix the attitude in question.

see the error(s) of their ways, despite the best efforts of those on the side of truth (as she sees it). And this conclusion, in turn, should tell Ramirez something about the discernibility of the sort(s) of truth and falsity that are at issue here. Even as she continues to endorse and defend her views, still, given the persisting systematic disagreement, she must acknowledge that truth and falsity here are *not easily discernible by very many people as smart as she is, as knowledgeable of the relevant arguments and evidence, who have had a good deal of time thinking about the relevant issues, who work in a manner that is at least somewhat independent of others, who are as highly motivated to endorse what is true as she is, and so on.* In these circumstances, I submit, she should not be particularly confident that she does have the truth on her side.[7]

I have just argued that when Ramirez holds views under conditions in which she acknowledges that there is systematic (peer) disagreement, she ought not to be particularly confident of the truth of her views. Then it seems to me that to precisely this degree her situation is like that of someone who regards the evidence bearing on whether p to be such as not to decisively tell in favor of either [p] or its negation. This is not to say that she regards it as an open question which side is better supported; to repeat, if that were her attitude, she should not have views on the matter at all.[8] Rather, my claim is that her views on the second-order question—which side is better supported by the total evidence?—do not have the sort of confidence that goes along with the attitude of *belief*. And if this is so, then Ramirez ought not to believe that p: such an attitude would be normatively inappropriate given the evidence.

Perhaps it will be wondered how it can be *reasonable* for one to continue to "have a view" on a matter regarding which one acknowledges that the total evidence does not warrant belief in either the hypothesis that p or its negation. But it is easy to see that these worries are misguided. Consider the attitude of *speculation*. (Or, if one thinks that speculation is a speech act, not an attitude, consider the attitude-type that constitutes the sincerity condition for this speech act. Call this "attitudinal speculation.") It is consistent with one's (attitudinally) speculating that p that one acknowledges that the total set of reasons and evidence bearing on whether p fail to warrant belief either way. To be sure, one who speculates that p will regard the balance of reasons as tipping in favor of the truth of [p], as against its negation.[9] Still, such a person might happily

---

[7] Compare the reasoning in Hajek (2007).

[8] I am not sure this is correct. Might not I defend a view which I regard as a "long shot," even as I acknowledge that it is less well supported by current evidence than is one of its competitors? Would this alone convict me of unreasonableness or irrationality? I do not think so. It seems to me that the decision to defend a view on a controversial matter in philosophy is as much a normative status—I thereby inherit the burden of defending it, that is, of providing positive reasons on its behalf, and fending off objections from other parties—as it is a judgment made on the basis of evidence. To be sure, if I do not think that it will turn out that the view I favor will ultimately be better supported by the evidence—perhaps by evidence to which no one currently has access, or by reasons which no one has thought of to date—then there seems something slightly perverse about my defending that view. In any case, I leave these details for future work.

[9] We might then construe attitudinal speculation as a matter of having a degree of belief that is above 0.5 (or at least above that of any of its competitors) but which is below the threshold for outright belief. I am sympathetic to this construal, but do not have the space to argue for it here.

concede that this balance in favor of [p] is not sufficiently strong as to warrant outright belief in [p]. Hence the attitude of speculation that p: one who attitudinally speculates that p regards [p] as more likely than [not-p], though also regards the total evidence as stopping short of warranting belief in [p]. It should be obvious that one's attitude on this score can be more or less reasonable: it is more reasonable to the degree that the evidential situation is as one takes it to be: namely, such as to make it more likely that [p], even as the evidence stops short of being supportive enough to warrant outright belief in [p]. What this shows is that there is a truth-directed attitude which can be reasonable even in the face of evidence which one acknowledges to fall short of warranting outright belief. The objection that there can be no such attitude, then, is groundless.

Still, it might be wondered whether the sort of attitude I am describing—an attitude in the family of *attitudinal speculation*—is anything like the attitude of those who have views on contested matters in philosophy. Many will object immediately that they believe their theories, *period*; to such folks, any attempt to characterize their attitude as other than belief is to be false to the facts.[10] However, my claims here are that they *should not* believe, and that in any case there is an attitudinal cousin of belief which is reasonable to have even under conditions of systematic disagreement and which captures much, if perhaps not all, of the things that are involved in "having a view" in philosophy.

To make good on this claim, I need to revisit what is involved in "having a view" in philosophy. (Here I ask the reader to keep in mind that "having a view" in philosophy is a stand-in for the sort of attitude that is appropriate towards a proposition under conditions of diminished epistemic hope.) Typically, the attitude present when one "has a view" in philosophy involves endorsing the view, and also being its *champion*[11]— which includes being committed to defending it as the occasion arises. This, I want to suggest, is the core of the attitude associated with having a view in philosophy: it is *to regard the view as defensible*. The attitude of regarding a view as defensible stretches a long way across a confidence interval. At one extreme, S regards a view as defensible when S regards it as true (perhaps because she has what she regards as decisive evidence in favor of the view). At the other extreme, S regards a view as defensible when, although S acknowledges that the reasons and evidence bearing on the question do not settle matters, and so do not warrant outright belief, still, the balance of reasons supports [p] over [not-p].[12] (There are cases between these extremes as well, of course.) One might take the latter sort of attitude in the face of acknowledged systematic disagreement. It is when one does so, I submit, that one's doxastic attitude should be seen as a species of (attitudinal) speculation—at least with respect to one's assessment of the evidential situation.

---

[10] I thank Diego Machuca for this point.
[11] I thank David Chalmers for suggesting (in conversation) the notion of *championing*, as capturing the sort of attitude I am trying to describe here.
[12] But see fn. 8 for a potentially very important qualification.

Still, there are some important differences between attitudinal speculation (*simpliciter*, as it were) and the attitude that corresponds to the endorsement and championing of a philosophical view (when this is done under conditions of systematic disagreement). One who endorses and champions a philosophical view is typically more motivated to persist in defense of the view when challenged, than is one who merely speculates that p. (We are more committed, and perhaps more emotionally attached, to our philosophical views, than we are to our speculations.) I grant this, but deny that it establishes anything very substantial. For even granting the point, it might only suggest that endorsing and championing a view under conditions of systematic disagreement is a *special case* of attitudinal speculation—one whose specialness consists (in part) of characteristic emotional overtones and the associated practical commitments. As noted, having a view in philosophy is in part a matter of championing the view, whereas one does not necessarily champion what one speculates to be the case. What is more, it is not hard to see how a species of attitudinal speculation with this sort of emotional-and-practical-commitment profile might emerge. If one takes oneself to have a deep appreciation of the total evidence bearing on the question of which one is speculating, one might well feel motivated to defend one's speculation against those who would speculate that the contrary is true. (It is in this way that it makes sense to speak of your being the view's champion.) What is more, there is also a sociological dimension to philosophical practice in this regard: since it is common knowledge that those who defend their views well do better in the profession, generally speaking, one will have a clear motive (and emotional investment) in defending one's views in philosophy. Finally, there is also a psychological dimension to philosophical practice in this regard: since many of the views we defend are views about such things as the nature of the good life, or justice, or beauty, or what is of ultimate value, and so on, and since such matters are the sort of things around which one can orient one's life, one will be animated to defend these views when they are put under pressure. In short, we have many motives for being emotionally involved in, and motivated to defend, our philosophical views; and we can make sense of these motives even on the assumption that having a philosophical view on a contested issue is a species of attitudinal speculation. We can make sense of all of this on the assumption that having a view is not merely a cognitive affair but also a commitment of sorts: you are your view's champion.

There is one other aspect of philosophical practice that becomes intelligible on the hypothesis that having a philosophical view on a controversial topic is a matter of attitudinal speculation: we can make sense of the possibility of (cases of) "reasonable disagreement in philosophy." If having a view is a matter of attitudinal speculation, and if attitudinal speculation is a matter of having a degree of confidence above 0.5 but below the threshold warranting outright belief, then disagreements over the truth-value of a given proposition can be formulated as disagreements over the point *within the confidence interval between disbelief and belief* which the total evidence warrants. But as the disagreeing sides get closer and closer to one another—one side a little above 0.5, the other side a little below 0.5—it becomes harder and harder to discern from the total evidence which side is correct. In this way we might be able to make sense of reasonable disagreement regarding contested propositions, even if we assume that for any body of evidence and any proposition there is a unique degree of confidence one ought to have in that proposition given that evidence.[13] For, in precisely the same way that it can be very hard for anyone to discern whether the total evidence warrants a degree of confidence in [p] which is 0.9, as opposed to 0.89 or 0.88 or ... so too it can be very hard to discern whether the total evidence warrants a 0.55 degree of confidence in [p], as opposed to 0.45 (or some other close value less than 0.5). Even if the uniqueness thesis is true, we can in this way still make sense of the reasonableness of (some) philosophical disagreements. Note, though, that if the uniqueness thesis is true, and if having a view in philosophy involves having an outright belief in the truth of the view, reasonable disagreement in philosophy is a non-starter. In that case the disagreement is one in which the confidence levels of the disputing parties are at a great distance from one another, and so the disagreement over whether p cannot be rationalized as a matter of the difficulty of discerning where *within some small interval* the evidence warrants.

In sum: I tentatively endorse the hypothesis that, when one defends a view in the face of acknowledged systematic disagreement, one's attitude is—or should be!—a species of *attitudinal speculation* as to the truth of the view, and one's commitment to it is that of being a *champion* of the view, defending it as the occasion calls for this. The advantage of such a proposal is that it enables us to see how one's attitude can continue to be reasonable, even when one acknowledges (as one should) that the state of evidence fails to warrant outright belief on either side.[14] And since "having a view" in philosophy is only a special case of the more general phenomenon of advancing a claim in a context of diminished epistemic hope, we now have what is wanted: a characterization of the attitude that is appropriate to assertions of contested propositions. (End of the extended digression.)

We have all that we need to construct an account of sincerity in the assertion of contested propositions. In particular, sincerity is a matter of having the attitude corresponding to what is properly expected of one who is participating in this sort of activity. To see this, consider again the case of philosophy. Sincerity in the assertion of a contested philosophical proposition is a matter of regarding the proposition as defensible (and being committed to defending it). Since mutual belief among philosophers includes beliefs regarding how difficult it is in this domain to arrive at a belief that is doxastically justified, let alone knowledgeable, hearers will not in general expect that speakers believe what they say—with the further result that mere lack of belief does not constitute insincerity. Rather, insincerity is a matter of advancing a claim under

---

[13] This is, of course, one version of the uniqueness thesis, familiar in debates in the epistemology of disagreement.

[14] It also promises to enable us to see how certain cases of reasonable disagreement in philosophy are possible.

conditions in which one does not regard it as defensible (or where one is not committed to defending it).

Clearly, such an account of assertoric sincerity clashes with tradition. Bernard Williams captures tradition well when he writes that sincerity "consists in a disposition to make sure that one's assertion expresses what one actually believes" (Williams 2002: 96). But it is worth noting that my alternative account honors the core idea of sincerity as it is standardly understood: that of *not misrepresenting oneself (one's attitude)* in one's assertion. I suppose that Williams, like most, thought that not misrepresenting oneself in assertion requires that one believe what one asserts. But I think this is too quick. The idea of not misrepresenting oneself in assertion can be seen as involving two components. The first is in the idea of representing oneself in a certain way when one asserts. The second is in the idea of satisfying the very representation itself. In earlier chapters I argued that this talk of "representing oneself" in assertion can be understood in terms of MMENA itself: one who asserts that p does something regarding which it is mutually manifest that what one did is warranted only if one satisfied the standard E (provided by assertion's norm), and from here it is but a short inference to the conclusion that in asserting one represented oneself as satisfying E. If the norm of assertion is fixed in a context-sensitive fashion, in terms of what it is reasonable to suppose is mutually believed in the circumstance, then one's self-representation will be sensitive to—and in cases of full alignment, adjusted by—the contextually-fixed standard. And since that standard was fixed in terms of what it is reasonable to suppose is mutually believed in context, it will be reasonable to expect a competent hearer to discern that standard. Having such an attitude, then, satisfies the two-part component on sincerity: one represents oneself as having a certain attitude, and one has that attitude. Of course, in most cases—certainly all cases in which the "default" standard is in place—one's assertion represents oneself as knowing, and so sincerity will require the attitudinal component of knowledge (= belief). But there are exceptions to this, as when conversation persists under conditions of the mutual awareness of epistemically inhospitable conditions and the mutually acknowledged desire to persist. If my mutual-belief-based account is correct, assertions made in such contexts do not carry with them the promise of belief-worthiness. For this reason, assertions made in such contexts will not mislead people into thinking that one believes what one asserts, hence will not mislead another to regard one as having an attitude one does not have—*hence are not thereby insincere*. So long as one has the attitude in question—which in the case being discussed is the attitude of regarding the proposition asserted as defensible—one's assertion was not insincere. The very mutuality of the exchange ensures against fooling one's interlocutor into thinking that one has a certain attitude that in fact one lacks. This, it seems to me, just is the stuff of sincerity. That sincerity does not require belief in all cases, then, is an insight afforded by the view, not a problem for it.

Still, there are cases in the literature that might be thought to pose a problem for my view of assertoric sincerity. Consider for example the phenomenon that Lackey (2007b) calls "selfless assertion". In those cases, the speaker asserts, under conditions in which she is highly propositionally justified with respect to the asserted proposition, yet fails to believe what she asserts out of some, say, emotional condition. It is natural to think that these assertions are insincere, and yet we can concoct examples in which the selfless speaker regards the proposition as defensible—in which case it appears to follow that my account must regard such assertions as sincere.[15] But this objection is based on a confusion. Consider anyone who offers a selfless assertion under any circumstance in which it would be reasonable for the hearer to expect a robustly epistemic norm to be satisfied. (If my argument from Section 11.2 is correct, this will be most circumstances.) Such a speaker is thereby offering an assertion that *would* be insincere if not believed by the speaker. This is because in such circumstances, to assert is to represent oneself as satisfying a robustly epistemic condition, which condition will be satisfied only if one believes what one asserts. It is only when we are under conditions of epistemically diminished hope that the requirements on assertoric sincerity do not require belief. Of course, if a selfless assertion were made in such circumstances, my view would imply that it is not thereby insincere. But I submit that this is the right verdict in such a case: a selfless assertion made under conditions of diminished epistemic hope would be no more insincere than it is insincere of a philosopher to assert her view even though she does not believe it (owing to its being a highly contested matter). I conclude, then, that selfless assertion poses no difficulty for my proposed conception of assertoric sincerity.

11.5 Assertion and Moore's Paradox, Revisited

I want to conclude with two final objections to the context-sensitive picture on offer—or rather, to the coherence of that picture with the claims I have made on behalf of MMENA. They are the challenge from Moore-paradoxicality (revisited in this section), and the challenge from children's assertion (Section 11.6).

In Chapter 6 I discussed the role of MMENA in the diagnosis of the phenomena associated with Moore's paradox. I note that neither MMENA, nor indeed any norm of assertion, can diagnose all forms of Moore's paradox, for the simple reason that, whether or not one made the corresponding assertion, it would be Moore-paradoxical to judge or believe the content expressed by 'p, but I do not believe that p.' Since a proper diagnosis of Moore-paradoxicality will need to cover the case of Moore-paradoxicality *in (silent) belief and judgment*, in addition to that in assertion, we should not expect a complete treatment of these phenomena from any norm of assertion. But if the norm of assertion is context-sensitive, this might be thought to raise a problem. In particular, unless there is some other way to ensure that in any context of utterance the assertion of a Moore-paradoxical content[16] would be unwarranted, the context-sensitive

---

[15] I thank an anonymous referee for indicating the need to address this worry.
[16] Call any content whose judgment or assertion would standardly be taken to manifest the phenomena of Moore's paradox a "Moore-paradoxical content."

account will yield the verdict that some assertions of Moore-paradoxical content are warranted.

To this, several things can be said. First, it must be borne in mind that a proper diagnosis of the phenomenon of Moore-paradoxicality will have to cover more than just assertion, and it may well be that whatever the proper diagnosis is it will cover the cases in question—whatever our norm of assertion is. In addition, various proponents of assertion's norm have argued that the norm need not be knowledge, nor even anything belief-involving, to account for the unacceptability of assertions of Moore-paradoxical contents. As noted in Chapter 6, Kvanvig (2009) argues that the justified belief norm will capture all of the same data as captured by the knowledge norm; and Douven (2006: 473–76) argues that even a weaker norm, the rationality norm, can capture these data. Insofar as the context-sensitive proposal can embrace these norms (in particular contexts), it can avail itself of these accounts of Moore-paradoxicality. Still, the challenge facing the context-sensitive account remains, since I have argued that there are cases (involving contested propositions) in which belief in a proposition is not merely unjustified but *would be irrational*, and yet assertion of the proposition can still be warranted. In such cases neither the Kvanvig model nor the Douven model will be of any help. What should be said of such cases?

At this juncture, two further points can be made. One is that the considerations to which one can appeal in order to explain the unacceptability of the assertion of a Moore-paradoxical content appear to be perfectly general, and do not require that there be any corresponding justified or rational belief. (This is a point made by Douven 2006 but also by Weiner 2005, in defense of the truth norm, but the point is general.) Particular assertions, like particular instances of any speech act, have a point: they aim to achieve certain effects, and this is something that is known by any competent language user. The question can thus arise: what could be the point of an assertion of (what is expressed by) 'p, but I do not believe that p'? (The same question could be raised by focusing on the assertion of other Moore-paradoxical contents.) Now the objection I am considering is that, if the context-sensitive account of assertion's norm is correct, then there can be a warranted assertion of a Moore-paradoxical content. Note, however, that if such an assertion is to be warranted, it must satisfy the norm of assertion. So if the objection is to succeed, it must focus on a situation in which the norm is one that does not even require belief. To be sure, I have given at least one type of example of such a situation: the case of philosophical claims being made under conditions of systematic disagreement. But even here, we might wonder what the point would be to asserting 'p, but I do not believe that p.' Since it is already mutually manifest that conditions involve epistemically diminished hope, the hearer will already be entitled to regard the speaker as having a doxastic attitude weaker than belief. In such a context, the announcement that one does not believe p can only be jarring, calling out for further explanation. Arguably, this accounts for much of the sense of unacceptability of an assertion of 'p, but I do not believe that p' even in contexts of philosophical controversy.

Still, one might insist that we can come up with contexts in which there is a point to such an assertion in the envisaged context. I am not certain whether this is so. But for the sake of argument, let me grant this, if only to see what can be said in the worst-case scenario. This brings me to my final point. It would appear that under such conditions the assertion would be warranted. Interestingly, this idea has already been anticipated in the context of philosophy. Here I cite Alan Hajek's (2007) paper, "My Philosophical Position Says [p] and I Don't Believe [p]." His contention there is that "various prominent philosophers are committed to asserting and believing various Moore-paradoxical sentences in virtue of the very philosophical positions they hold" (2007: 217). Hajek is non-committal regarding what to conclude from this:

... [O]bserving the commitment may help lay bare what *we* find peculiar in these philosophical positions, where previously we may only have had vague feelings of unease; or we may regard the Moore-paradoxical commitments as further *reductios* of the positions; or we may conclude that not all Moore sentences are paradoxical after all. (217; italics in original)

But he anticipates the possibility that it is in the nature of having a view in philosophy that, when one holds a view under conditions of controversy,[17] something other than belief is involved—with the result that the cost of advancing one's view (making an assertion) is that we have to acknowledge cases of warranted assertion of a Moore-paradoxical content. Unlike Hajek, I am embracing this possibility as actual. I am not certain that there is ever a point to the assertion of Moore-paradoxical content; but if (in keeping with the objection's contention) there are contexts in which such a point can be discerned, I would defend the acceptability of the assertions themselves.

It might be added that there are other cases in which Moore-paradoxical contents are warranted (and even acceptable all-things-considered). Matthew Weiner's (2005) example involves an assertion of the form 'p, but I do not know that p.' He offers the following dialogue as an illustration:

AUDREY: The French will attack at nightfall.
PULLINGS: How do you know that?
AUDREY: I don't—we haven't intercepted their orders—but my prediction is that they will attack at nightfall.

On the assumption that predictions are assertions, Audrey's last statement is an assertion of the form 'p, but I do not know that p.' Yet it seems warranted for all that. I mention this if only to undermine the strength of the intuition that there are never any contexts in which the assertion of a Moore-paradoxical content is warranted.

---

[17] Hajek does not defend a claim of this general form; his claim rather regards specific (highly controversial!) claims in philosophy which by their very content (such as regarding the non-existence of belief or truth) are such that endorsement of them commits its defender to something like Moore-paradoxical contents.

As noted in Chapter 10, Benton (2012) responds to Weiner's case of predictions, arguing that the knowledge norm of assertion can accommodate these data. I repeat his comment here:

[P]redictions only *seem* permissible because they are naturally and normally made in contexts of acknowledged practical urgency wherein it is recognized that knowledge won't be had, yet predictions still must be made. Given such urgent contexts, it is understandable why we often enough don't enforce the knowledge requirement with predictions. (104–5; italics in original)

But in Chapter 10 I pointed out that Benton's proposal suffers from one key weakness. Even if we grant that the knowledge requirement is not enforced with predictions, even so, we *still* need a standard for warranted (prediction-constituting) assertions in these cases. After all, it is not as if, once we have agreed to waive the knowledge requirement, it is *anything goes*. As a result, Benton must further complicate his story so as to include standards that are in place when we (assert so as to) make predictions. Benton might think to deny that these are standards of assertion. But if so, his proposal begins to seem unmotivated. After all, we have an alternative (context-sensitive) proposal for the norm of assertion—one which captures the data without need for postulating a standard specific to prediction.

In sum, I do not know whether the assertion of a Moore-paradoxical content can ever have a conversational point. If it can't, then the proponent of the context-sensitive account of assertion's norm can appeal to broadly Gricean considerations to account for the unacceptability of these assertions. But if there is a point, then the proponent will have to embrace the possibility of warranted assertions of Moore-paradoxical contents. Given the restricted contexts in which there could be such a point, however, these cases are likely to conform to situations in which it is not entirely implausible to think that the assertions are warranted. In any case they will be like the sort of case Hajek (2007) describes. I recognize that it is still rather bold to say that the assertions are warranted. I regard this as a cost of the view. But given that the cost is not as great as we would otherwise have imagined, that there would appear to be other cases in which assertions of the form 'p, but I do not know that p' are warranted (the case of predictions), and that the view has the various other virtues I have been claiming on its behalf in the previous two chapters, the cost is worth paying.

11.6 Children's Assertion

I turn, finally, to the objection from children's assertion.[18] To set up the challenge I will be making two assumptions. The first is that very young (cognitively immature) children are not cognitively sophisticated enough to have mutual beliefs. The second is that even so such children make warranted assertions. I should say that these assumptions

---

[18] This objection was brought to my attention by Jennifer Lackey, in conversation.

are concessive: if these assumptions are false, then the objection I am about to consider does not get off the ground. Still, the assumptions are plausible, so I will grant them without further ado. Given these two assumptions, it would appear that the RMBS account of assertion, according to which the standard is fixed by what is reasonably regarded as mutually believed in context, will have to deliver the verdict that very young children are not warranted in their assertions.

Why think that the mutual belief account cannot deliver a "warranted" verdict in cases involving very young children? Well, one might think that in contexts in which it is reasonable to suppose that there are *no* mutual beliefs, this account cannot deliver *any* verdict. But this is not so. For the very reasoning I used in Chapter 10 to defend the idea of knowledge as a default setting would appear to be in place here too: this, after all, is a special case of the scenario in which mutual belief is minimal. Thus the mutual-belief account will deliver the verdict that the child's assertion is warranted iff the default standard (knowledge) is met. So long as the child knows, her assertion is warranted.

But perhaps the objection can be transformed. Perhaps what is objectionable is not that the account cannot offer the right verdicts in these cases, but rather that the child in question cannot take advantage of the mechanisms of mutual belief, and so cannot participate in any assertoric practice save those whose standards are just the default standards. In response I embrace this implication. I think that the sort of adjustments of assertoric standards I have been describing in the previous two chapters require quite a little cognitive sophistication. It should come as no surprise that cognitively immature (but still linguistic) children cannot participate in them. On the contrary, we might think that they need to be initiated into the simplest version of our assertoric practice, prior to being in a position to enter the practice in its more complicated manifestations. Thus, far from being an objection, the case from young children's assertoric practice would appear to be in conformity with the predictions made by my context-sensitive account.

11.7 Conclusion

I have no doubt but that my context-sensitive account of assertion's norm gives way to some rather radical lessons. Chief among these is its implication that there can be cases of warranted assertion of propositions that the subject is not justified in believing. I admit that such an implication is initially jarring. I admit further that accommodating this implication requires tinkering with a variety of the claims I have made on behalf of this book's core thesis: MMENA. Still, none of these tinkerings undermines the case for MMENA; and in most cases, the tinkerings required are independently plausible. What emerges from this is a picture of assertion governed by the mutuality of conversation. It is not merely the various features of what is communicated, but also some features of the force with which things are communicated, that are determined in the context of the conversation itself.

Bibliography

Adams, R. (1985). "Involuntary Sins," *Philosophical Review* 94(1): 3–31.
Adler, J. (1997). "Lying, Deceiving, or Falsely Implicating," *Journal of Philosophy* 94(9): 435–52.
Adler, J. (2002). *Belief's Own Ethics* (Cambridge, MA: MIT Press).
Adler, J. and Armour-Garb, B. (2007). "Moore's Paradox and the Transparency of Belief," in M. Green and J. Williams (eds.), *Moore's Paradox: New Essays on Belief, Rationality, and the First Person* (Oxford: Oxford University Press), pp. 146–64.
Alston, W. (2000). *Illocutionary Acts and Sentence Meaning* (Ithaca, NY: Cornell University Press).
Anscombe, E. (1979). "What is it to Believe Someone?" in C. F. Delaney (ed.), *Rationality and Religious Belief* (South Bend, IN: University of Notre Dame Press).
Atlas, J. (2007). "What Reflexive Pronouns Tell Us about Belief: A New Moore's Paradox *De Se*, Rationality, and Privileged Access," in M. Green and J. Williams (eds.), *Moore's Paradox: New Essays on Belief, Rationality, and the First Person* (Oxford: Oxford University Press), pp. 117–45.
Audi, R. (1997). "The Place of Testimony in the Fabric of Knowledge and Justification," *American Philosophical Quarterly* 34(4): 405–22.
Bach, K. (1997). "The Semantics–Pragmatics Distinction: What it is and Why it Matters," in *Pragmatik* (VS Verlag für Sozialwissenschaften), pp. 33–50.
Bach, K. (2008). "Applying Pragmatics to Epistemology," *Philosophical Issues* 18: 68–88.
Bach, K. and Harnish, R. (1979). *Linguistic Communication and Speech Acts* (Cambridge, MA: MIT Press).
Baker, J. (1987). "Trust and Rationality," *Pacific Philosophical Quarterly* 68: 1–13.
Baldwin, T. (1990). *G. E. Moore* (London: Routledge).
Baldwin, T. (2007). "The Normative Character of Belief," in M. Green and J. Williams (eds.), *Moore's Paradox: New Essays on Belief, Rationality, and the First Person* (Oxford: Oxford University Press), pp. 76–89.
Benton, M. (2012). "Assertion, Knowledge and Predictions," *Analysis* 72(1): 102–5.
Benton, M. (forthcoming). "Gricean Quality," *Noûs*.
Bergmann, M. (2006). *Justification Without Awareness* (Oxford: Oxford University Press).
Bergmann, M. (2009). "Rational Disagreement after Full Disclosure," *Episteme* 6(3): 336–53.
Bernecker, S. (2009). *Memory: A Philosophical Study* (Oxford: Oxford University Press).
Bird, A. (2007). "Justified Judging," *Philosophy and Phenomenological Research* 74(1): 81–110.
Black, M. (1952). "Saying and Disbelieving," *Analysis* 13: 25–33.
Blome-Tillmann, M. (2013). "Contextualism and the Knowledge Norms," *Pacific Philosophical Quarterly* 94(1): 89–100.
Brandom, R. (1983). "Asserting," *Noûs* 17(44): 637–50.
Brandom, R. (1994). *Making It Explicit* (Cambridge, MA: Harvard University Press).
Brewer, B. (1999). *Perception and Reason* (Oxford: Oxford University Press).
Brown, J. and Cappelen, H. (eds.) (2010). *Assertion: New Philosophical Essays* (Oxford: Oxford University Press).

Burge, T. (1979). "Individualism and the Mental," *Midwest Studies in Philosophy* 4(1): 73–121.
Burge, T. (1993). "Content Preservation," *Philosophical Review* 102(4): 457–88.
Buss, S. (1997). "Justified Wrongdoing," *Noûs* 31(3): 337–69.
Calhoun, C. (1989). "Responsibility and Reproach," *Ethics* 99: 386–406.
Cappelen, H. (2010). "Against Assertion," in J. Brown and H. Cappelen (eds.), *Assertion: New Philosophical Essays* (Oxford: Oxford University Press), pp. 21–48.
Cappelen, H. and Lepore, E. (2005). *Insensitive Semantics: A Defense of Semantic Minimalism and Speech Act Pluralism* (Oxford: Blackwell).
Chan, T. (2006). "Belief, Assertion, and Moore's Paradox," *Philosophical Studies* 139(3): 395–414.
Christiansen, D. (2007). "Epistemology of Disagreement: The Good News," *Philosophical Review* 116(2): 187–217.
Christiansen, D. (2011). "Disagreement, Question-Begging, and Epistemic Self-Criticism," *Philosophers' Imprint* 11(6): 1–22.
Chudnoff, E. (2011). "The Nature of Intuitive Justification," *Philosophical Studies* 153: 313–33.
Clifford, W. (1999). "The Ethics of Belief," *The Ethics of Belief and Other Essays* (New York: Prometheus Books).
Coady, C. (1992). *Testimony: A Philosophical Study* (Oxford: Oxford University Press).
Cohen, S. (2004). "Knowledge, Assertion, and Practical Reasoning," *Philosophical Issues* 12: 482–91.
Conee, E. and Feldman, R. (2004). *Evidentialism: Essays in Epistemology* (Oxford: Oxford University Press).
Craig, E. (1990). *Knowledge and the State of Nature* (Oxford: Clarendon Press).
Darwall, S. (2006). *The Second-Person Standpoint* (Cambridge, MA: Harvard University Press).
Davidson, D. (1969). "On Saying That," reprinted in Davidson (1984a), pp. 93–108.
Davidson, D. (1973). "Radical Interpretation," reprinted in Davidson (1984a), pp. 125–40.
Davidson, D. (1974a). "Belief and the Basis of Meaning," reprinted in Davidson (1984a), pp. 141–54.
Davidson, D. (1974b). "On the Very Idea of a Conceptual Scheme," reprinted in Davidson (1984a), pp. 183–98.
Davidson, D. (1975). "Thought and Talk," reprinted in Davidson (1984a), pp. 155–70.
Davidson, D. (1979). "Moods and Performances," reprinted in *Inquiries into Truth and Interpretation* (Oxford: Oxford University Press, 1991), pp. 109–21.
Davidson, D. (1984a). *Inquiries into Truth and Interpretation* (Oxford: Oxford University Press).
Davidson, D. (1984b). "Communication and Convention," *Synthese* 59(1): 3–17.
Davidson, D. (1991). "Three Varieties of Knowledge," reprinted in Davidson (2001), pp. 205–20.
Davidson, D. (1992). "The Second Person," reprinted in Davidson (2001), pp. 107–22.
Davidson, D. (1999a). "Reply to Tyler Burge," in L. Hahn (ed.), *The Philosophy of Donald Davidson* (Chicago, IL: Open Court), pp. 251–54.
Davidson, D. (1999b). "The Emergence of Thought," reprinted in Davidson (2001), pp. 123–34.
Davidson, D. (2001). *Subjective, Intersubjective, Objective* (Oxford: Oxford University Press).
DeRose, K. (1991). "Epistemic Possibilities," *Philosophical Review* 100: 581–605.
DeRose, K. (1996). "Knowledge, Assertion, and Lotteries," *Australasian Journal of Philosophy* 74: 568–80.
DeRose, K. (2002). "Assertion, Knowledge, and Context," *Philosophical Review* 111: 167–203.

Dias, M. and Harris, P. (1990). "The Influence of the Imagination on Reasoning by Young Children." *British Journal of Developmental Psychology* 8: 305–18.
Donnellan, K. (1966). "Reference and Definite Descriptions," in G. Ostertag (ed.), *Definite Descriptions: A Reader* (Cambridge, MA: MIT Press), pp. 173–94.
Douven, I. (2006). "Assertion, Knowledge, and Rational Credibility," *Philosophical Review* 115: 449–85.
Dretske. F. (1997). *Naturalizing the Mind* (Cambridge, MA: MIT Press).
Dummett, M. (1973). *Frege's Philosophy of Language* (New York: Harper & Row).
Dummett, M. (1981). *Frege: Philosophy of Language* (Oxford: Duckworth).
Dummett, M. (1993). "Mood, Force, and Convention," in *The Seas of Language* (Oxford: Clarendon Press), pp. 202–23.
Dummett, M. (1994). "Testimony and Memory," in B. K. Matilal and A. Chakrabarti (eds.), *Knowing from Words* (Amsterdam: Kluwer Academic Publishers), pp. 251–72.
Elga, A. (2007). "Reflection and Disagreement," *Noûs* 41(3): 478–502.
Elgin, K. (2004). "True Enough," *Philosophical Issues* 14: 113–31.
Elgin, K. (2007). "Understanding and the Facts," *Philosophical Studies* 132: 33–42.
Elgin, K. (2009a). "Exemplification, Idealization, and Understanding," in M. Suarez (ed.), *Fictions in Science: Essays on Idealization and Modeling* (London: Routledge), pp. 77–90.
Elgin, K. (2009b). "Is Understanding Factive?" in D. Pritchard, A. Millar, and A. Haddock (eds.), *Epistemic Value* (Oxford: Oxford University Press), pp. 322–30.
Fallis, D. (2008). "Toward an Epistemology of Wikipedia," *Journal of the American Society for Information Science and Technology* 59(10): 1662–74.
Fantl, J. and McGrath, M. (2009). *Knowledge in an Uncertain World* (Oxford: Oxford University Press).
Farkas, K. (2007). *The Subject's Point of View* (Oxford: Oxford University Press).
Faulkner, P. (2000). "The Social Character of Testimonial Knowledge," *Journal of Philosophy* 97(11): 581–601.
Faulkner, P. (2007). "A Geneology of Trust," *Episteme* 4(3): 305–21.
Faulkner, P. (2011). *Knowledge on Trust* (Oxford: Oxford University Press).
Feldman, R. (2006). "Epistemological Puzzles about Disagreement," in S. Hetherington (ed.), *Epistemology Futures* (Oxford: Oxford University Press), pp. 216–36.
Feldman, R. and Conee, E. (1985). "Evidentialism," *Philosophical Studies* 48(1): 15–34.
FitzPatrick, W. (2008). "Moral Responsibility and Normative Ignorance: Answering a New Skeptical Challenge," *Ethics* 118: 589–613.
Foley, R. (1994). "Egoism in Epistemology," in F. Schmitt (ed.), *Socializing Epistemology* (Lanham, MD: Rowman & Littlefield), pp. 53–73.
Foley, R. (2001). *Intellectual Trust in Oneself and Others* (Cambridge: Cambridge University Press).
Frances, B. (2005). *Scepticism Comes Alive* (Oxford: Oxford University Press).
Fricker, E. (1987). "The Epistemology of Testimony," *Proceedings of the Aristotelian Society*, Supplemental Vol. 61: 57–83.
Fricker, E. (1994). "Against Gullibility," in B. K. Matilal and A. Chakrabarti (eds.), *Knowing from Words* (Amsterdam: Kluwer Academic Publishers), pp. 125–61.
Fricker, E. (1995). "Telling and Trusting: Reductionism and Anti-Reductionism in the Epistemology of Testimony," *Mind* 104: 393–411.

Fricker, E. (2003). "Understanding and Knowledge of What is Said," in A. Barber (ed.), *The Epistemology of Language* (Oxford: Oxford University Press), pp. 325–66.
Fricker, E. (2006). "Testimony and Epistemic Autonomy," in J. Lackey and E. Sosa (eds.), *The Epistemology of Testimony* (Oxford: Oxford University Press), pp. 225–52.
Fricker, M. (2007). *Epistemic Injustice: Power and the Ethics of Knowing* (Oxford: Oxford University Press).
Fumerton, R. (2006). "The Epistemic Role of Testimony: Internalist and Externalist Perspectives," in J. Lackey and E. Sosa (eds.), *The Epistemology of Testimony* (Oxford: Oxford University Press), pp. 77–92.
Fumerton, R. (2010). "You Can't Trust a Philosopher," in R. Feldman and T. Warfield (eds.), *Disagreement* (Oxford: Oxford University Press), pp. 91–110.
Garnham, A. and Perner, J. (1990). "Does Manifestness Solve Problems of Mutuality?" *Behavioral and Brain Sciences* 13: 178–79.
Gauker, C. (2001). "Situated Inference versus Conversational Implicature," *Noûs* 35: 163–89.
Gendler, T. (2011). "On the Epistemic Costs of Implicit Bias," *Philosophical Studies* 156(1): 33–63.
Gibbons, J. (2006). "Access Externalism," *Mind* 115(457): 19–39.
Gibbons, J. (2013). *The Norm of Belief* (Oxford: Oxford University Press).
Goldberg, S. (2004). "Radical Interpretation, Understanding, and Testimonial Transmission," *Synthese* 138(3): 387–416.
Goldberg, S. (2005). "Testimonial Knowledge from Unsafe Testimony," *Analysis* 65(4): 302–11.
Goldberg, S. (2006). "Reductionism and the Distinctiveness of Testimonial Knowledge," in J. Lackey and E. Sosa (eds.), *The Epistemology of Testimony* (Oxford: Oxford University Press), pp. 127–44.
Goldberg, S. (2007a). *Anti-Individualism: Mind and Language, Knowledge and Justification* (Cambridge: Cambridge University Press).
Goldberg, S. (2007b). "How Lucky Can You Get?" *Synthese* 158: 315–27.
Goldberg, S. (2009a). "The Knowledge Account of Assertion and the Conditions on Testimonial Knowledge," in D. Pritchard and P. Greenough (eds.), *Williamson on Knowledge* (Oxford: Oxford University Press), pp. 60–72.
Goldberg, S. (2009b). "Experts, Semantic and Epistemic," *Noûs* 43(4): 581–98.
Goldberg, S. (2009c). "Reliabilism in Philosophy," *Philosophical Studies* 124(1): 105–17.
Goldberg, S. (2010a). *Relying on Others: An Essay in Epistemology* (Oxford: Oxford University Press).
Goldberg, S. (2010b). "Assertion, Testimony, and the Epistemic Significance of Speech," *Logos and Episteme* 1(1): 59–65.
Goldberg, S. (2011). "Interpreting Assertions," in G. Preyer and C. Amoretti (eds.), *Triangulation: From an Epistemic Point of View* (New York: Ontos Publishers), pp. 153–76.
Goldberg, S. (forthcoming a). "What is the Subject-Matter of the Theory of Epistemic Justification?" in J. Greco and D. Henderson (eds.), *The Point and Purpose of Epistemic Evaluation* (Oxford: Oxford University Press).
Goldberg, S. (forthcoming b). "Should Have Known," *Synthese*.
Goldberg, S. and Henderson, D. (2006). "Monitoring and Anti-Reductionism in the Epistemology of Testimony," *Philosophy and Phenomenological Research* 72(3): 576–93.
Goldman, A. (1986). *Epistemology and Cognition* (Cambridge, MA: Harvard University Press).
Graham, P. (1997). "What is Testimony?" *Philosophical Quarterly* 47(187): 227–32.

Graham, P. (2000a). "Conveying Information," *Synthese* 123(3): 365–92.
Graham, P. (2000b). "Transferring Knowledge," *Noûs* 34(1): 131–52.
Graham, P. (2000c). "The Reliability of Testimony," *Philosophy and Phenomenological Research* 61(3): 695–709.
Graham, P. (2004). "Metaphysical Libertarianism and the Epistemology of Testimony," *American Philosophical Quarterly* 41: 37–50.
Graham, P. (2006a). "Liberal Fundamentalism and its Rivals," in J. Lackey and E. Sosa (eds.), *The Epistemology of Testimony* (Oxford: Oxford University Press), pp. 93–115.
Graham, P. (2006b). "Testimonial Justification: Inferential or Non-inferential?" *Philosophical Quarterly* 56(222): 84–95.
Graham, P. (2010). "Testimonial Entitlement and the Function of Comprehension," in A. Haddock, A. Millar, and D. Pritchard (eds.), *Social Epistemology* (Oxford: Oxford University Press), pp. 148–74.
Grandy, R. (1973). "Reference, Meaning, and Belief," *Journal of Philosophy* 70(14): 439–52.
Green, M. and Williams, J. (eds.) (2007). *Moore's Paradox: New Essays on Belief, Rationality, and the First Person* (Oxford: Oxford University Press).
Greenough, P. and Pritchard, D. (eds.) (2009). *Williamson on Knowledge* (Oxford: Oxford University Press).
Grice, P. (1957). "Meaning," *Philosophical Review* 66: 377–88.
Grice, P. (1968a). "Utterer's Meaning, Sentence-Meaning, and Word-Meaning," reprinted in *Studies in the Way of Words* (Cambridge, MA: Harvard University Press, 1989), pp. 117–37.
Grice, P. (1968b/1989). "Logic and Conversation," reprinted in *Studies in the Way of Words* (Cambridge, MA: Harvard University Press, 1989), pp. 22–40.
Grimm, S. (2009). "Epistemic Normativity," in A. Haddock, A. Millar, and D. Pritchard (eds.), *Epistemic Value* (Oxford: Oxford University Press), pp. 243–64.
Hajek, A. (2007). "My Philosophical Position Says [p] and I Don't Believe [p]," in M. Green and J. Williams (eds.), *Moore's Paradox: New Essays on Belief, Rationality, and the First Person* (Oxford: Oxford University Press), pp. 217–31.
Harman, E. (2011). "Does Moral Ignorance Exculpate?" *Ratio* 24(4): 443–68.
Harman, G. (1986). *Change in View* (Cambridge, MA: MIT Press).
Harris, P. (2002). "Checking our Sources: The Origins of Trust in Testimony," *Studies in History and Philosophy of Science* 33(2): 315–33.
Hawthorne, J. (2005). *Knowledge and Lotteries* (Oxford: Oxford University Press).
Hawthorne, J. and Srinivasan, A. (2013). "Disagreement Without Transparency: Some Bleak Thoughts," in D. Christensen and J. Lackey (eds.), *The Epistemology of Disagreement: New Essays* (Oxford: Oxford University Press), pp. 9–30.
Henderson, D. and Horgan, T. (2007). "Some Ins and Outs of Transglobal Reliabilism," in S. Goldberg (ed.), *Internalism and Externalism in Semantics and Epistemology* (Oxford: Oxford University Press), pp. 100–29.
Hill, C. and Schechter, J. (2007). "Hawthorne's Lottery Puzzle and the Nature of Belief," *Philosophical Issues* 17: 102–22.
Hinchman, T. (2005). "Telling as Inviting to Trust," *Philosophy and Phenomenological Research* 70(3): 562–87.
Insole, C. (2000). "Seeing Off the Local Threat to Irreducible Knowledge by Testimony," *Philosophical Quarterly* 50(198): 44–56.

Jack, J. (1994). "The Role of Comprehension," in B. K. Matilal and A. Chakrabarti (eds.), *Knowing from Words* (Amsterdam: Kluwer Academic Publishers), pp. 163–93.
Jary, M. (2010). *Assertion* (Basingstoke: Palgrave Macmillan).
Jones, O. (1991). "Moore's Paradox, Assertion and Knowledge," *Analysis* 51: 182–86.
Kant, I. (2002). *Groundwork for the Metaphysics of Morals* (New Haven, CT: Yale University Press).
Kelly, T. (2005). "The Epistemic Significance of Disagreement," in T. Gendler and J. Hawthorne (eds.), *Oxford Studies in Epistemology* (Oxford: Oxford University Press), vol. 1, pp. 167–97.
Kelly, T. (2010). "Peer Disagreement and Higher-Order Evidence," in R. Feldman and T. Warfield (eds.), *Disagreement* (Oxford: Oxford University Press), pp. 111–74.
Kenyon, T. (2012). "The Informational Richness of Testimonial Contexts," *Philosophical Quarterly* 63: 58–80.
Kornblith, H. (2010). "Belief in the Face of Controversy," in R. Feldman and T. Warfield (eds.), *Disagreement* (Oxford: Oxford University Press), pp. 29–52.
Kornblith, H. (2012). "Is Philosophical Knowledge Possible?" in D. Machuca (ed.), *Disagreement and Skepticism* (New York: Routledge), pp. 260–76.
Kotzen, M. (2013). "Multiple Studies and Evidential Defeat," *Noûs* 47(1): 154–80.
Kriegel, U. (2011). *The Sources of Intentionality* (Oxford: Oxford University Press).
Kriegel, U. (2013). *Phenomenal Intentionality* (Oxford: Oxford University Press).
Kripke, S. (1977). "Speaker Reference and Semantic Reference," *Midwest Studies in Philosophy* 2(1): 255–76.
Kusch, M. (2009). "Testimony and the Value of Knowledge," in A. Haddock, A. Millar, and D. Pritchard (eds.), *Epistemic Value* (Oxford: Oxford University Press), pp. 60–94.
Kvanvig, J. (2009). "Assertion, Knowledge and Lotteries," in D. Pritchard and P. Greenough (eds.), *Williamson on Knowledge* (Oxford: Oxford University Press), pp. 140–60.
Lackey, J. (1999). "Testimonial Knowledge and Transmission," *Philosophical Quarterly* 49(197): 471–90.
Lackey, J. (2006). "It Takes Two to Tango: Beyond Reductionism and Non-Reductionism in the Epistemology of Testimony," in J. Lackey and E. Sosa (eds.), *The Epistemology of Testimony* (Oxford: Oxford University Press), pp. 160–92.
Lackey, J. (2007a). "Learning From Words," *Philosophy and Phenomenological Research* 73(1): 77–101.
Lackey, J. (2007b). "Norms of Assertion," *Noûs* 41(4): 594–628.
Lackey, J. (2008). *Learning From Words* (Oxford: Oxford University Press).
Lackey, J. (2010). "A Justificationist's View of Disagreement's Epistemic Significance," in A. Haddock, A. Millar, and D. Pritchard (eds.), *Social Epistemology* (Oxford: Oxford University Press), pp. 298–325.
Lackey, J. (2011). "Assertion and Isolated Secondhand Knowledge," in J. Brown and H. Cappelen (eds.), *Assertion: New Philosophical Essays* (Oxford: Oxford University Press), pp. 251–75.
Lackey, J. (2014). "Taking Religious Disagreement Seriously," in T. O'Connor and L. F. Goins (eds.), *Religious Faith and Intellectual Virtue* (Oxford: Oxford University Press), pp. 299–316.
Lawlor, K. (2013). *Assurance: An Austinian View of Knowledge and Knowledge Claims* (Oxford: Oxford University Press).
Leite, A. (2007). "How to Link Assertion and Knowledge without Going Contextualist," *Philosophical Studies* 134: 111–29.

Levin, J. (2008). "Assertion, Practical Reason, and Pragmatic Theories of Knowledge," *Philosophy and Phenomenological Research* 76(2): 359–84.
Lewis, D. (1974/1983). "Radical Interpretation," *Synthese* 23: 331–44; reprinted in D. Lewis, *Philosophical Papers* (Oxford: Oxford University Press, 1983), pp. 108–18.
Lewis, D. (1975/2001). "Language and Languages," in A. Martinich (ed.), *The Philosophy of Language*, 4th edition (Oxford: Oxford University Press), pp. 562–81.
Lewis, D. (1979). "Scorekeeping in a Language Game," *Journal of Philosophical Logic* 8: 339–59.
Lipton, P. (1998). "The Epistemology of Testimony," *Studies in History and Philosophy of Science* 29(1): 1–31.
Lipton, P. (2007). "Alien Abduction: Inference to the Best Explanation and the Epistemology of Testimony," *Episteme* 4(3): 238–51.
Littlejohn, C. (2010). "Moore's Paradox and Epistemic Norms," *Australasian Journal of Philosophy* 88(1): 79–100.
Littlejohn, C. (2013). "Disagreement and Defeat," in D. Machuca (ed.), *Disagreement and Skepticism* (New York: Routledge), pp. 169–92.
Loar, B. (2003). "Phenomenal Intentionality as the Basis of Mental Content," in M. Hahn and B. Ramberg (eds.), *Reflections and Replies: Essays on the Philosophy of Tyler Burge* (Cambridge, MA: MIT Press), pp. 229–58.
Lyons, J. (2009). *Perception and Basic Beliefs* (Oxford: Oxford University Press).
MacFarlane, J. (2003). "Future Contingents and Relative Truth," *Philosophical Quarterly* 53(212): 321–36.
MacFarlane, J. (2005). "Making Sense of Relative Truth," *Proceedings of the Aristotelian Society* 105: 321–39.
MacFarlane, J. (2010). "What is an Assertion?" in J. Brown and H. Cappelen (eds.), *Assertion: New Philosophical Essays* (Oxford: Oxford University Press), pp. 79–96.
Maher, P. (1993). *Betting on Theories* (Cambridge: Cambridge University Press).
Maitra, I. (2010). "Assertion, Norms, and Games," in J. Brown and H. Cappelen (eds.), *Assertion: New Philosophical Essays* (Oxford: Oxford University Press), pp. 277–96.
Maitra, I. and Weatherson, B. (2010). "Assertion, Knowledge, and Action," *Philosophical Studies* 149: 99–118.
Matheson, J. (2009). "Conciliatory Views of Disagreement and Higher-Order Evidence," *Episteme: A Journal of Social Philosophy* 6(3): 269–79.
McDowell, J. (1980). "Meaning, Communication, and Knowledge," reprinted in J. McDowell, *Meaning, Knowledge, and Reality* (Cambridge, MA: Harvard University Press, 1998), pp. 29–50.
McDowell, J. (1994a). *Mind and World* (Oxford: Oxford University Press).
McDowell, J. (1994b). "Knowledge by Hearsay," in B. K. Matilal and A. Chakrabarti (eds.), *Knowing from Words* (Amsterdam: Kluwer Academic Publishers), pp. 195–224.
McGinn, C. (1986). "Radical Interpretation and Epistemology," in E. Lepore (ed.), *Truth and Interpretation: Perspectives on the Philosophy of Donald Davidson* (Oxford: Basil Blackwell), pp. 356–68.
McGlynn, A. (2012). "Interpretation and Knowledge Maximization," *Philosophical Studies* 160: 391–405.
McKinnon, R. (2012). "How do You Know that 'How do You Know?' Challenges a Speaker's Knowledge?" *Pacific Philosophical Quarterly* 93: 65–83.

McKinnon, R. (2013). "The Supportive Reasons Norm of Assertion," *American Philosophical Quarterly* 50(2): 121–34.
McKinnon, R. and Simard Smith, P. (2013). "Sure the Emperor Has No Clothes, but You Shouldn't Say That," *Philosophia* 41(3): 825–29.
McMyler, B. (2011). *Testimony, Trust, and Authority* (Oxford: Oxford University Press).
Millikan, R. (2000). *On Clear and Confused Ideas: An Essay about Substance Concepts* (Cambridge: Cambridge University Press).
Millikan, R. (2004). "Existence Proof for a Viable Externalism," in R. Schantz (ed.), *The Externalist Challenge* (Berlin: Walter de Gruyter), pp. 227–38.
Montmarquet, J. (1992). "Epistemic Virtue and Doxastic Responsibility," *American Philosophical Quarterly* 29(4): 331–41.
Montminy, M. (2013). "The Single Norm of Assertion," in *Perspectives on Pragmatics and Philosophy* (Dordrecht: Springer International Publishing), pp. 35–52.
Moody-Adams, M. (1994). "Culture, Responsibility, and Affected Ignorance," *Ethics* 104: 291–309.
Moore, G. E. (1993). "Moore's Paradox," in T. Baldwin (ed.), *G. E. Moore: Selected Writings* (London: Routledge), pp. 207–12.
Moran, R. (2006). "Getting Told and Being Believed," in J. Lackey and E. Sosa (eds.), *The Epistemology of Testimony* (Oxford: Oxford University Press), pp. 272–306.
Nelkin, D. (2000). "The Lottery Paradox, Knowledge, and Rationality," *Philosophical Review* 109: 373–409.
Neta, R. (2006). "Epistemology Factualized: New Contractarian Foundations for Epistemology," *Synthese* 150: 247–80.
Neta, R. (2009). "Treating Something as a Reason for Acting," *Noûs* 43(4): 684–99.
Owens, D. (2000). *Reason without Freedom: The Problem of Epistemic Normativity* (London: Routledge).
Owens, D. (2006). "Testimony and Assertion," *Philosophical Studies* 130: 105–29.
Pagin, P. (2011). "Information and Assertoric Force," in J. Brown and H. Cappelen (eds.), *Assertion: New Philosophical Essays* (Oxford: Oxford University Press), pp. 97–136.
Pettit, P. (1995). "The Cunning of Trust," *Philosophy and Public Affairs* 24(3): 202–25.
Pierce, C. (1934). "Belief and Judgment," in C. Hartshorne and P. Weiss (eds.), *Collected Papers, Volume V* (Cambridge, MA: Harvard University Press).
Price, H. (1998). "Three Norms of Assertibility, or, How the MOA Became Extinct," *Philosophical Perspectives* 12: 241–54.
Pryor, J. (2000). "The Skeptic and the Dogmatist," *Noûs* 34(4): 517–49.
Recanati, R. (1987). *Mood and Force* (Cambridge: Cambridge University Press).
Reid, Thomas (1997). *An Inquiry into the Human Mind on the Principles of Common Sense* (Edinburgh: Edinburgh University Press).
Rescorla, M. (2009). "Assertion and its Constitutive Norms," *Philosophy and Phenomenological Research* 79(1): 98–130.
Reynolds, S. (2002). "Testimony, Knowledge, and Epistemic Goals," *Philosophical Studies* 110(2): 139–61.
Richards, C. and Sanderson, J. (1999). "The Role of the Imagination in Facilitating Deductive Reasoning in 2-, 3-, and 4-Year-Olds," *Cognition* 72: B1–B9.
Ridge, M. (2006). "Sincerity and Expressivism," *Philosophical Studies* 131: 487–510.
Rosen, G. (2002). "Culpability and Ignorance," *Proceedings of the Aristotelian Society* 103(1): 61–84.

Ross, A. (1986). "Why do we Believe what we are Told?" *Ratio* 28(1): 69–88.
Ross, J. (1975). "Testimonial Evidence," in K. Lehrer (ed.), *Analysis and Metaphysics: Essays in Honor of R. M. Chisholm* (Dordrecht: Reidel), pp. 35–55.
Rotondo, A. (2013). "Undermining, Circularity, and Disagreement," *Synthese* 190: 563–84.
Rysiew, P. (2007a). "Beyond Words: Communication, Truthfulness, and Understanding," *Episteme* 4(3): 285–304.
Rysiew, P. (2007b). "Speaking of Knowing," *Noûs* 41(4): 627–62.
Sayward, C. (1966). "Assertion and Belief," *Philosophical Studies* 17(5): 74–78.
Sayward, C. (1971). "More on Assertion and Belief," *Philosophical Studies* 22: 20–24.
Schaffer, J. (2008). "Knowledge in the Image of Assertion," *Philosophical Issues* 18(1): 1–19.
Schmitt, F. (2002). "Testimony, Justification, and the Parity Argument," *Studies in the History and Philosophy of Science* 33: 385–406.
Schmitt, F. (2006). "Testimonial Justification and Transindividual Reasons," in J. Lackey and E. Sosa (eds.), *The Epistemology of Testimony* (Oxford: Oxford University Press), pp. 193–224.
Schmitt, F. (2010). "The Assurance View of Testimony," in A. Haddock, A. Millar, and D. Pritchard (eds.), *Social Epistemology* (Oxford: Oxford University Press), pp. 216–42.
Searle, J. (1969). *Speech Acts* (Cambridge: Cambridge University Press).
Searle, J. (1979). "A Taxonomy of Illocutionary Acts," in *Expression and Meaning* (Cambridge: Cambridge University Press), pp. 1–29.
Shogenji, T. (2006). "A Defense of Reductionism about Testimonial Justification of Beliefs," *Noûs*, 40(2): 331–46.
Slote, M. (1979). "Assertion and Belief," in J. Dancy (ed.), *Papers on Language and Logic* (Keele: Keele University Library), pp. 177–90.
Smith, A. (2005). "Responsibility for Attitudes: Activity and Passivity in Mental Life," *Ethics* 115(2): 236–71.
Smith, H. (1983). "Culpable Ignorance," *Philosophical Review* 92(4): 543–71.
Sobel, J. (1987). "On the Evidence of Testimony for Miracles: A Bayesian Interpretation of David Hume's Analysis," *Philosophical Quarterly* 37(147): 166–86.
Sorensen, R. (1988). *Blindspots* (Oxford: Oxford University Press).
Sorensen, R. (2007). "Baldfaced Lies! Lying Without the Intent to Deceive," *Pacific Philosophical Quarterly* 88: 251–64.
Sosa, D. (2009). "Dubious Assertion," *Philosophical Studies* 146: 269–72.
Sosa, D. (forthcoming). "The Unimportance of Being Earnest," *Noûs*.
Sosa, E. (1994). "Testimony and Coherence," in B. K. Matilal and A. Chakrabarti (eds.), *Knowing from Words* (Amsterdam: Kluwer Academic Publishers), pp. 59–67.
Sosa, E. (2007). *A Virtue Epistemology: Apt Belief and Reflective Knowledge, Volume 1* (Oxford: Oxford University Press).
Sosa, E. (2009). *A Virtue Epistemology: Apt Belief and Reflective Knowledge, Volume 2* (Oxford: Oxford University Press).
Sperber, D. and Wilson, D. (1986). *Relevance: Communication and Cognition* (London: Blackwell).
KSperber, D. and Wilson, D. (1990). "Spontaneous Deduction and Mutual Knowledge," *Behavioral and Brain Sciences* 13: 179–84.
Stalnaker, R. (1974). "Pragmatic Presuppositions," in M. K. Munitz and P. K. Unger (eds.), *Semantics and Philosophy* (New York: New York University Press), pp. 197–214.

Stalnaker, R. (1978). "Assertion," in P. Cole (ed.), *Syntax and Semantics, Vol. 9: Pragmatics* (New York: Academic Press), pp. 315–22; reprinted in Stalnaker (1999), pp. 78–95; page references to reprinted version.
Stalnaker, R. (1999). *Context and Content* (Oxford: Oxford University Press).
Stanley, J. (2005). *Knowledge and Practical Interests* (Oxford: Oxford University Press).
Stanley, J. (2008). "Knowledge and Certainty," *Philosophical Issues* 18: 34–57.
Stevenson, L. (1993). "Why Believe What People Say?" *Synthese* 94: 429–51.
Stone, J. (2007). "Contextualism and Warranted Assertion," *Pacific Philosophical Quarterly* 88(1): 92–113.
Strawson, P. (1994). "Knowing from Words," in B. K. Matilal and A. Chakrabarti (eds.), *Knowing from Words* (Amsterdam: Kluwer Academic Publishers), pp. 23–27.
Sutton, J. (2007). *Without Justification* (Cambridge, MA: MIT Press).
Thune, M. (2010). "'Partial Defeaters' and the Epistemology of Disagreement," *Philosophical Quarterly* 60(239): 355–72.
Turri, J. (2010a). "Epistemic Invariantism and Speech Act Contextualism," *Philosophical Review* 119(1): 77–95.
Turri, J. (2010b). "Prompting Challenges," *Analysis* 70(3): 456–62.
Turri, J. (2011). "The Express Knowledge Account of Assertion," *Australasian Journal of Philosophy* 89(2): 37–45.
Turri, J. (2014). "Knowledge and Suberogatory Assertion," *Philosophical Studies* 167: 557–67.
Unger, P. (1975). *Ignorance: A Case for Skepticism* (Oxford: Clarendon Press).
Van Fraasen, B. (2002). *The Empirical Stance* (New Haven, CT: Yale University Press).
Wanderer, J. (2011). "Addressing Testimonial Injustice: Being Ignored and Being Rejected," *Philosophical Quarterly* 62: 148–69.
Watson, G. (2004). "Asserting and Promising," *Philosophical Studies* 117(1/2): 57–77.
Weatherson, B. (2003). "What Good are Counterexamples?" *Philosophical Studies* 115(1): 1–31.
Wedgewood, R. (2007). *The Nature of Normativity* (Oxford: Oxford University Press).
Weiner, M. (2005). "Must We Know What We Say?" *Philosophical Review* 114: 227–51.
Weiner, M. (2007). "Norms of Assertion," *Philosophical Compass* 2: 187–95.
Welbourne, M. (1994). "Testimony, Knowledge, and Belief," in B. K. Matilal and A. Chakrabarti (eds.), *Knowing From Words* (Amsterdam: Kluwer Academic Publishers), pp. 297–313.
White, R. (2005). "Epistemic Permissiveness," *Philosophical Perspectives* 19: 445–59.
Williams, B. (2002). *Truth and Truthfulness* (Princeton: Princeton University Press).
Williams, J. (1994). "Moorean Absurdity and the Intentional 'Structure' of Assertion," *Analysis* 54: 160–66.
Williamson, T. (1996). "Knowing and Asserting," *Philosophical Review* 105: 489–523.
Williamson, T. (2000). *Knowledge and Its Limits* (Oxford: Oxford University Press).
Williamson, T. (2005). "Contextualism, Subject-Sensitive Invariantism, and Knowledge of Knowledge," *Philosophical Quarterly* 55(219): 213–35.
Williamson, T. (2007). *The Philosophy of Philosophy* (London: Blackwell).
Wright, C. (1992). *Truth and Objectivity* (Cambridge, MA: Harvard University Press).
Zagzebski, L. (2003). "Intellectual Motivation and the Good of Truth," in M. DePaul and L. Zagzebski (eds.), *Intellectual Virtue: Perspectives from Ethics and Epistemology* (Oxford: Oxford University Press), pp. 135–54.

Index

ABL, 197, 200
AB≡, 197, 199
Adams, Robert, 178 (fn 17)
Adler, Jonathan, 61, 161 (fn 33), 162 (fn 38), 164 (fn 40), 166
Affirm, vii, 3
AGRB, 42; see also Assertion and the generation of reasons to believe
AIP, 108, 109, 112–18
Akrasia, 178
Alston, William, 155 (fn 22)
Ambiguity, 128–29
Amour-Garb, Bradley, 161 (fn 33)
Anonymity, see Assertion, anonymous
 – defined, 206
Anscombe, Elizabeth, 180 (fn 19), 186, 188
Anti-individualism, see Justification, anti-individualism about testimonial –; Externalism, epistemic
ARB, 155, 157–58
ARK, 155, 156
Assent, 9, 97, 101, 104–06, 110
Assertion
 Acceptance of –, see Justification, non-reductionism about testimonial –; Justification, reductionism about testimonial –
 Accountability in –, 86, 90; see also Assertion-generated responsibilities
 Anonymous –, 169, 204–21
 – and argument, 246
 – and assent, 105–06, 110; see also Assent
 – and audience, 63, 66, 88–89, 174–75, 179, 187, 218, 258–59, 262, 267, 269
 – and authorization, 8, 13–14, 27, 77–80
 – and belief, 10, 12–13, 18, 20, 30, 78, 99, 144–70, 192–203, 213, 226, 248, 278, 284
 – and claims on hearer's attention, 182–85
 – and declarative sentences, 4–5
 – and disagreement, 229–31
 – and duty, see Assertion and responsibilities-to-assert
 – and epistemic authority, 28–30, 34, 69, 70, 72, 77–80, 87–88, 106–12, 118–22, 124–26, 129–45, 146–47, 149, 167, 169, 172–75, 177–89, 190, 201–02, 204, 207, 218, 257, 259, 263 (fn 11), 274, 276, 283
 – and knowledge communication, see Knowledge communication
 – and prediction, 252–53; see also Prediction
 – and promising, 63–64, 174–75
 – and representing oneself as epistemically authoritative, 149, 155–57, 181–89, 201, 276, 283, 284
 – and representing oneself as knowing, 7, 16, 18, 19, 155, 284; see also ARK
 – and respect, 181–89
 – and responsibilities-for-having-asserted, 179, 193, 201
 – and responsibilities-to-assert, 179, 189–203
 – and retraction, 8, 14–15, 18, 20–21, 166
 – and telling, 77–80, 86–89; see also Tell
 – and testimony, 20 (fn 23), 46, 48, 51 (fn 19), 54–58, 62, 72–92, 143, 146 (fn 5)
 – and the communication of knowledge, see Knowledge communication
 – and the division of epistemic labor, 57
 – and the generation of reasons to believe, 42, 43, 46–70; see also AGRB, PRR
 – as a source of justification, 59–62; see also Justification, non-reductionism about testimonial –
 – as evidence, 41, 43–58 (see esp. 43–45), 89–91, 202
 – by spokesperson, 220
 – in philosophy, 30–34, 245–48, 251, 254, 259, 260, 264, 267, 276–77, 283, 285, 286–87
 – in private diaries, 65–66
 – in professions, 30–33
 – in teaching, 30–33, 165, 170
 – versus speculation, 55–58, 78–80, 81
 -belief link, 197–203; see also ABL
 -generated entitlements, 6, 7–8, 11, 13–14, 16–17, 20, 29, 39, 56, 63–64, 67, 68, 69, 70, 72–80, 80–91, 98, 130, 171–203, 273, 275, 276, 277
 -generated responsibilities, 6, 7–8, 11, 13–14, 20, 29, 39, 67, 72–80, 80–91, 123–43, 171–203, 205, 210, 215–16, 218, 258, 273, 275, 276, 277; see also Assertion and responsibilities-for-having-asserted; Assertion and responsibilities-to-assert
Bald –, 246
Belief-worthiness of –, 7, 12–13, 15, 18, 19, 32, 51–53, 70–71, 72, 147, 151, 152, 155–57, 167, 183, 202, 204, 217–21, 273, 275, 276, 277–78
Challenges to –, 7, 13, 17–18
Cheating in –, 26–28
Children's –, 52, 107–08, 285, 288–89

302 INDEX

Assertion (*Cont.*)
  Comprehension of the content of –, 118–22, 125 (fn 3), 127–29, 132, 137, 139, 141–42, 191
  Consumers of –, 119–20
  Content of –, 96, 123–43
  Conventional nature of –, 80–82
  Credibility of –, 209–10, 215, 217
  Duty to –, 189–92
  Epistemic Significance of –, 6, 37–91, 39, 51–54, 144, 156, 174, 276–78
  Ethics of –, 83–84, 90, 171–203
  Examples of –, vii, 4
  Face-to-face vs. other types of –, 209–13, 216–19
  Features of –, 6–9
  Felicity of –, 8 (fn 5)
  Garrulousness in –, 183–85
  Goodness of –, 146 (fn 6)
  Group –, 220
  Hedged –, 149, 163–64, 247, 252
  Legal –, 30–31
  Modal features of –, 28–30, 54
  Norm of –, see Norm of Assertion; Rule, Constitutive – Account of Assertion
  Philosophical –, see Assertion in philosophy
  Policing of –, 205, 210–11, 213–16, 218, 219–21, 253
  Practical aim of –, 213
  Propriety of –, see Norm of assertion and warrantedness; Propriety, primary and secondary
  Public nature of – , 167–69, 174, 204–05, 215 (fn 15), 218–19, 220, 221, 269
  Reckless –, 148–50
  Reliability of –, 27–28, 51–54, 60–61, 87–88
  Representational dimension of –, 53
  Reputation in –, 210–11
  Selfless –, 20 (fn 23), 151, 284–85
  Sexism and –, 183, 219
  Sincerity of –, see Sincerity
  Suberogatory –, 146 (fn 6)
  Theories of –, 9–21
  Understanding –, 52; see also Assertion, comprehension of the content of –
  Warrantedness of –, see Norm of assertion and warrantedness
Assertoric force, 5–6, 10, 77–80
Assurance, 39, 78
  – view of testimony, 63–66, 69–70, 72, 76, 77, 82–91, 175 (fn 9), 179
Attention, see Assertion and claims on hearer's attention
Attest, see testify
Attitudinal account (of assertion), 10, 12–15
Audi, Robert, 44 (fn 6), 52 (fn 22), 59
Austin, John, 8 (fn 5), 213 (fn 12)
Authority, see Assertion and epistemic authority
Authorize, see Assertion and authorization

Avow, vii, 3, 166
AWSPD, 251–53, 254, 255

Bach, Kent, ix (fn 4), 8 (fn 6), 10, 12–15, 128 , 144–45, 154, 256, 272 (fn 1)
Baldwin, Thomas, 144 (fn 2), 161
Basis Assumption, 40, 41, 43
Bayesianism, see Justification, Bayesian theory of
Belief, 6, 8, 144–55, 162–70, 199–201, 226, 279–80, 282; see also Assertion and belief; Expression (of belief)
  – and credence, see Belief, degrees of
  – and judgment, 162–63, 164
  Degrees of –, 231, 280 (fn 9), 282–83,
  Ethics of –, 74, 168, 171–72, 192–203
  First-order –, 191, 196–201
  Higher-order –, 193–96
  Mutual –, 255–72, 274, 288, 289; see also MBS; RMBS
  Norm of –, 105 (fn 14), 162–64, 272 (fn 1), 279–80
  Voluntarism about –, 167
Belief-worthiness, see Assertion, belief-worthiness of
Belief-worthiness purport, 51–53, 70–72; see also Assertion, belief-worthiness of
Benton, Matthew, 252–53, 258 (fn 8), 266 (fn 18), 276, 288
Bergmann, Michael, 227 (fn 4), 230 (fn 13), 241 (fn 30)
Bernecker, Sven, 165 (fn 42)
Bilgrami, Akeel, 138 (fn 13)
Bird, Alexander, 164, 169–70
Black, Max, 155 (fn 22)
Blair, Jason, 211 (fn 10)
Blame, 75–77, 80, 84–85, 87, 89, 123–24, 143, 173, 175–76; see also assertion-generated entitlements; assertion-generated responsibilities
  Moral –, 175–80
Blogs, 205 (fn 2), 219–20
Blome-Tilman, Michael, 193 (fn 37)
Bloomfield, Paul, 183 (fn 22)
Brady, Michael, 264 (fn 15)
Brandom, Robert, 11, 63 (fn 36), 74 (fn 5), 82 (fn 19), 155 (fn 22)
Buck-passing, 8, 75–77, 80, 87; see also assertion-generated entitlements; assertion-generated responsibilities
Bullshit, 110–11, 185
Burge, Tyler, 51, 52 (fn 22), 119, 121 (fn 31), 125 (fn 3), 129 (fn 5), 130, 135–36, 165
Buss, Sarah, 178 (fn 17)

Calhoun, Cheshire, 178 (fn 17)
Cappelen, Herman, 26–30, 34, 44 (fn 5), 131, 133 (fn 9), 164

Certainty, 67
Chalmers, David, 281 (fn 11)
Championing, 18, 281–82, 283
Charity, see Principle of Charity
Cheating, see Assertion, Cheating in
Christensen, David, 228 (fn 6), 229, 231, 233
Chudnoff, Eli, 60
CK-aptness, 6, 9, 15; see also Knowledge communication
Clifford, William, 168, 172
Coady, Tony, 49–50, 51 (fn 19), 52 (fn 22), 53, 54, 59, 118 (fn 28), 119, 121 (fn 31), 125 (fn 3)
Cohen, Stew, viii (fn 3), 35 (fn 30)
Coherentism, see Justification, Coherence theory of
Commitment account of assertion, 11–12, 17–19, 31; see also assertion-generated entitlements; assertion-generated responsibilities
Common Ground, 10, 15, 181
 – account of Assertion, 10–11, 15–17
Common Knowledge, see Norm of assertion and common knowledge
Communication systems, 29–30
Connee, Earl, 43, 121 (fn 32)
Conspiracy theories, 268–71
Content, see Assertion, Content
 – ascription, 133, 138, 142
 – individuation, 137
 – preservation, 142
 Face-value – ascription, 133 (fn 8), 143; see also Face-value interpretation, face-value* interpretation
 Mental –, 140
 Metalinguistic –, 134–35
Contention, The, 133
Contextualism, ix (fn 5), 74 (fn 4), 243
Convention, see Assertion, conventional nature of
Conversational score, 11
Convey, 172 (fn 1), 181–89, 190, 202, 218
Cooperative Principle, 255–56, 264, 275
Craig, Edward, 168
Culpable ignorance, 178, 192, 195–96

Darwall, Stephen, 63 (fn 37)
Davidson, Donald, 8–9, 53, 95, 97–103, 155 (fn 22)
Declarative mood, 5, 99–100, 145
DEF, 242
Defeaters, see also Justification and defeat
 No – condition in epistemology, 228
 Types of –, 227, 228 (fn 7)
DeRose, Keith, ix (fn 5), 74 (fn 4), 155 (fn 22), 176, 177, 193 (fn 36)
Descartes, René, 30–31
Descriptions, 152–53
DIF, 217, 218

Diminished epistemic hope, 251–53, 255, 259, 270 (fn 20), 276, 278, 283, 284, 285
Disagreement, see also Assertion and disagreement
 Conformism regarding –, 230
 – about what is mutually believed in context, 265
 – in Philosophy, see Philosophy, Disagreement in
 Entrenched –, 229, 232, 238, 242, 244
 Epistemology of –, 226, 231–48
 Isolated –, 228 (fn 8)
 Non-conformism regarding –, 230, 231, 237, 242
 Non-localized –, 229, 232, 238, 242, 244
 One-off –, 228, 238, 239
 Peer –, 228, 230, 232 (fn 18), 238, 241, 242, 244, 247, 248
 p-relevant –, 228, 241, 242, 247
 Problem of –, 250–55, 258
 Systematic –, 225, 226, 228–48, 250–55, 271, 273, 275, 278–80, 281
 Widespread –, 229, 232, 244
Division of Epistemic Labor, see Assertion and the division of epistemic labor
Dogmatism, see Justification, Dogmatism about –
Donnellan, Keith, 152–53
Dorr, Cian, 237 (fn 27), 247 (fn 36)
Douven, Igor, 11–12, 67, 69, 160, 162 (fn 37), 162 (fn 38), 286
Dretske, Fred, 40–41
Dummett, Michael, 44 (fn 7), 52 (fn 22), 99, 144 (fn 1), 145 (fn 4), 162 (fn 38), 169
Duty, see Assertion and responsibilities-to-assert

Early vision, 113
EA≡, 197, 199
Ebels-Duggan, Kyla, 188 (fn 28)
Ebels-Duggan, Sean, 236 (fn 26)
EC-susceptibility, 7, 16, 17; see also Assertion, challenges to
EHOB, 196
Elga, Adam, 228 (fn 8)
Elgin, Kate, 164 (fn 41)
ENA, 96, 146–47, 153, 154, 158, 161, 172, 190, 207, 250–51, 253, 254, 255, 257, 273
Entitlements, see assertion-generated –; Justification, non-reductionism about testimonial –; Justification, reductionism about testimonial –
 – in assertion and belief, 163–65, 170
 – in perception, 46
 – in testimony, 68, 73–77, 83–85, 180–81, 186, 211–13; see also Assertion-generated entitlements;
 Moral –, 84

Epistemic Injustice, 182–89, 210 (fn 8)
ESSPD, 251, 254, 255, 259
Ethics of belief, see Belief, ethics of
Evidence, 43, 167, 197–203, 230, 279, 281, 283; see also Assertion as evidence; Justification, Evidentialist theory of
– and reasons, 43, 211
Evidentialism, see Justification, Evidentialist Theory of
EWB, 199, 200
Excuse, 192
Expert, 134–35, 140, 141–42, 211, 214, 235
Expertise, see Expert
Expression (of belief), 10, 12–15, 144, 151; see also Assertion and Belief, Belief
Externalism, Epistemic, 176, 179, 211–12, 236 (fn 26), 243; see also Justification, anti-individualism about testimonial –
Externalism, Semantic, 135, 243

Face-value interpretation, 123–32, 141, 143
– as a useful fiction, 130–32
– defined, 126–27
Face-value* interpretation, 132, 136–38, 140, 141, 142
Fallis, Don, 220 (fn 16)
False Belief Test, 107 (fn 18)
Fantl, Jeremy, 199 (fn 44)
Farkas, Katya, 137 (fn 11), 140 (fn 15)
Faulkner, Paul, 47 (fn 11), 48 (fn 14), 62, 70
Feldman, Rich, 43, 121 (fn 31)
Felicity, see Assertion, felicity of
Fitzpatrick, William, 178
Foley, Richard, 51
Force, 256; see also Assertoric force
Foundationalism, see Justification, Foundationalist theory of
Foundationalist Phenomenalism, 138; see also FP
FP, 138, 140–42
Frances, Bryan, 225 (fn 1), 230 (fn 13), 248 (fn 39)
Free Enrichment, 128–29
Fricker, Elizabeth, 43 (fn 4), 44 (fn 7), 47, 49–50, 51 (fn 19), 53, 77, 209 (fn 5)
Fricker, Miranda, 180–89, 210 (fn 8), 263 (fn 13), 266 (fn 18)
Fumerton, Richard, 43, 121 (fn 31), 225 (fn 1)
FV* Constraint, 137, 142

Game theory, 29–30
Gendler, Tamar, 236 (fn 24)
Gettier cases, 48, 160, 175–76, 194, 210 (fn 9), 246, 254
Gibbons, John, 162 (fn 34), 227 (fn 5)
Goldberg, Sanford, 8 (fn 4), 28 (fn 27), 41 (fn 2), 43 (fn 4), 47 (fn 12), 50, 51, 59 (fn 29), 60, 61, 64, 68, 75, 77 (fn 10), 81 (fn 17), 82 (fn 19), 90 (fn 27), 121 (fn 33), 123–24, 125 (fn 2), 125 (fn 3), 129 (fn 5), 143, 162 (fn 36), 165, 175 (fn 10), 176 (fn 11), 177 (fn 15), 192 (fn 32), 192 (fn 33), 209 (fn 6), 225 (fn 1), 230 (fn 13), 234, 236 (fn 25), 248 (fn 39)
Graham, Peter, 54, 60 (fn 31), 118 (fn 28), 120 (fn 30), 125 (fn 3), 152 (fn 16), 165 (fn 43), 185 (fn 24)
Grandy, Richard, 13 (fn 15), 106, 108
Green, Mitch, 158 (fn 25)
Greenough, Patrick, 75 (fn 7)
Grice, Paul, 10, 58, 89, 250, 255–56, 258, 262, 264, 266, 271, 275, 288
Grimm, Stephen, 168
Groups, epistemic, 259–64, 267–68
  Degenerate –, 268–71
Gullibility, 47

Hajek, Al, 280 (fn 7), 287, 288
Harman, Elizabeth, 177 (fn 16)
Harnish, Robert, ix (fn 4), 8 (fn 6), 10, 12–15, 144–45, 154, 256
Hawthorne, John, viii (fn 3), 35 (fn 30), 155 (fn 22), 230 (fn 13)
Hearer-FV* requirement, 138, 139–42; see also FV* constraint
Henderson, David, 47 (fn 12), 121 (fn 33), 137 (fn 11), 140 (fn 15), 209 (fn 6)
Hill, Chris, 147 (fn 8)
Hinchman, Ted, 63, 64 (fn 39), 75, 77, 174 (fn 6), 180, 186, 188, 202 (fn 49)
Holism, Radical, 138–39
Horgan, Terry, 137 (fn 11), 140 (fn 15)

IAC, 137, 138
Illocutionary Act, 256; see also Assertoric force
Implicature, 125 (fn 2), 130 (fn 6), 191, 256, 275
Implicit Bias, 236
Inferential Role Semantics, 138; see also IRS
Inform, vii, 3
INS, 148–49
Insole, Chris, 50, 59
Intention
  Communicative –, 30; see also R-intentions
Internalism about assertoric content, 123, 142; see also IAC
Internalism, epistemic, 211–12, 236 (fn 26), 243
Internalism, semantic, see Internalism about assertoric content; IAC
Interpretation, see Radical Interpretation
Irony, 5 (fn 2), 176 (fn 14)
IRS, 138, 139–40

Jack, Julie, 43 (fn 4)
James, William, 168
Jary, Mark, 99–100, 144 (fn 1), 145 (fn 4)
Justification, 162, 167, 174, 246, 248, 254

Anti-individualism about testimonial –, 61
Basic –, 48 (fn 14), 50–58, 58–62
Bayesian Theory of –, 43
Coherence Theory of –, 40, 246
Dogmatism about –, 59–60
Doxastic vs. propositional –, 254, 285
Evidentialist Theory of –, 39, 42, 43–58, 230
Externalism about –, see Externalism, epistemic
Foundationalist Theory of –, 43
Internalism about –, see Internalism, epistemic
– and defeat, 47–48, 59, 125 (fn 3), 160–61, 182 (fn 20), 226, 227–28, 230, 231–37, 241–42, 250–55
– and evidence, 43
– and inference to the best explanation, 43, 50
– and reasons, 40–43
– and reliability, 230–45; see also Justification, Reliabilist Theory of
– and the norm of belief, 162
– of memorial belief, 61
– of perceptual belief, 41, 45, 46, 47–48, 113, 239
– versus blameworthiness, 85
Non-reductionism about testimonial –, 45, 50–58, 58–62, 64–65, 67–69, 76, 83–86, 90, 118–22, 125 (fn 3), 207–09, 211 (fn 11)
Prima facie –, 60, 211
Reductionism about testimonial –, 46–58, 67–68, 86, 90, 119–22, 125 (fn 3), 185 (fn 24), 207–09
Reliabilist Theory of –, 41, 60–62, 233 (fn 19), 234, 239; see also Justification and reliability

Kelly, Tom, 230 (fn 11), 237–38, 241 (fn 29)
Kenyon, Tim, 49, 185 (fn 24), 214 (fn 14)
Kim, Jerry, 24
King, Braydon, 24
KNA, 175, 176
Knowledge communication, 6–7, 12–13, 15, 17–18, 19–20, 39–70, 73, 74, 126–30, 133, 137, 142, 152, 154, 169, 216, 258, 273, 275, 276
Kornblith, Hilary, 225 (fn 1), 228 (fn 8), 243 (fn 32), 248 (fn 39)
Kotzen, Matthew, 230 (fn 13)
Kriegel, Uriah, 137 (fn 11), 140 (fn 15)
Kripke, Saul, 152 (fn 17), 153
Kusch, Martin, 168
Kvanvig, John, 8 (fn 7), 11, 14 (fn 16), 67, 147 (fn 8), 159, 161, 164 (fn 40), 165 (fn 44), 172 (fn 2), 286

Lackey, Jennifer, ix (fn 5), 11–12, 20 (fn 23), 47 (fn 11), 48 (fn 14), 49–50, 64, 65, 67, 78 (fn 12), 79, 88 (fn 22), 147 (fn 8), 151, 152 (fn 15), 152 (fn 16), 153, 154, 160 (fn 31), 165 (fn 43), 176 (fn 12),
185 (fn 24), 230 (fn 13), 230 (fn 14), 230 (fn 15), 232 (fn 16), 237 (fn 27), 239 (fn 28), 275 (fn 2), 284
Lackey cases, 152–53
Language
  Idiolectial –, 140, 141
  – norms (of meaning), 126, 131; see also Rules, semantic
  Public –, 124, 127–30, 132, 139–40
Lawlor, Krista, 62 (fn 34), 266 (fn 16)
Leite, Adam, ix (fn 5), 74 (fn 4), 193 (fn 36)
Leonard, Nick, 242 (fn 31)
Lepore, Ernie, 44 (fn 5), 131, 133 (fn 9), 164
Lewis, David, 11, 100 (fn 10)
Lies, 26, 87, 110
  Bald-faced –, 5, 25, 145, 150, 154, 176 (fn 14)
Lipton, Peter, 43, 50, 121 (fn 31)
Littlejohn, Clayton, 159 (fn 29), 161 (fn 33), 230 (fn 13)
Loar, Brian, 137 (fn 11), 140 (fn 15)
Lottery propositions, 199 (fn 43)
Luck, epistemic 176, 194, 212; see also Gettier cases
Ludlow, Peter, 235 (fn 23), 247 (fn 36)
Lyons, Jack, 41

MacFarlane, John, 8 (fn 6), 8 (fn 7), 9–12, 166, 170, 253 (fn 4)
Machuca, Diego, 281 (fn 10)
Maitra, Ishani, viii (fn 3), ix (fn 5), 21–26, 35 (fn 30),164
Matheson, Jon, 230 (fn 13)
Maxim
  – of Quality, 256, 257, 258, 264
MBS, 257, 258, 261 (fn 10), 262–66; see also Belief, mutual; RMBS
McDowell, John, 41 (fn 1), 51, 58 (fn 28)
McGinn, Colin, 100 (fn 10)
McGlynn, Aidan, 112 (fn 23), 117
McGrath, Matthew, 199 (fn 44)
McKinnon, Rachel, ix (fn 5), 20 (fn 23), 34 (fn 29), 69 (fn 43), 99 (fn 8), 146 (fn 6), 156, 159 (fn 29), 160 (fn 30), 161 (fn 33), 164, 170, 172 (fn 2), 276 (fn 3)
McMyler, Ben, 63, 64 (fn 39)
Meaning; see also Assertion, content of; Face-value interpretation;
  Sentence- vs. speaker- –, 123–24
Millikan, Ruth, 40–41
MMENA, 96, 98, 100, 103–12, 123, 124–30, 134, 135, 136, 142, 143, 144, 146, 148, 150, 154, 155, 156, 158, 170, 171–72, 177, 180, 182, 183, 184 (fn 23), 187, 189, 190, 193, 201, 203, 204, 205, 218, 221, 257, 272, 273, 284, 285, 289
Montmarquet, James, 178
Montminy, Martin, 193 (fn 37)

Moody-Adams, Michele, 178 (fn 17)
Moore, G. E., 144, 157–58, 166
Moore's paradox, viii, 35 (fn 30), 157–62, 170, 263 (fn 12), 285–88
Moran, Richard, 58, 63, 64 (fn 39), 73 (fn 2), 75, 77, 84 (fn 20), 86–91, 174 (fn 6), 180, 186, 188, 202 (fn 49)
MPB1, 158, 159, 161
MPB2, 158, 161
MPK, 159, 160–62
Mullins, Matthew, 244 (fn 34)
Mutual belief, 255–65, 267–68, 270–72, 274–77, 283–84, 288–89
Mutual knowledge, 67

NA, 96
Negligence, 195–96; see also Culpable ignorance
Neta, Ram, 12, 20 (fn 23), 147 (fn 8)
Non-reductionism, see Justification, non-reductionism about testimonial –
Normativity, 13–14, 73–74, 88, 167, 173, 181, 243, 279
Norm of assertion, vii, 11–12, 21–35, 39, 66–70, 80–89, 143, 146, 168–69, 173, 175, 177–80, 192, 195, 203, 205, 250–51, 253–54, 259, 264, 272, 274; see also Assertion; Normativity; Rule, Constitutive – Account of Assertion
  Candidates for –, viii, 67, 96 (fn 2), 108–09, 136 (fn 11), 146–47, 150–51, 207, 275
  "Default" setting of –, 262–63, 265, 267–68, 274, 276, 277, 284
  Invariant nature of –, 146 (fn 6)
  Knowledge –, 68, 147, 156, 159, 164 (fn 40), 175, 210 (fn 9), 253, 254, 262–63, 274; see also KNA
  – and norm of belief, 161, 162–70, 200 (fn 46)
  – and norm of judgment, 164
  – and norm of practical reasoning, viii (fn 3), 35 (fn 30)
  – and the methodology of Radical Interpretation, 112–18
  – and warrantedness, 73–80, 88, 96, 106, 146, 173, 175–76, 227 (fn 3), 246, 254, 255–59, 263, 272–91
  – as a rule of language, 67, 76, 83
  – as common knowledge, 80–82, 96
  – as norm of permission, 193, 213
  – is context-sensitive, 29, 33, 34, 146 (fn 6), 225, 226, 250, 255, 260–64, 271, 272–91
  Objections to –, 21–35

Observation sentences, 112–14
Owens, David, 63 (fn 36), 67 (fn 41), 74, 174 (fn 6)

Pagin, Peter, 34, 253 (fn 4)
PASD, 245, 247
Perlocutionary act, 213 (fn 12)
Pettit, Philip, 62
Phenomenalism, see Foundationalist Phenomenalism; FP
Philosophy,
  Disagreement in –, 229–30, 233, 235–37, 242–48, 260, 278–79, 282–83, 287
  Having a view in –, 281–82, 283
  Methodology of –, 225 (fn 1), 235–36, 244, 245–49
  – as an epistemic group, 260–64
  Practice of –, 225 (fn 1), 245–49, 252–53, 260–62, 280–82
Pierce, Charles Sanders, 11
Positive Reasons Requirement, 46–58
Pragmatic encroachment, 167
Pragmatics, 152 (fn 17), 155–57
  Wide –, 128–29, 131
Prediction, 181, 252–53, 276, 287–88
Preface paradox, 228 (fn 6)
Presentation-as-true, 5, 181–82, 190, 202
Presupposition, 125 (fn 2), 181, 191
Principle of Charity, 9, 97, 101, 112, 114–16, 122
Principle of Humanity, 13 (fn 15), 106, 108, 117, 119
Principle of Knowledge-Maximization, 109 (fn 20), 116–17, 122
Pritchard, Duncan, 75 (fn 7), 166 (fn 44)
Privacy, 184
Promise, see Assertion and promising
Propriety, primary versus secondary, 176–77, 254 (fn 5)
PRR, 47, 185 (fn 24); see also Positive Reasons Requirement
Pryor, Jim, 60
Putnam, Hilary, 139–40

QD, 127
Quine, Willard, 97, 101, 112

RA, 11
Radical Interpretation, 8–9, 13, 17, 19, 20, 54, 95–122, 132, 137
  Evidence for –, 101–02, 109–14
  Justification of methodology for –, 101, 103, 115–16
  Methodological Principles of –, see AIP; Principle of Charity; Principle of Humanity, Principle of Knowledge Maximization
  Semantic vs. epistemic methods of –, 113
  Triangulation in –, 101 (fn 11), 102
Rationality, epistemic, 197, 199
Realisticness condition, 48–49
Reasons, see Reasons Assumption; Evidence
  Moral –, 189–90, 193

Reasons assumption, 40, 43
Reductionism, see Justification, reductionism about testimonial –
  Global vs. local –, 49–50, 53, 59
Reed, Baron, 242 (fn 31)
Refereeing, 219
Reference, 128, 152 (fn 17)
Regarding-as-defensible, 279–80, 281
Reid, Thomas, 51, 60; see also Justification, non-reductionism about testimonial –
Relevance Theory, 184 (fn 23)
Relevant Alternatives, 195, 198–200
Reliabilism, see Justification, Reliabilist theory of
Report, vii, 3, 4, 112
Representing oneself as knowing, see Assertion and representing oneself as knowing
Reputation, see Assertion, reputation in
Rescorla, Michael, 11
Respect, 181–89, 201
Responsibility, see assertion-generated-
Retraction, see Assertion and retraction
Reynolds, Stephen, 146 (fn 5), 155 (fn 22)
RH, 138–39, 140
Ridge, Michael, 183 (fn 22), 278 (fn 5)
RI-evidential feature (of assertion), 9, 13
Right of Complaint, see Assertion-generated entitlements
R-intentions, 10, 12; see also Intention, communicative
Risk, 167, 198, 201
RMBS, 266–71, 273, 275, 289; see also MBS; Belief, mutual
Rosen, Gideon, 176 (fn 13), 177–78
Ross, Angus, 58, 75, 83–86, 89–91, 173, 174 (fn 6), 202 (fn 49)
Rotondo, Andrew, 230 (fn 13)
Rule, 11, 83, 85–86, 173
  Baseball –, 21–26
  Breaches of –, 22–24
  Constitutive –, 11, 21–30
  Constitutive – account of assertion, 11–12, 19–36, 62, 66–70, 95, 98–99, 155; see also Norm of assertion
  – of language, 83, 85; see also Norm of assertion as rule of language
  Semantic –, 127, 129
Rysiew, Patrick, 43 (fn 4), 52 (fn 21), 120 (fn 30), 155 (fn 21), 155 (fn 22), 164 (fn 40)

Say, 58, 62, 256
Schaffer, Jonathan, 15
Schechter, Josh, 147 (fn 8)
Schmitt, Fred, 51, 61
Searle, John, 11, 155 (fn 22)
Second-person perspective, see Assertion and audience; Assertion, ethics of; Testimony, ethics of; Testimony, overhearers of
Secret, 204 (fn 1)
Security wall model, 220
Shafer-Landau, Russ, 242 (fn 31)
Signal, 29, 103
Silence, 195–96
Simard Smith, Paul, 34 (fn 29), 69 (fn 43), 156, 159 (fn 29), 160 (fn 30), 161 (fn 33)
Sincerity, 8, 12, 18, 20, 98–99, 104–06, 107, 110–11, 118, 144–45, 147–50, 174, 176 (fn 14), 182 (fn 20), 200, 210, 212, 214, 273, 275, 278, 283–85
  – defined, 148; see also INS
Skepticism, 108–10, 166, 227, 230 (fn 11), 242 (fn 31), 243, 248 (fn 39), 269
Slote, Michael, 11, 155 (fn 22)
Smith, Angela, 178 (fn 17)
Smith, Holly, 178 (fn 17)
Sobel, Jordan, 43
Sorensen, Roy, 145, 154, 158 (fn 25), 161
Sosa, David, 74
Sosa, Ernie, 51 (fn 19), 77, 167, 183 (fn 22)
Speaker-FV* requirement, 138, 139–42; see also FV* constraint
Speculation, 55–58, 77, 78–80, 81, 280–82
Speech Act Pluralism, see Speech Acts, pluralism about
Speech Acts, 100, 105–06, 191, 212, 252
  Individuation of –, 21–26
  Pluralism about –, 44 (fn 5), 131, 133 (fn 9)
Speech Context, 273–76
Sperber, Dan, 184 (fn 23)
Spokesperson, see Assertion by spokesperson
Srinivasan, Amia, 230 (fn 13)
Stalnaker, Robert, 10–11, 155 (fn 22), 180–81, 202 (fn 48)
Stanley, Jason, viii (fn 3), 11, 35 (fn 30), 67, 155 (fn 22), 165
State, vii, 3, 4, 158
Stevenson, Leslie, 50, 52 (fn 22), 118 (fn 28), 119, 121 (fn 31), 125 (fn 3)
Stone, Jim, 159 (fn 29), 172 (fn 2)
Strawson, Peter, 51, 52 (fn 22), 61
Strong Evidentialism, 45, 46–58, 86, 90–91, 202
Superstition, 168

Tell, 3, 4, 63, 70, 72, 74, 76, 77–80, 86–89, 186
Testify, vii, 3, 54–58, 77–80, 81, 169, 187
Testimony, 72–92, 187
  Assurance view of –, see Assurance view of testimony
  Epistemology of –, 43–70, 74, 89–91, 118–22, 125 (fn 3), 179, 185, 209–14; see also Justification, Non-reductionism

Testimony (*Cont.*)
    about testimonial –; Justification, Reductionism about testimonial –
    Ethics involved in –, 62–66, 73 (fn 3), 83–86, 88, 90, 171–203
    Hearer –, 79
    Interpersonal views of –, 62–66
    Non-reductionism about –, see Justification, Non-reductionism about testimonial –
    Overhearers of –, 63, 88–89, 179
    Reductionism about –, see Justification, Reductionism about testimonial –
    Religious –, 77
    Speaker –, 79
    Stranger –, 213–14, 215 (fn 15)
    – and assertion, see Assertion and testimony
    – and displaced perception, 40–41
    – and memory, 61
    – and promising, 63–64
    – and testimonial injustice, 187
    – and the generation of warrant, 165
    – weakens warrant, 165
Thune, Michael, 230 (fn 13)
Transindividual reasons, 61
Transparency, 194
Troll, 205
Trust, 39, 62–66, 70, 72, 84, 186, 188, 221, 239, 265, 274
    – and self-trust, 51
Trustworthiness, 62, 70, 87, 119, 186, 188, 218, 219, 264
Truth, 5, 51, 77, 79–80, 83, 97–98, 113, 115, 160, 165, 170, 183, 185, 239–40, 254 (fn 5), 272 (fn 1), 280, 286

Turri, John, 34 (fn 29), 74, 75 (fn 7), 146 (fn 6), 147 (fn 7), 172 (fn 2)
TWW, 165

Unger, Peter, 11, 155 (fn 22)
Uniqueness, 283

Van Fraassen, Bas, 166

Wanderer, Jeremy, 180 (fn 19), 187–88
Warrant, see Norm of assertion and warrantedness
Warranting Condition, 48–49
Watson, Gary, 11, 63 (fn 36)
WBW, 155
Weatherson, Brian, viii (fn 3), ix (fn 5), 35 (fn 30), 164, 246
Weiner, Matthew, 12, 83, 254 (fn 5), 286, 287
What it's like to be a woman in philosophy (blog), 205 (fn 2), 219
Wikipedia, 220
Williams, Bernard, 30, 54 (fn 25), 145, 154, 284
Williams, John, 158 (fn 25)
Williamson, Tim, viii (fn 3), 11, 35 (fn 30), 67, 74, 75 (fn 7), 96 (fn 1), 99, 109 (fn 20), 112, 116–17, 122, 155 (fn 22), 157 (fn 24), 159–60, 162–63, 169, 172 (fn 2), 176, 177, 237 (fn 27), 275 (fn 2)
Wilson, Deirdre, 184 (fn 23)
WPE, 129, 130–32
Wright, Crispin, 11

Zagzebski, Linda, 168, 200 (fn 47)